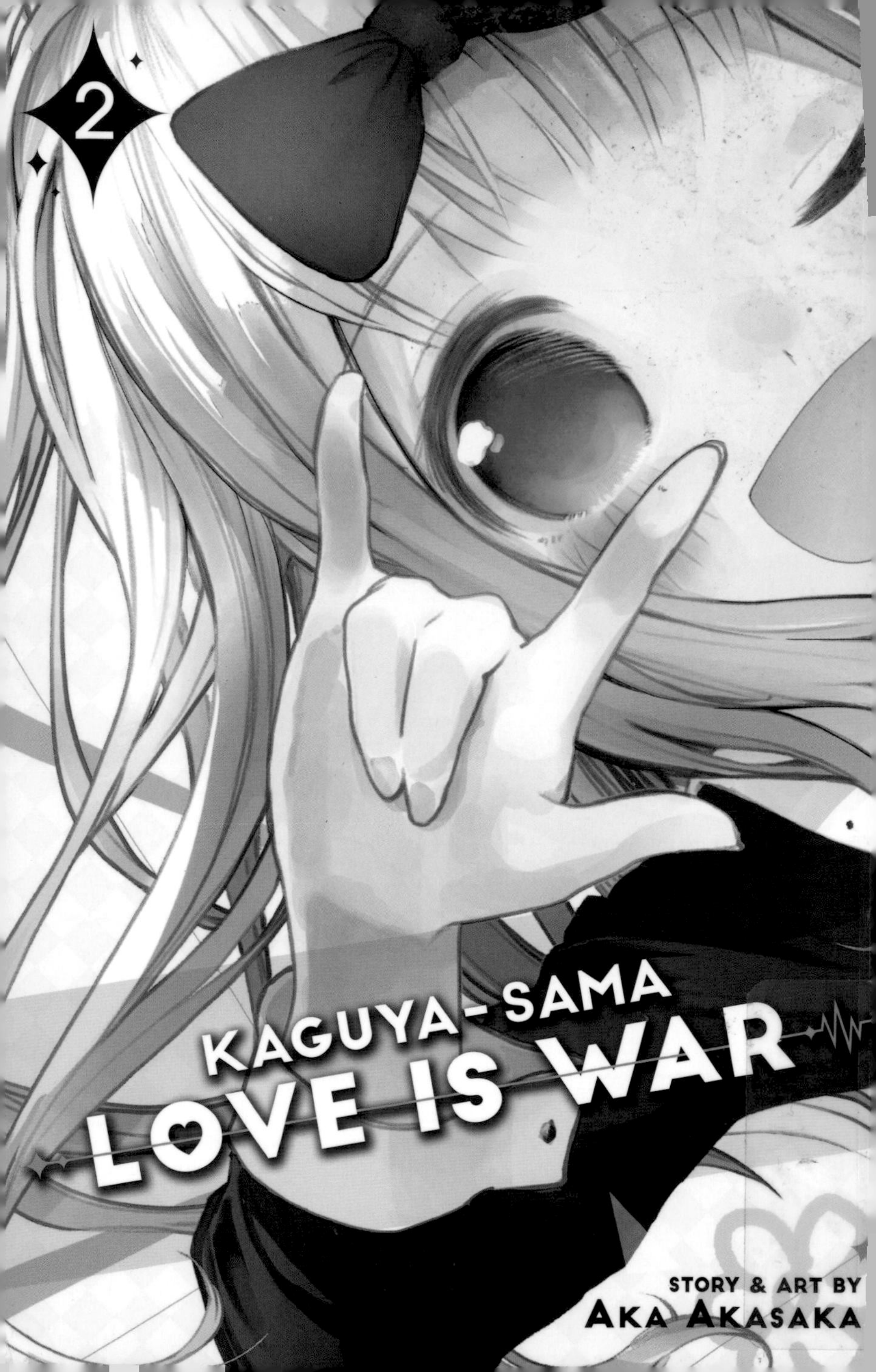

2
KAGUYA-SAMA
LOVE IS WAR
STORY & ART BY
AKA AKASAKA

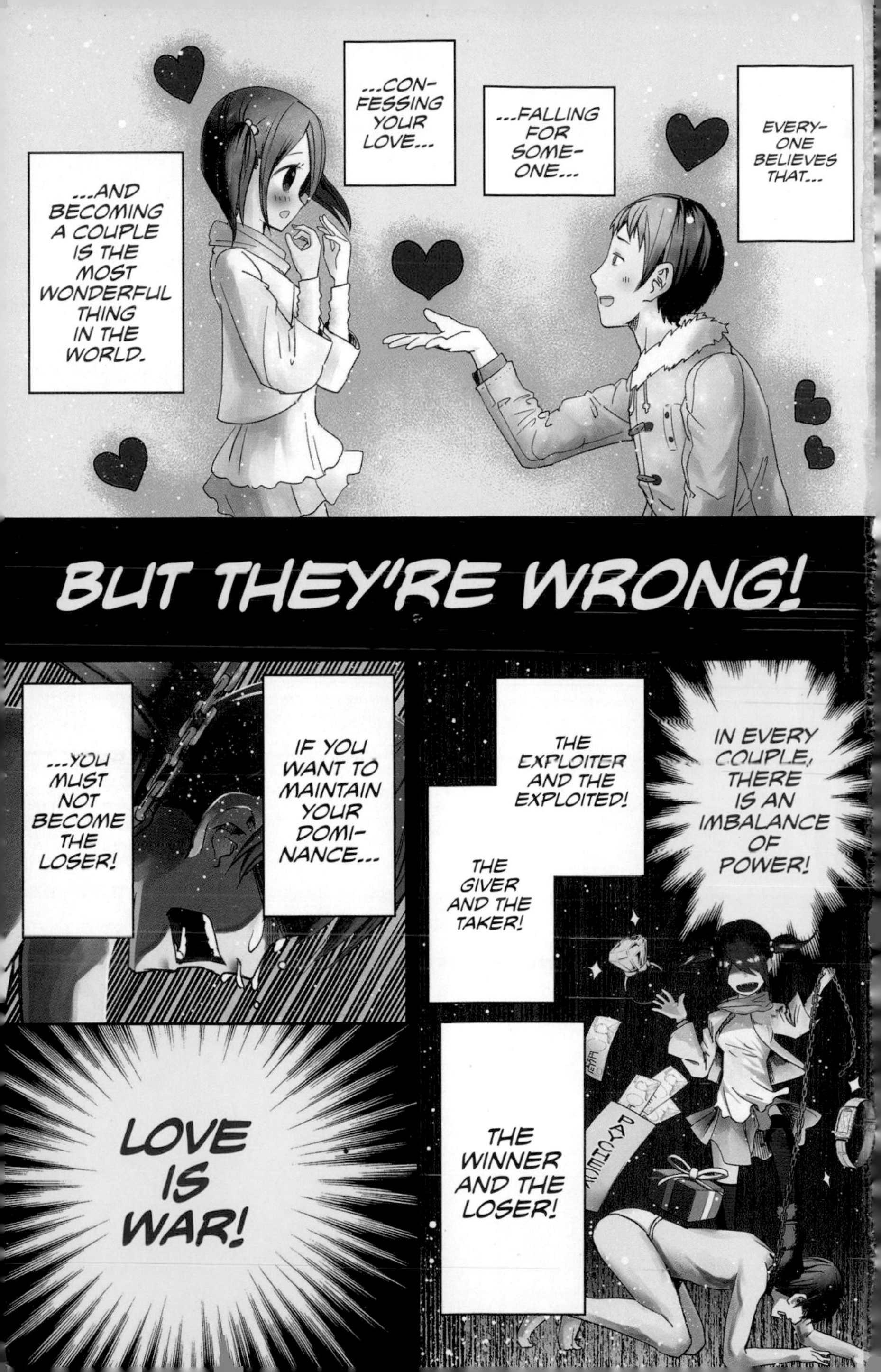
EVERYONE BELIEVES THAT...
...FALLING FOR SOMEONE...
...CONFESSING YOUR LOVE...
...AND BECOMING A COUPLE IS THE MOST WONDERFUL THING IN THE WORLD.
BUT THEY'RE WRONG!
IN EVERY COUPLE, THERE IS AN IMBALANCE OF POWER!
THE EXPLOITER AND THE EXPLOITED!
THE GIVER AND THE TAKER!
THE WINNER AND THE LOSER!
IF YOU WANT TO MAINTAIN YOUR DOMINANCE...
...YOU MUST NOT BECOME THE LOSER!
LOVE IS WAR!

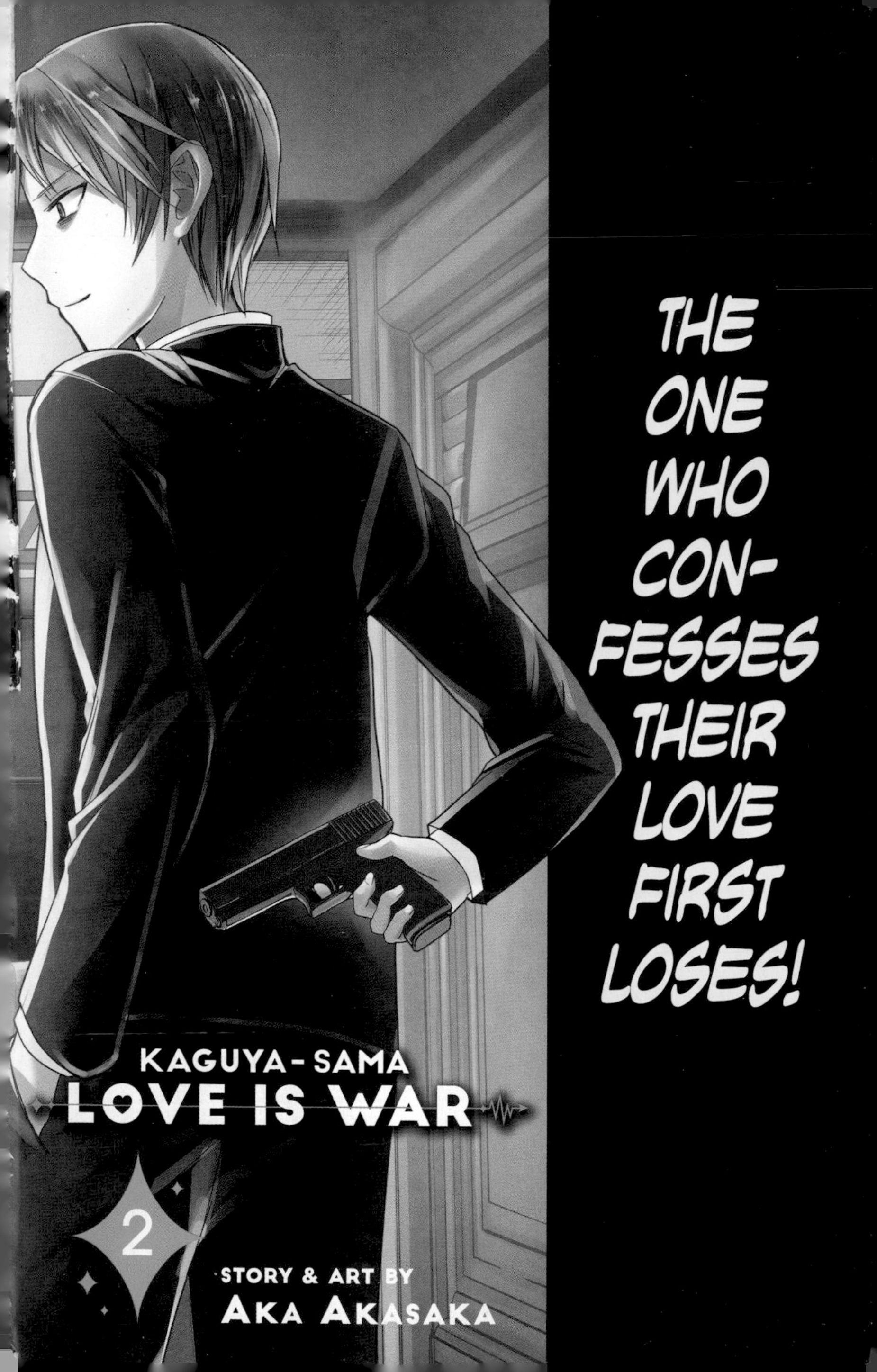
THE ONE WHO CON-FESSES THEIR LOVE FIRST LOSES!
KAGUYA-SAMA
LOVE IS WAR
2
STORY & ART BY
Aka Akasaka

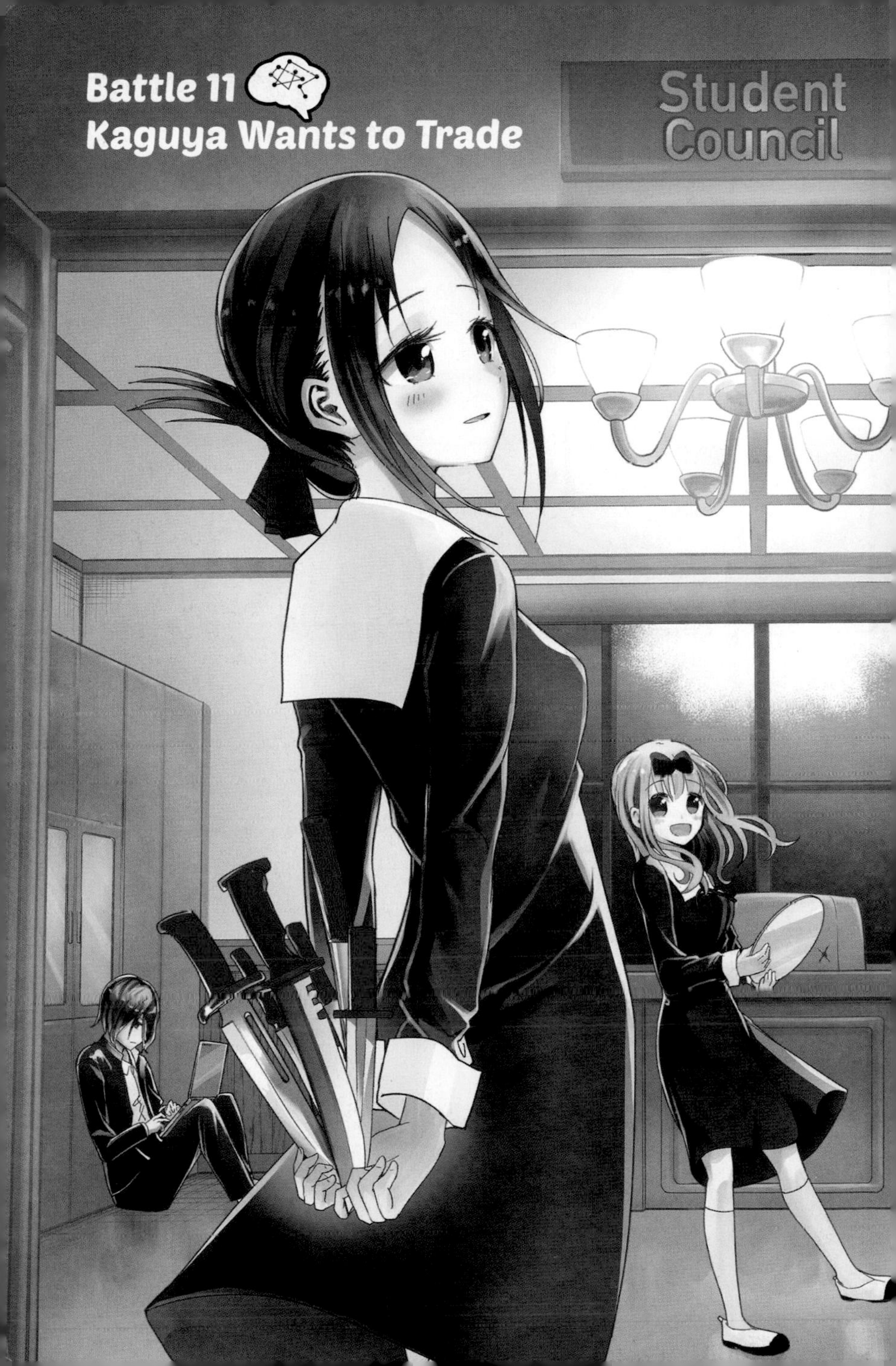
Battle 11
Kaguya Wants to Trade
Student Council

KAGUYA-SAMA LOVE IS WAR

BATTLE CAMPAIGNS 2

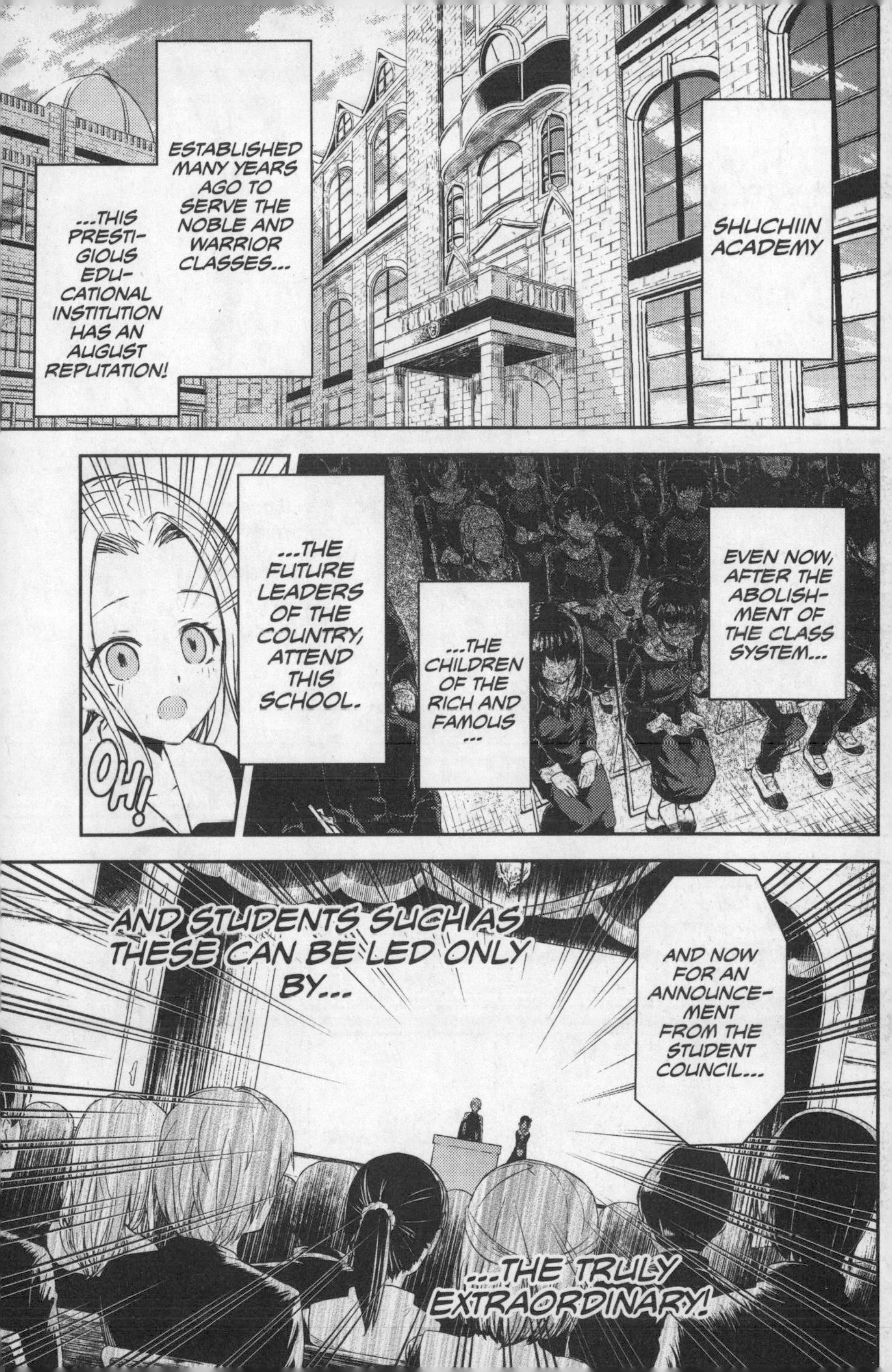
SHUCHIIN ACADEMY
ESTABLISHED MANY YEARS AGO TO SERVE THE NOBLE AND WARRIOR CLASSES...
...THIS PRESTIGIOUS EDUCATIONAL INSTITUTION HAS AN AUGUST REPUTATION!
EVEN NOW, AFTER THE ABOLISHMENT OF THE CLASS SYSTEM...
...THE CHILDREN OF THE RICH AND FAMOUS...
...THE FUTURE LEADERS OF THE COUNTRY, ATTEND THIS SCHOOL.
OH!
AND NOW FOR AN ANNOUNCEMENT FROM THE STUDENT COUNCIL...
AND STUDENTS SUCH AS THESE CAN BE LED ONLY BY...
...THE TRULY EXTRAORDINARY!

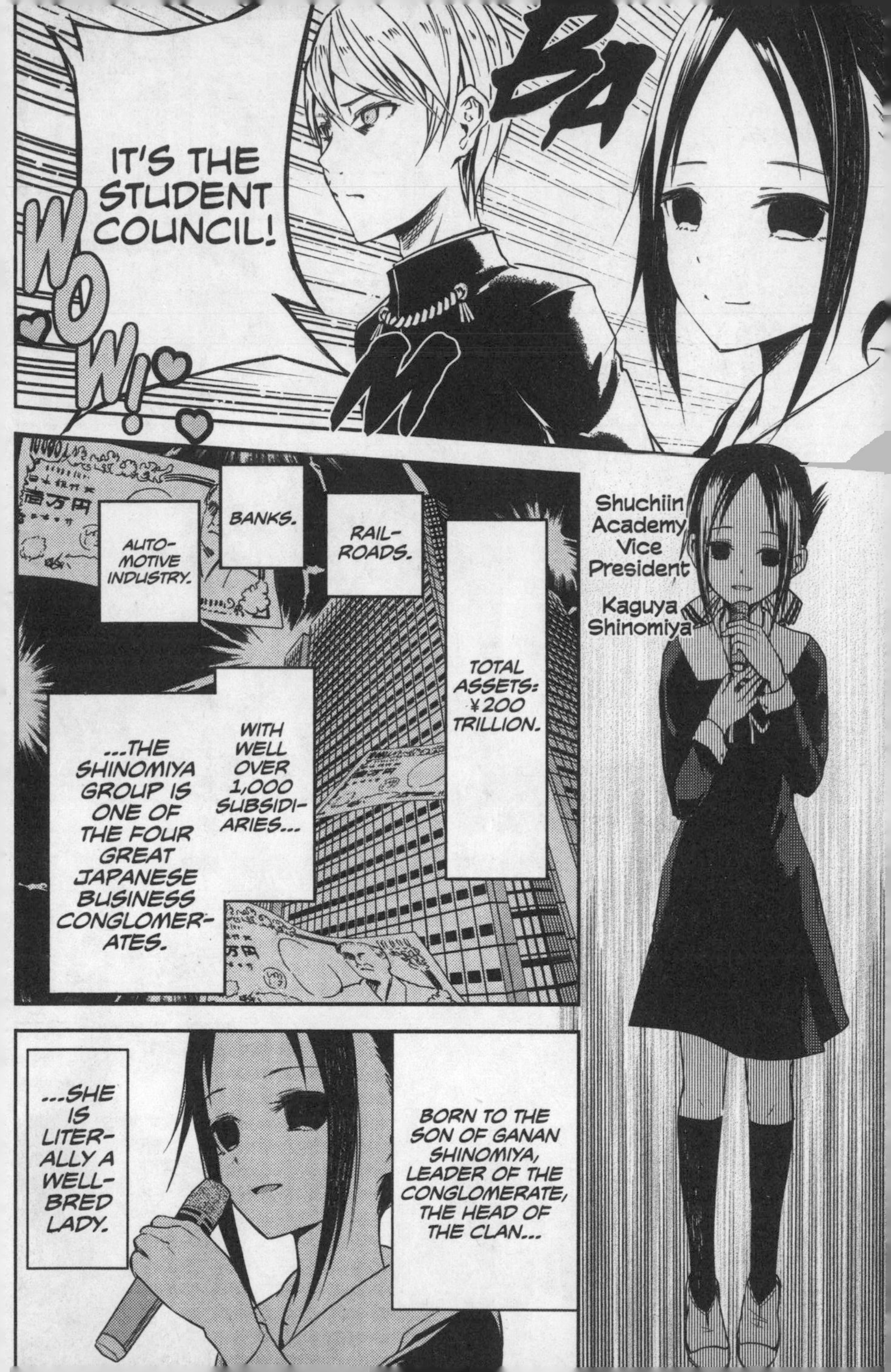
BAM
IT'S THE STUDENT COUNCIL!
WOW!
Shuchiin Academy Vice President
Kaguya Shinomiya
RAIL-ROADS.
BANKS.
AUTO-MOTIVE INDUSTRY.
TOTAL ASSETS: ¥200 TRILLION.
WITH WELL OVER 1,000 SUBSIDI-ARIES...
...THE SHINOMIYA GROUP IS ONE OF THE FOUR GREAT JAPANESE BUSINESS CONGLOMER-ATES.
BORN TO THE SON OF GANAN SHINOMIYA, LEADER OF THE CONGLOMERATE, THE HEAD OF THE CLAN...
...SHE IS LITER-ALLY A WELL-BRED LADY.

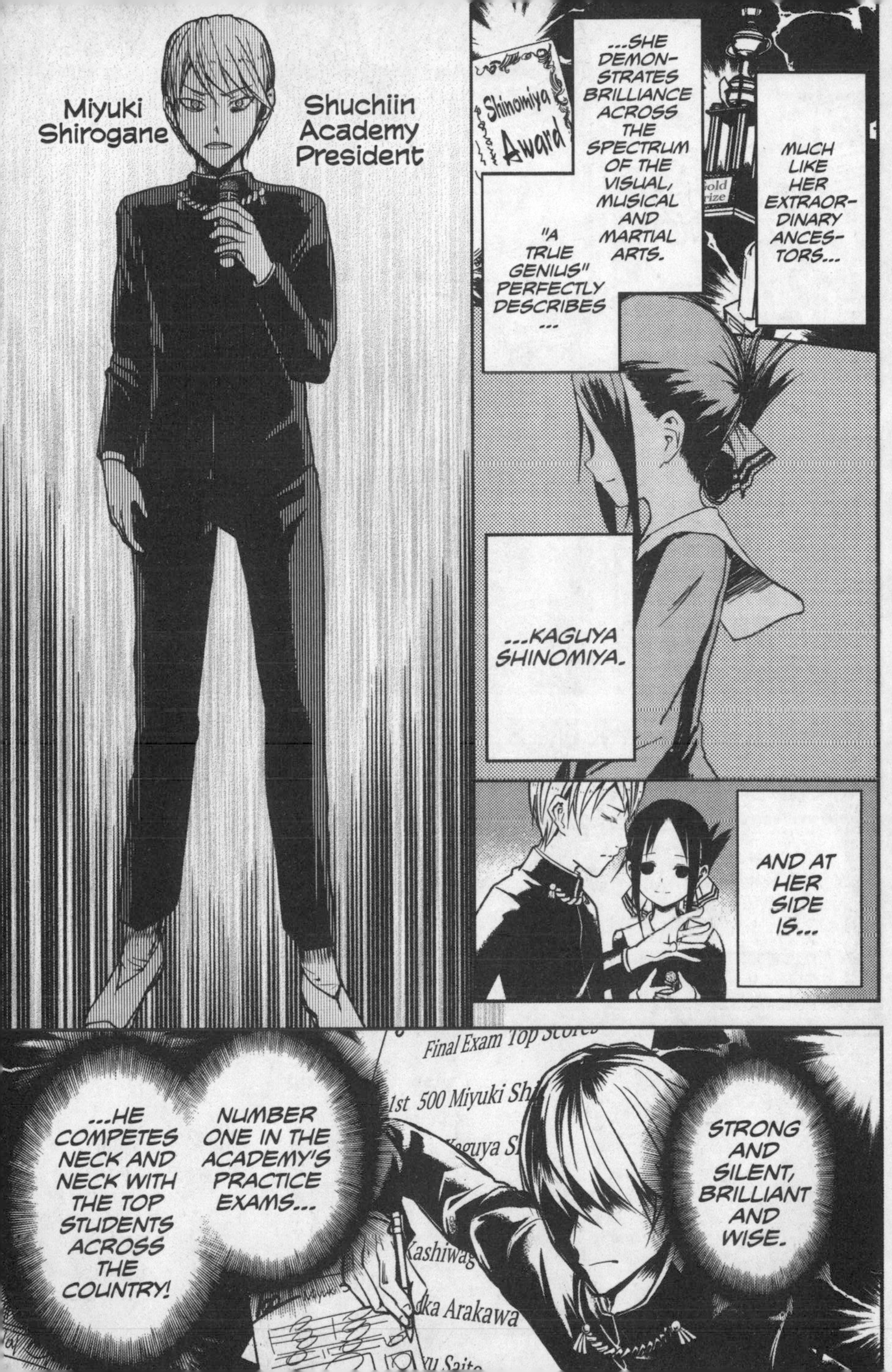
MUCH LIKE HER EXTRAORDINARY ANCESTORS...
...SHE DEMONSTRATES BRILLIANCE ACROSS THE SPECTRUM OF THE VISUAL, MUSICAL AND MARTIAL ARTS.
Shinomiya Award
"A TRUE GENIUS" PERFECTLY DESCRIBES...
...KAGUYA SHINOMIYA.
AND AT HER SIDE IS...
Shuchiin Academy President
Miyuki Shirogane
STRONG AND SILENT, BRILLIANT AND WISE.
Final Exam Top Scores
NUMBER ONE IN THE ACADEMY'S PRACTICE EXAMS...
...HE COMPETES NECK AND NECK WITH THE TOP STUDENTS ACROSS THE COUNTRY!

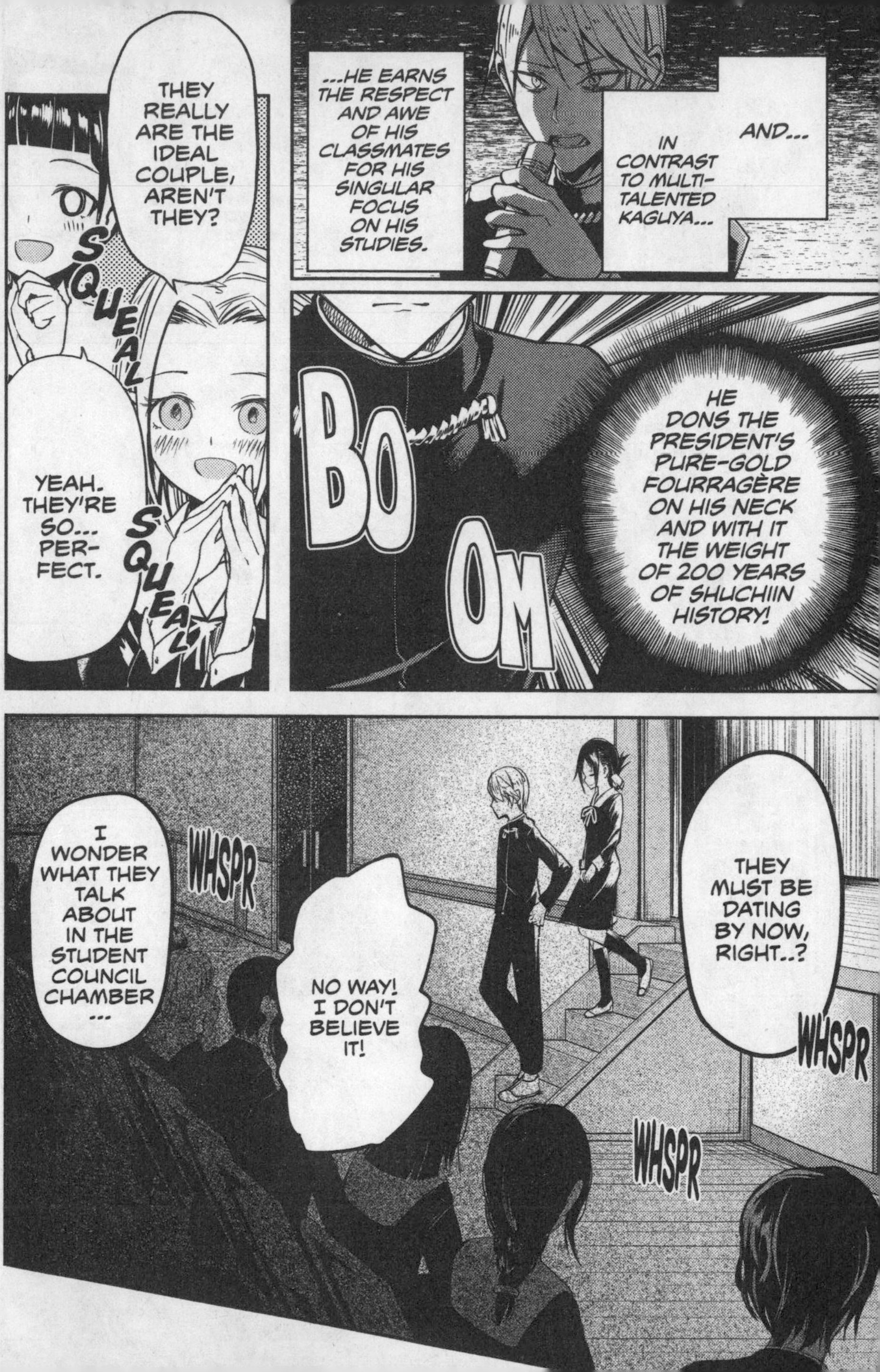
AND...
IN CONTRAST TO MULTI-TALENTED KAGUYA...
...HE EARNS THE RESPECT AND AWE OF HIS CLASSMATES FOR HIS SINGULAR FOCUS ON HIS STUDIES.
HE DONS THE PRESIDENT'S PURE-GOLD FOURRAGÈRE ON HIS NECK AND WITH IT THE WEIGHT OF 200 YEARS OF SHUCHIIN HISTORY!
BOOM
THEY REALLY ARE THE IDEAL COUPLE, AREN'T THEY?
SQUEAL
YEAH. THEY'RE SO... PER-FECT.
SQUEAL
THEY MUST BE DATING BY NOW, RIGHT..?
WHSPR
WHSPR
NO WAY! I DON'T BELIEVE IT!
I WONDER WHAT THEY TALK ABOUT IN THE STUDENT COUNCIL CHAMBER...
WHSPR

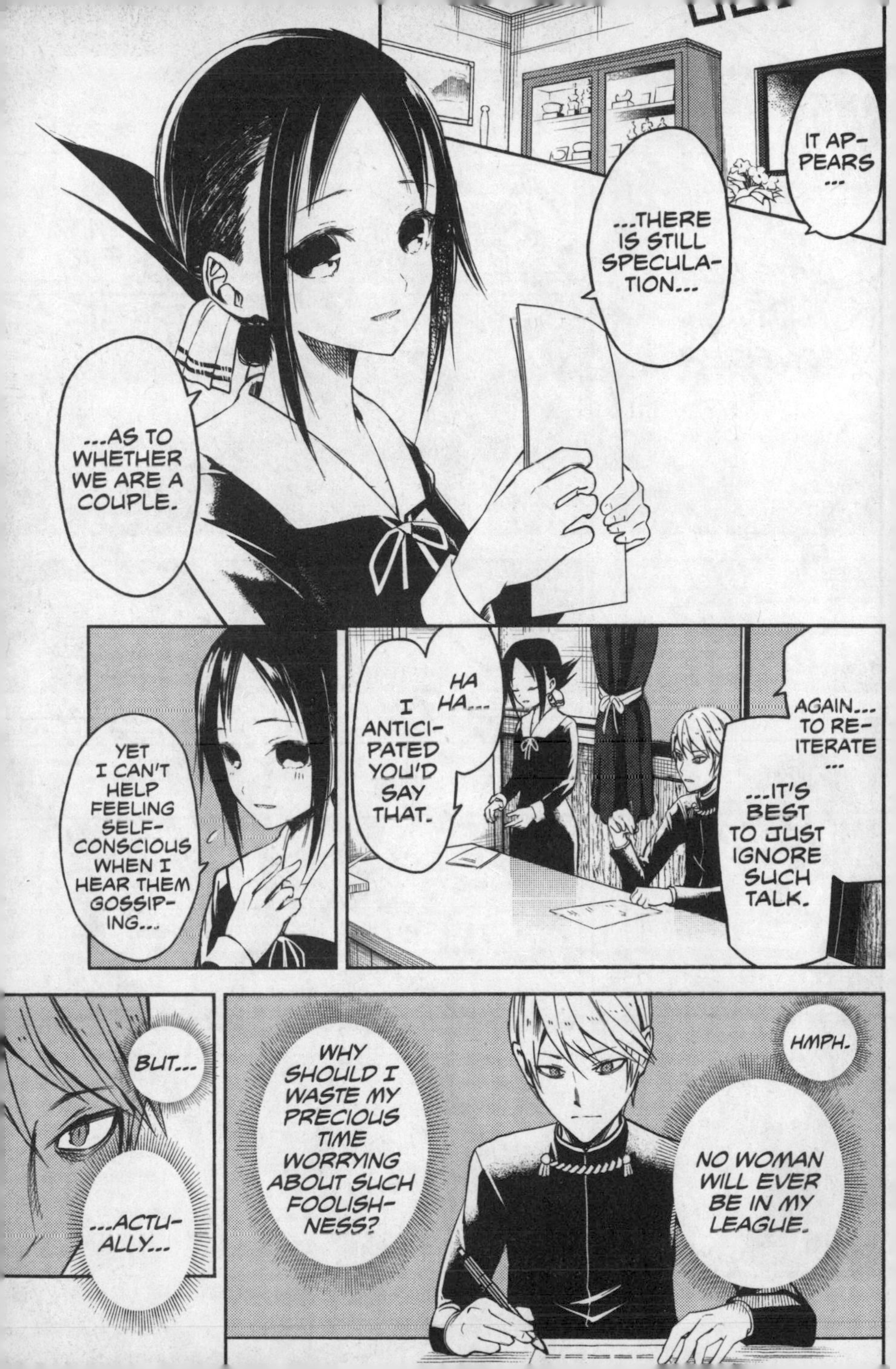
IT APPEARS...
...THERE IS STILL SPECULATION...
...AS TO WHETHER WE ARE A COUPLE.
AGAIN... TO REITERATE...
...IT'S BEST TO JUST IGNORE SUCH TALK.
HA HA... I ANTICIPATED YOU'D SAY THAT.
YET I CAN'T HELP FEELING SELF-CONSCIOUS WHEN I HEAR THEM GOSSIPING...
HMPH.
NO WOMAN WILL EVER BE IN MY LEAGUE.
WHY SHOULD I WASTE MY PRECIOUS TIME WORRYING ABOUT SUCH FOOLISHNESS?
BUT...
...ACTUALLY...

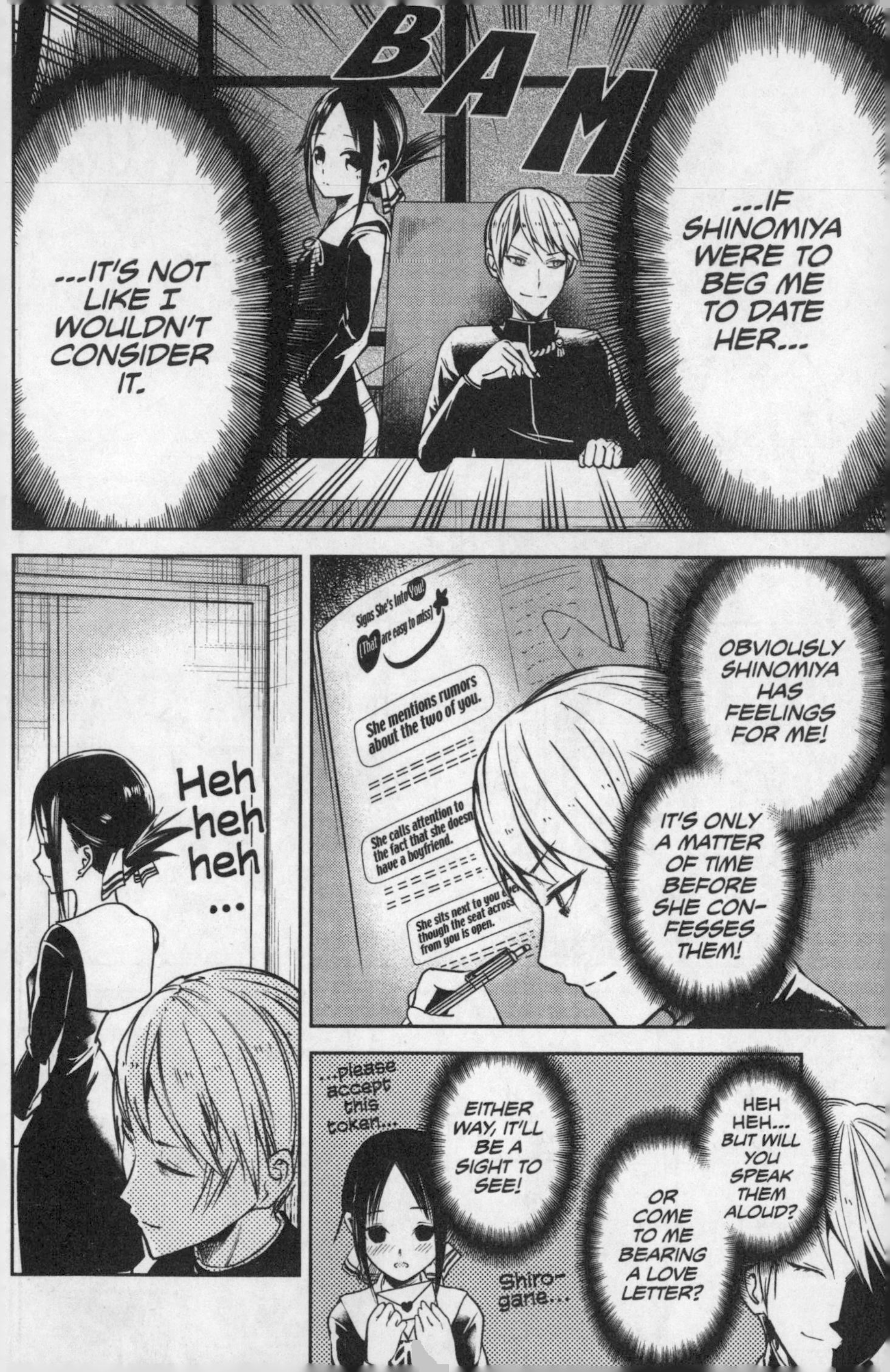
...IF SHINOMIYA WERE TO BEG ME TO DATE HER...
BAM
...IT'S NOT LIKE I WOULDN'T CONSIDER IT.
OBVIOUSLY SHINOMIYA HAS FEELINGS FOR ME!
IT'S ONLY A MATTER OF TIME BEFORE SHE CON-FESSES THEM!
Signs She's Into You!
(That are easy to miss)
She mentions rumors about the two of you.
She calls attention to the fact that she doesn
have a boyfriend.
She sits next to you ev
though the seat across
from you is open.
HEH HEH... BUT WILL YOU SPEAK THEM ALOUD?
OR COME TO ME BEARING A LOVE LETTER?
EITHER WAY, IT'LL BE A SIGHT TO SEE!
Shiro-gane...
...please accept this token...
Heh heh heh...

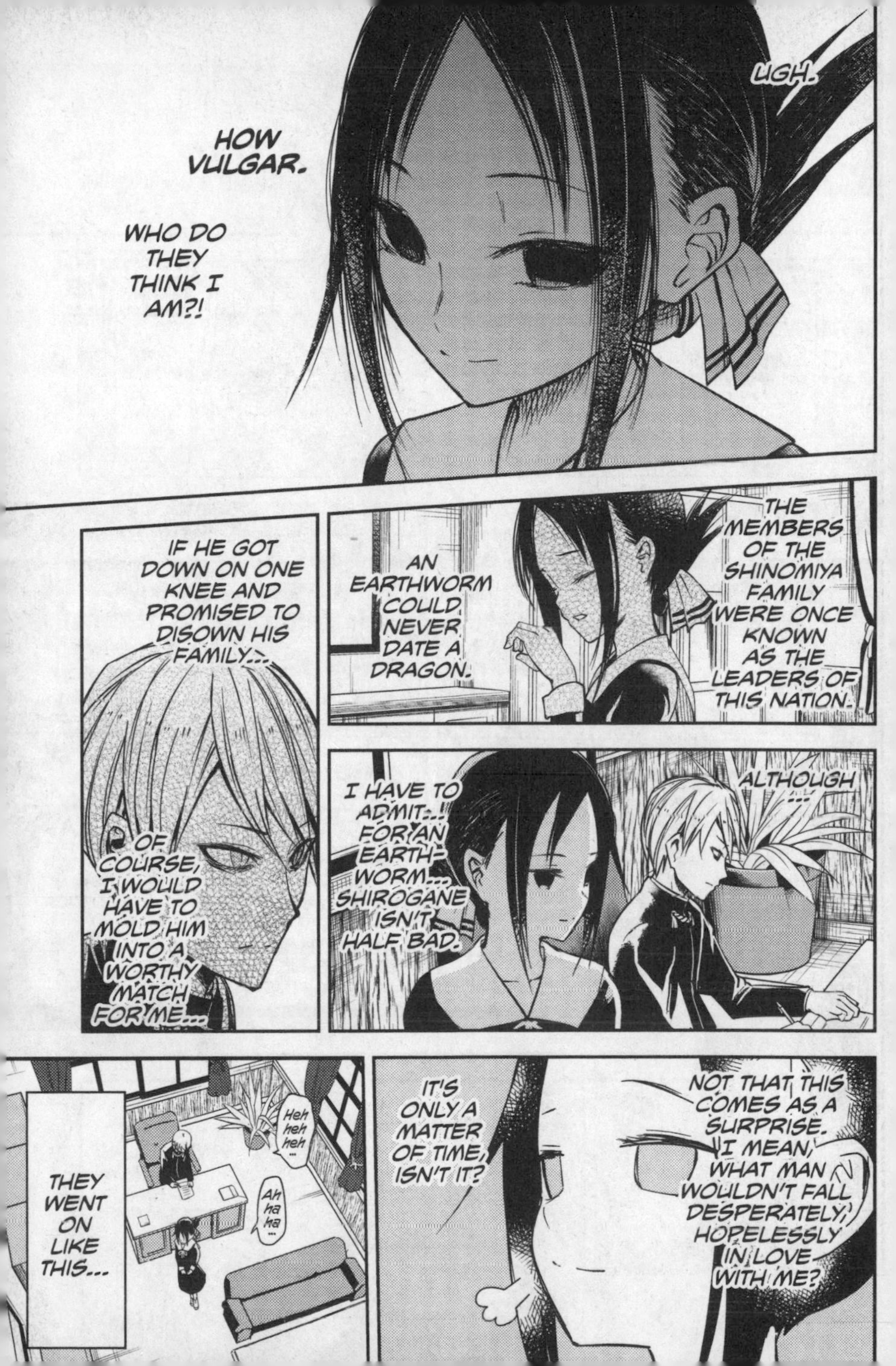
UGH.
HOW VULGAR.
WHO DO THEY THINK I AM?!
THE MEMBERS OF THE SHINOMIYA FAMILY WERE ONCE KNOWN AS THE LEADERS OF THIS NATION.
AN EARTHWORM COULD NEVER DATE A DRAGON.
ALTHOUGH...
I HAVE TO ADMIT... FOR AN EARTHWORM... SHIROGANE ISN'T HALF BAD.
IF HE GOT DOWN ON ONE KNEE AND PROMISED TO DISOWN HIS FAMILY...
OF COURSE, I WOULD HAVE TO MOLD HIM INTO A WORTHY MATCH FOR ME...
NOT THAT THIS COMES AS A SURPRISE. I MEAN, WHAT MAN WOULDN'T FALL DESPERATELY, HOPELESSLY IN LOVE WITH ME?
IT'S ONLY A MATTER OF TIME, ISN'T IT?
Heh heh heh...
Ah ha ha...
THEY WENT ON LIKE THIS...

...FOR HALF A YEAR!

...NOTHING HAPPENED!

AND IN ALL THAT TIME...

While I am trying to avoid gender bias, I firmly believe in the power of the maternal instinct. The essence of the maternal instinct is to bring another under one's wing, to possess, identify with, complement one's sense of self, to compensate for what one lacking. I thought that attraction to members of the complimentary difference possesses many of these aspects; the adult who the glitter...

EVENTUALLY, THE GEOLOGY STORE NEAR MY HOUSE BOUGHT MY COLLECTION.

WHEN I WAS LITTLE, I LIKED TO COLLECT BEAUTIFUL STONES. AS I GREW, THE STONES THAT I BROUGHT HOME ALSO GREW.

The gain-loss principle states th compared to the first impression, it presents a more favorable impress down the road, it will lead to a mo favorable impression overall. Rece terms of character development, phenomena is known as an act of communicatio already been establish havior patt actionable ploying th rough st k in whi intinu wh

THE OTHER DAY, WE GAVE HER A SURPRISE BIRTHDAY PARTY, AND SHE WAS THRILLED. IT'S RATHER IRONIC, SINCE THAT'S A KIND OF PRANK TOO.

AS A CHILD, I WAS OFTEN SCOLDED FOR PLAYING PRANKS ON MY NANNY.

...TO "I HAVE TO FORCE HIM/HER TO PROFESS HIS/HER LOVE TO ME"!

...''I GUESS I'D BE WILLING TO GO OUT WITH HIM/ HER IF THAT'S WHAT HE/ SHE REALLY WANTS"...

WITHOUT ANY ACTUAL PROGRESS, THEIR THINKING SHIFTED FROM...

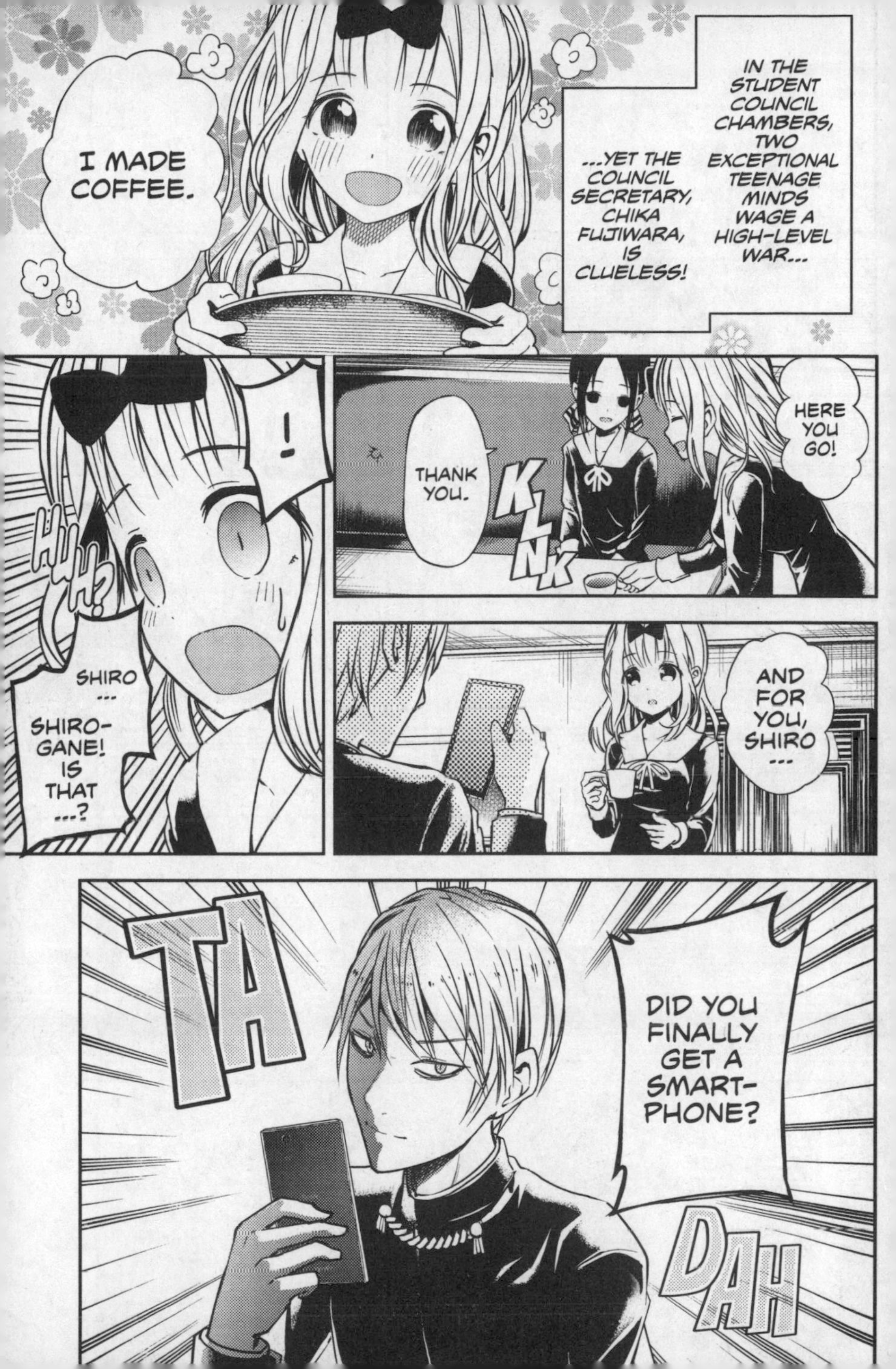
IN THE STUDENT COUNCIL CHAMBERS, TWO EXCEPTIONAL TEENAGE MINDS WAGE A HIGH-LEVEL WAR...
...YET THE COUNCIL SECRETARY, CHIKA FUJIWARA, IS CLUELESS!
I MADE COFFEE.
HERE YOU GO!
KLNK
THANK YOU.
AND FOR YOU, SHIRO---
!
HUH?
SHIRO--- SHIRO-GANE! IS THAT---?
TA
DID YOU FINALLY GET A SMART-PHONE?
DAH

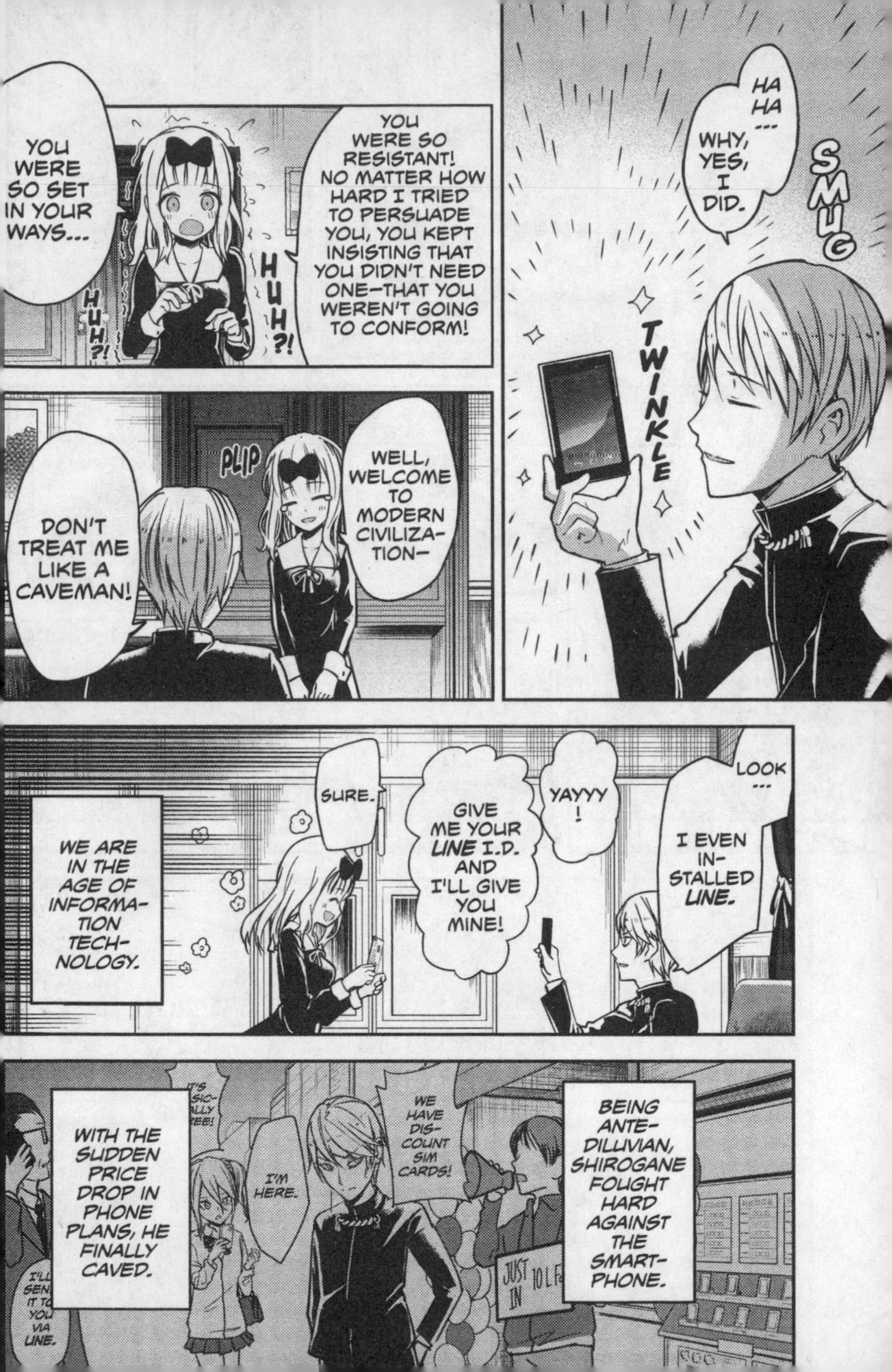
SMUG
HA HA... WHY, YES, I DID.
TWINKLE
YOU WERE SO RESISTANT! NO MATTER HOW HARD I TRIED TO PERSUADE YOU, YOU KEPT INSISTING THAT YOU DIDN'T NEED ONE—THAT YOU WEREN'T GOING TO CONFORM!
HUH HUH?!
HUH HUH?!
YOU WERE SO SET IN YOUR WAYS...
WELL, WELCOME TO MODERN CIVILIZA-TION—
PLIP
DON'T TREAT ME LIKE A CAVEMAN!
LOOK... I EVEN IN-STALLED LINE.
YAYYY!
GIVE ME YOUR LINE I.D. AND I'LL GIVE YOU MINE!
SURE.
WE ARE IN THE AGE OF INFORMA-TION TECH-NOLOGY.
BEING ANTE-DILUVIAN, SHIROGANE FOUGHT HARD AGAINST THE SMART-PHONE.
WE HAVE DIS-COUNT SIM CARDS!
JUST IN
I'M HERE.
WITH THE SUDDEN PRICE DROP IN PHONE PLANS, HE FINALLY CAVED.

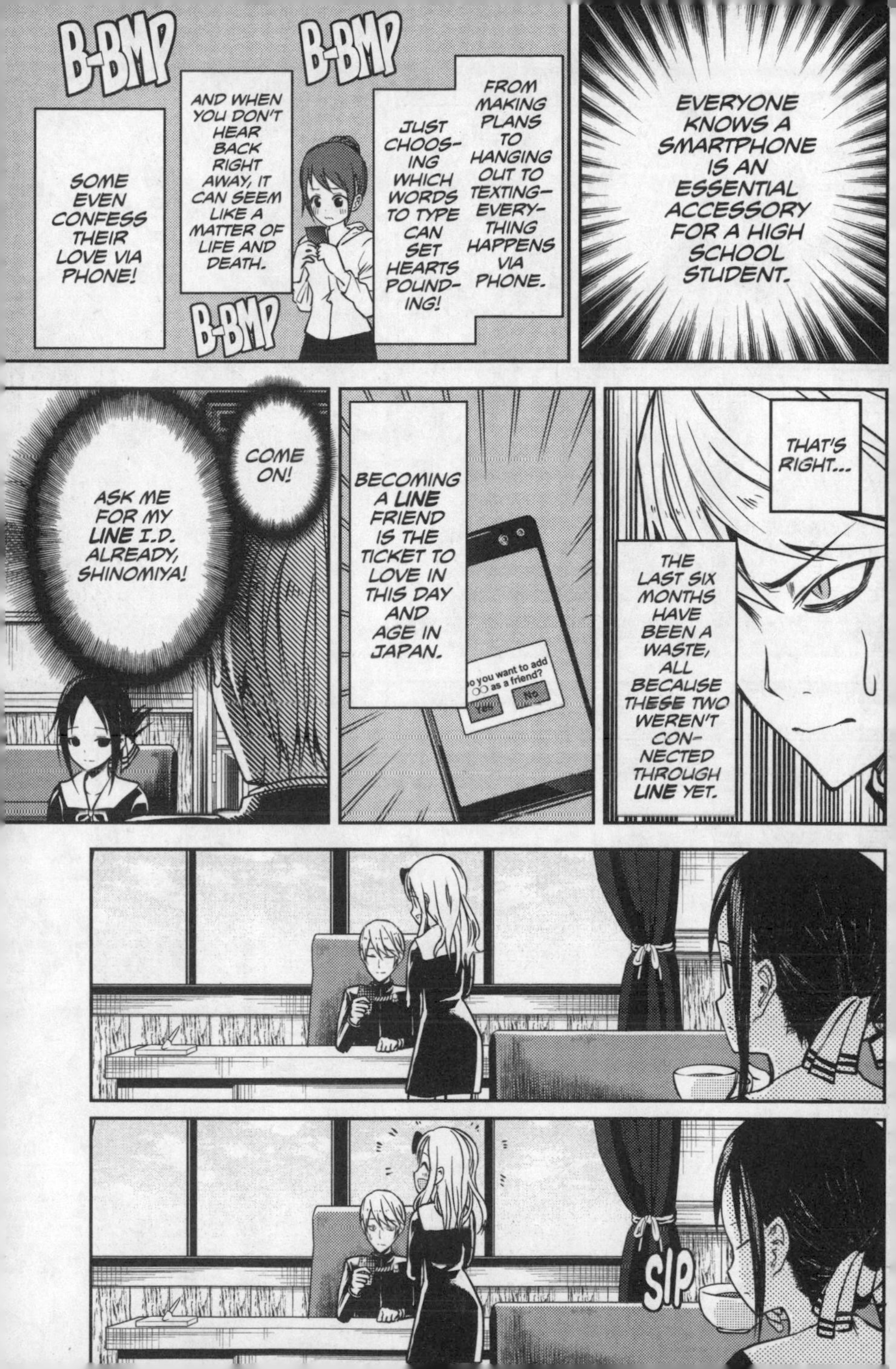
EVERYONE KNOWS A SMARTPHONE IS AN ESSENTIAL ACCESSORY FOR A HIGH SCHOOL STUDENT.
FROM MAKING PLANS TO HANGING OUT TO TEXTING—EVERYTHING HAPPENS VIA PHONE.
JUST CHOOSING WHICH WORDS TO TYPE CAN SET HEARTS POUNDING!
B-BMP
AND WHEN YOU DON'T HEAR BACK RIGHT AWAY, IT CAN SEEM LIKE A MATTER OF LIFE AND DEATH.
B-BMP
SOME EVEN CONFESS THEIR LOVE VIA PHONE!
B-BMP
THAT'S RIGHT...
THE LAST SIX MONTHS HAVE BEEN A WASTE, ALL BECAUSE THESE TWO WEREN'T CONNECTED THROUGH LINE YET.
BECOMING A LINE FRIEND IS THE TICKET TO LOVE IN THIS DAY AND AGE IN JAPAN.
as a friend?
No
COME ON!
ASK ME FOR MY LINE I.D. ALREADY, SHINOMIYA!
SIP

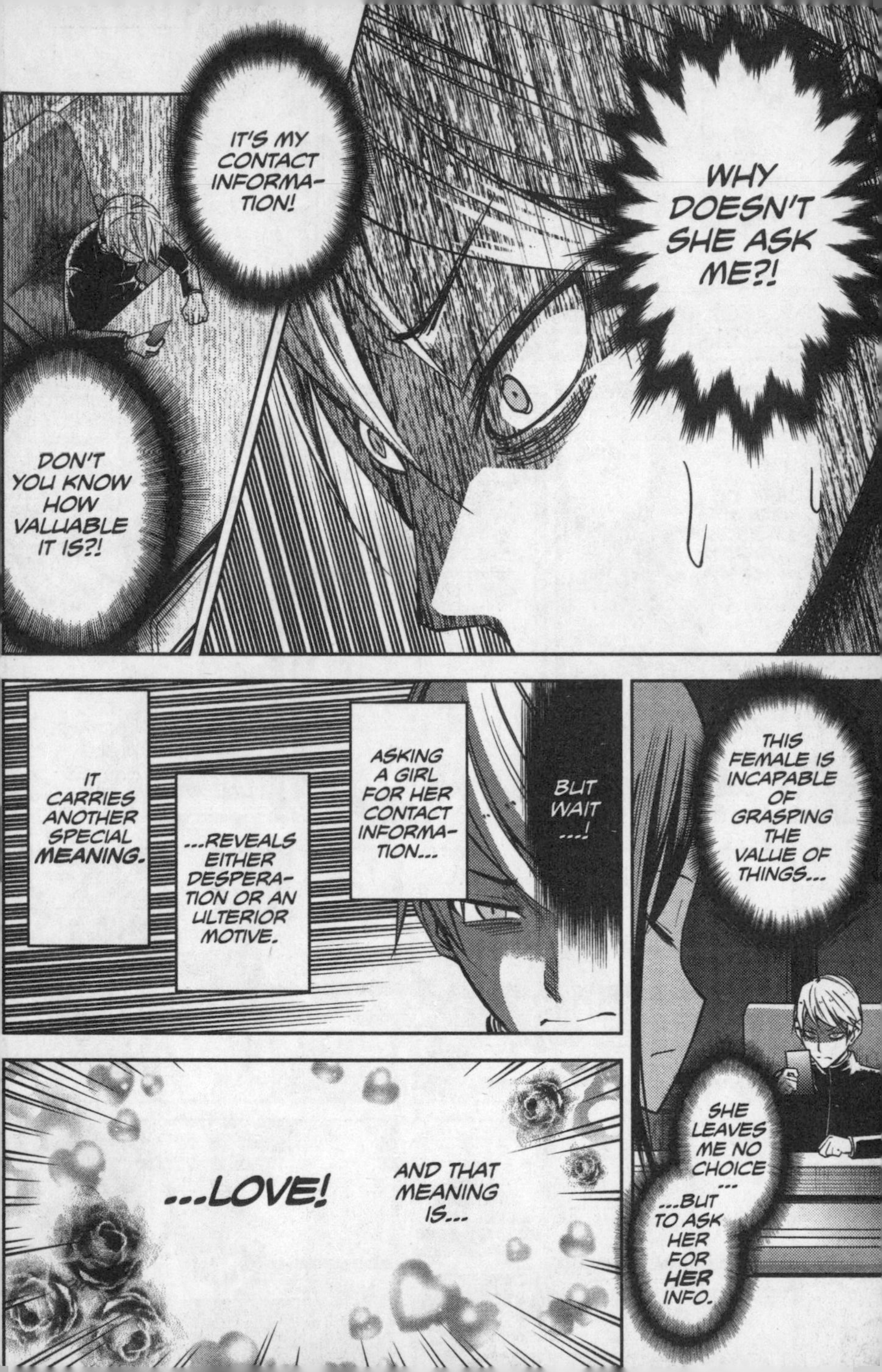
WHY DOESN'T SHE ASK ME?!
IT'S MY CONTACT INFORMATION!
DON'T YOU KNOW HOW VALUABLE IT IS?!
THIS FEMALE IS INCAPABLE OF GRASPING THE VALUE OF THINGS...
SHE LEAVES ME NO CHOICE...
...BUT TO ASK HER FOR HER INFO.
BUT WAIT...!
ASKING A GIRL FOR HER CONTACT INFORMATION...
...REVEALS EITHER DESPERATION OR AN ULTERIOR MOTIVE.
IT CARRIES ANOTHER SPECIAL MEANING.
AND THAT MEANING IS...
...LOVE!

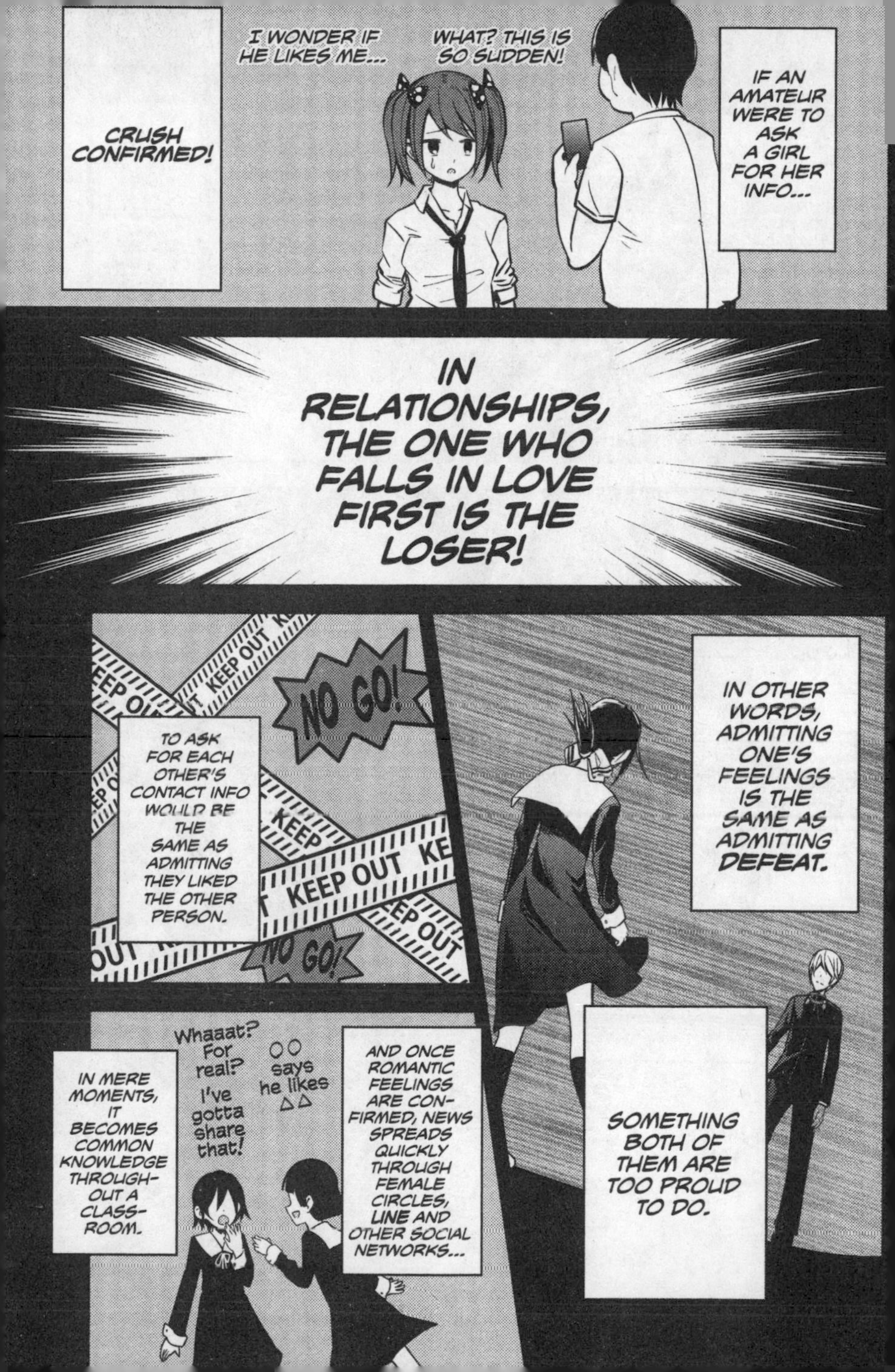
IF AN AMATEUR WERE TO ASK A GIRL FOR HER INFO...
WHAT? THIS IS SO SUDDEN!
I WONDER IF HE LIKES ME...
CRUSH CONFIRMED!
IN RELATIONSHIPS, THE ONE WHO FALLS IN LOVE FIRST IS THE LOSER!
IN OTHER WORDS, ADMITTING ONE'S FEELINGS IS THE SAME AS ADMITTING DEFEAT.
SOMETHING BOTH OF THEM ARE TOO PROUD TO DO.
NO GO!
KEEP OUT
TO ASK FOR EACH OTHER'S CONTACT INFO WOULD BE THE SAME AS ADMITTING THEY LIKED THE OTHER PERSON.
NO GO!
AND ONCE ROMANTIC FEELINGS ARE CONFIRMED, NEWS SPREADS QUICKLY THROUGH FEMALE CIRCLES, LINE AND OTHER SOCIAL NETWORKS...
○○ says he likes △△
Whaaat? For real? I've gotta share that!
IN MERE MOMENTS, IT BECOMES COMMON KNOWLEDGE THROUGHOUT A CLASSROOM.

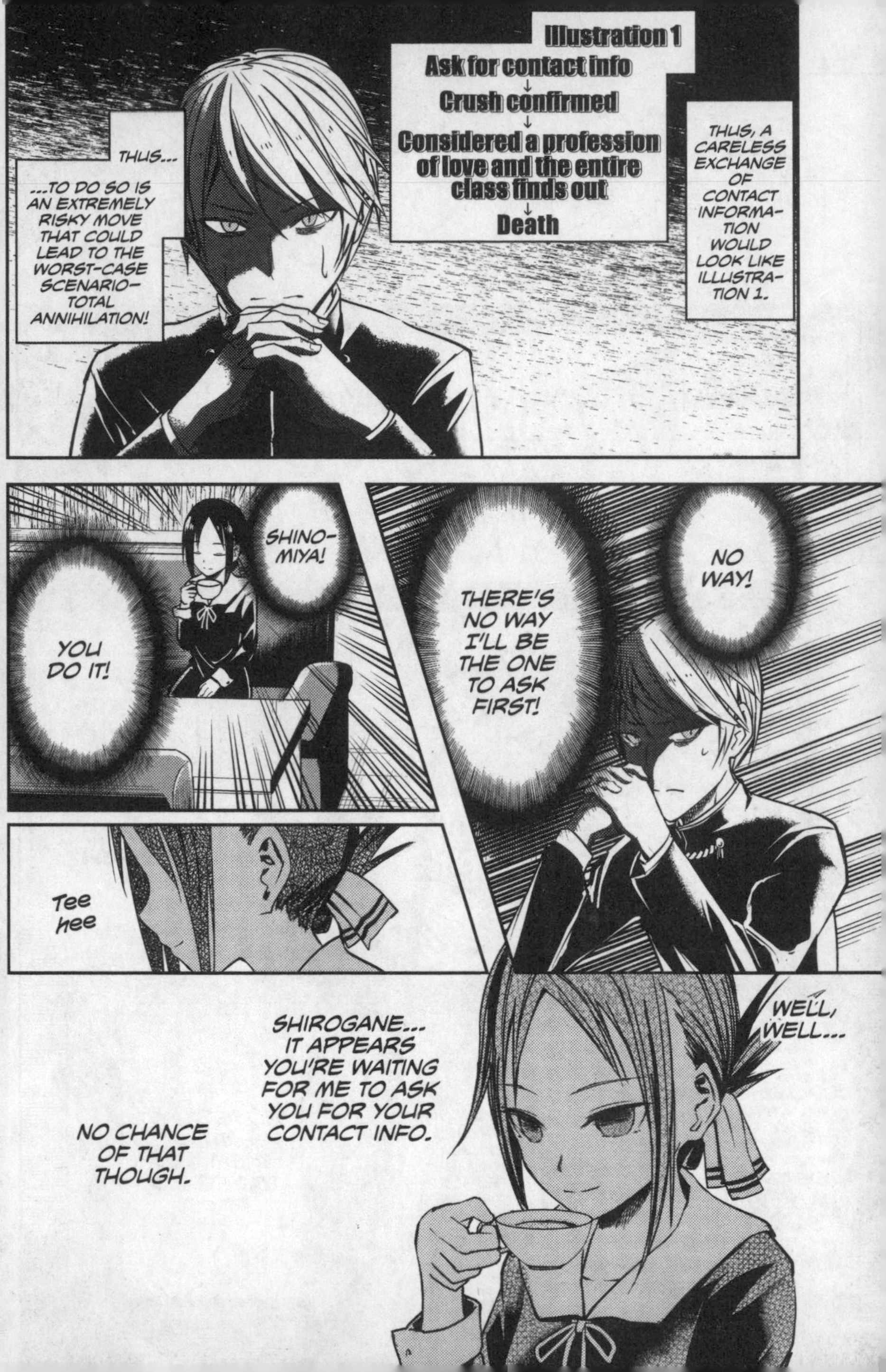
THUS, A CARELESS EXCHANGE OF CONTACT INFORMATION WOULD LOOK LIKE ILLUSTRATION 1.
Illustration 1
Ask for contact info
↓
Crush confirmed
↓
Considered a profession of love and the entire class finds out
↓
Death
THUS...
...TO DO SO IS AN EXTREMELY RISKY MOVE THAT COULD LEAD TO THE WORST-CASE SCENARIO—TOTAL ANNIHILATION!
NO WAY!
THERE'S NO WAY I'LL BE THE ONE TO ASK FIRST!
SHINOMIYA!
YOU DO IT!
Tee hee
WELL, WELL...
SHIROGANE... IT APPEARS YOU'RE WAITING FOR ME TO ASK YOU FOR YOUR CONTACT INFO.
NO CHANCE OF THAT THOUGH.

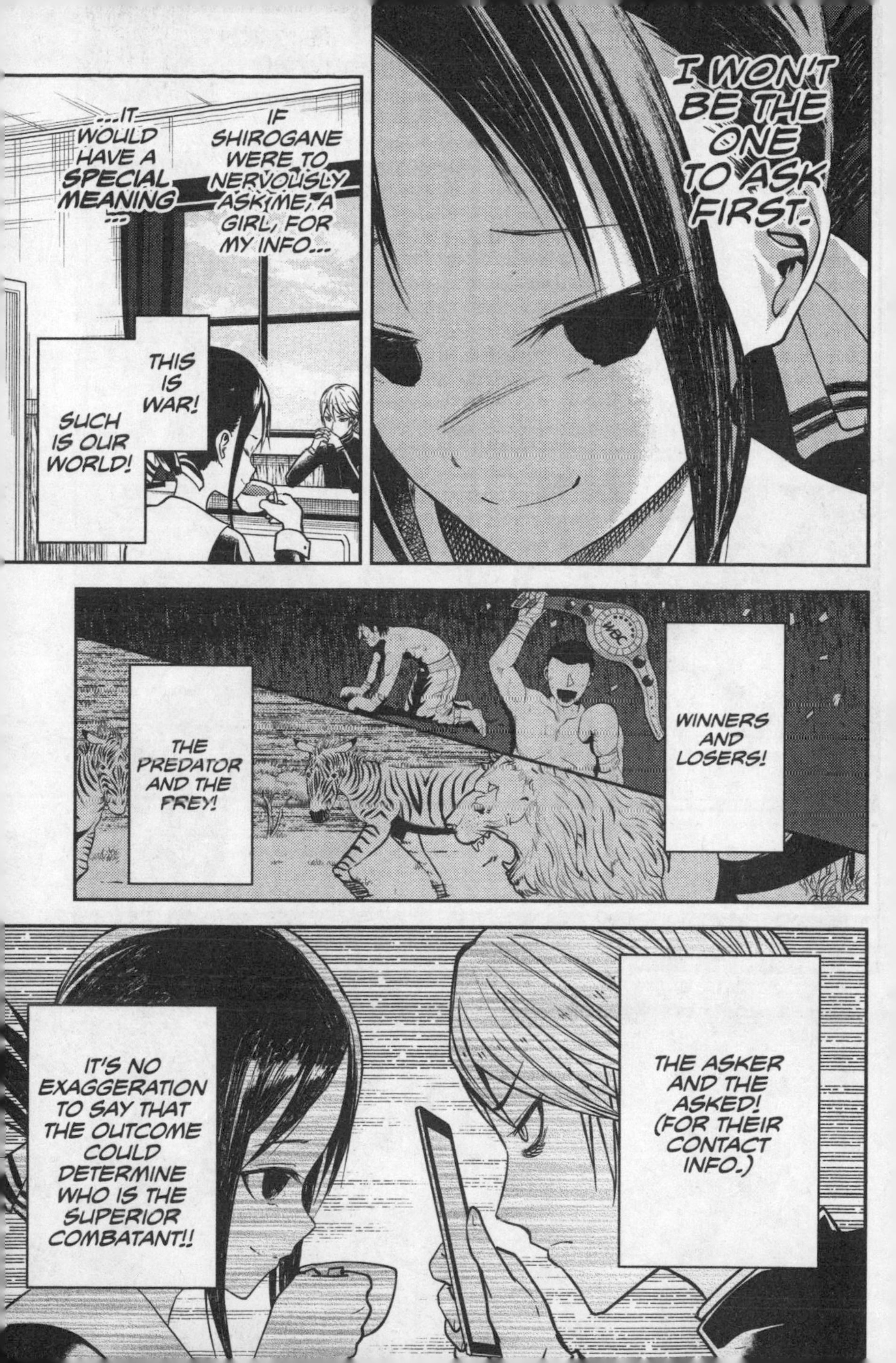
I WON'T BE THE ONE TO ASK FIRST.
IF SHIROGANE WERE TO NERVOUSLY ASK ME, A GIRL, FOR MY INFO...
...IT WOULD HAVE A SPECIAL MEANING...
THIS IS WAR!
SUCH IS OUR WORLD!
WINNERS AND LOSERS!
THE PREDATOR AND THE PREY!
THE ASKER AND THE ASKED! (FOR THEIR CONTACT INFO.)
IT'S NO EXAGGERATION TO SAY THAT THE OUTCOME COULD DETERMINE WHO IS THE SUPERIOR COMBATANT!!

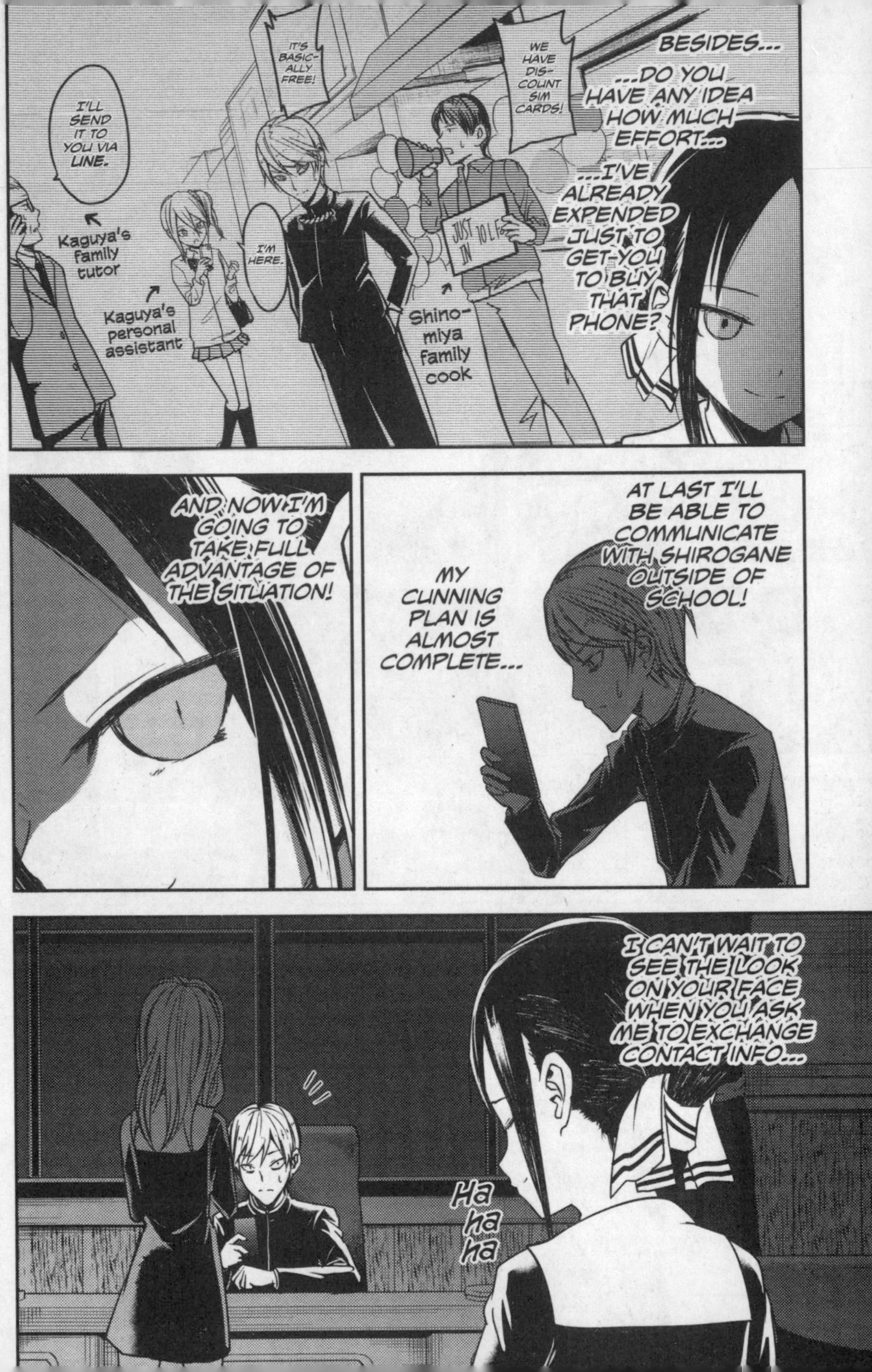
BESIDES...
...DO YOU HAVE ANY IDEA HOW MUCH EFFORT...
...I'VE ALREADY EXPENDED JUST TO GET YOU TO BUY THAT PHONE?
WE HAVE DIS-COUNT SIM CARDS!
JUST IN
Shino-miya family cook
IT'S BASIC-ALLY FREE!
I'M HERE.
Kaguya's personal assistant
I'LL SEND IT TO YOU VIA LINE.
Kaguya's family tutor
AT LAST I'LL BE ABLE TO COMMUNICATE WITH SHIROGANE OUTSIDE OF SCHOOL!
MY CUNNING PLAN IS ALMOST COMPLETE...
AND NOW I'M GOING TO TAKE FULL ADVANTAGE OF THE SITUATION!
I CAN'T WAIT TO SEE THE LOOK ON YOUR FACE WHEN YOU ASK ME TO EXCHANGE CONTACT INFO...
Ha ha ha

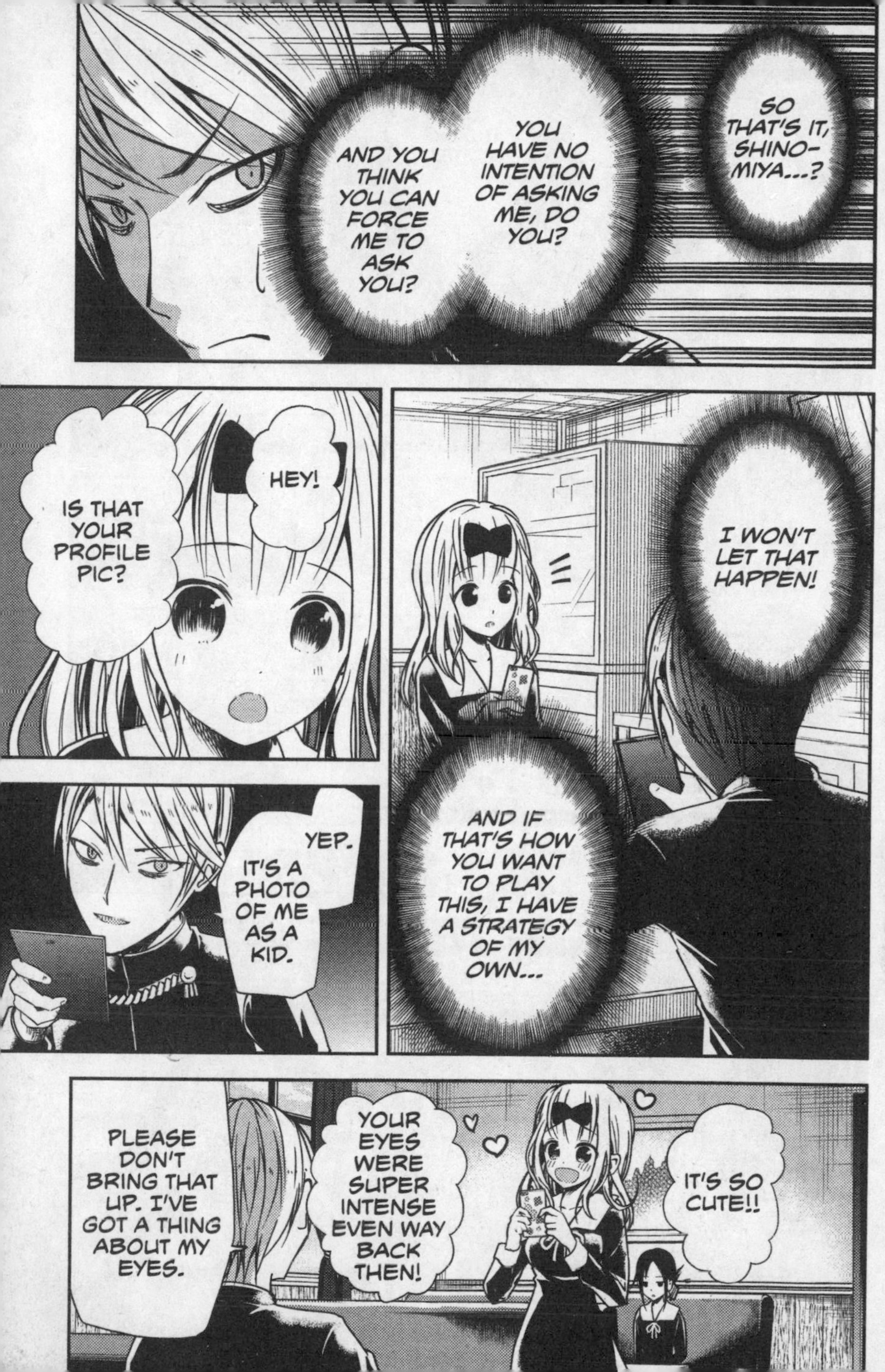
SO THAT'S IT, SHINO-MIYA...?
YOU HAVE NO INTENTION OF ASKING ME, DO YOU?
AND YOU THINK YOU CAN FORCE ME TO ASK YOU?
I WON'T LET THAT HAPPEN!
AND IF THAT'S HOW YOU WANT TO PLAY THIS, I HAVE A STRATEGY OF MY OWN...
HEY!
IS THAT YOUR PROFILE PIC?
YEP.
IT'S A PHOTO OF ME AS A KID.
IT'S SO CUTE!!
YOUR EYES WERE SUPER INTENSE EVEN WAY BACK THEN!
PLEASE DON'T BRING THAT UP. I'VE GOT A THING ABOUT MY EYES.

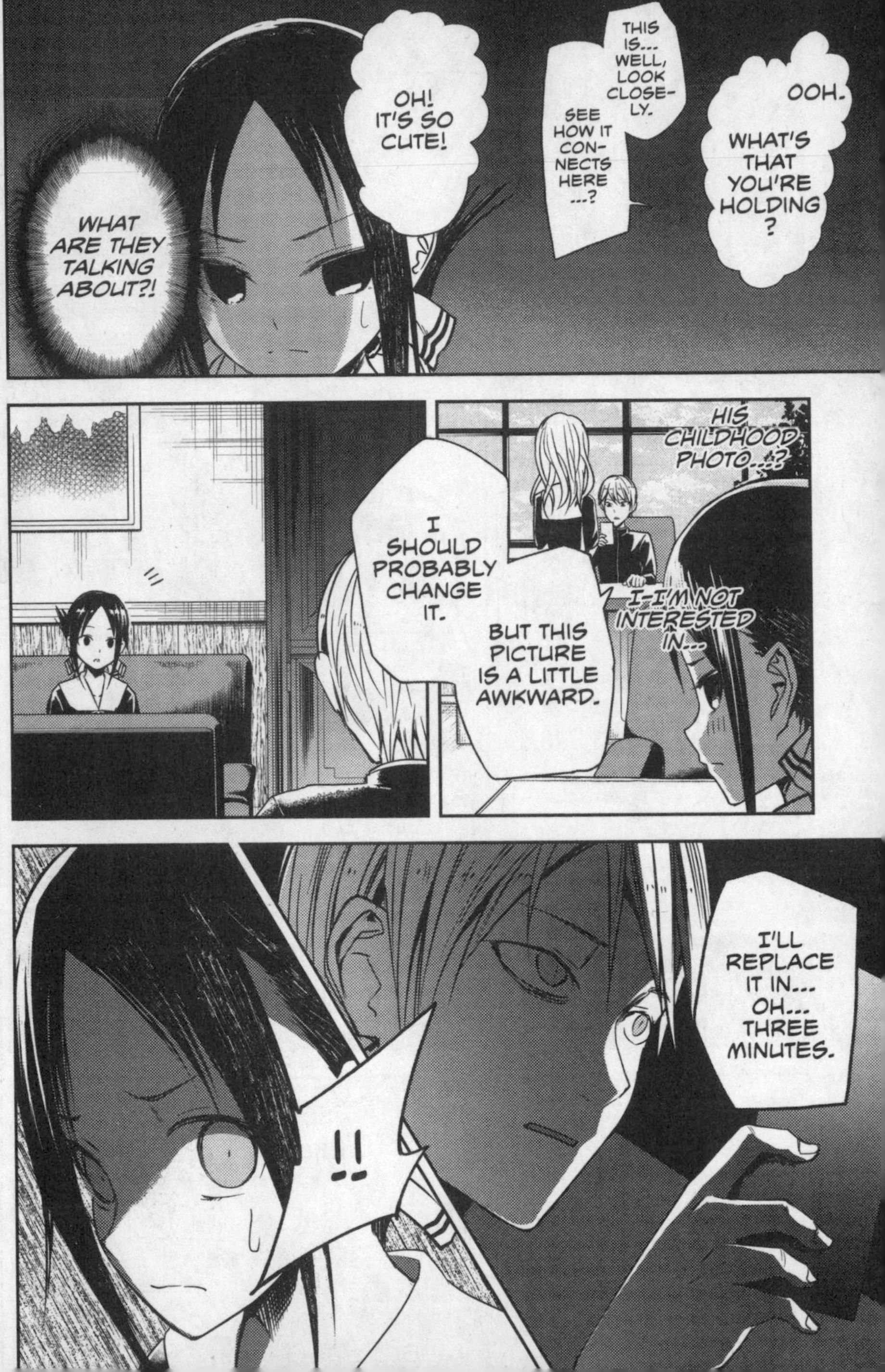
OOH. WHAT'S THAT YOU'RE HOLDING?
THIS IS... WELL, LOOK CLOSE-LY.
SEE HOW IT CON-NECTS HERE...?
OH! IT'S SO CUTE!
WHAT ARE THEY TALKING ABOUT?!
HIS CHILDHOOD PHOTO...?
I SHOULD PROBABLY CHANGE IT.
BUT THIS PICTURE IS A LITTLE AWKWARD.
I-I'M NOT INTERESTED IN...
I'LL REPLACE IT IN... OH... THREE MINUTES.
!!

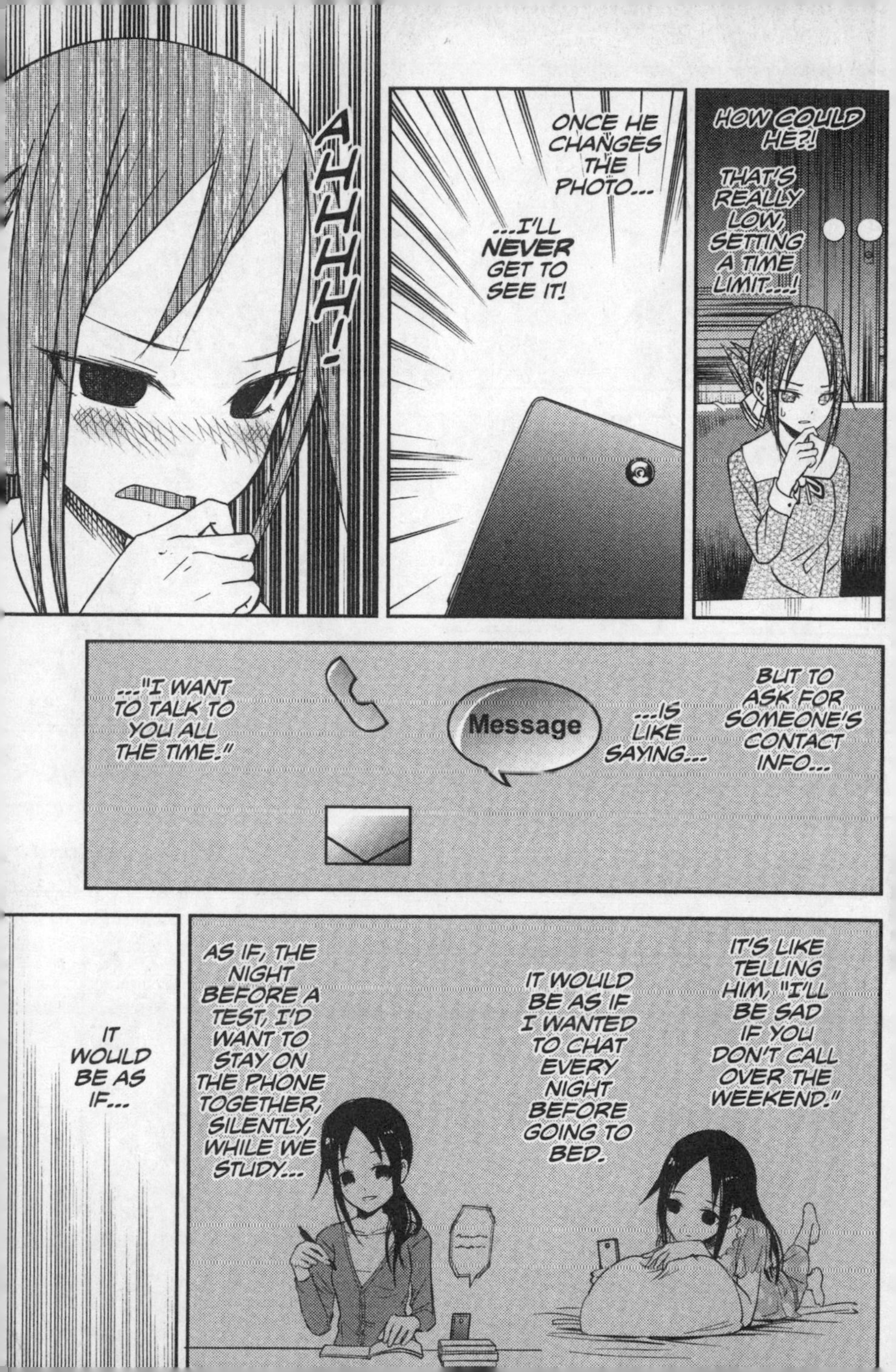
HOW COULD HE?!
THAT'S REALLY LOW, SETTING A TIME LIMIT...!
ONCE HE CHANGES THE PHOTO...
...I'LL NEVER GET TO SEE IT!
AHHHH!
BUT TO ASK FOR SOMEONE'S CONTACT INFO...
...IS LIKE SAYING...
Message
..."I WANT TO TALK TO YOU ALL THE TIME."
IT'S LIKE TELLING HIM, "I'LL BE SAD IF YOU DON'T CALL OVER THE WEEKEND."
IT WOULD BE AS IF I WANTED TO CHAT EVERY NIGHT BEFORE GOING TO BED.
AS IF, THE NIGHT BEFORE A TEST, I'D WANT TO STAY ON THE PHONE TOGETHER, SILENTLY, WHILE WE STUDY...
IT WOULD BE AS IF...

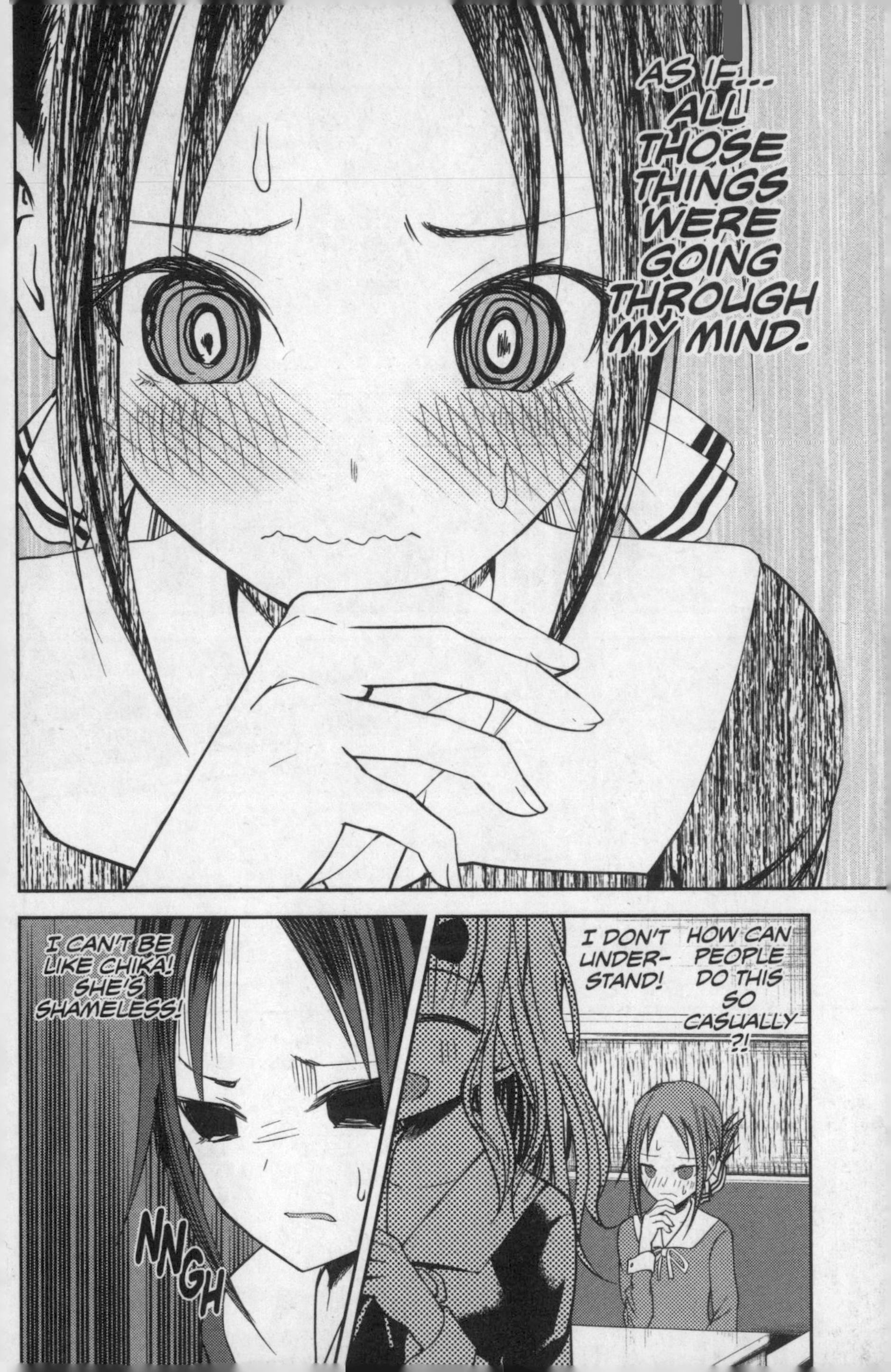
AS IF... ALL THOSE THINGS WERE GOING THROUGH MY MIND.
HOW CAN PEOPLE DO THIS SO CASUALLY?!
I DON'T UNDER-STAND!
I CAN'T BE LIKE CHIKA! SHE'S SHAMELESS!
NNGH

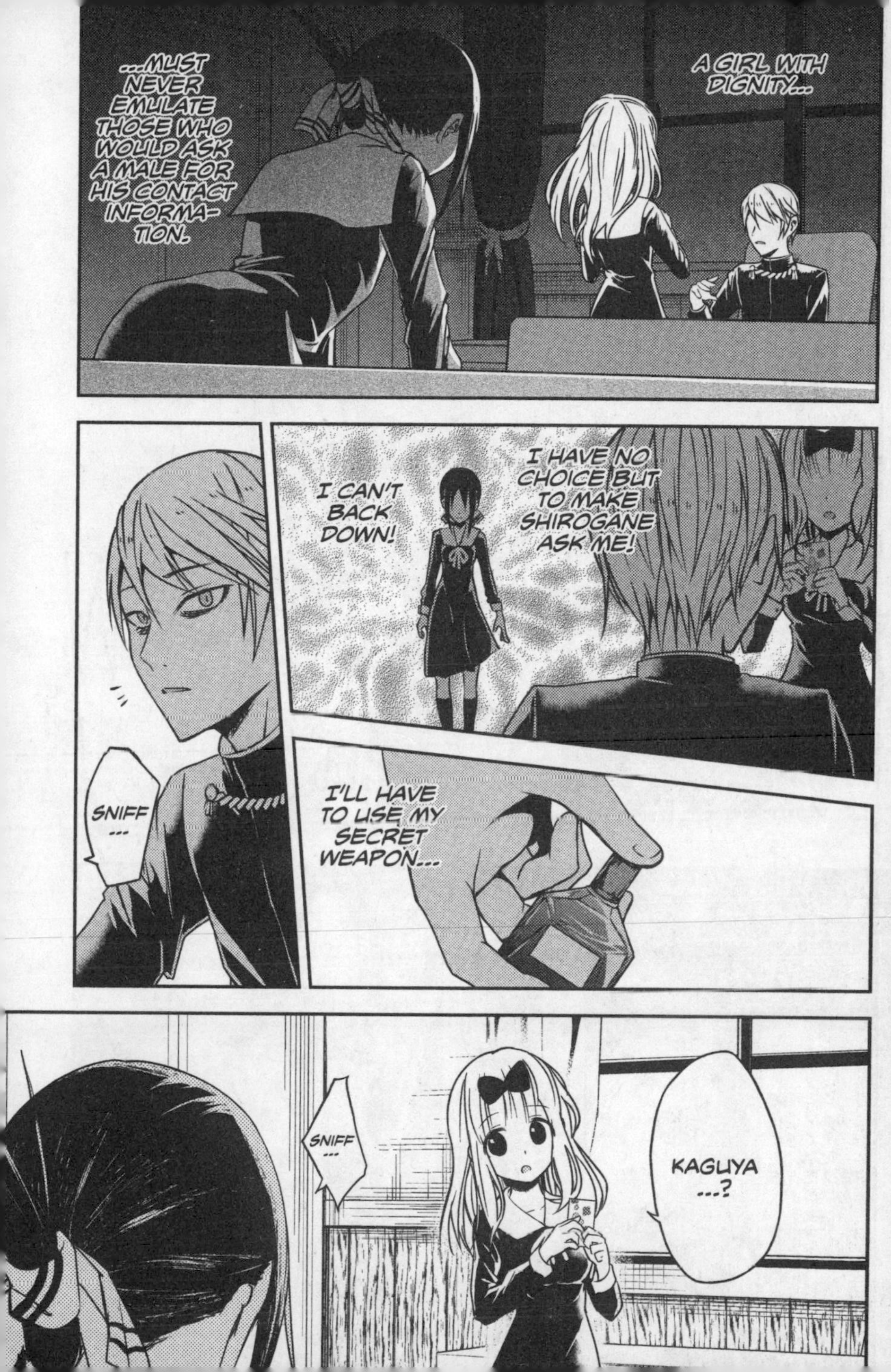
A GIRL WITH DIGNITY...
...MUST NEVER EMULATE THOSE WHO WOULD ASK A MALE FOR HIS CONTACT INFORMATION.
I HAVE NO CHOICE BUT TO MAKE SHIROGANE ASK ME!
I CAN'T BACK DOWN!
I'LL HAVE TO USE MY SECRET WEAPON...
SNIFF...
KAGUYA...?
SNIFF...

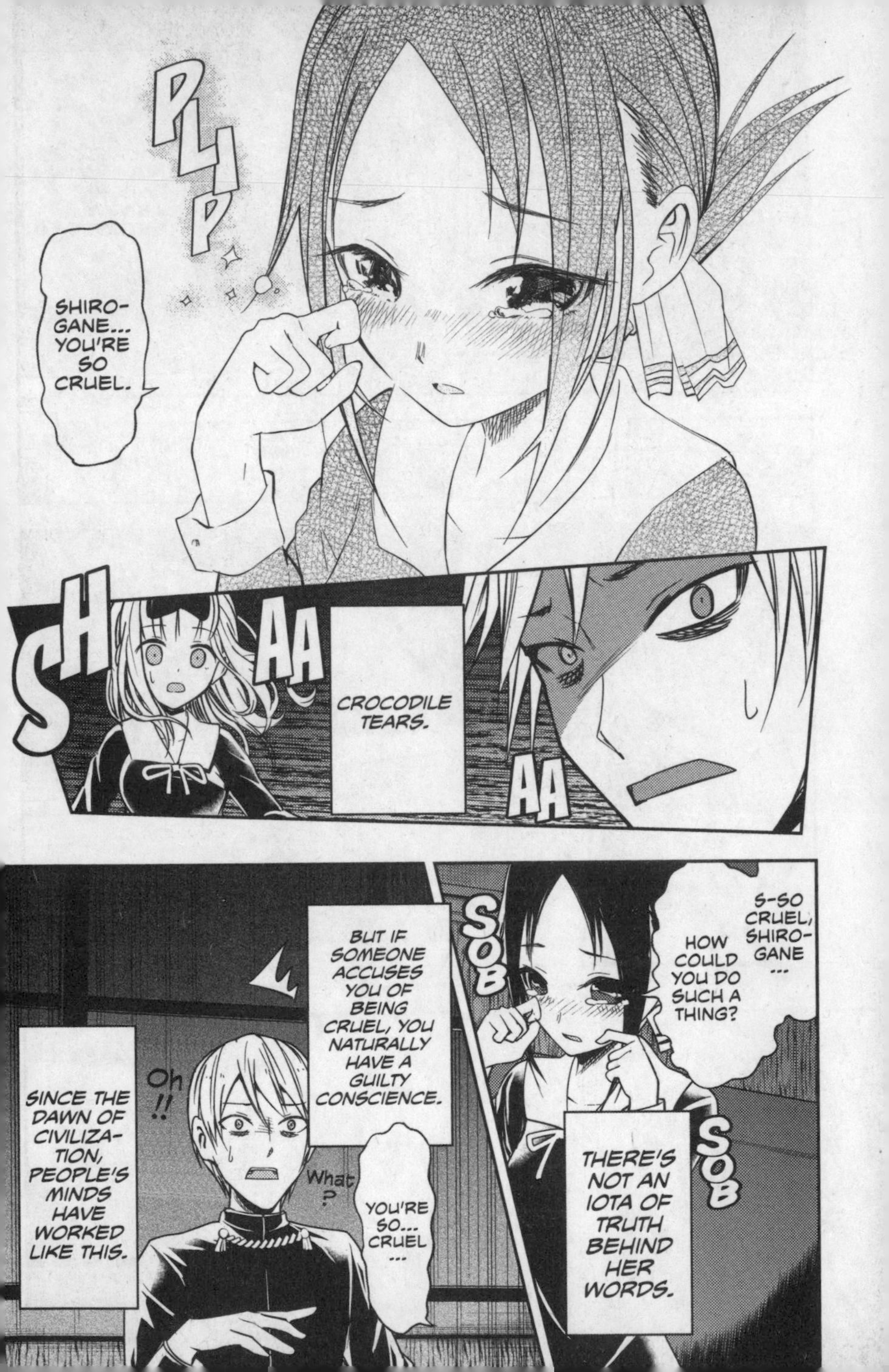

PLIP
SHIRO-GANE... YOU'RE SO CRUEL.
SHAA
CROCODILE TEARS.
AA
S-SO CRUEL, SHIRO-GANE...
HOW COULD YOU DO SUCH A THING?
SOB
SOB
THERE'S NOT AN IOTA OF TRUTH BEHIND HER WORDS.
BUT IF SOMEONE ACCUSES YOU OF BEING CRUEL, YOU NATURALLY HAVE A GUILTY CONSCIENCE.
YOU'RE SO... CRUEL...
What?
Oh!!
SINCE THE DAWN OF CIVILIZA-TION, PEOPLE'S MINDS HAVE WORKED LIKE THIS.

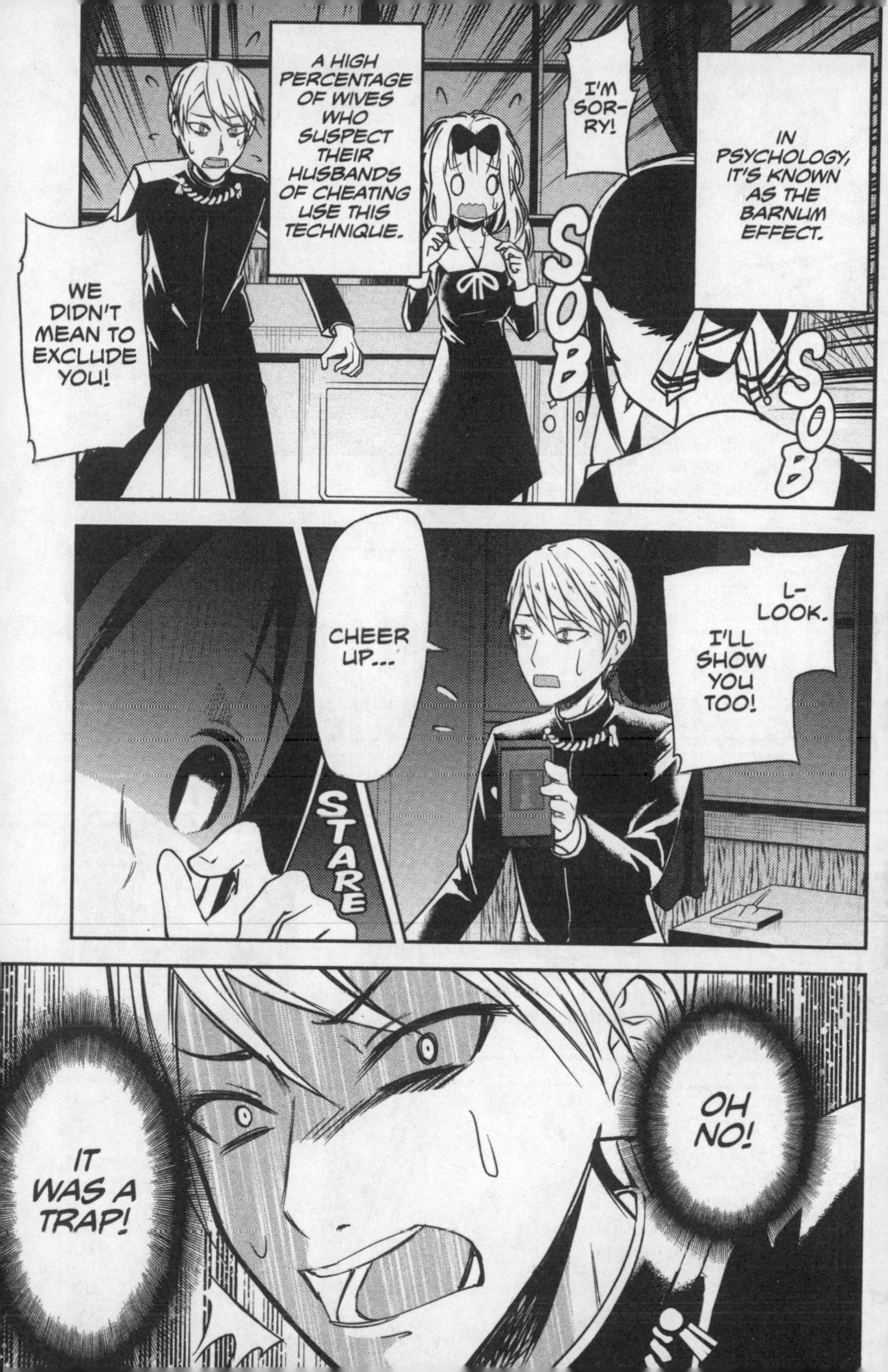
IN PSYCHOLOGY, IT'S KNOWN AS THE BARNUM EFFECT.
SOB
SOB
I'M SORRY!
SOB
A HIGH PERCENTAGE OF WIVES WHO SUSPECT THEIR HUSBANDS OF CHEATING USE THIS TECHNIQUE.
WE DIDN'T MEAN TO EXCLUDE YOU!
L- LOOK.
I'LL SHOW YOU TOO!
CHEER UP...
STARE
OH NO!
IT WAS A TRAP!

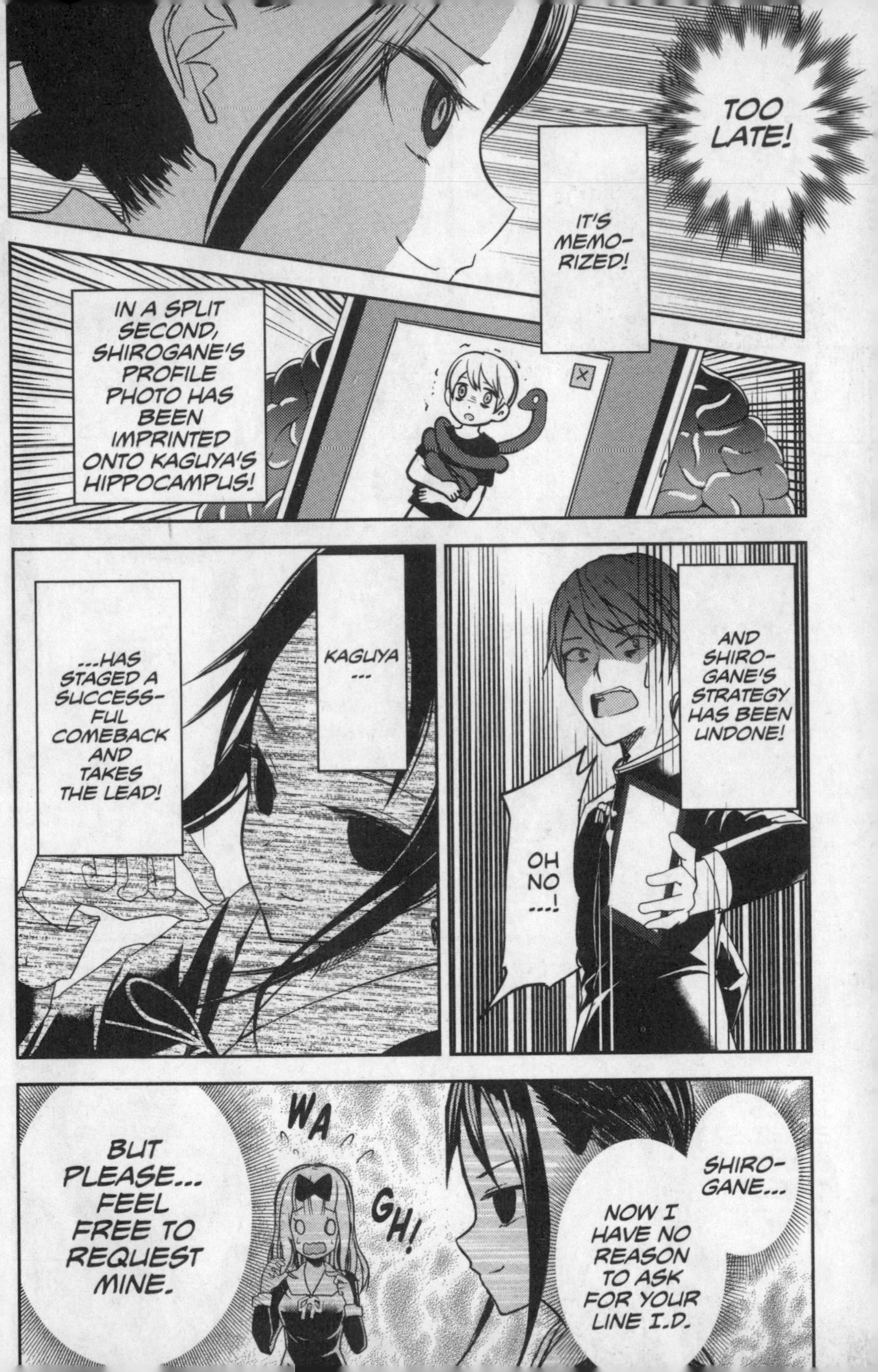
TOO LATE!
IT'S MEMORIZED!
IN A SPLIT SECOND, SHIROGANE'S PROFILE PHOTO HAS BEEN IMPRINTED ONTO KAGUYA'S HIPPOCAMPUS!
AND SHIROGANE'S STRATEGY HAS BEEN UNDONE!
OH NO ...!
KAGUYA ...
...HAS STAGED A SUCCESSFUL COMEBACK AND TAKES THE LEAD!
SHIROGANE...
NOW I HAVE NO REASON TO ASK FOR YOUR LINE I.D.
WAGH!
BUT PLEASE... FEEL FREE TO REQUEST MINE.

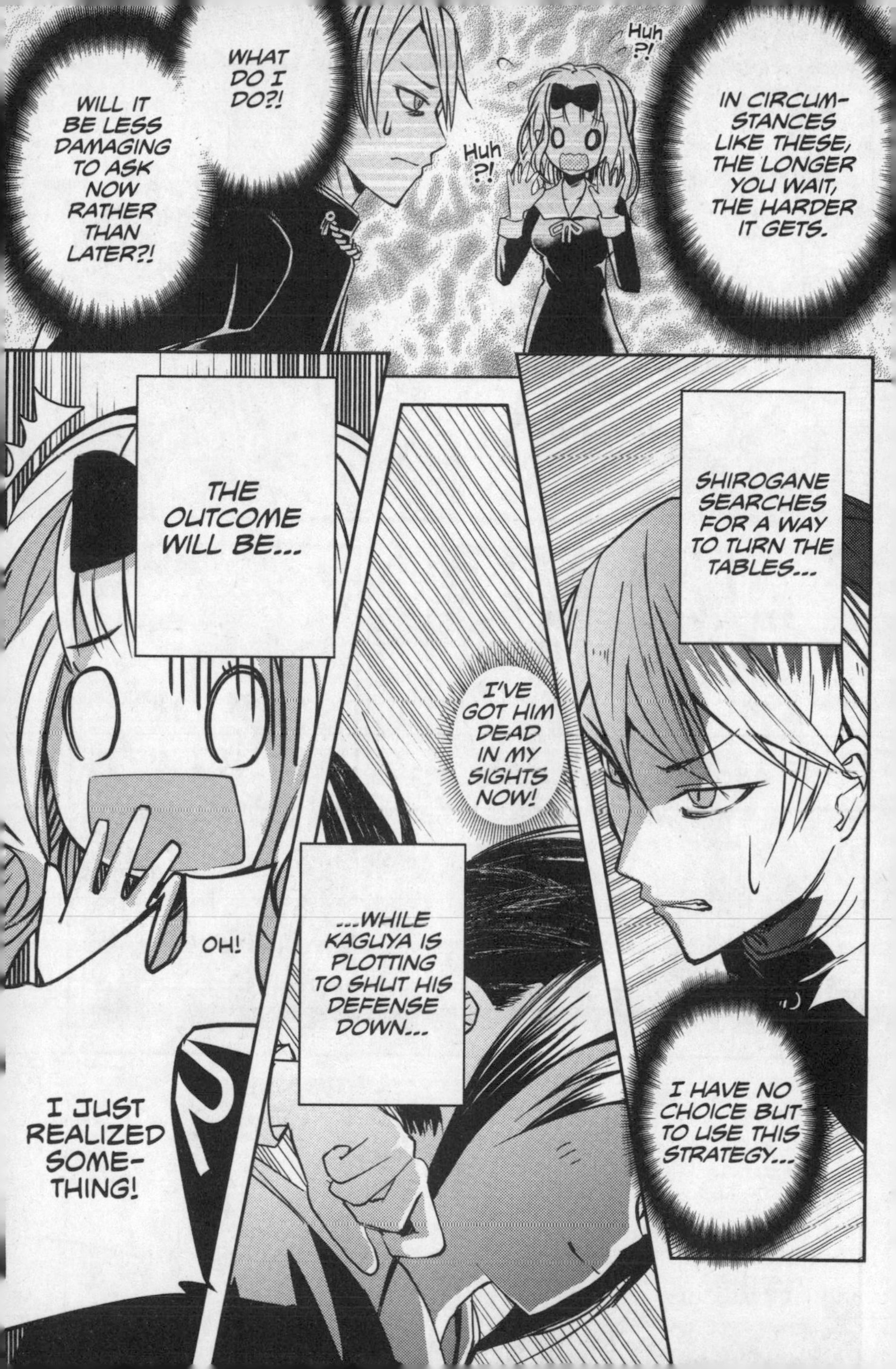
IN CIRCUM-STANCES LIKE THESE, THE LONGER YOU WAIT, THE HARDER IT GETS.
Huh ?!
Huh ?!
WHAT DO I DO?!
WILL IT BE LESS DAMAGING TO ASK NOW RATHER THAN LATER?!
SHIROGANE SEARCHES FOR A WAY TO TURN THE TABLES...
I HAVE NO CHOICE BUT TO USE THIS STRATEGY...
I'VE GOT HIM DEAD IN MY SIGHTS NOW!
...WHILE KAGUYA IS PLOTTING TO SHUT HIS DEFENSE DOWN...
THE OUTCOME WILL BE...
OH!
I JUST REALIZED SOME-THING!

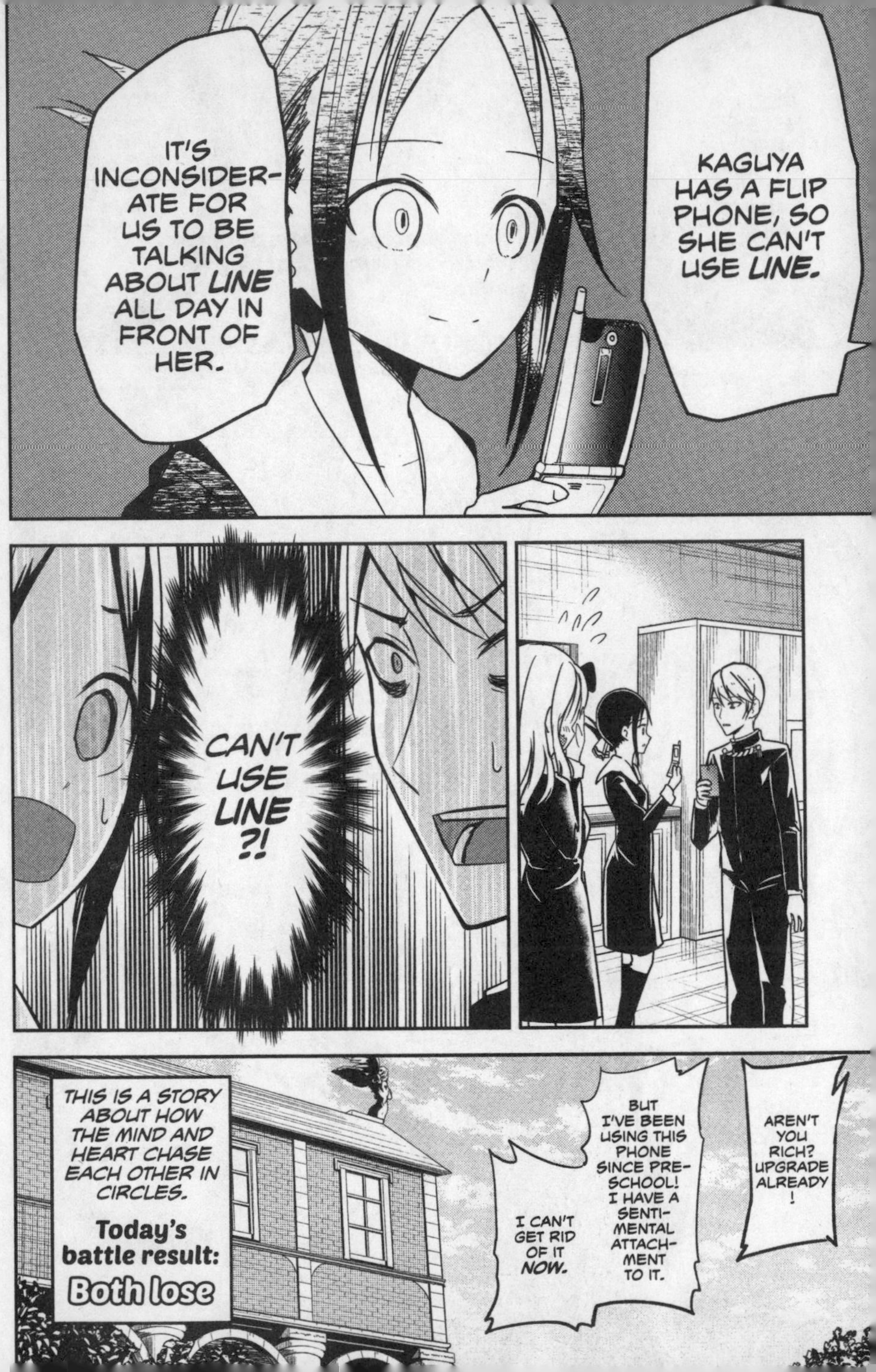

KAGUYA HAS A FLIP PHONE, SO SHE CAN'T USE *LINE*.
IT'S INCONSIDERATE FOR US TO BE TALKING ABOUT *LINE* ALL DAY IN FRONT OF HER.
CAN'T USE LINE?!
AREN'T YOU RICH? UPGRADE ALREADY!
BUT I'VE BEEN USING THIS PHONE SINCE PRESCHOOL! I HAVE A SENTIMENTAL ATTACHMENT TO IT.
I CAN'T GET RID OF IT *NOW*.
THIS IS A STORY ABOUT HOW THE MIND AND HEART CHASE EACH OTHER IN CIRCLES.
Today's battle result:
Both lose

Beginning with this chapter in Japan, this series transferred from *Miracle Jump* magazine to *Weekly Young Jump*.

There are no changes to the setting, sequence, etc. Please just consider this a continuation of the *Miracle* version.

I'm having a lot of déjà vu!

KAGUYA-SAMA

LOVE IS WAR

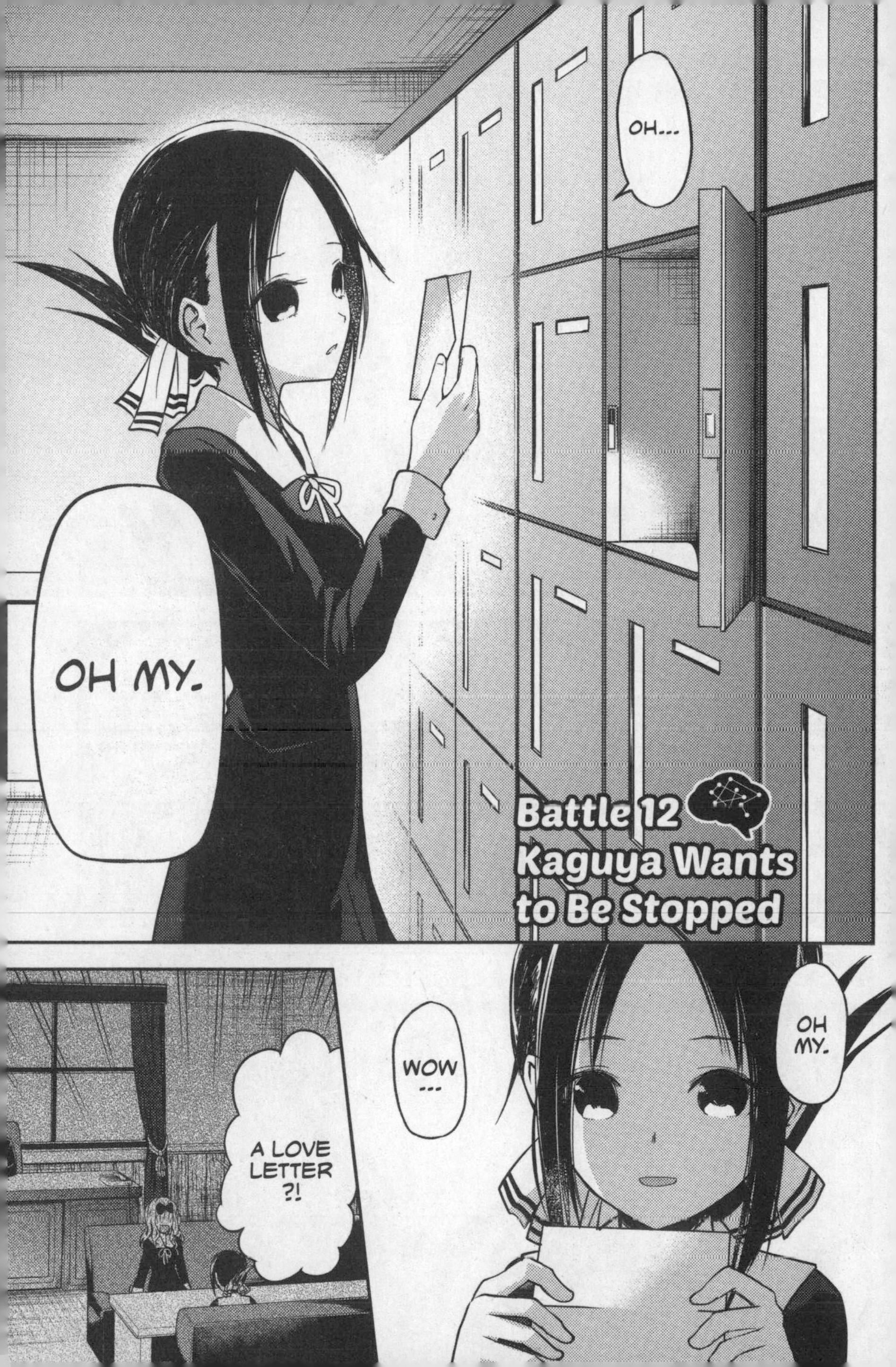
OH...
OH MY.
Battle 12
Kaguya Wants to Be Stopped
OH MY.
WOW ...
A LOVE LETTER ?!

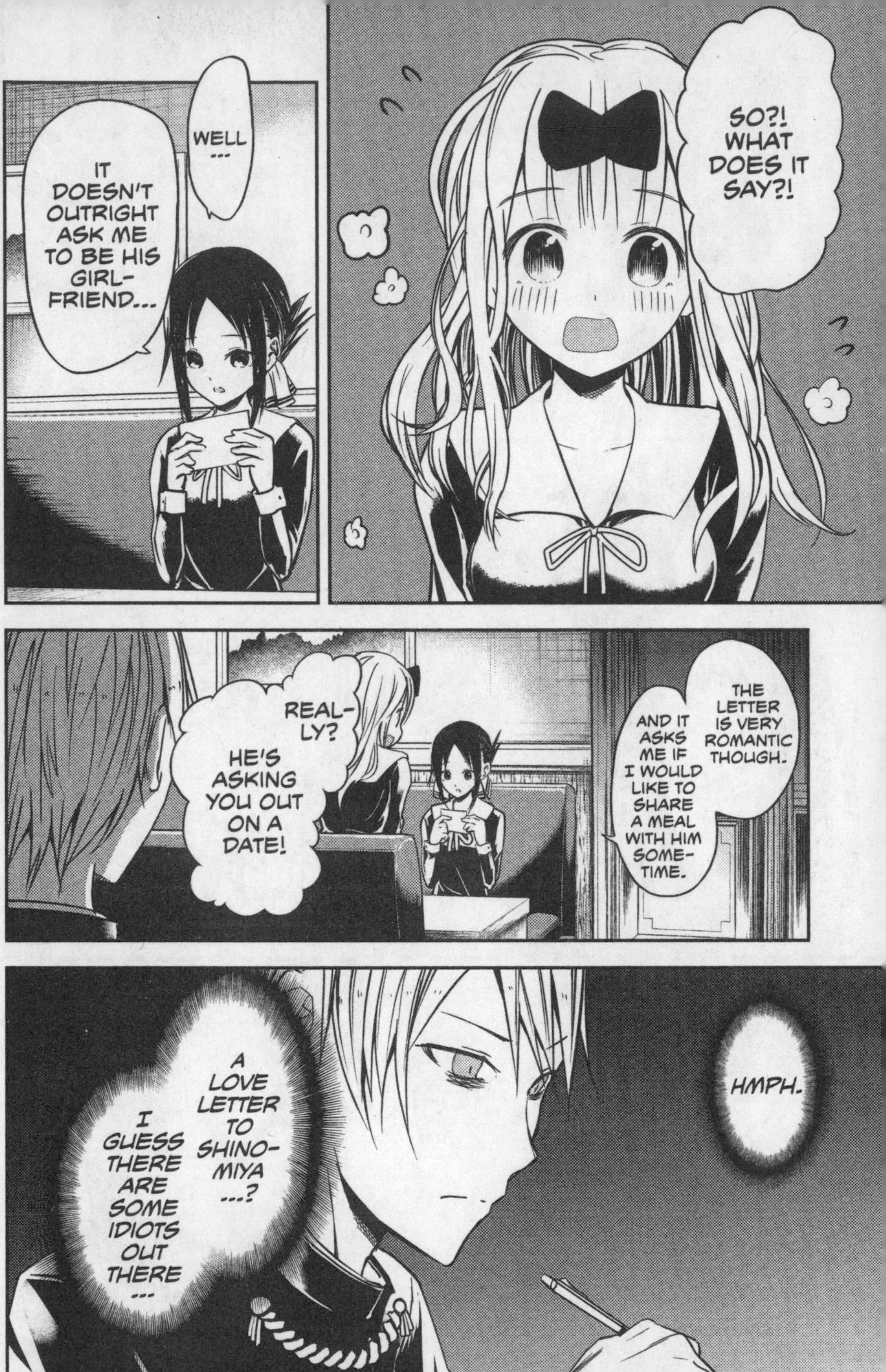
SO?! WHAT DOES IT SAY?!
WELL ---
IT DOESN'T OUTRIGHT ASK ME TO BE HIS GIRL-FRIEND...
THE LETTER IS VERY ROMANTIC THOUGH.
AND IT ASKS ME IF I WOULD LIKE TO SHARE A MEAL WITH HIM SOME-TIME.
REAL-LY?
HE'S ASKING YOU OUT ON A DATE!
HMPH.
A LOVE LETTER TO SHINO-MIYA ---?
I GUESS THERE ARE SOME IDIOTS OUT THERE ---

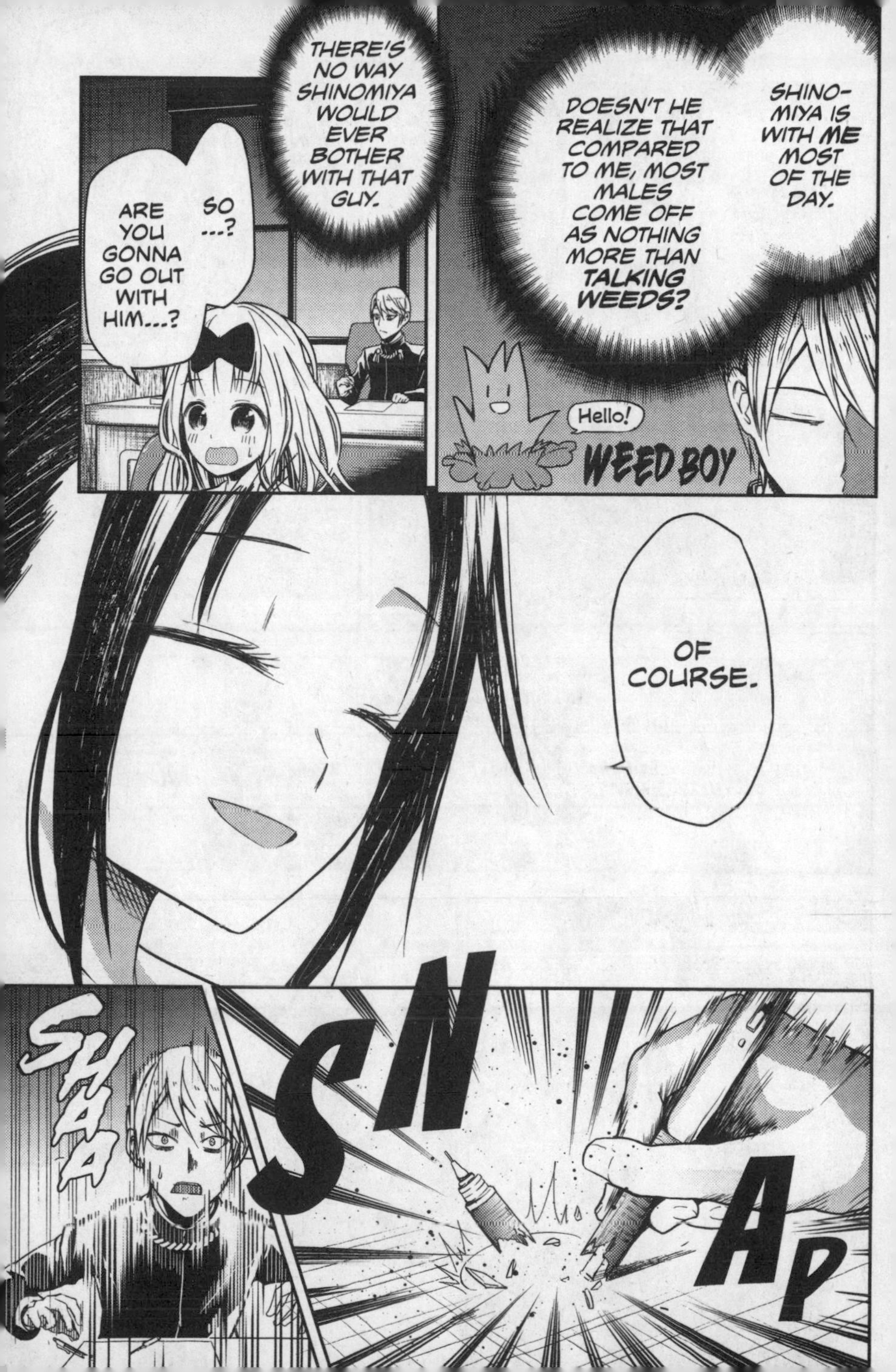
SHINOMIYA IS WITH ME MOST OF THE DAY.
DOESN'T HE REALIZE THAT COMPARED TO ME, MOST MALES COME OFF AS NOTHING MORE THAN TALKING WEEDS?
Hello!
WEED BOY
THERE'S NO WAY SHINOMIYA WOULD EVER BOTHER WITH THAT GUY.
SO ...?
ARE YOU GONNA GO OUT WITH HIM...?
OF COURSE.
SNAP
SHAA

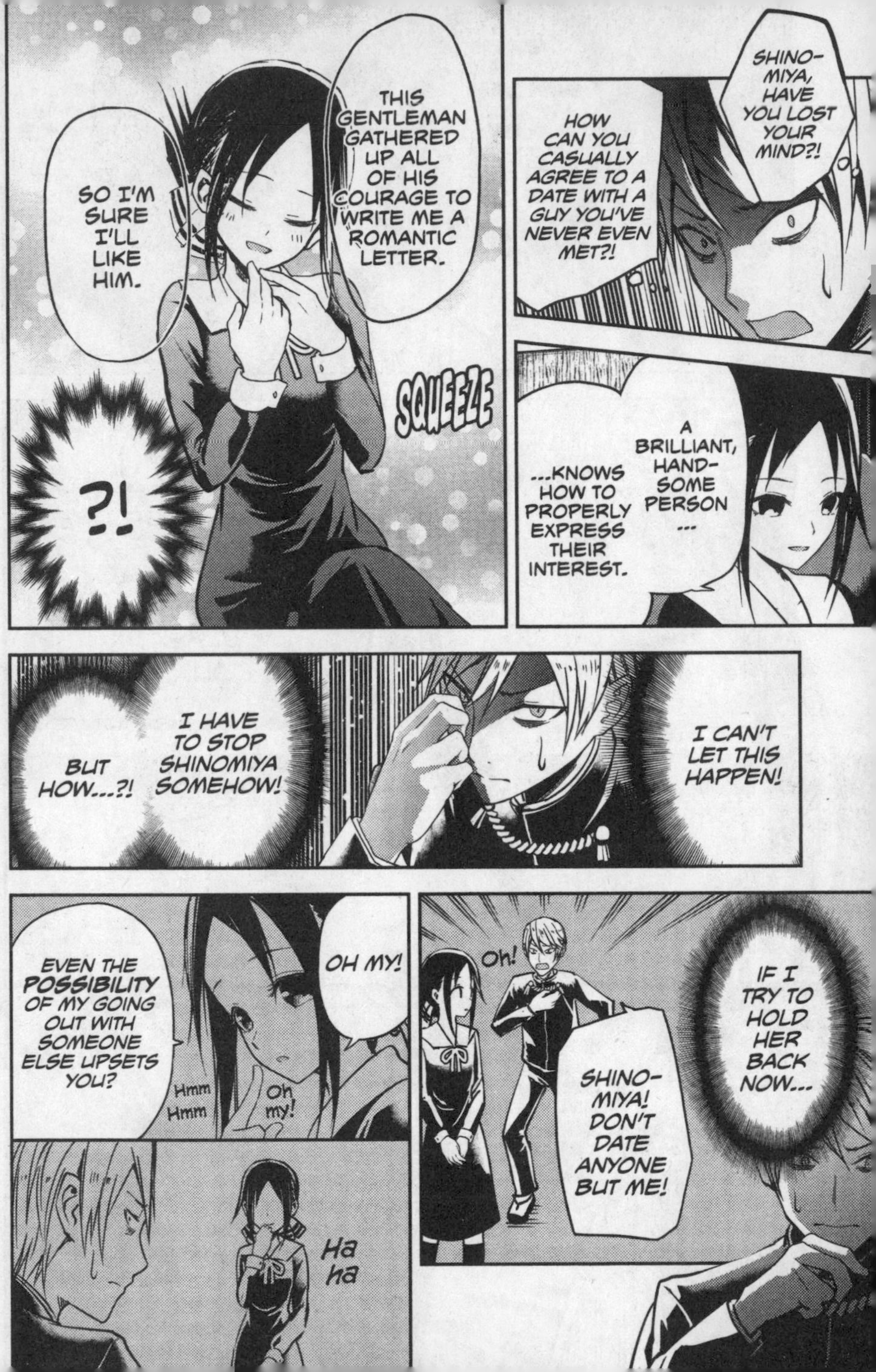
SHINO-MIYA, HAVE YOU LOST YOUR MIND?!
HOW CAN YOU CASUALLY AGREE TO A DATE WITH A GUY YOU'VE NEVER EVEN MET?!
A BRILLIANT, HAND-SOME PERSON...
...KNOWS HOW TO PROPERLY EXPRESS THEIR INTEREST.
THIS GENTLEMAN GATHERED UP ALL OF HIS COURAGE TO WRITE ME A ROMANTIC LETTER.
SO I'M SURE I'LL LIKE HIM.
SQUEEZE
?!
I CAN'T LET THIS HAPPEN!
I HAVE TO STOP SHINOMIYA SOMEHOW!
BUT HOW...?!
IF I TRY TO HOLD HER BACK NOW...
SHINO-MIYA! DON'T DATE ANYONE BUT ME!
Oh!
OH MY!
EVEN THE POSSIBILITY OF MY GOING OUT WITH SOMEONE ELSE UPSETS YOU?
Hmm Hmm
Oh my!
Ha ha

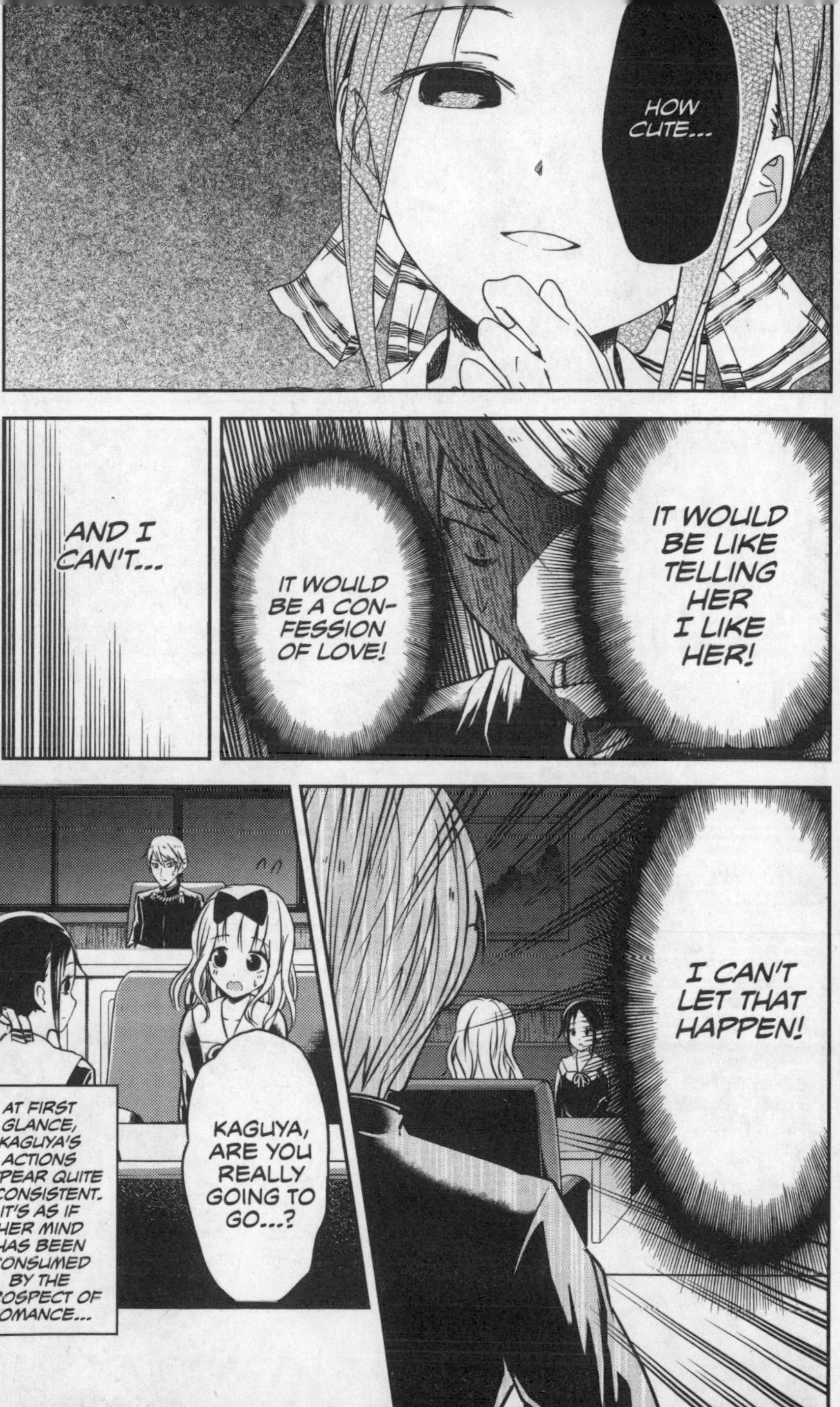
HOW CUTE...
IT WOULD BE LIKE TELLING HER I LIKE HER!
IT WOULD BE A CON-FESSION OF LOVE!
AND I CAN'T...
I CAN'T LET THAT HAPPEN!
KAGUYA, ARE YOU REALLY GOING TO GO...?
AT FIRST GLANCE, KAGUYA'S ACTIONS APPEAR QUITE INCONSISTENT. IT'S AS IF HER MIND HAS BEEN CONSUMED BY THE PROSPECT OF ROMANCE...

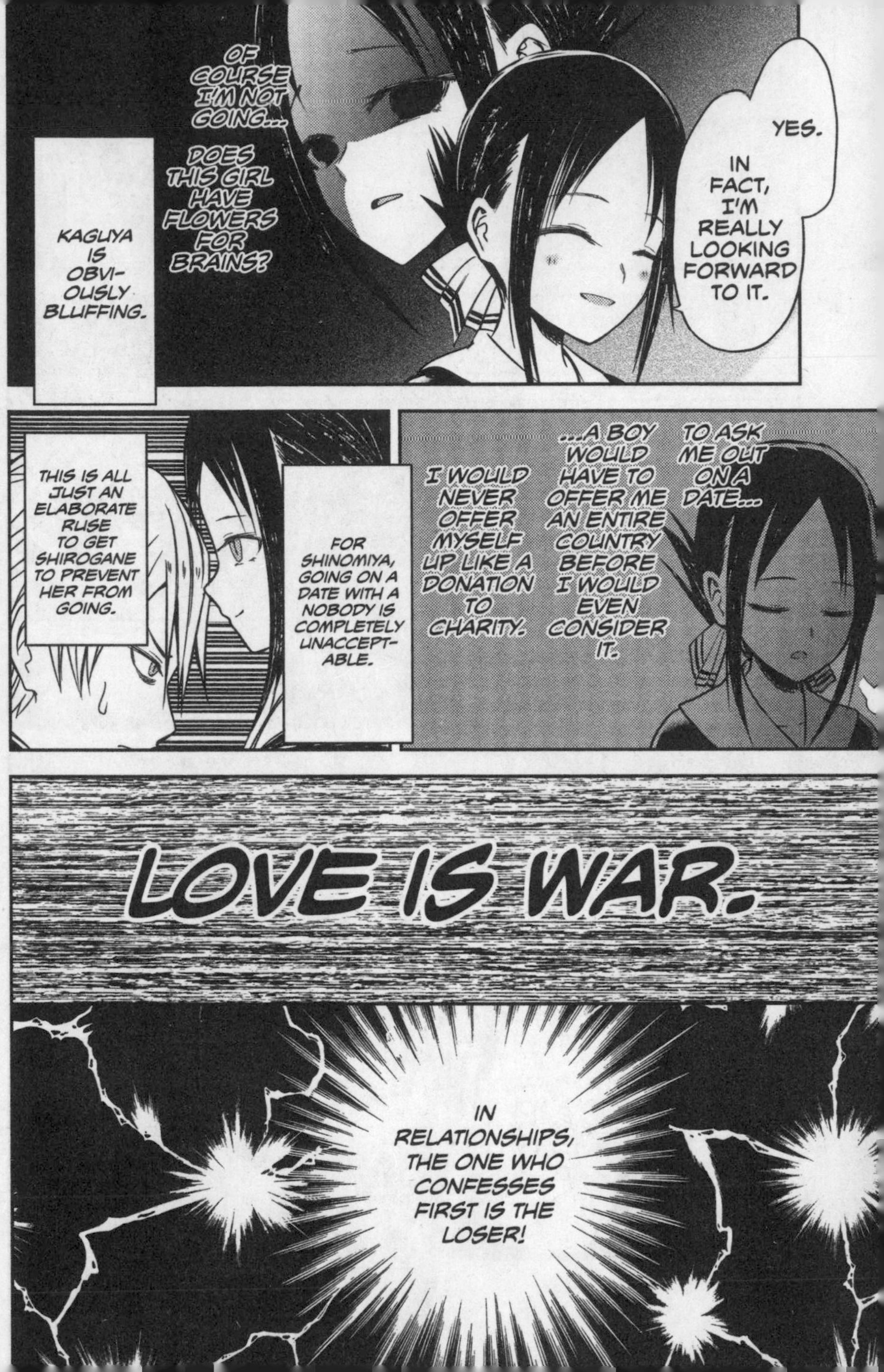
YES. IN FACT, I'M REALLY LOOKING FORWARD TO IT.
OF COURSE I'M NOT GOING... DOES THIS GIRL HAVE FLOWERS FOR BRAINS?
KAGUYA IS OBVIOUSLY BLUFFING.
TO ASK ME OUT ON A DATE...
...A BOY WOULD HAVE TO OFFER ME AN ENTIRE COUNTRY BEFORE I WOULD EVEN CONSIDER IT.
I WOULD NEVER OFFER MYSELF UP LIKE A DONATION TO CHARITY.
FOR SHINOMIYA, GOING ON A DATE WITH A NOBODY IS COMPLETELY UNACCEPTABLE.
THIS IS ALL JUST AN ELABORATE RUSE TO GET SHIROGANE TO PREVENT HER FROM GOING.
LOVE IS WAR.
IN RELATIONSHIPS, THE ONE WHO CONFESSES FIRST IS THE LOSER!

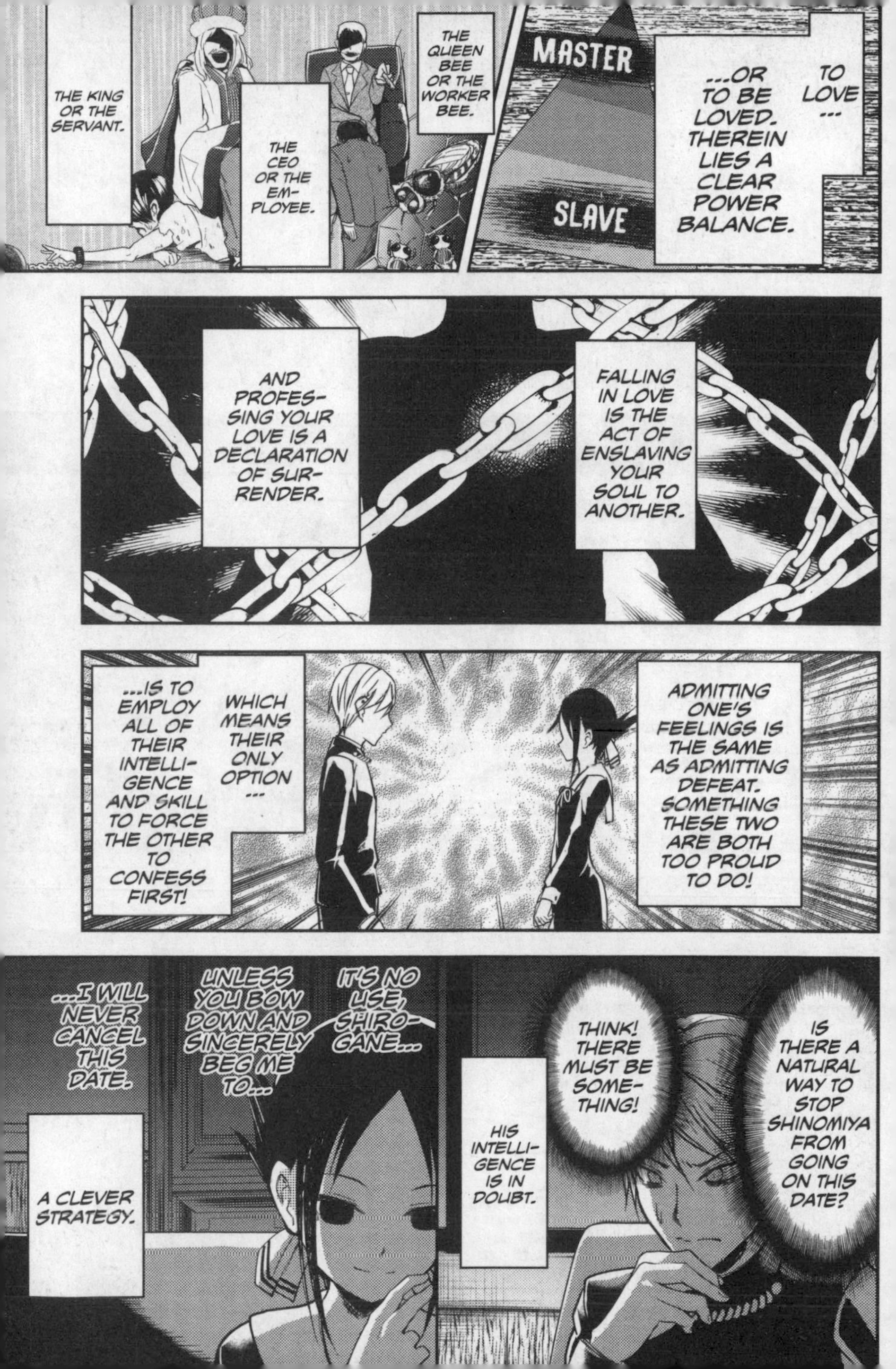
MASTER
SLAVE
TO LOVE ---
...OR TO BE LOVED. THEREIN LIES A CLEAR POWER BALANCE.
THE QUEEN BEE OR THE WORKER BEE.
THE CEO OR THE EMPLOYEE.
THE KING OR THE SERVANT.
FALLING IN LOVE IS THE ACT OF ENSLAVING YOUR SOUL TO ANOTHER.
AND PROFESSING YOUR LOVE IS A DECLARATION OF SURRENDER.
ADMITTING ONE'S FEELINGS IS THE SAME AS ADMITTING DEFEAT. SOMETHING THESE TWO ARE BOTH TOO PROUD TO DO!
WHICH MEANS THEIR ONLY OPTION ---
...IS TO EMPLOY ALL OF THEIR INTELLIGENCE AND SKILL TO FORCE THE OTHER TO CONFESS FIRST!
IS THERE A NATURAL WAY TO STOP SHINOMIYA FROM GOING ON THIS DATE?
THINK! THERE MUST BE SOMETHING!
HIS INTELLIGENCE IS IN DOUBT.
IT'S NO USE, SHIROGANE...
UNLESS YOU BOW DOWN AND SINCERELY BEG ME TO...
...I WILL NEVER CANCEL THIS DATE.
A CLEVER STRATEGY.

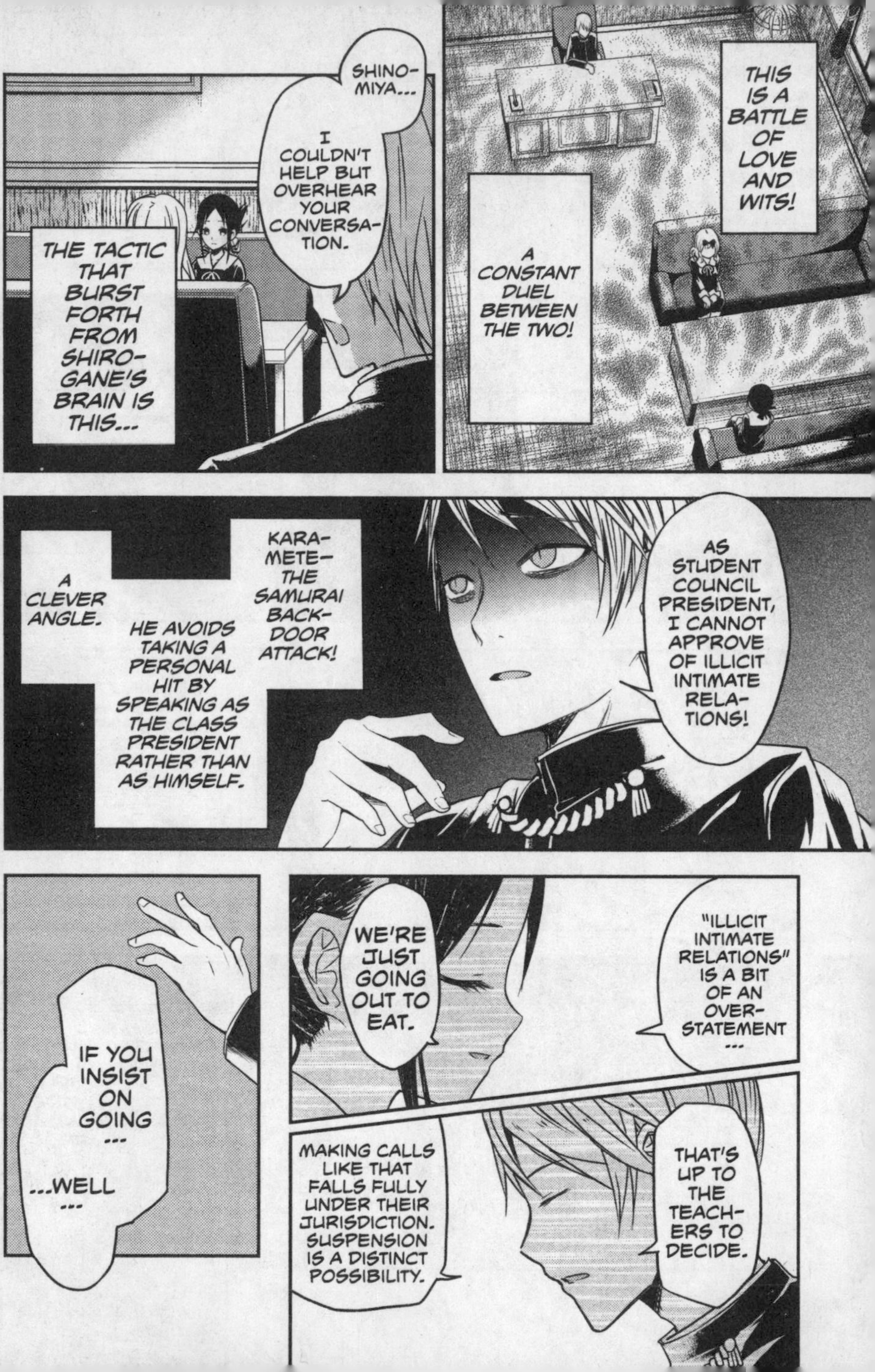
THIS IS A BATTLE OF LOVE AND WITS!
A CONSTANT DUEL BETWEEN THE TWO!
SHINOMIYA... I COULDN'T HELP BUT OVERHEAR YOUR CONVERSATION.
THE TACTIC THAT BURST FORTH FROM SHIROGANE'S BRAIN IS THIS...
AS STUDENT COUNCIL PRESIDENT, I CANNOT APPROVE OF ILLICIT INTIMATE RELATIONS!
KARAMETE—THE SAMURAI BACKDOOR ATTACK!
A CLEVER ANGLE.
HE AVOIDS TAKING A PERSONAL HIT BY SPEAKING AS THE CLASS PRESIDENT RATHER THAN AS HIMSELF.
"ILLICIT INTIMATE RELATIONS" IS A BIT OF AN OVERSTATEMENT...
WE'RE JUST GOING OUT TO EAT.
THAT'S UP TO THE TEACHERS TO DECIDE.
MAKING CALLS LIKE THAT FALLS FULLY UNDER THEIR JURISDICTION. SUSPENSION IS A DISTINCT POSSIBILITY.
IF YOU INSIST ON GOING...
...WELL...

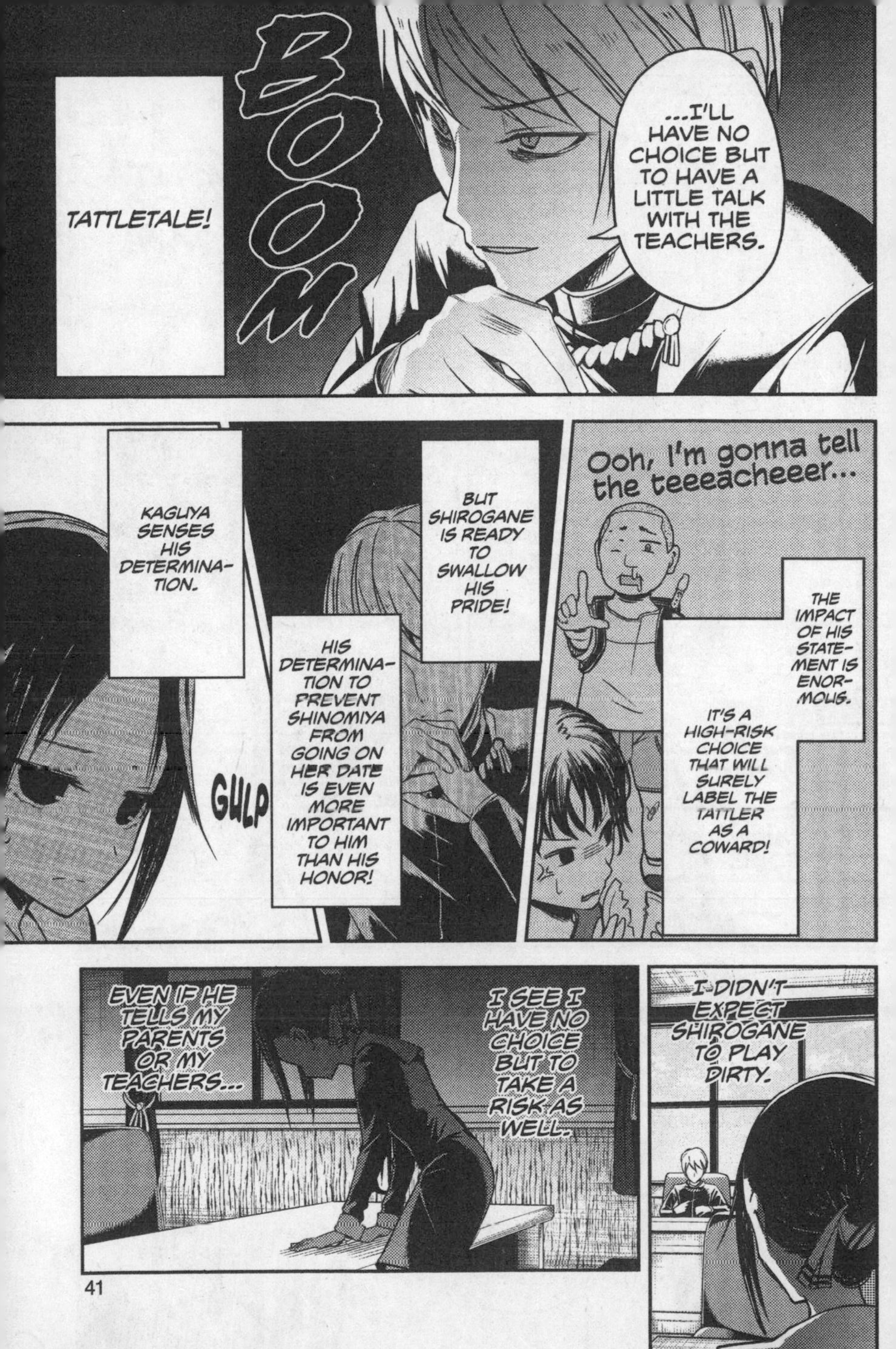
...I'LL HAVE NO CHOICE BUT TO HAVE A LITTLE TALK WITH THE TEACHERS.
BOOM
TATTLETALE!
Ooh, I'm gonna tell the teeeacheeer...
THE IMPACT OF HIS STATEMENT IS ENORMOUS.
IT'S A HIGH-RISK CHOICE THAT WILL SURELY LABEL THE TATTLER AS A COWARD!
BUT SHIROGANE IS READY TO SWALLOW HIS PRIDE!
HIS DETERMINATION TO PREVENT SHINOMIYA FROM GOING ON HER DATE IS EVEN MORE IMPORTANT TO HIM THAN HIS HONOR!
KAGUYA SENSES HIS DETERMINATION.
GULP
I DIDN'T EXPECT SHIROGANE TO PLAY DIRTY.
I SEE I HAVE NO CHOICE BUT TO TAKE A RISK AS WELL.
EVEN IF HE TELLS MY PARENTS OR MY TEACHERS...

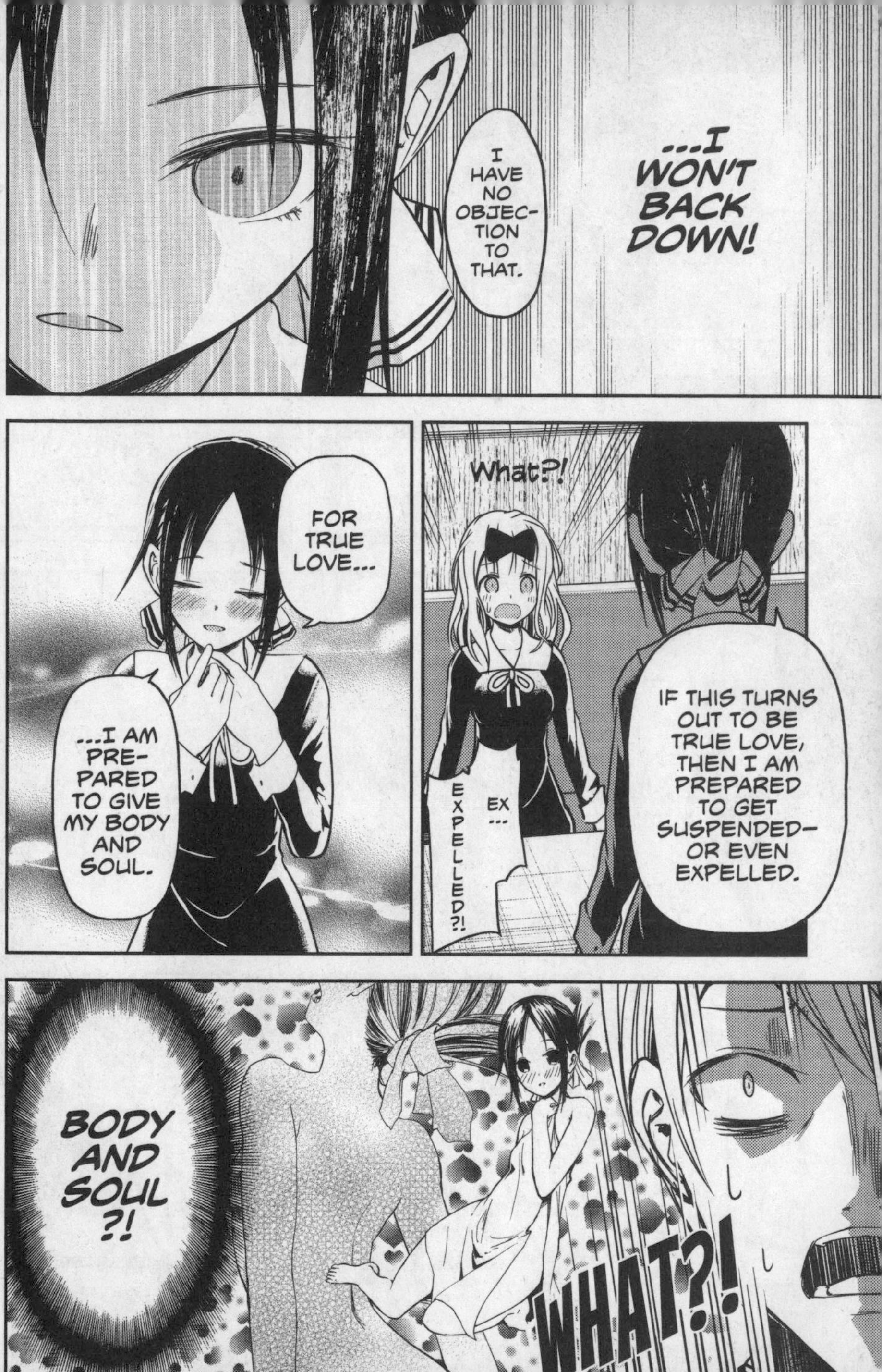
...I WON'T BACK DOWN!
I HAVE NO OBJECTION TO THAT.
What?!
IF THIS TURNS OUT TO BE TRUE LOVE, THEN I AM PREPARED TO GET SUSPENDED—OR EVEN EXPELLED.
EX...
EXPELLED?!
FOR TRUE LOVE...
...I AM PREPARED TO GIVE MY BODY AND SOUL.
WHAT?!
BODY AND SOUL?!

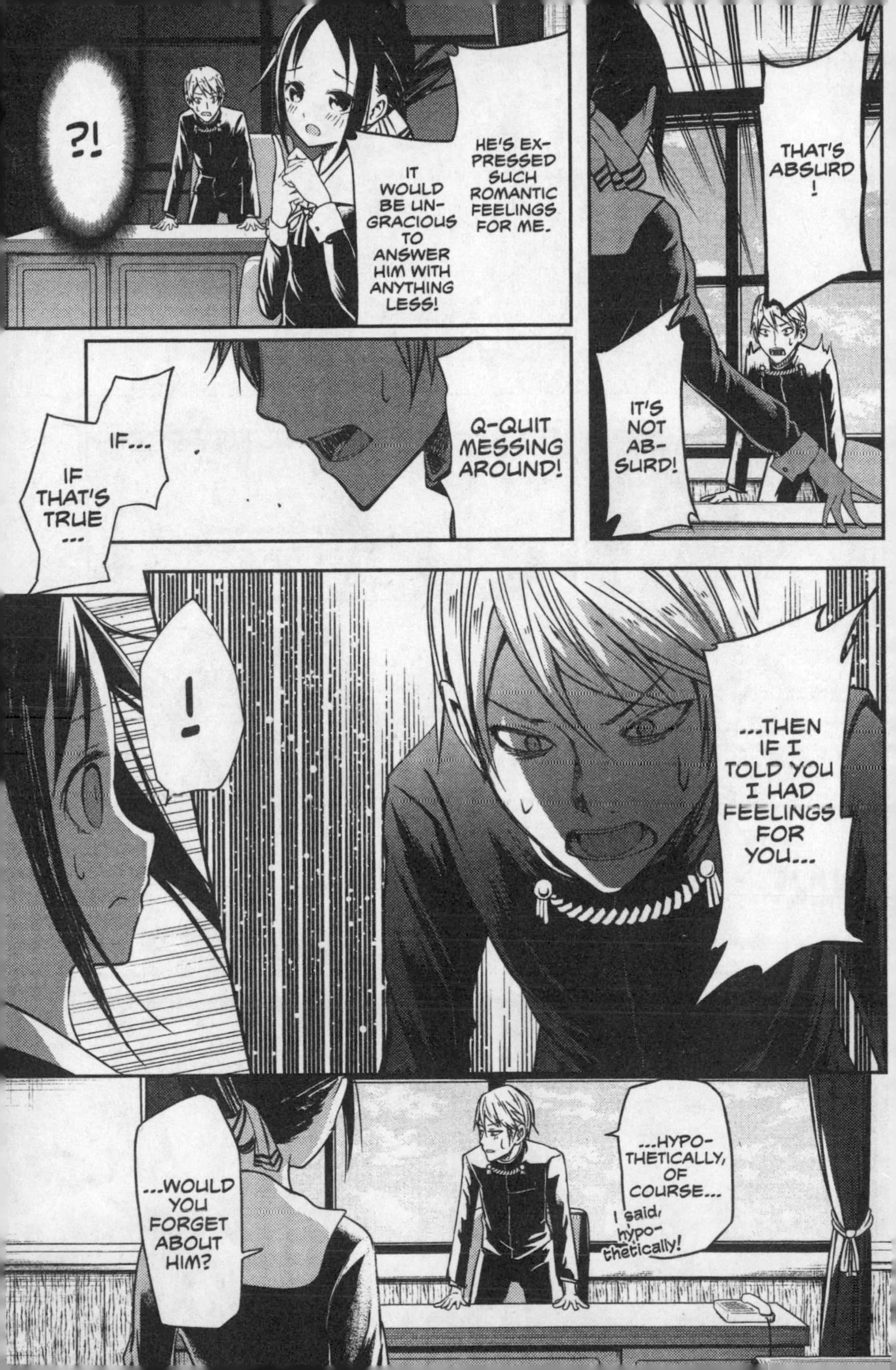
THAT'S ABSURD!
IT'S NOT ABSURD!
HE'S EXPRESSED SUCH ROMANTIC FEELINGS FOR ME.
IT WOULD BE UNGRACIOUS TO ANSWER HIM WITH ANYTHING LESS!
?!
Q-QUIT MESSING AROUND!
IF...
IF THAT'S TRUE...
...THEN IF I TOLD YOU I HAD FEELINGS FOR YOU...
!
...HYPOTHETICALLY, OF COURSE...
I said, hypothetically!
...WOULD YOU FORGET ABOUT HIM?

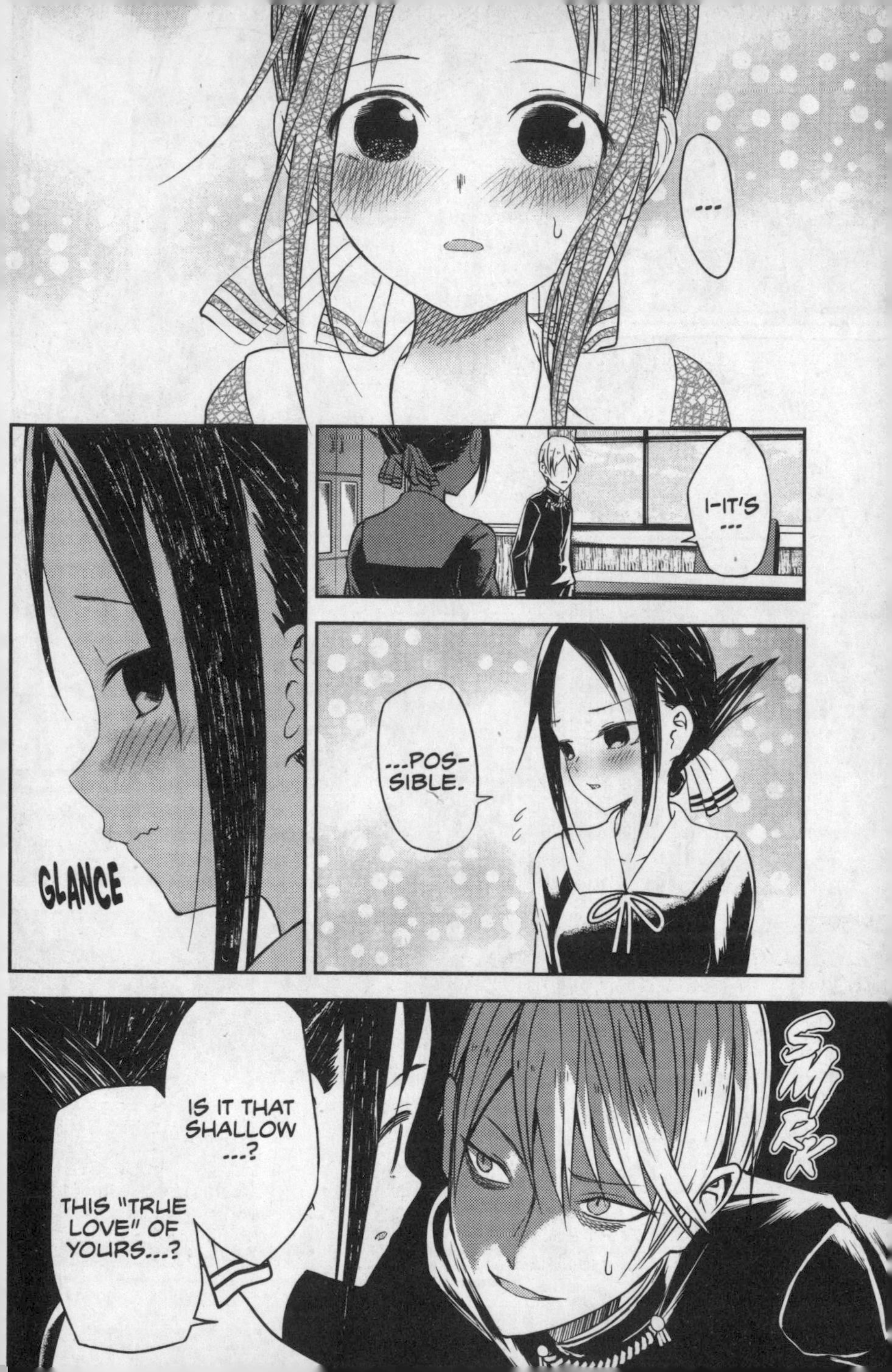
...
I-IT'S ...
...POS-SIBLE.
GLANCE
SMIRK
IS IT THAT SHALLOW ...?
THIS "TRUE LOVE" OF YOURS...?

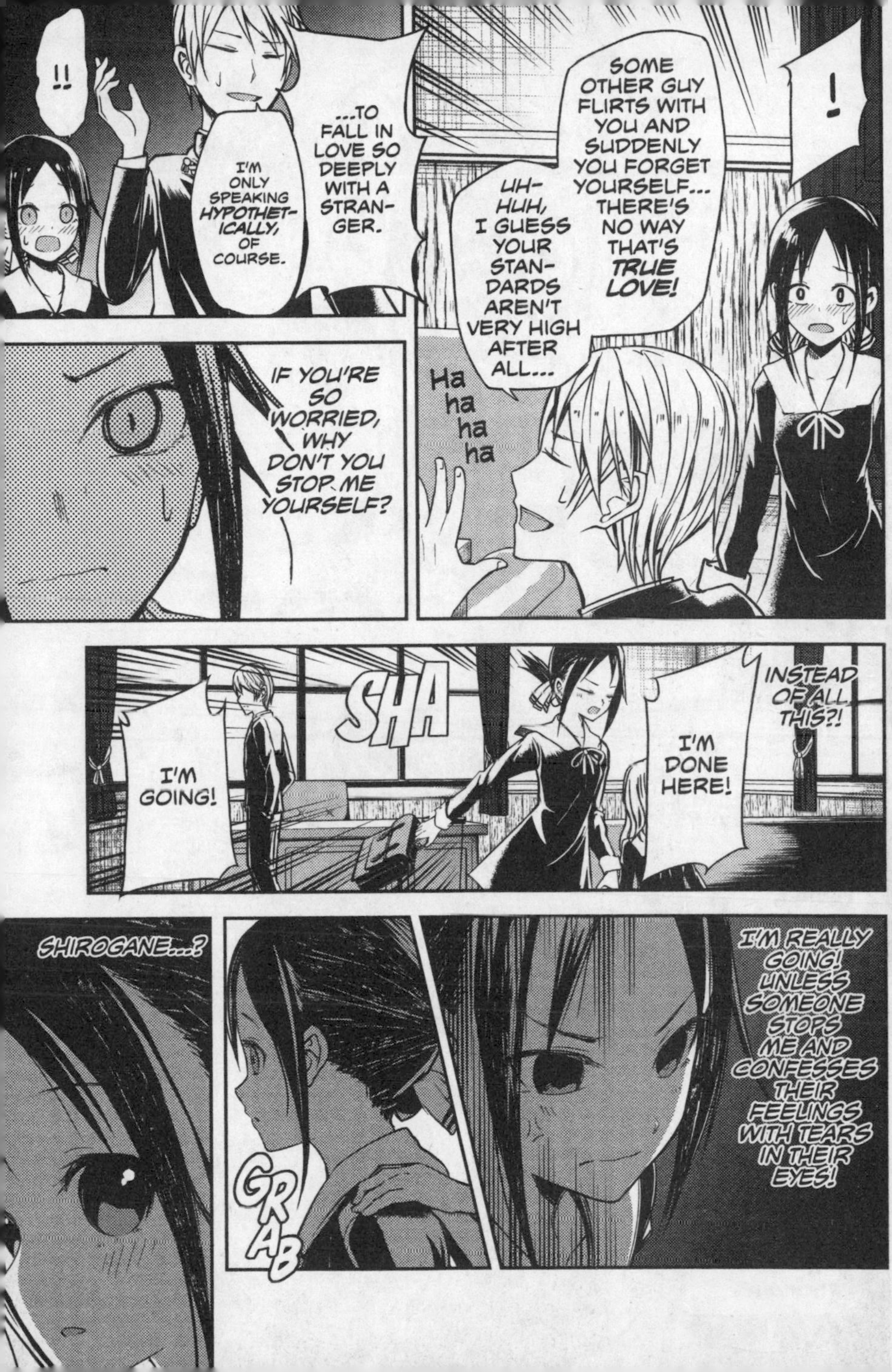

!
SOME OTHER GUY FLIRTS WITH YOU AND SUDDENLY YOU FORGET YOURSELF... THERE'S NO WAY THAT'S TRUE LOVE!
UH-HUH, I GUESS YOUR STANDARDS AREN'T VERY HIGH AFTER ALL...
Ha ha ha ha
...TO FALL IN LOVE SO DEEPLY WITH A STRANGER.
I'M ONLY SPEAKING HYPOTHETICALLY, OF COURSE.
!!
IF YOU'RE SO WORRIED, WHY DON'T YOU STOP ME YOURSELF?
INSTEAD OF ALL THIS?!
I'M DONE HERE!
SHA
I'M GOING!
I'M REALLY GOING! UNLESS SOMEONE STOPS ME AND CONFESSES THEIR FEELINGS WITH TEARS IN THEIR EYES!
GRAB
SHIROGANE...?

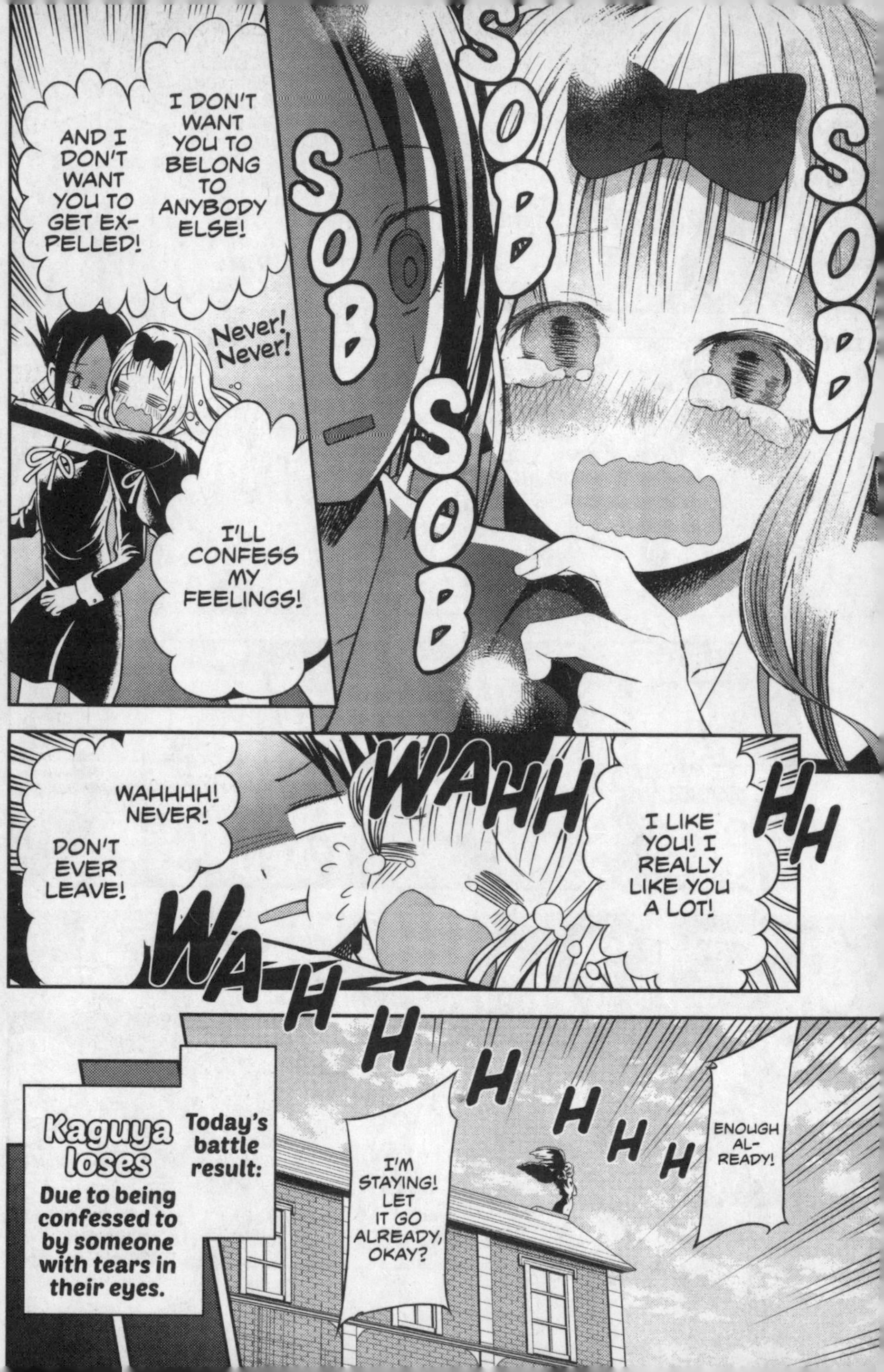
SOB
SOB
SOB
SOB
I DON'T WANT YOU TO BELONG TO ANYBODY ELSE!
AND I DON'T WANT YOU TO GET EX-PELLED!
Never! Never!
I'LL CONFESS MY FEELINGS!
I LIKE YOU! I REALLY LIKE YOU A LOT!
WAHHHH
WAHHHHH! NEVER!
DON'T EVER LEAVE!
WAHHHHHHHH
ENOUGH AL-READY!
I'M STAYING! LET IT GO ALREADY, OKAY?
Today's battle result:
Kaguya loses
Due to being confessed to by someone with tears in their eyes.

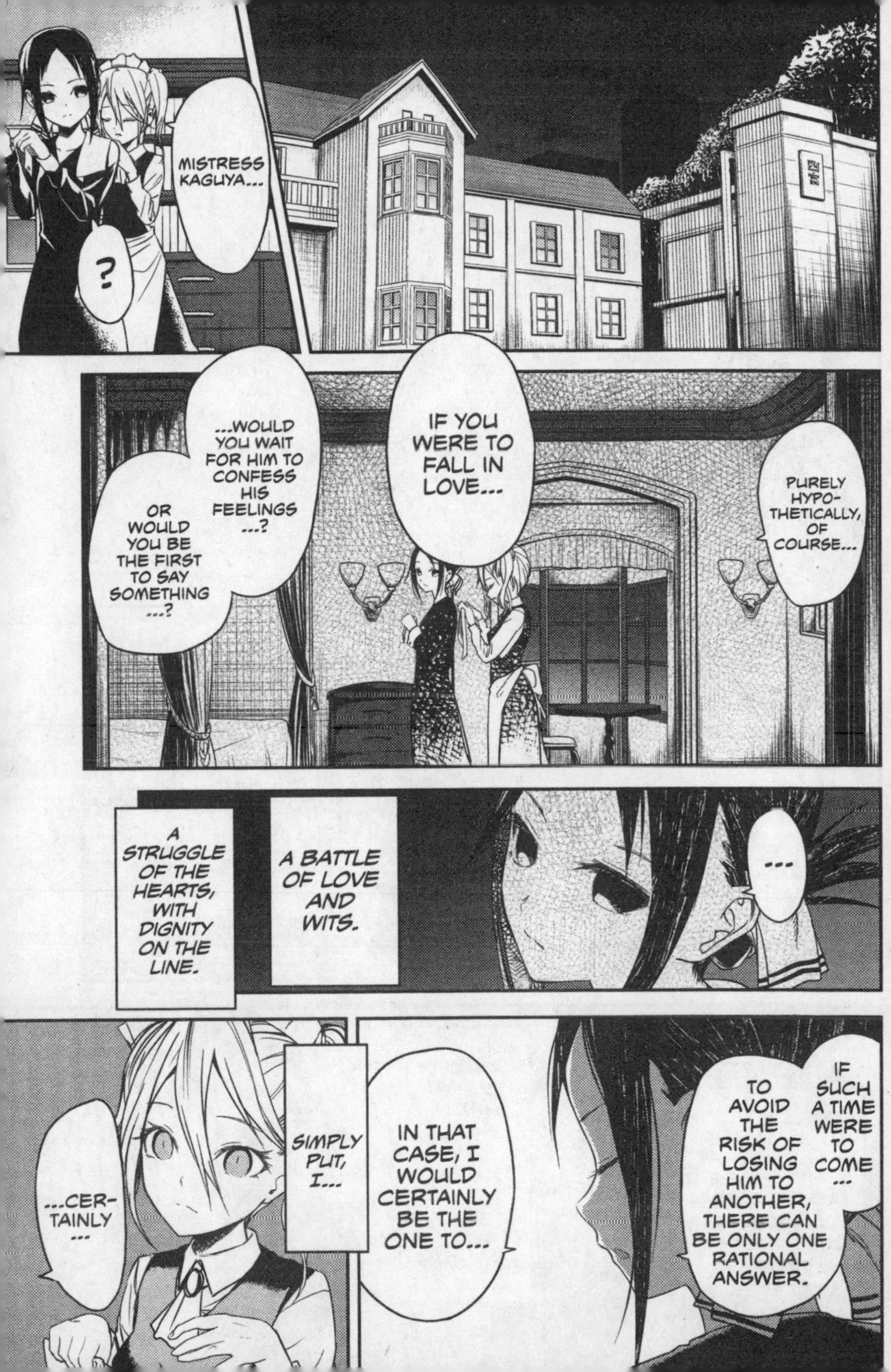
MISTRESS KAGUYA...
?
PURELY HYPOTHETICALLY, OF COURSE...
IF YOU WERE TO FALL IN LOVE...
...WOULD YOU WAIT FOR HIM TO CONFESS HIS FEELINGS...?
OR WOULD YOU BE THE FIRST TO SAY SOMETHING...?
...
A BATTLE OF LOVE AND WITS.
A STRUGGLE OF THE HEARTS, WITH DIGNITY ON THE LINE.
IF SUCH A TIME WERE TO COME...
TO AVOID THE RISK OF LOSING HIM TO ANOTHER, THERE CAN BE ONLY ONE RATIONAL ANSWER.
IN THAT CASE, I WOULD CERTAINLY BE THE ONE TO...
SIMPLY PUT, I...
...CERTAINLY...

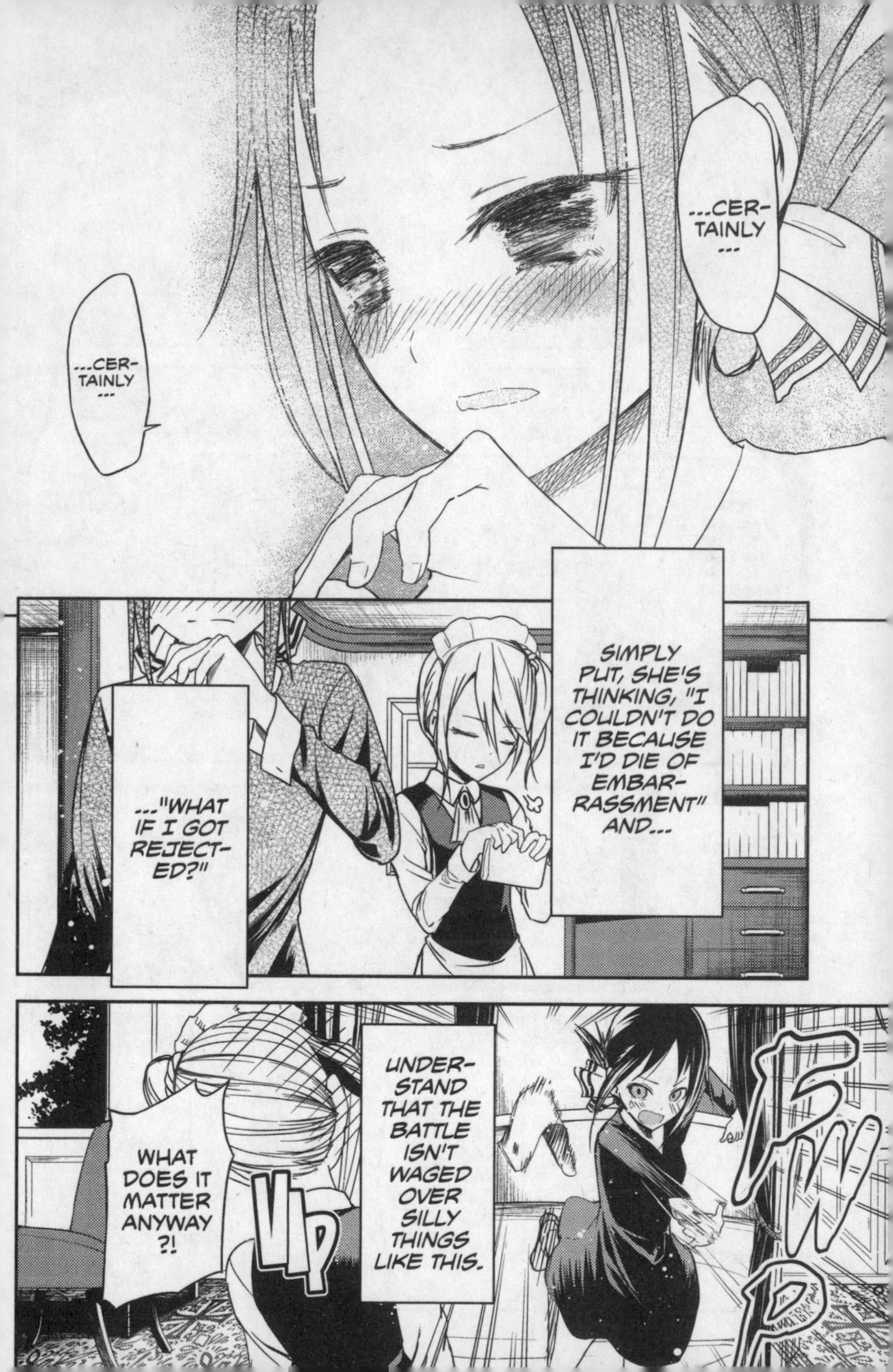
...CER-TAINLY...
...CER-TAINLY...
SIMPLY PUT, SHE'S THINKING, "I COULDN'T DO IT BECAUSE I'D DIE OF EMBAR-RASSMENT" AND...
..."WHAT IF I GOT REJECT-ED?"
FWP
UNDER-STAND THAT THE BATTLE ISN'T WAGED OVER SILLY THINGS LIKE THIS.
WHAT DOES IT MATTER ANYWAY?!

A passionate love letter
has arrived...

Dear Kaguya Shinomiya,

You are beautiful and precious.

Once solitary and unapproachable, you were like ice, and you stole my heart.

The person you have become is also beautiful. Like the melting snow in spring, in you I see the kindness and the beauty of the world.

But that beauty won't last forever. What awaits after the snow melts is mud. And what can you do with that but roll around in it?

I could never forgive that. If I could, I would preserve your beauty forever. Forever and ever and ever.

Together with me, we shall go on forever.

KAGUYA-SAMA

LOVE IS WAR

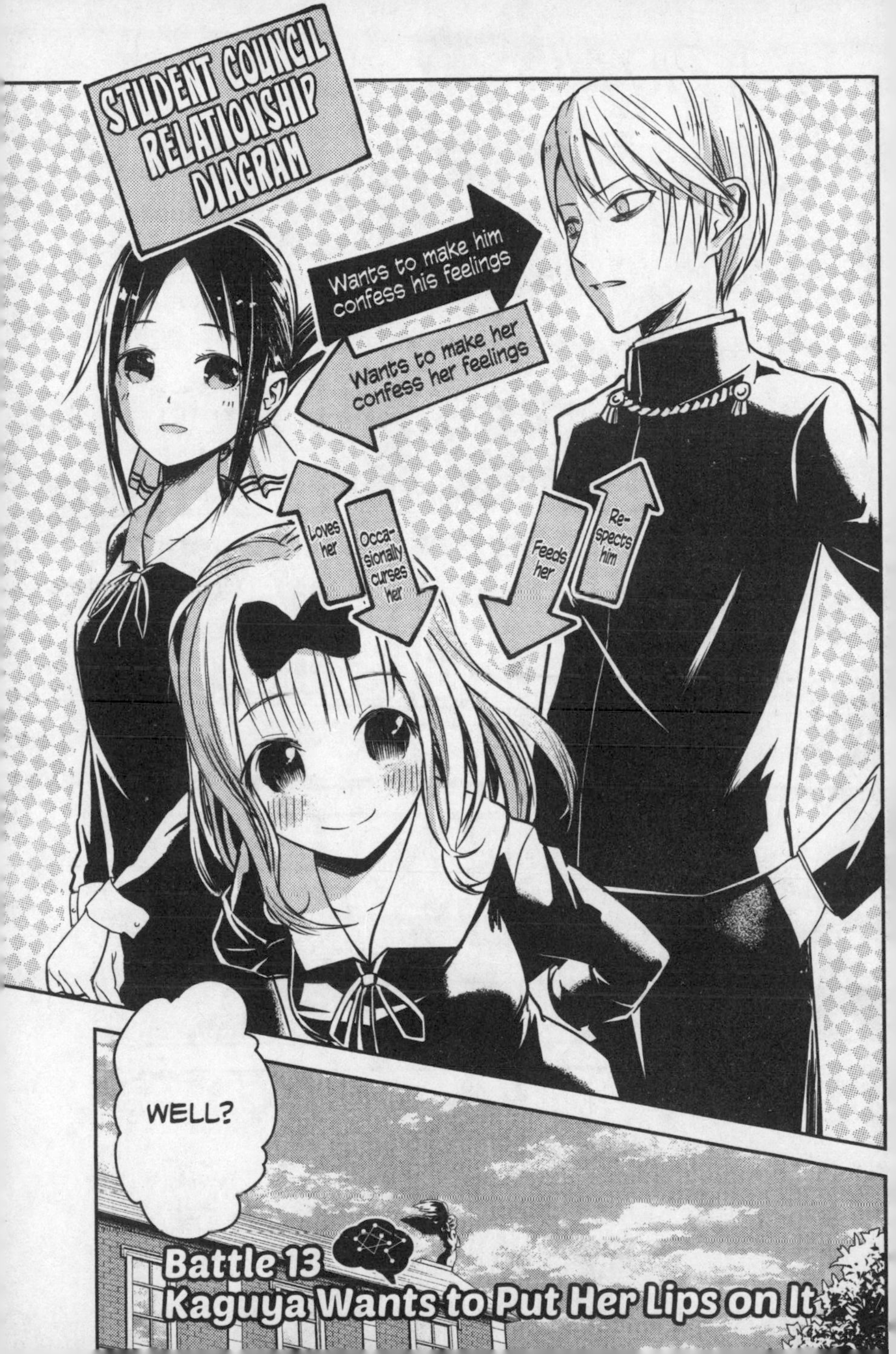
STUDENT COUNCIL RELATIONSHIP DIAGRAM
Wants to make him confess his feelings
Wants to make her confess her feelings
Re-spects him
Feeds her
Occa-sionally curses her
Loves her
WELL?
Battle 13
Kaguya Wants to Put Her Lips on It

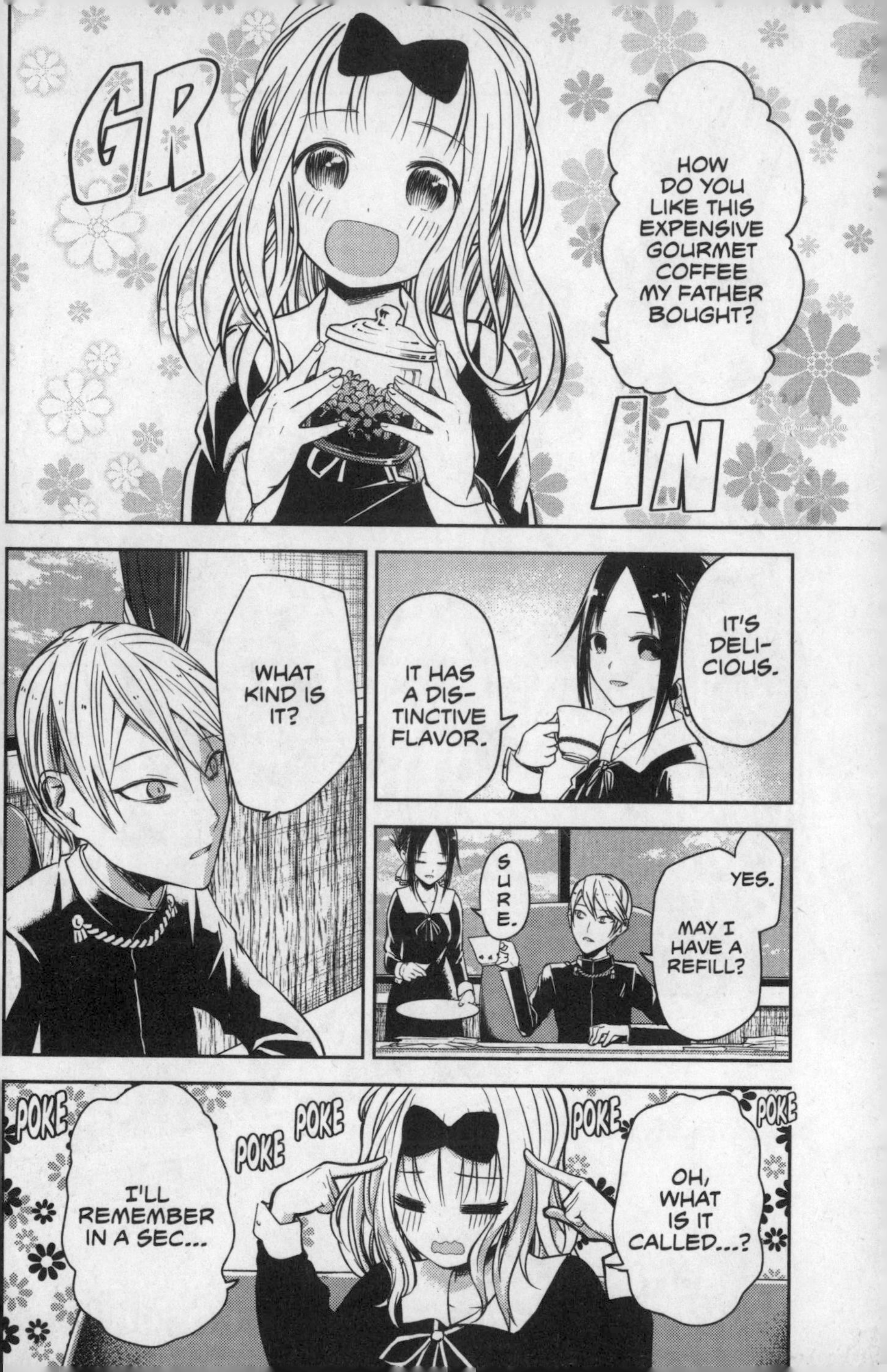
HOW DO YOU LIKE THIS EXPENSIVE GOURMET COFFEE MY FATHER BOUGHT?
GR
IN
IT'S DELI- CIOUS.
IT HAS A DIS- TINCTIVE FLAVOR.
YES.
MAY I HAVE A REFILL?
SURE.
WHAT KIND IS IT?
POKE
POKE
OH, WHAT IS IT CALLED...?
POKE
POKE
POKE
I'LL REMEMBER IN A SEC...

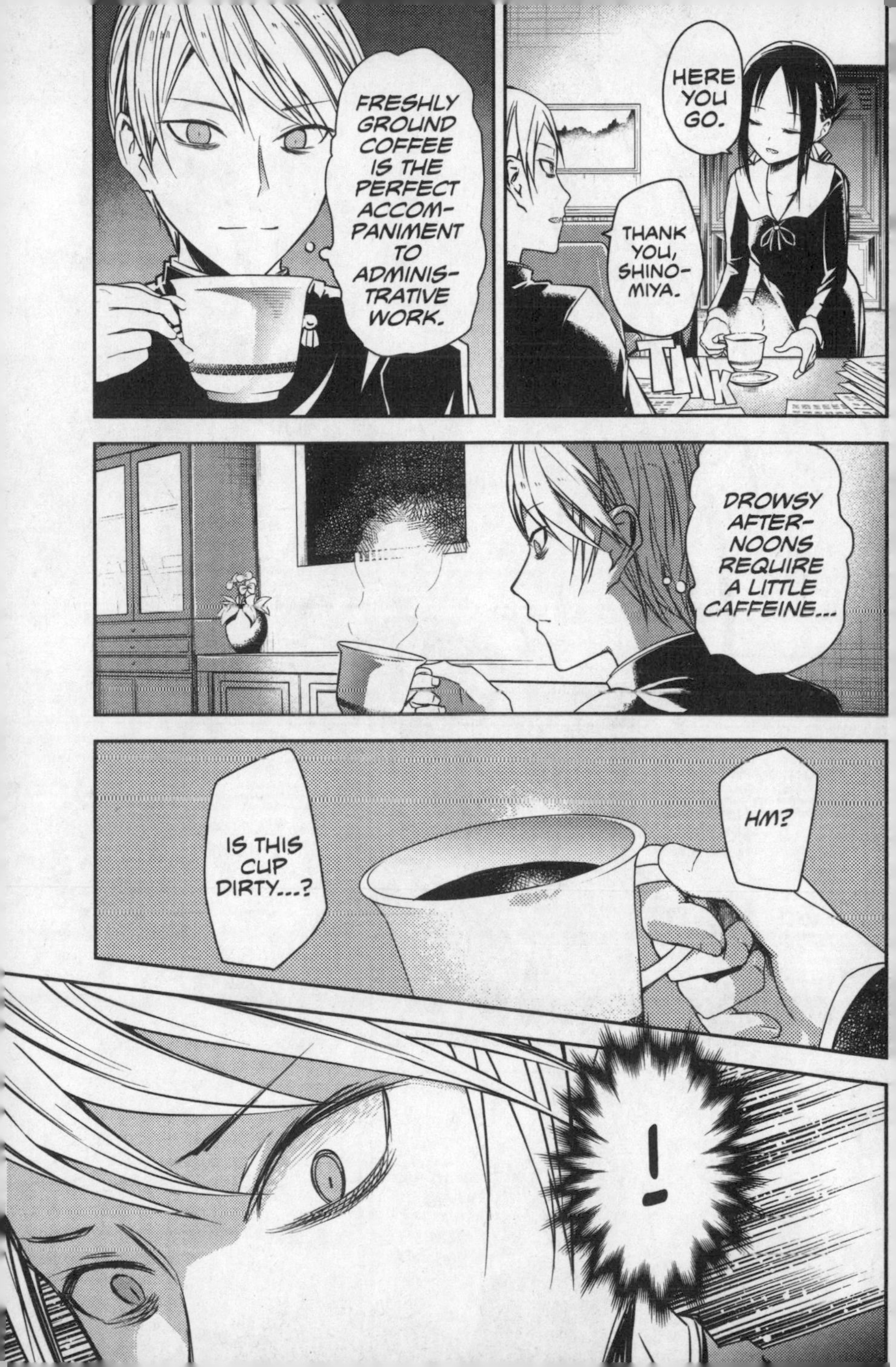
HERE YOU GO.
THANK YOU, SHINOMIYA.
TINK
FRESHLY GROUND COFFEE IS THE PERFECT ACCOMPANIMENT TO ADMINISTRATIVE WORK.
DROWSY AFTERNOONS REQUIRE A LITTLE CAFFEINE...
HM?
IS THIS CUP DIRTY...?
!

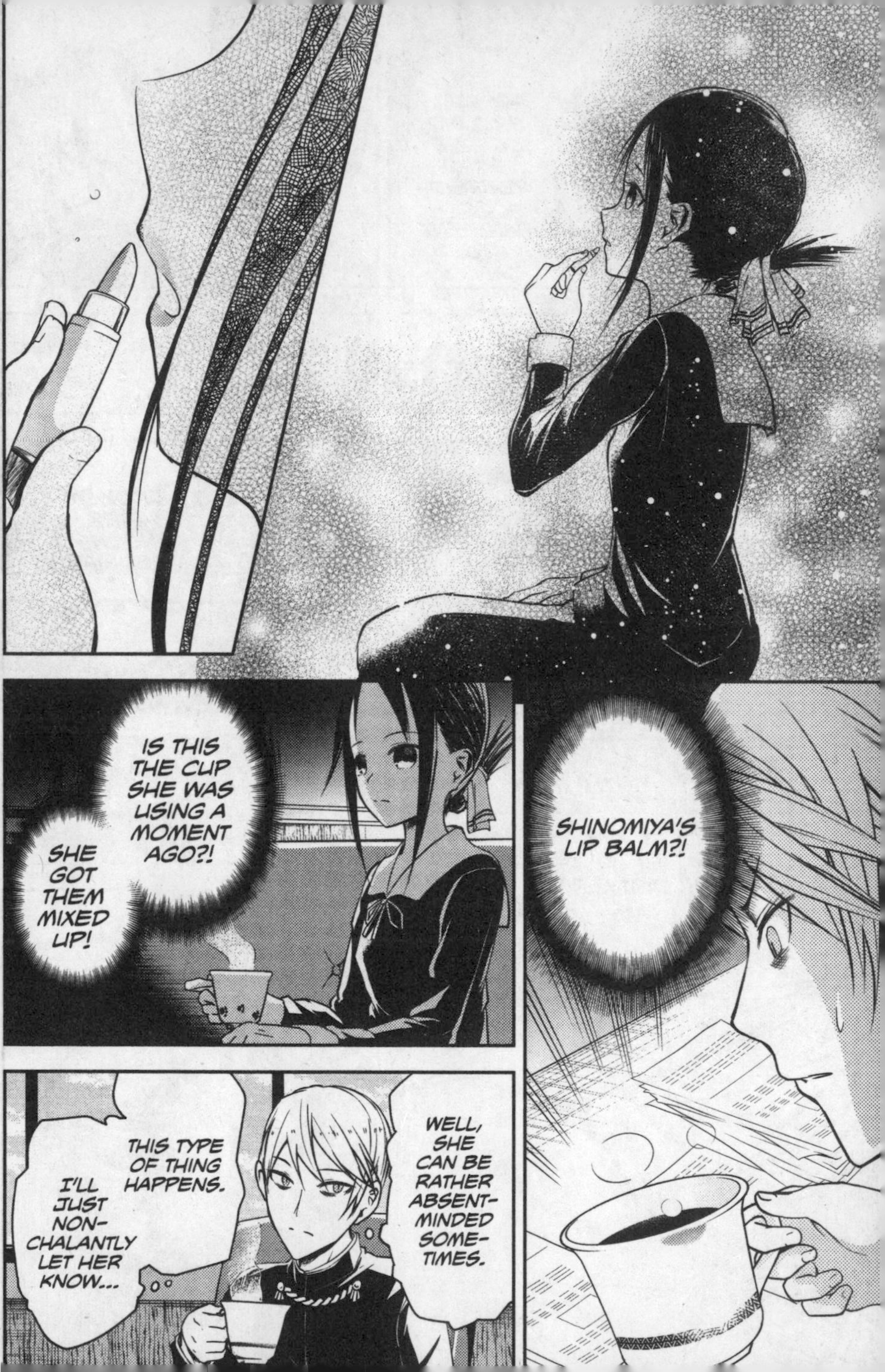
SHINOMIYA'S LIP BALM?!
IS THIS THE CUP SHE WAS USING A MOMENT AGO?!
SHE GOT THEM MIXED UP!
WELL, SHE CAN BE RATHER ABSENT-MINDED SOME-TIMES.
THIS TYPE OF THING HAPPENS.
I'LL JUST NON-CHALANTLY LET HER KNOW...

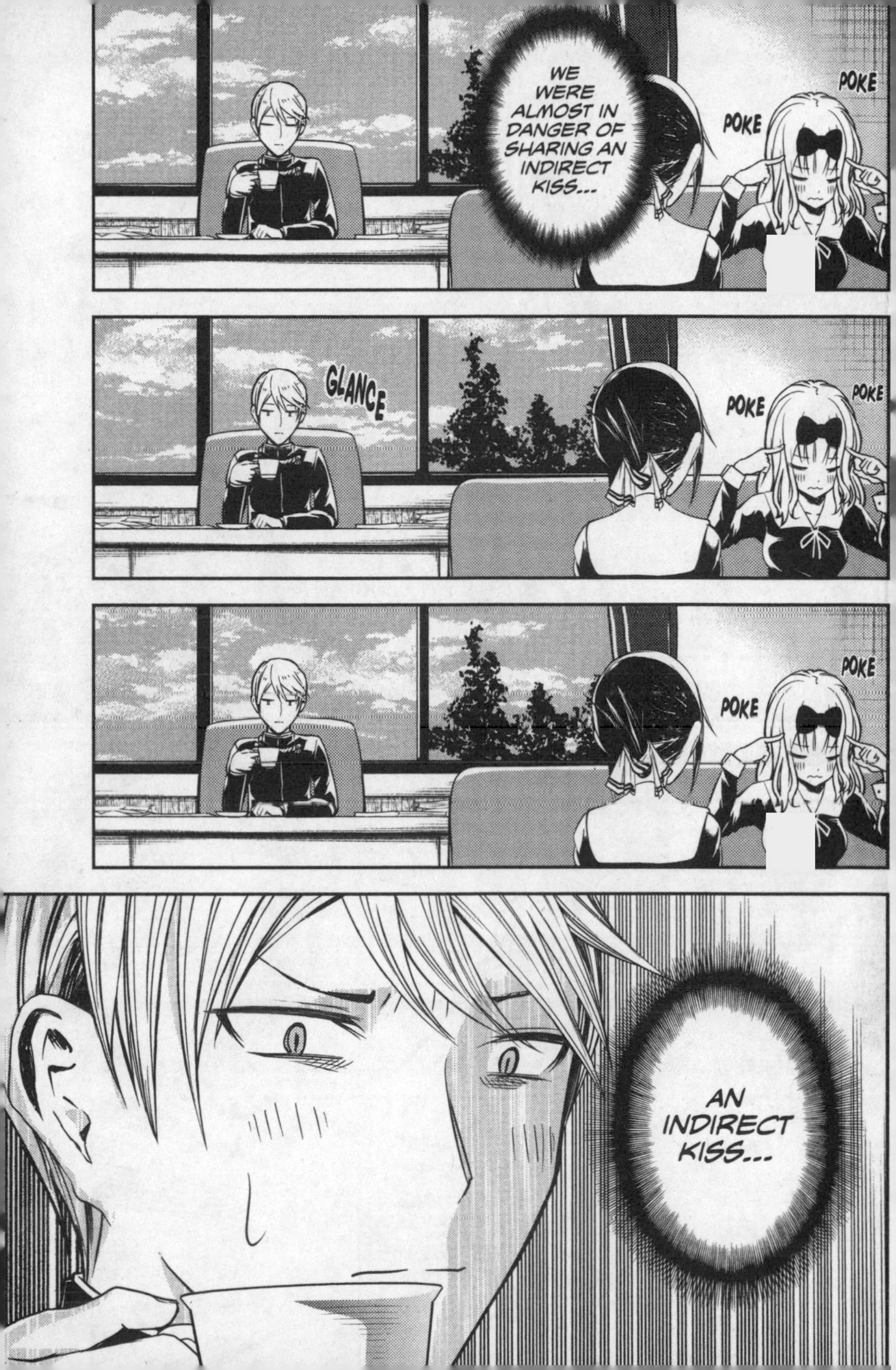
POKE
POKE
WE WERE ALMOST IN DANGER OF SHARING AN INDIRECT KISS...
POKE
POKE
GLANCE
POKE
POKE
AN INDIRECT KISS...

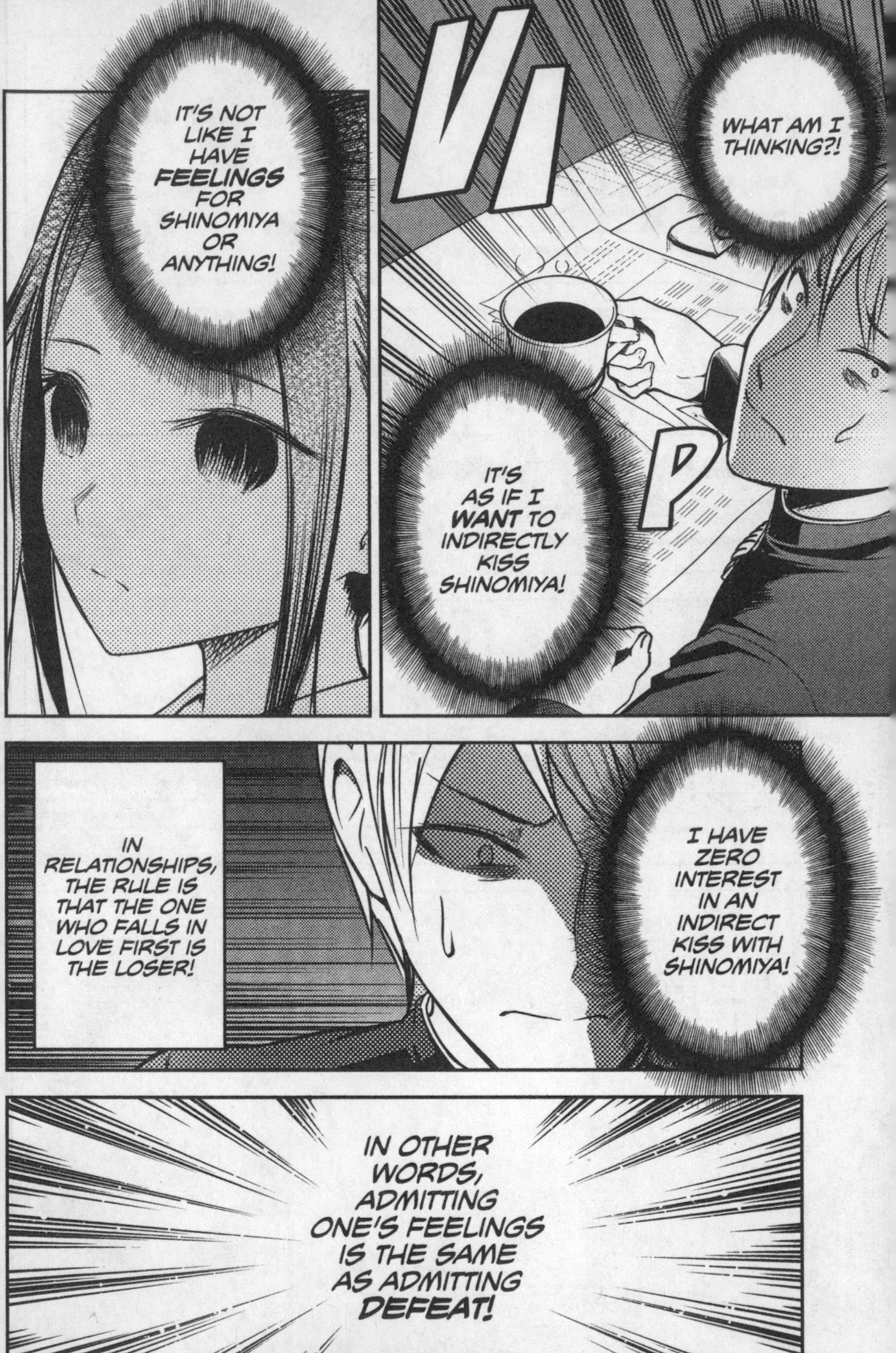
WHAT AM I THINKING?!
IT'S AS IF I WANT TO INDIRECTLY KISS SHINOMIYA!
IT'S NOT LIKE I HAVE FEELINGS FOR SHINOMIYA OR ANYTHING!
I HAVE ZERO INTEREST IN AN INDIRECT KISS WITH SHINOMIYA!
IN RELATIONSHIPS, THE RULE IS THAT THE ONE WHO FALLS IN LOVE FIRST IS THE LOSER!
IN OTHER WORDS, ADMITTING ONE'S FEELINGS IS THE SAME AS ADMITTING DEFEAT!

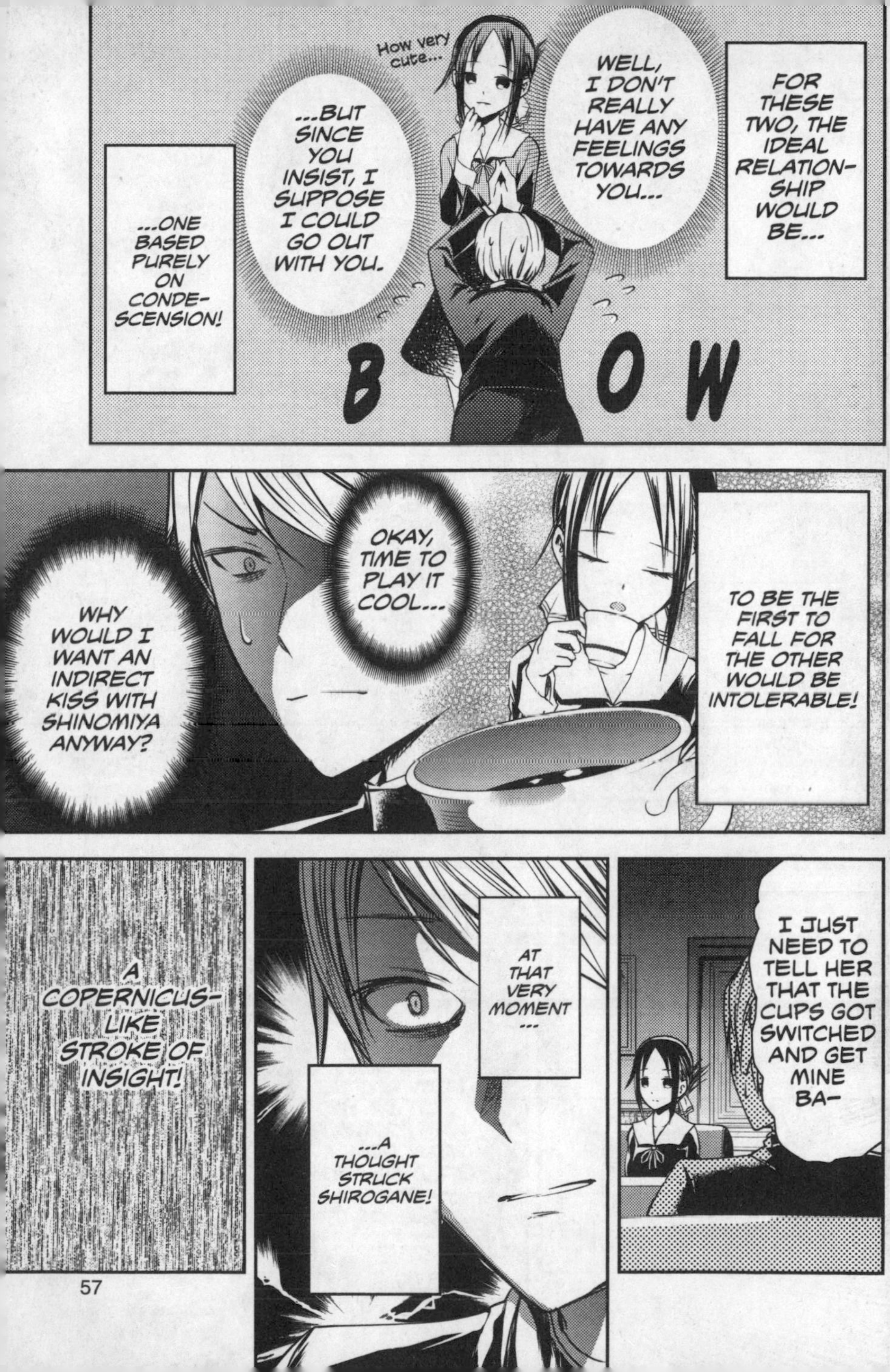
FOR THESE TWO, THE IDEAL RELATIONSHIP WOULD BE...
WELL, I DON'T REALLY HAVE ANY FEELINGS TOWARDS YOU...
How very cute...
...BUT SINCE YOU INSIST, I SUPPOSE I COULD GO OUT WITH YOU.
...ONE BASED PURELY ON CONDESCENSION!
BOW
TO BE THE FIRST TO FALL FOR THE OTHER WOULD BE INTOLERABLE!
OKAY, TIME TO PLAY IT COOL...
WHY WOULD I WANT AN INDIRECT KISS WITH SHINOMIYA ANYWAY?
I JUST NEED TO TELL HER THAT THE CUPS GOT SWITCHED AND GET MINE BA-
AT THAT VERY MOMENT...
...A THOUGHT STRUCK SHIROGANE!
A COPERNICUS-LIKE STROKE OF INSIGHT!

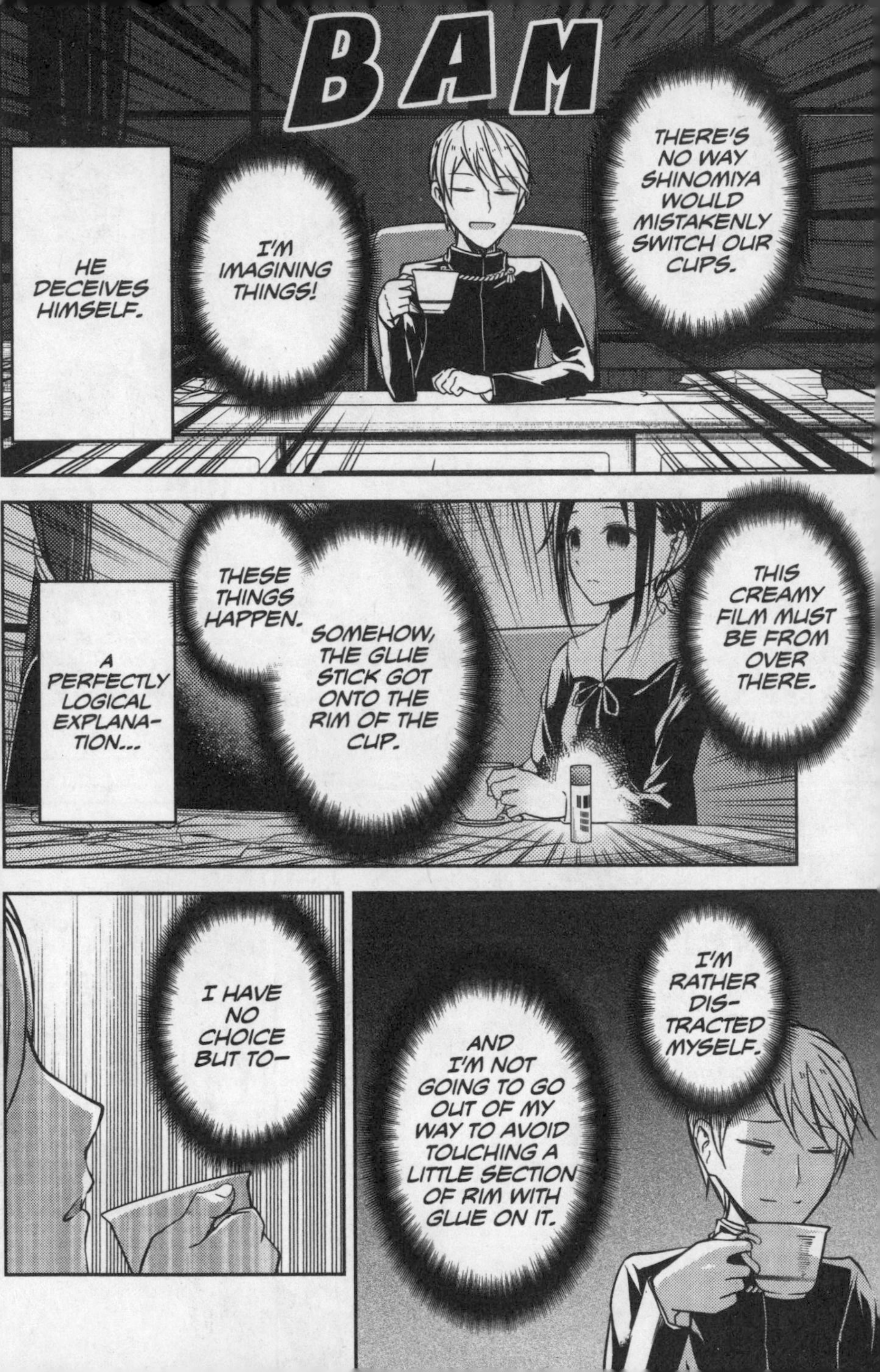
BAM
THERE'S NO WAY SHINOMIYA WOULD MISTAKENLY SWITCH OUR CUPS.
I'M IMAGINING THINGS!
HE DECEIVES HIMSELF.
THIS CREAMY FILM MUST BE FROM OVER THERE.
THESE THINGS HAPPEN.
SOMEHOW, THE GLUE STICK GOT ONTO THE RIM OF THE CUP.
A PERFECTLY LOGICAL EXPLANATION...
I'M RATHER DIS-TRACTED MYSELF.
AND I'M NOT GOING TO GO OUT OF MY WAY TO AVOID TOUCHING A LITTLE SECTION OF RIM WITH GLUE ON IT.
I HAVE NO CHOICE BUT TO—

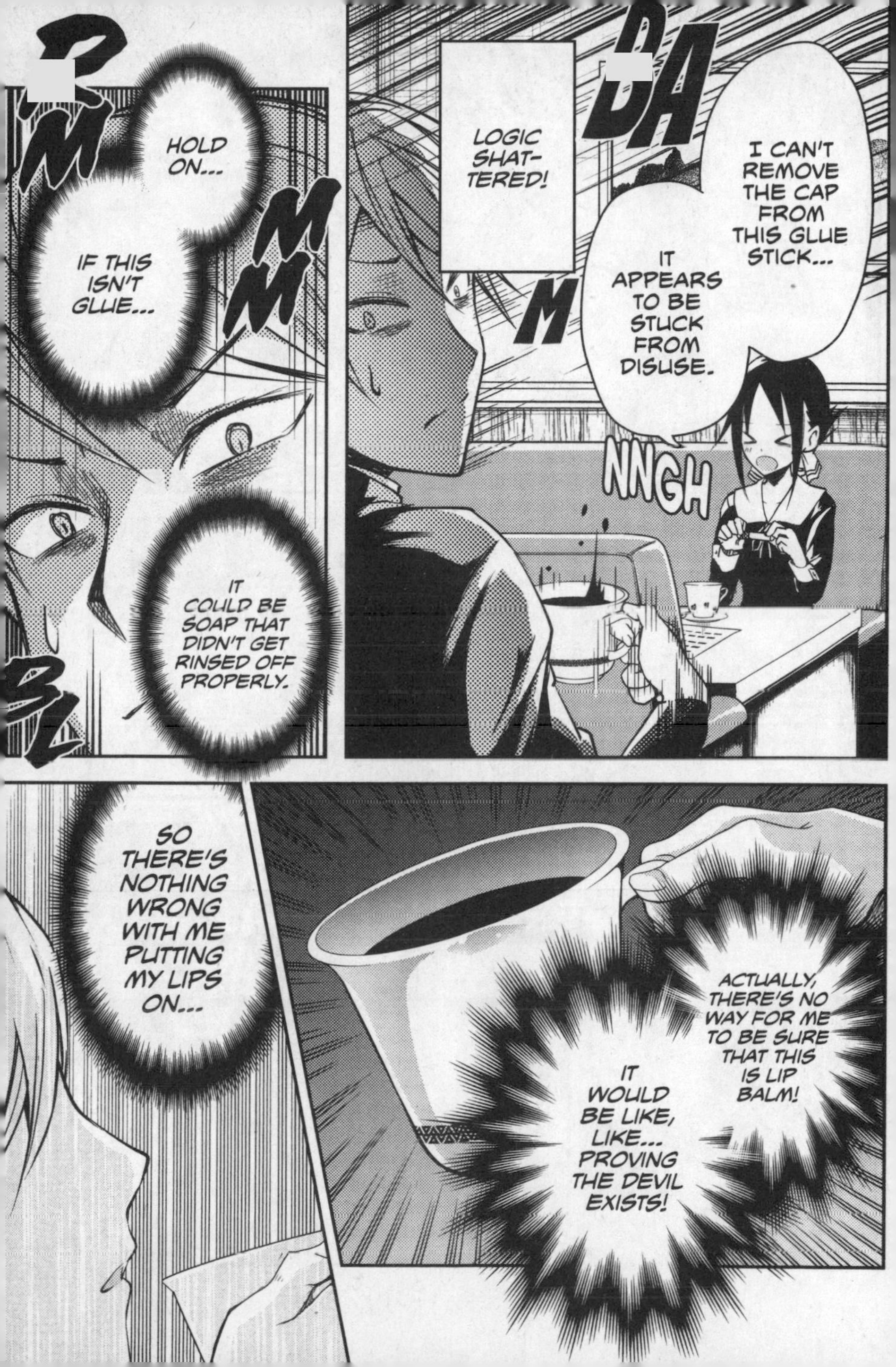
DA
M
LOGIC SHATTERED!
I CAN'T REMOVE THE CAP FROM THIS GLUE STICK...
IT APPEARS TO BE STUCK FROM DISUSE.
NNGH
HOLD ON...
IF THIS ISN'T GLUE...
IT COULD BE SOAP THAT DIDN'T GET RINSED OFF PROPERLY.
ACTUALLY, THERE'S NO WAY FOR ME TO BE SURE THAT THIS IS LIP BALM!
IT WOULD BE LIKE, LIKE... PROVING THE DEVIL EXISTS!
SO THERE'S NOTHING WRONG WITH ME PUTTING MY LIPS ON...

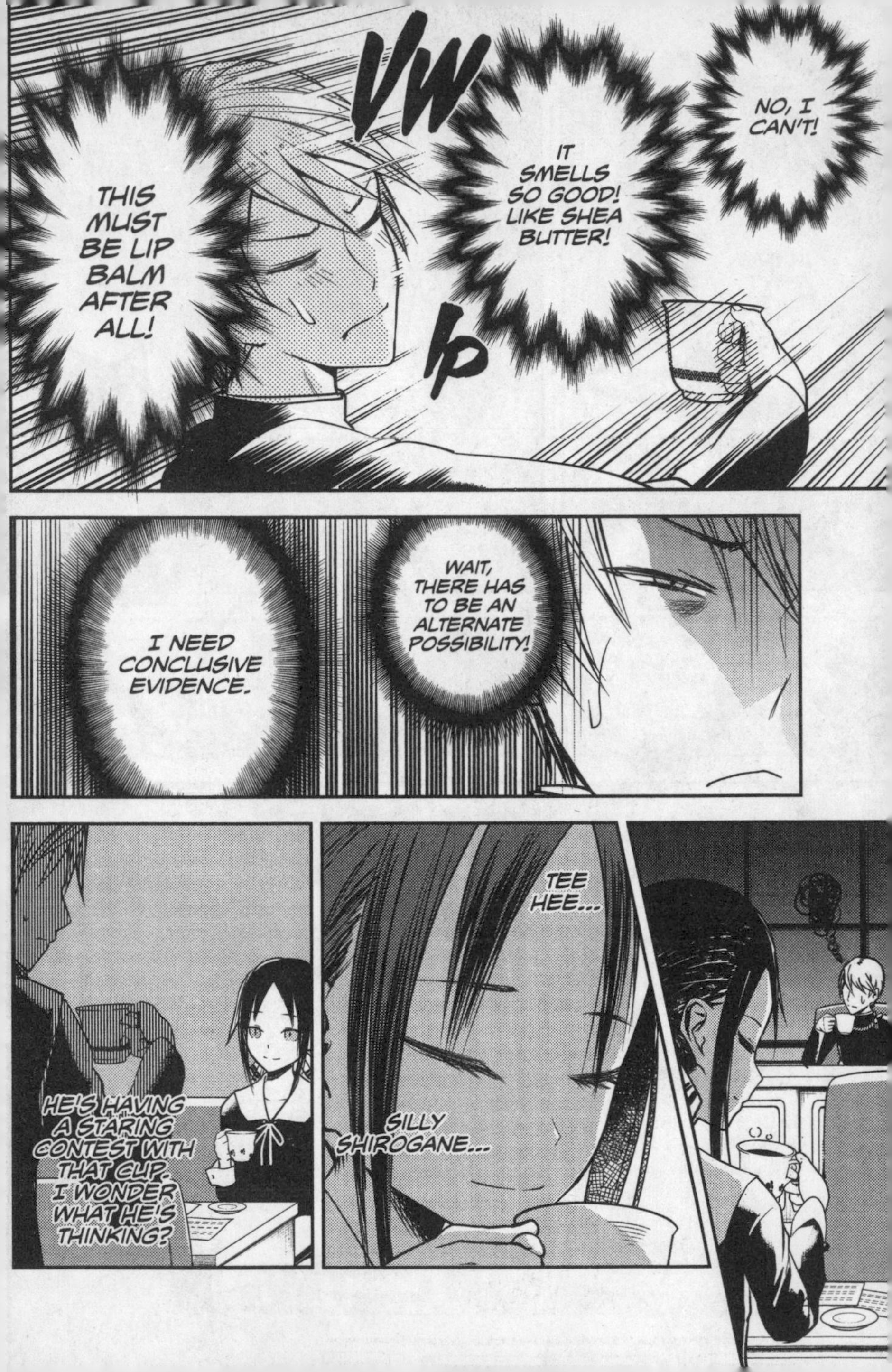
NO, I CAN'T!
IT SMELLS SO GOOD! LIKE SHEA BUTTER!
VW
THIS MUST BE LIP BALM AFTER ALL!
lp
WAIT, THERE HAS TO BE AN ALTERNATE POSSIBILITY!
I NEED CONCLUSIVE EVIDENCE.
TEE HEE...
SILLY SHIROGANE...
HE'S HAVING A STARING CONTEST WITH THAT CUP. I WONDER WHAT HE'S THINKING?

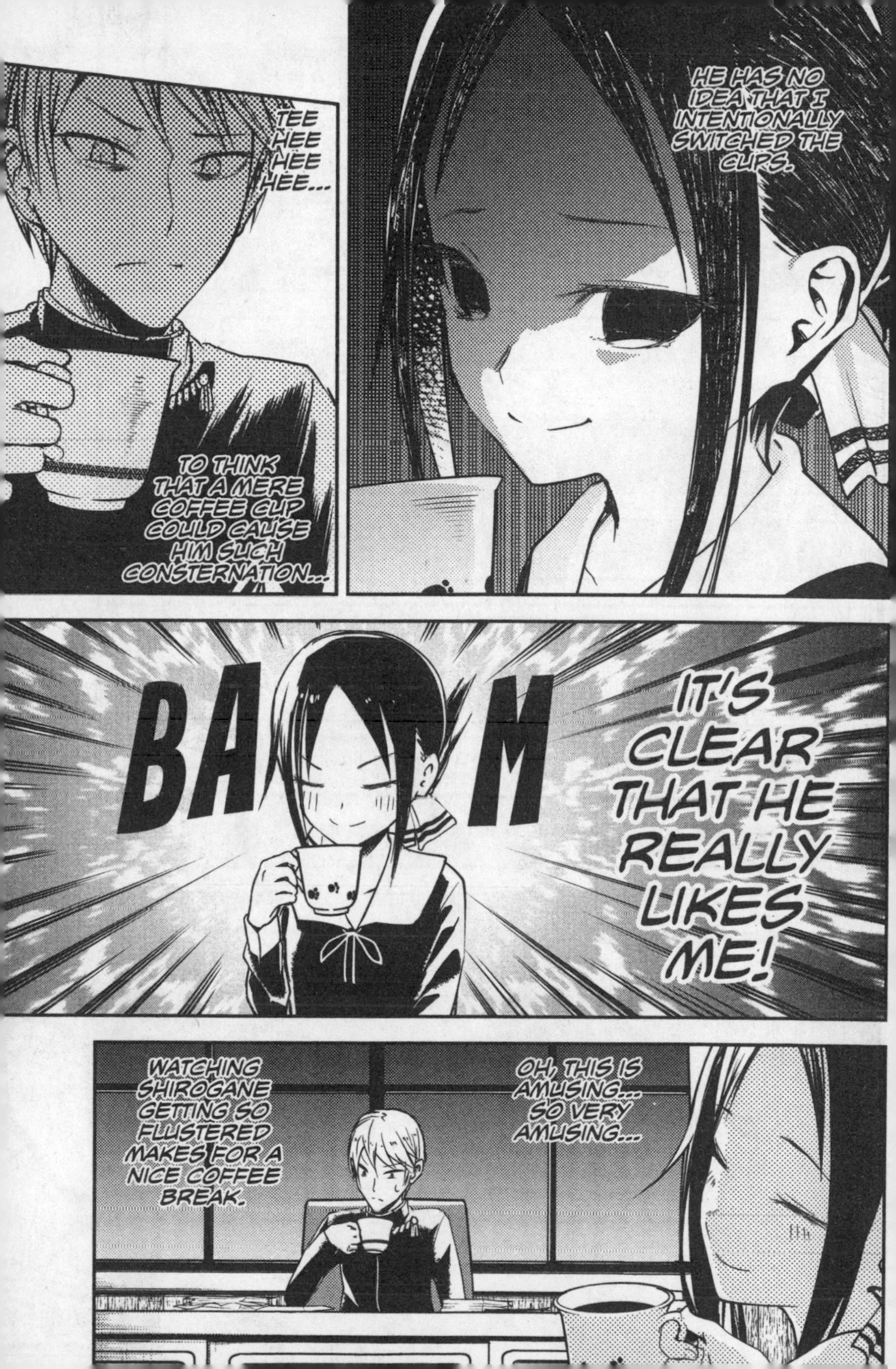
HE HAS NO IDEA THAT I INTENTIONALLY SWITCHED THE CUPS.
TEE HEE HEE HEE...
TO THINK THAT A MERE COFFEE CUP COULD CAUSE HIM SUCH CONSTERNATION...
IT'S CLEAR THAT HE REALLY LIKES ME!
BA M
OH, THIS IS AMUSING... SO VERY AMUSING...
WATCHING SHIROGANE GETTING SO FLUSTERED MAKES FOR A NICE COFFEE BREAK.

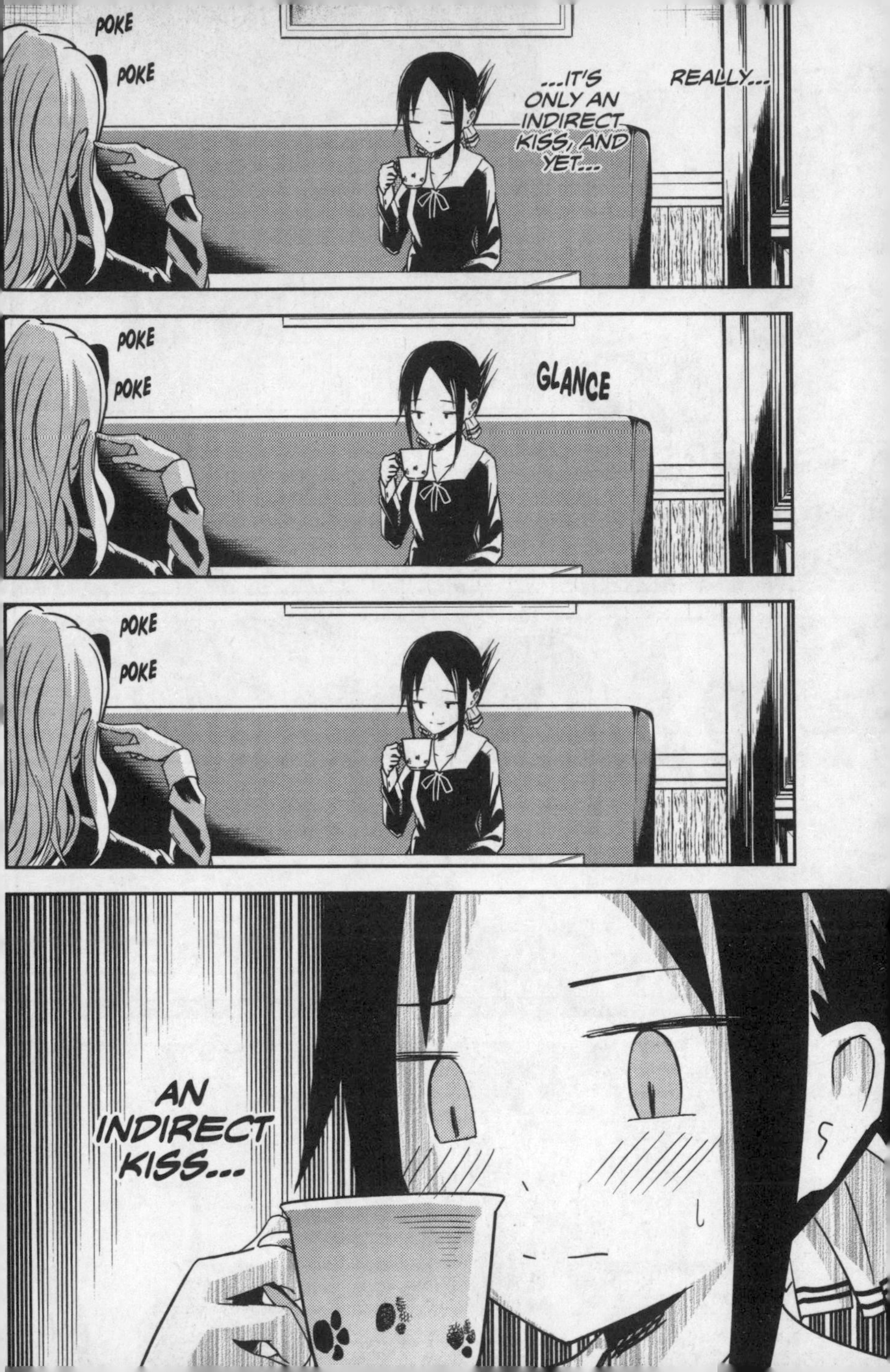
REALLY...
...IT'S ONLY AN INDIRECT KISS, AND YET...
POKE
POKE
GLANCE
POKE
POKE
POKE
POKE
AN INDIRECT KISS...

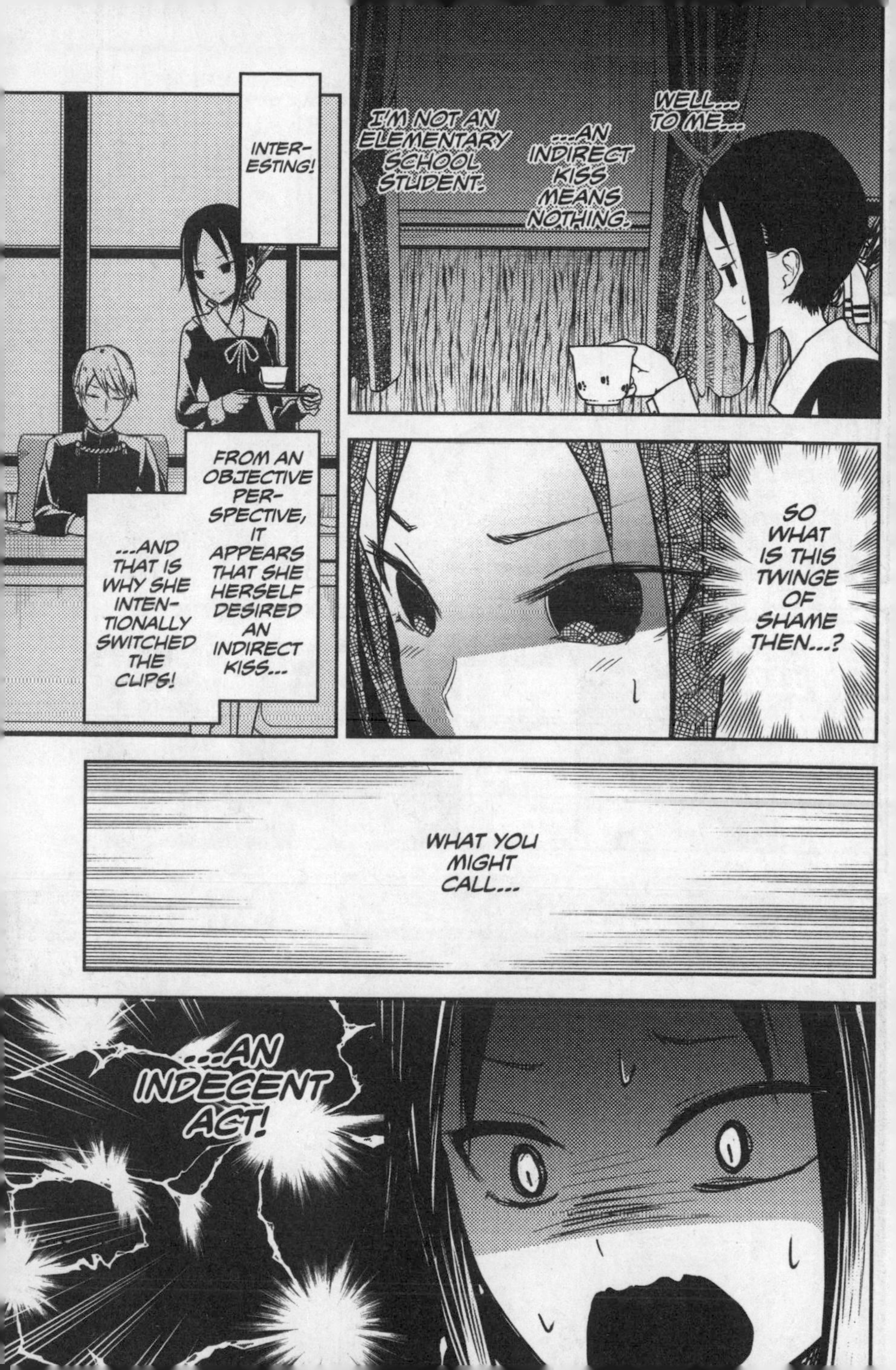
WELL... TO ME...
...AN INDIRECT KISS MEANS NOTHING.
I'M NOT AN ELEMENTARY SCHOOL STUDENT.
SO WHAT IS THIS TWINGE OF SHAME THEN...?
INTER-ESTING!
FROM AN OBJECTIVE PER-SPECTIVE, IT APPEARS THAT SHE HERSELF DESIRED AN INDIRECT KISS...
...AND THAT IS WHY SHE INTEN-TIONALLY SWITCHED THE CLIPS!
WHAT YOU MIGHT CALL...
...AN INDECENT ACT!

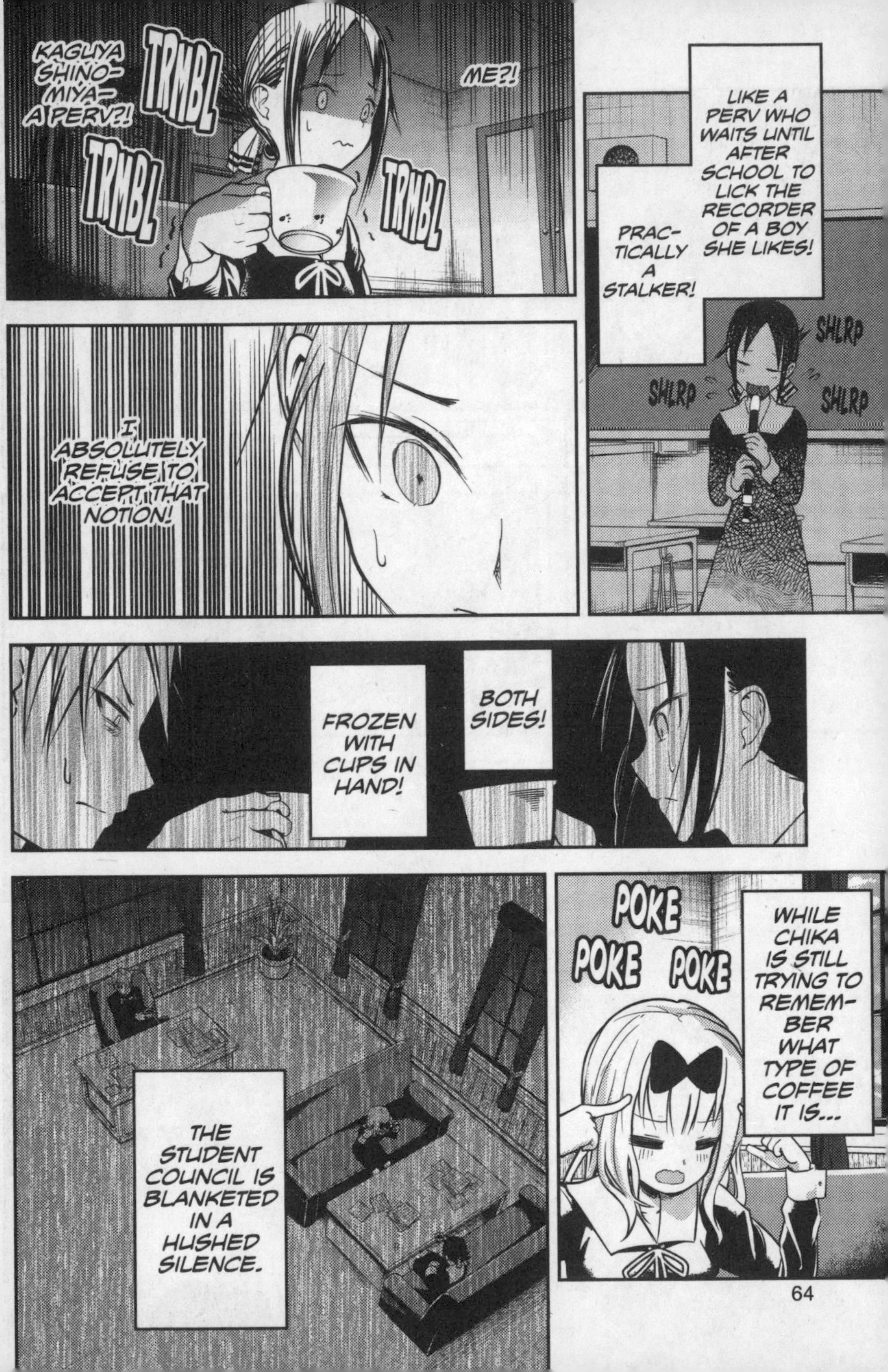
LIKE A PERV WHO WAITS UNTIL AFTER SCHOOL TO LICK THE RECORDER OF A BOY SHE LIKES!
PRAC-TICALLY A STALKER!
SHLRP
SHLRP
SHLRP
KAGUYA SHINO-MIYA— A PERV?!
TRMBL
TRMBL
TRMBL
ME?!
I ABSOLUTELY REFUSE TO ACCEPT THAT NOTION!
BOTH SIDES!
FROZEN WITH CUPS IN HAND!
POKE
POKE
POKE
WHILE CHIKA IS STILL TRYING TO REMEM-BER WHAT TYPE OF COFFEE IT IS...
THE STUDENT COUNCIL IS BLANKETED IN A HUSHED SILENCE.

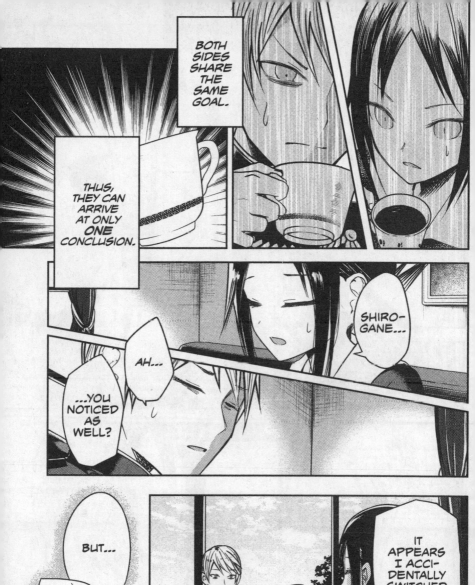

BOTH SIDES SHARE THE SAME GOAL.

THUS, THEY CAN ARRIVE AT ONLY ONE CONCLUSION.

SHIRO-GANE...

AH...

...YOU NOTICED AS WELL?

BUT...

WELL...

IT APPEARS I ACCI-DENTALLY SWITCHED OUR CUPS.

YES, IT DOES.

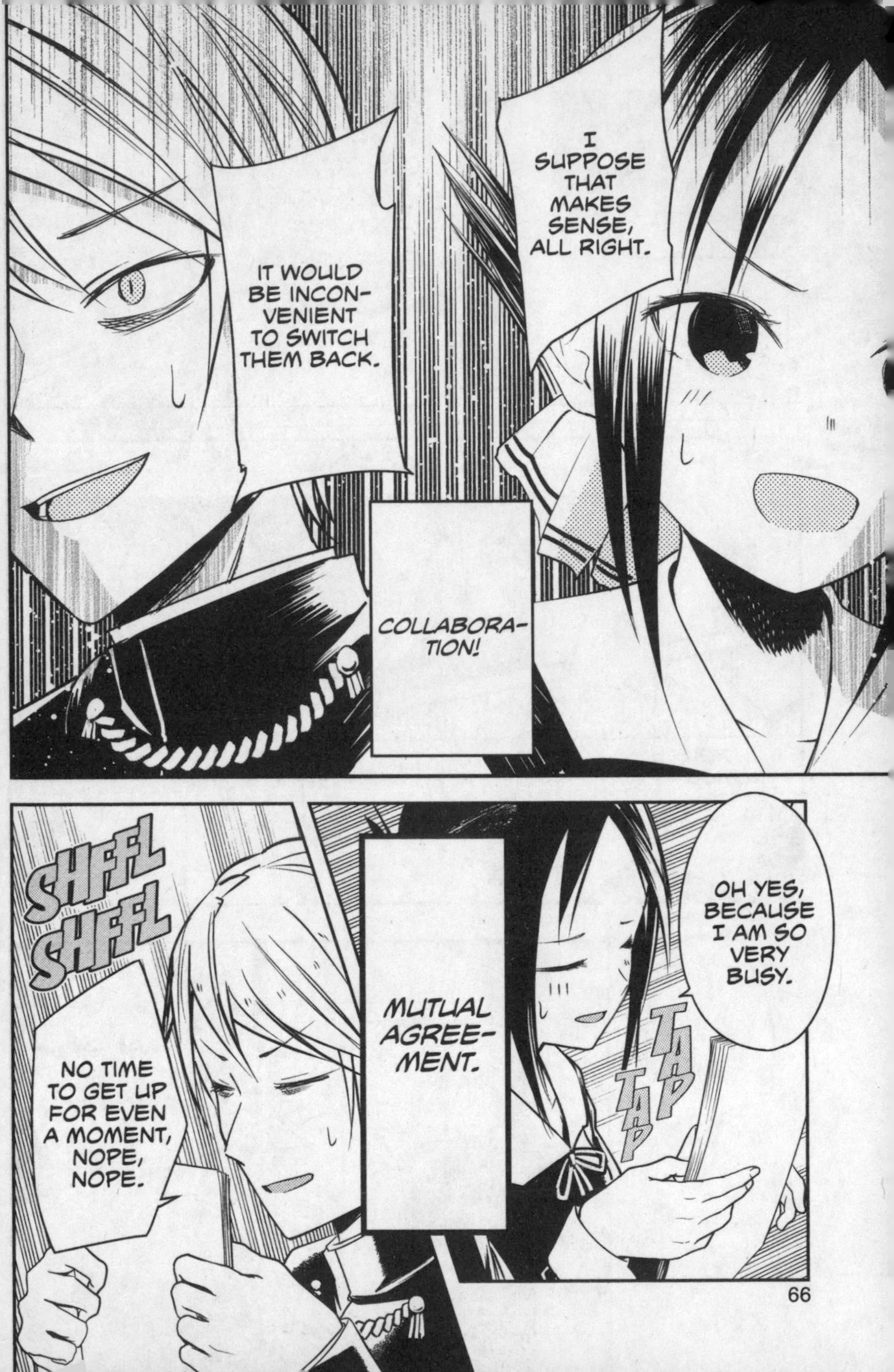
I SUPPOSE THAT MAKES SENSE, ALL RIGHT.
IT WOULD BE INCON-VENIENT TO SWITCH THEM BACK.
COLLABORA-TION!
OH YES, BECAUSE I AM SO VERY BUSY.
TAP TAP
MUTUAL AGREE-MENT.
SHFFL SHFFL
NO TIME TO GET UP FOR EVEN A MOMENT, NOPE, NOPE.

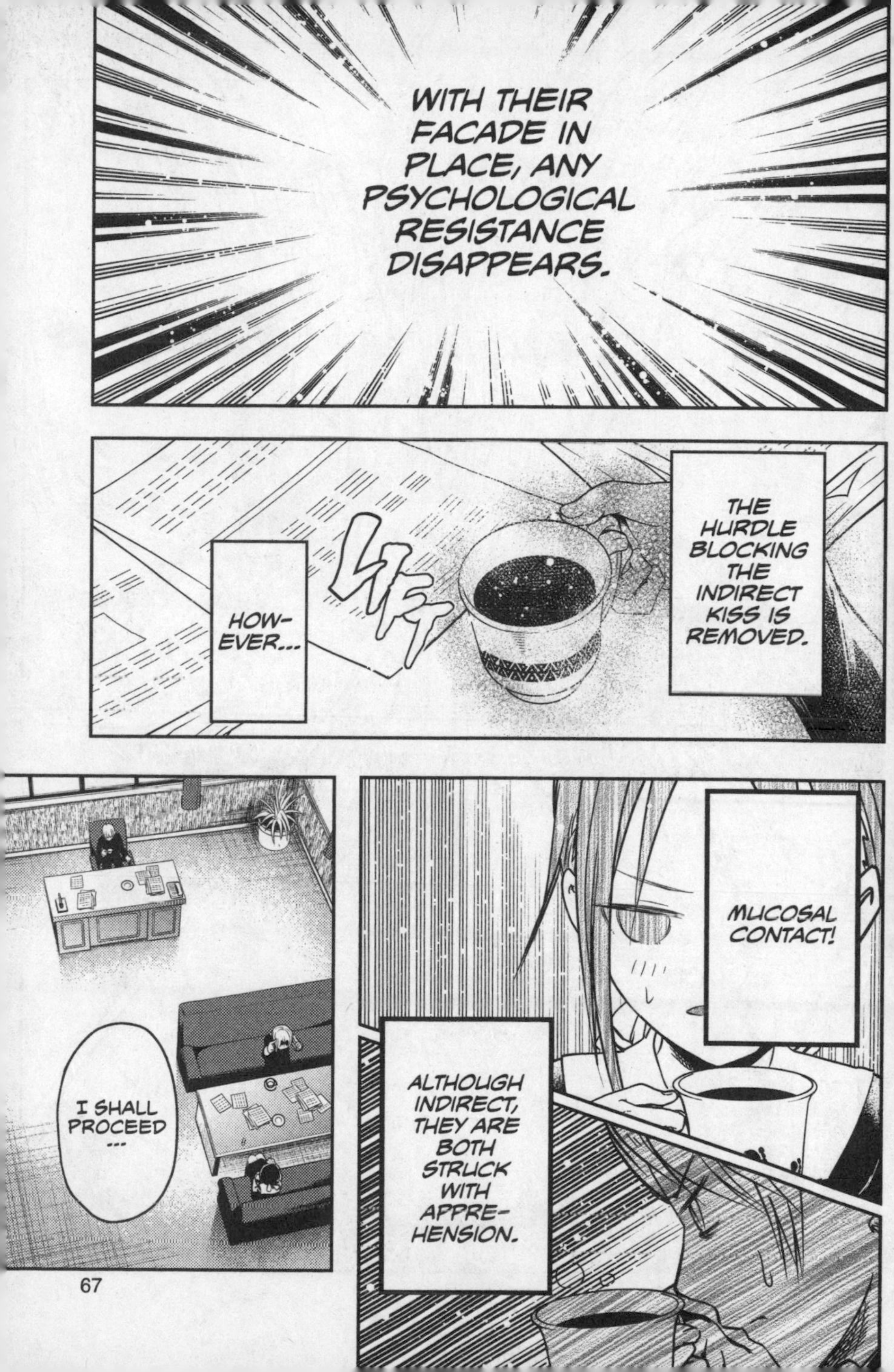
WITH THEIR FACADE IN PLACE, ANY PSYCHOLOGICAL RESISTANCE DISAPPEARS.
THE HURDLE BLOCKING THE INDIRECT KISS IS REMOVED.
LIFT
HOW-EVER...
MUCOSAL CONTACT!
ALTHOUGH INDIRECT, THEY ARE BOTH STRUCK WITH APPRE-HENSION.
I SHALL PROCEED...

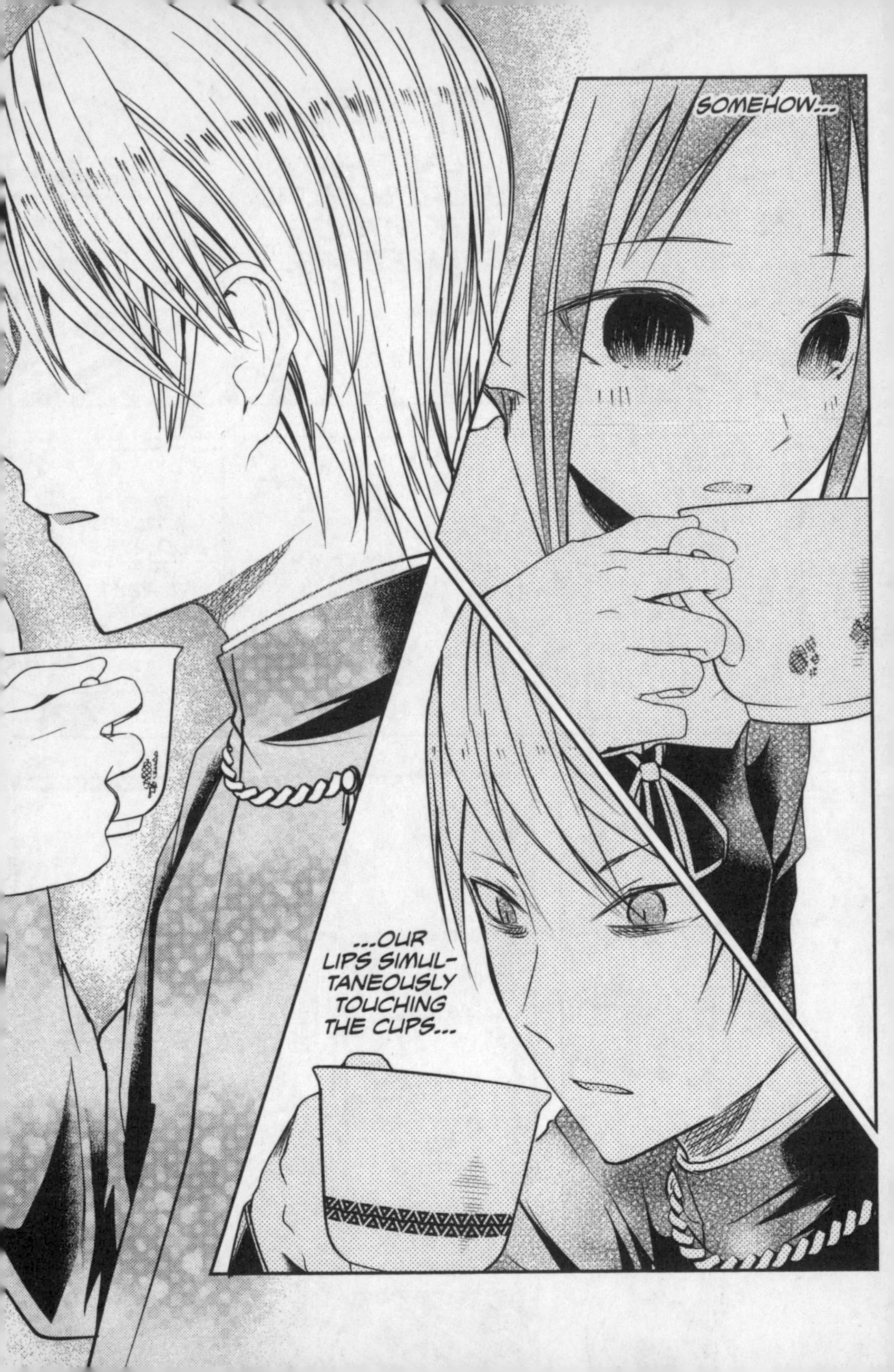
SOMEHOW...
...OUR LIPS SIMUL-TANEOUSLY TOUCHING THE CUPS...

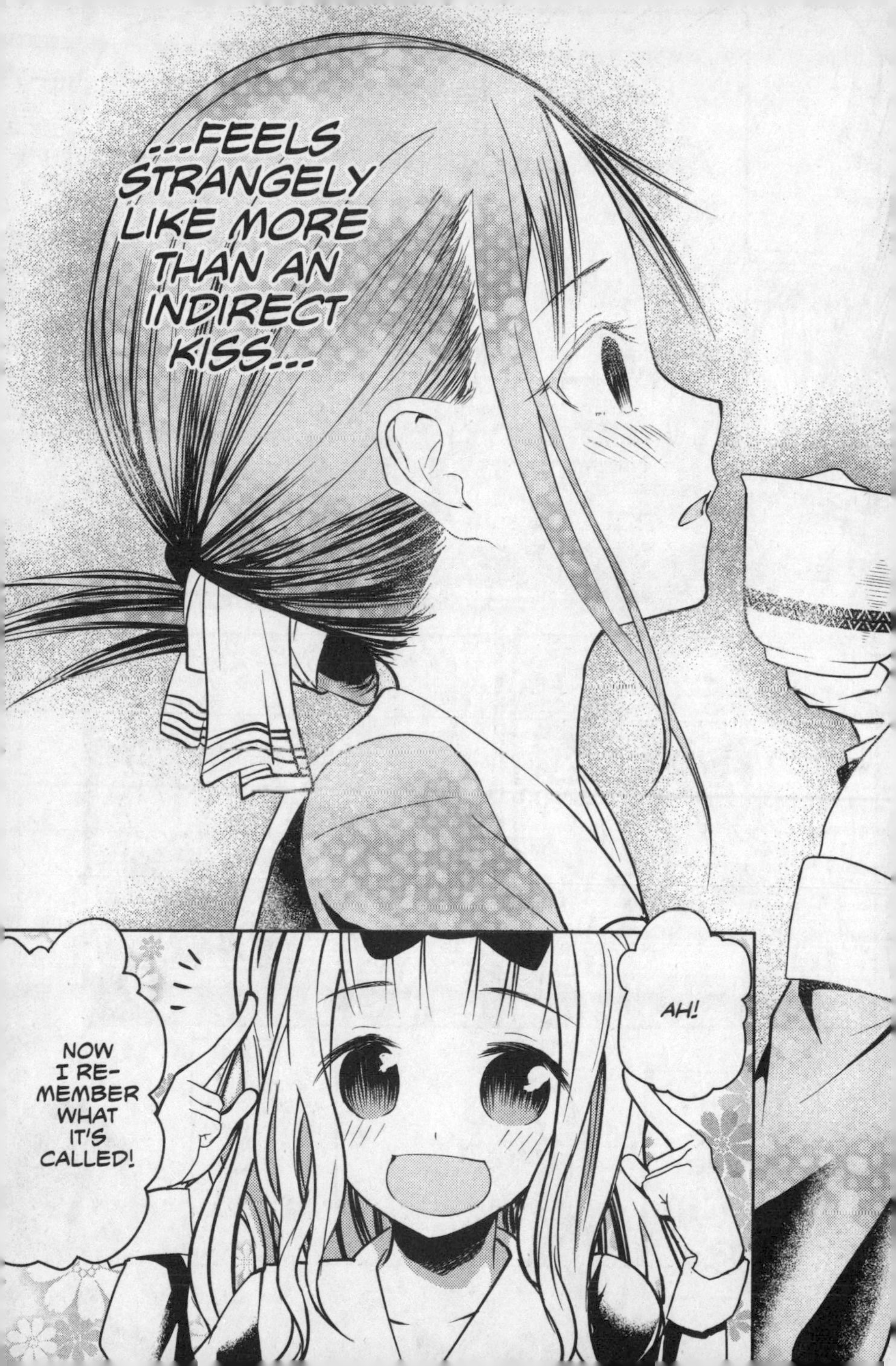
...FEELS STRANGELY LIKE MORE THAN AN INDIRECT KISS...
AH!
NOW I RE-MEMBER WHAT IT'S CALLED!

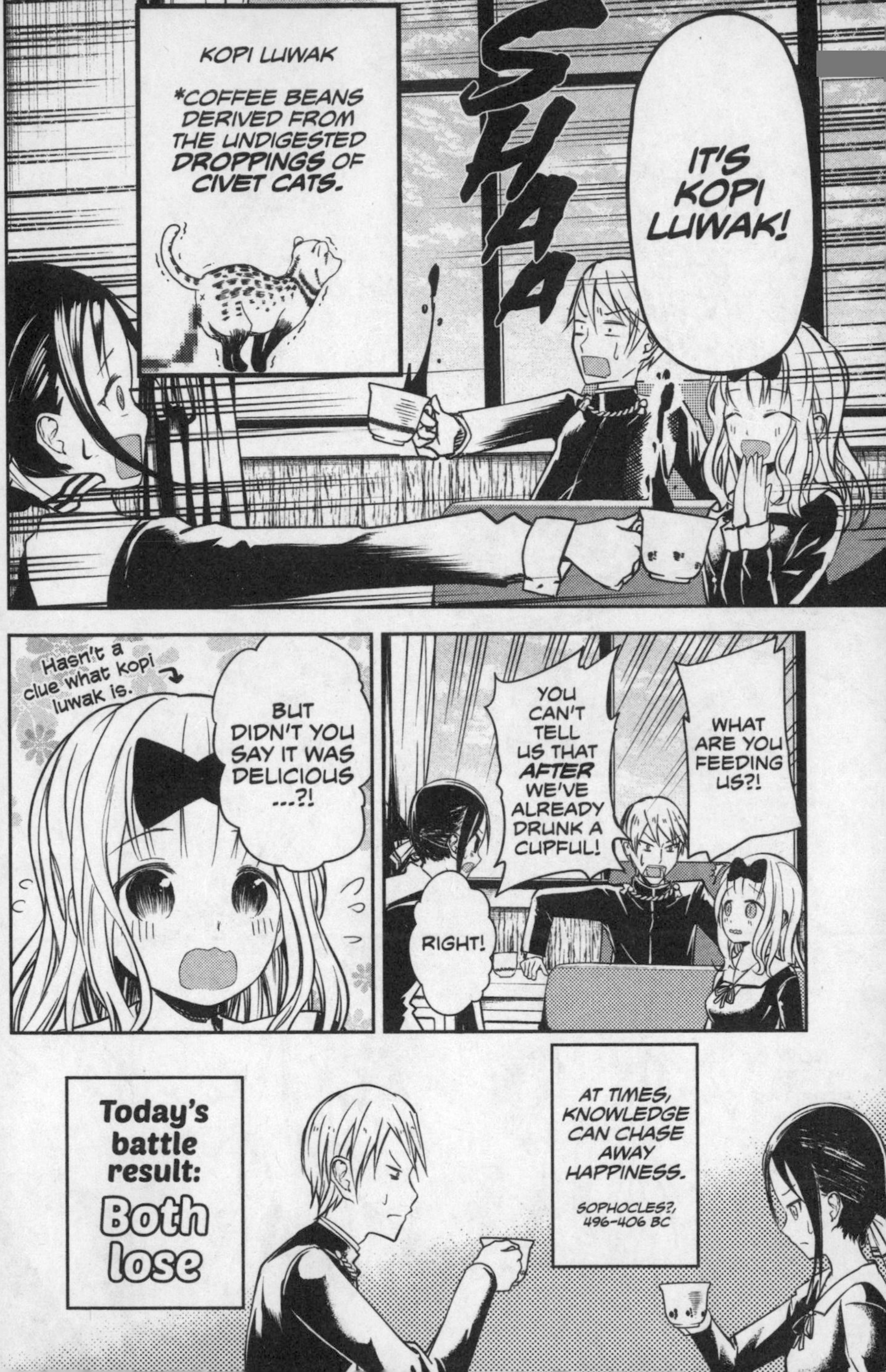
IT'S KOPI LUWAK!
SHAA
KOPI LUWAK
*COFFEE BEANS DERIVED FROM THE UNDIGESTED DROPPINGS OF CIVET CATS.
WHAT ARE YOU FEEDING US?!
YOU CAN'T TELL US THAT AFTER WE'VE ALREADY DRUNK A CUPFUL!
RIGHT!
BUT DIDN'T YOU SAY IT WAS DELICIOUS ...?!
Hasn't a clue what kopi luwak is.
AT TIMES, KNOWLEDGE CAN CHASE AWAY HAPPINESS.
SOPHOCLES?, 496-406 BC
Today's battle result: Both lose

In charge of coffee: Chika Fujiwara

In charge of tea: Kaguya Shinomiya

The one who just drinks: Miyuki Shirogane

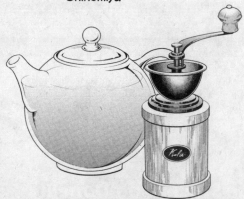

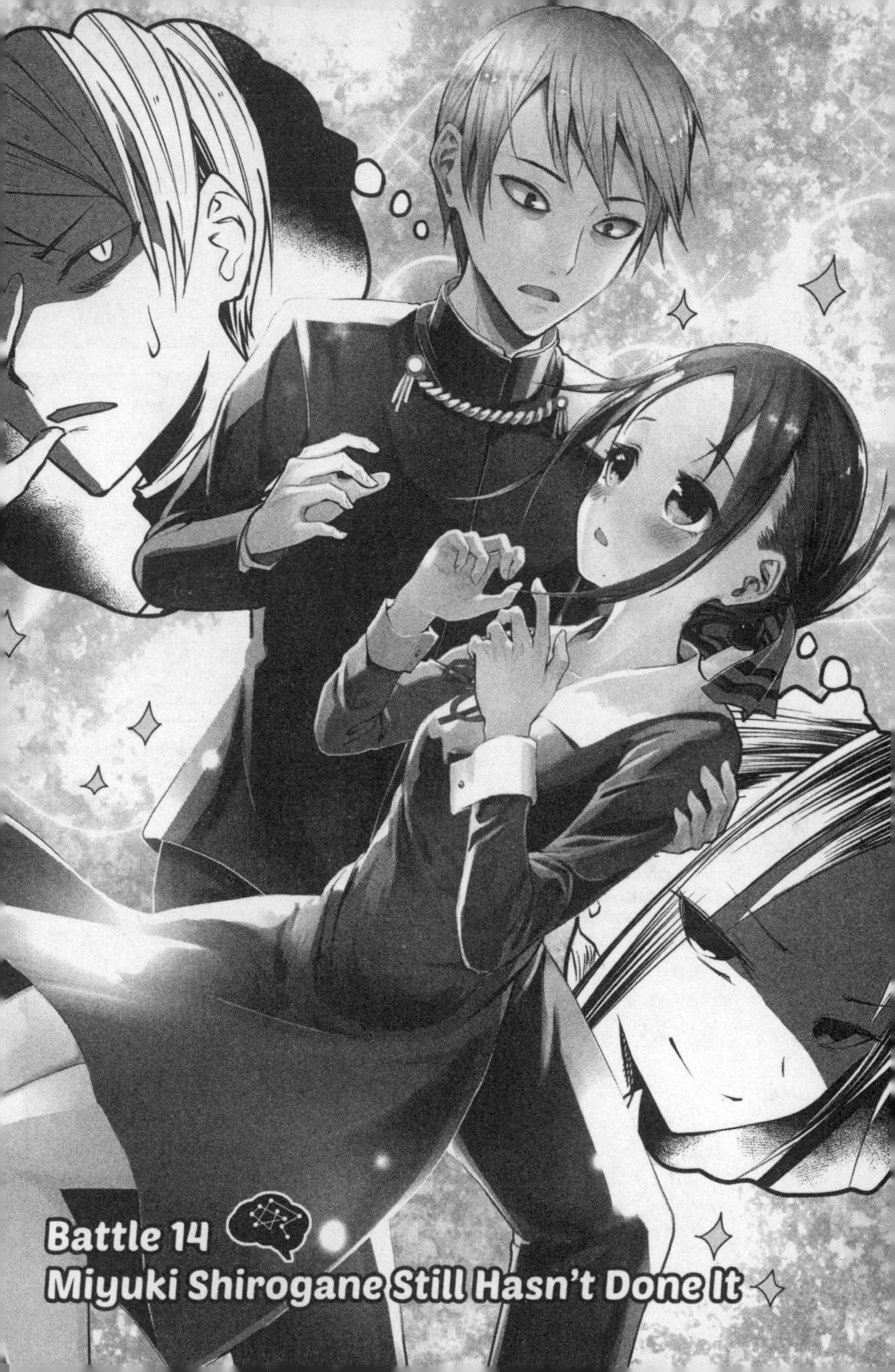
Battle 14
Miyuki Shirogane Still Hasn't Done It

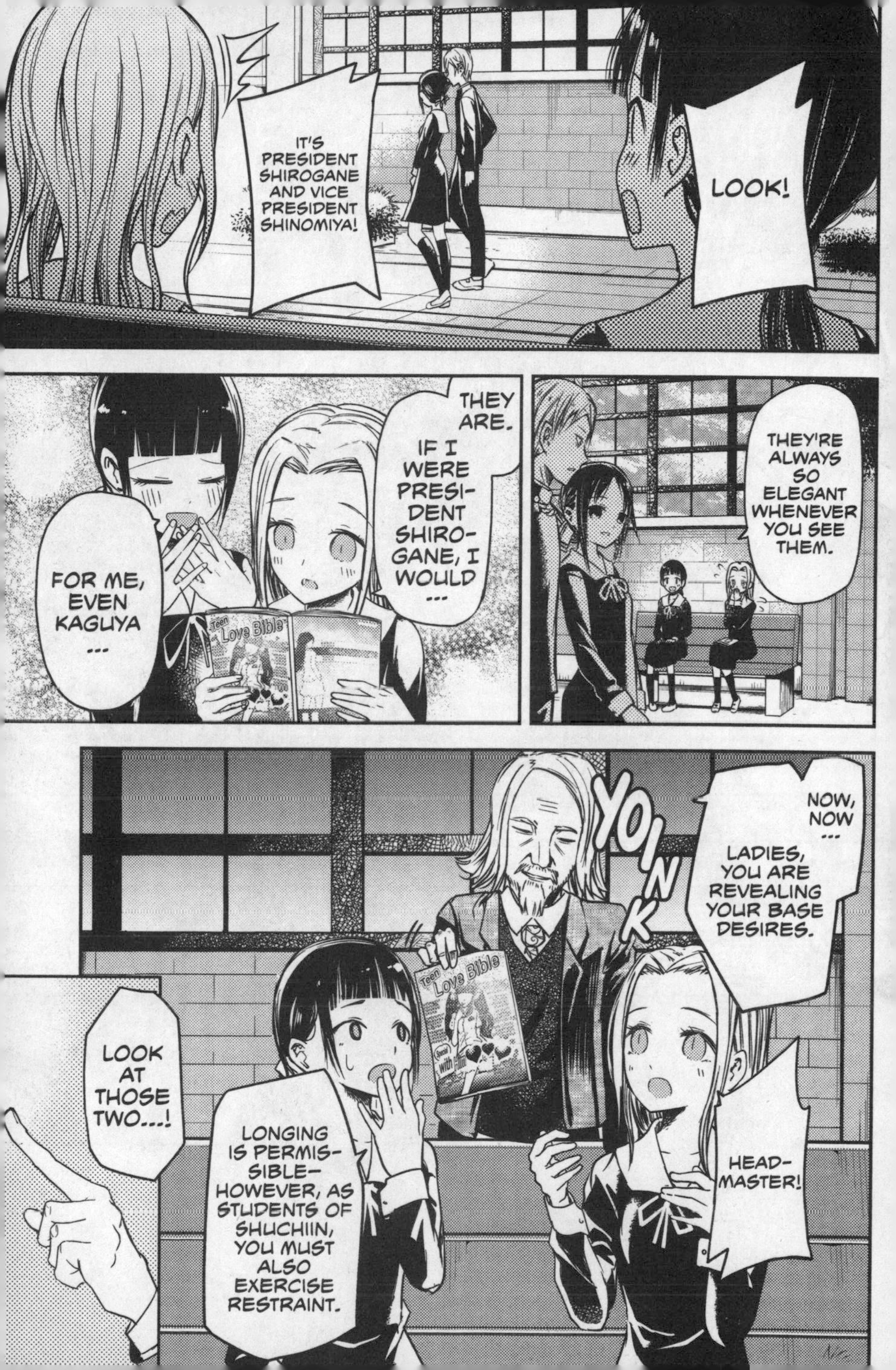
LOOK!
IT'S PRESIDENT SHIROGANE AND VICE PRESIDENT SHINOMIYA!
THEY'RE ALWAYS SO ELEGANT WHENEVER YOU SEE THEM.
THEY ARE.
IF I WERE PRESIDENT SHIROGANE, I WOULD...
FOR ME, EVEN KAGUYA...
Teen Love Bible
YOINK
NOW, NOW... LADIES, YOU ARE REVEALING YOUR BASE DESIRES.
HEADMASTER!
LONGING IS PERMISSIBLE— HOWEVER, AS STUDENTS OF SHUCHIIN, YOU MUST ALSO EXERCISE RESTRAINT.
LOOK AT THOSE TWO...!

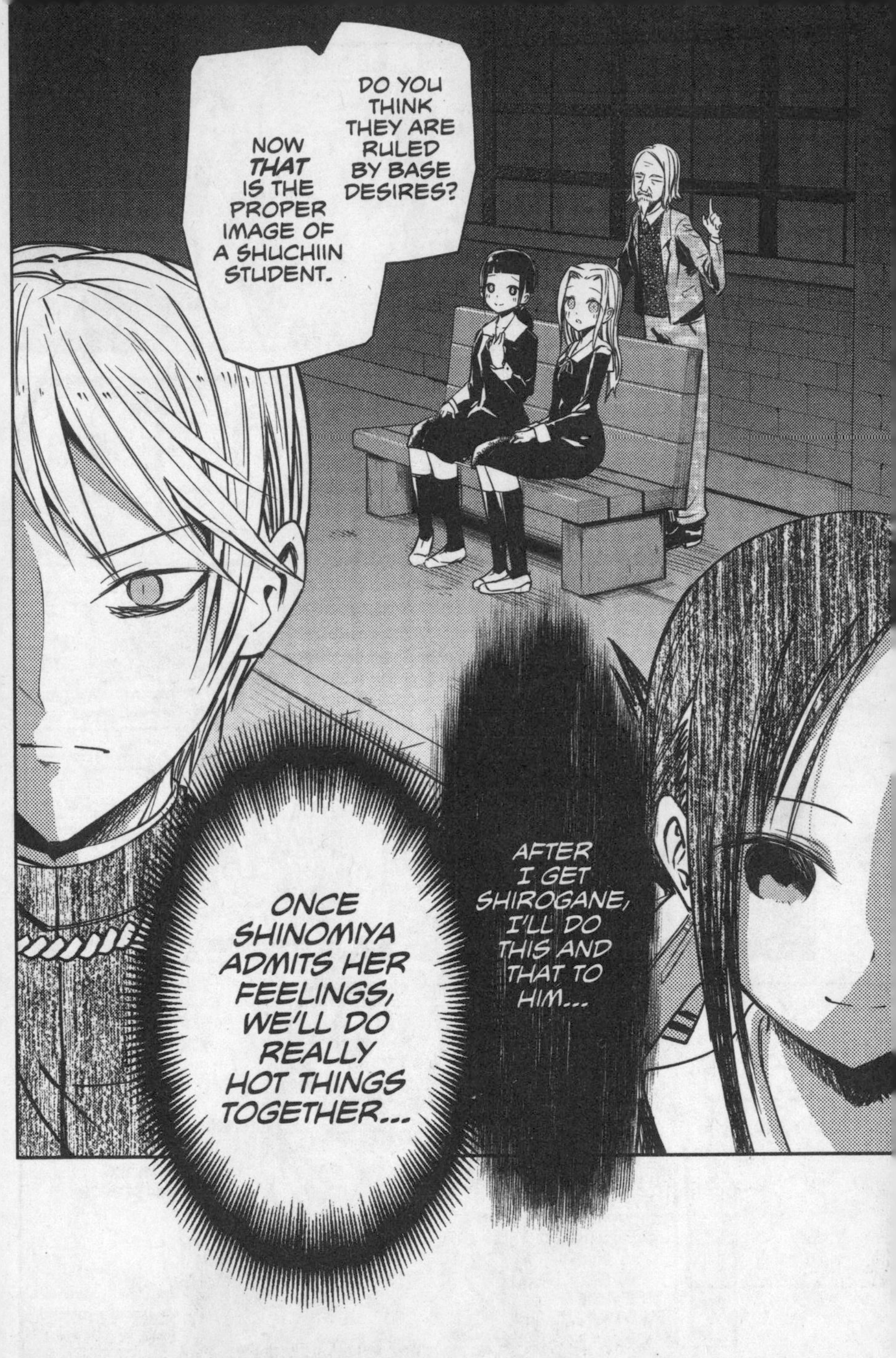
DO YOU THINK THEY ARE RULED BY BASE DESIRES?
NOW *THAT* IS THE PROPER IMAGE OF A SHUCHIIN STUDENT.
AFTER I GET SHIROGANE, I'LL DO THIS AND THAT TO HIM...
ONCE SHINOMIYA ADMITS HER FEELINGS, WE'LL DO REALLY HOT THINGS TOGETHER...

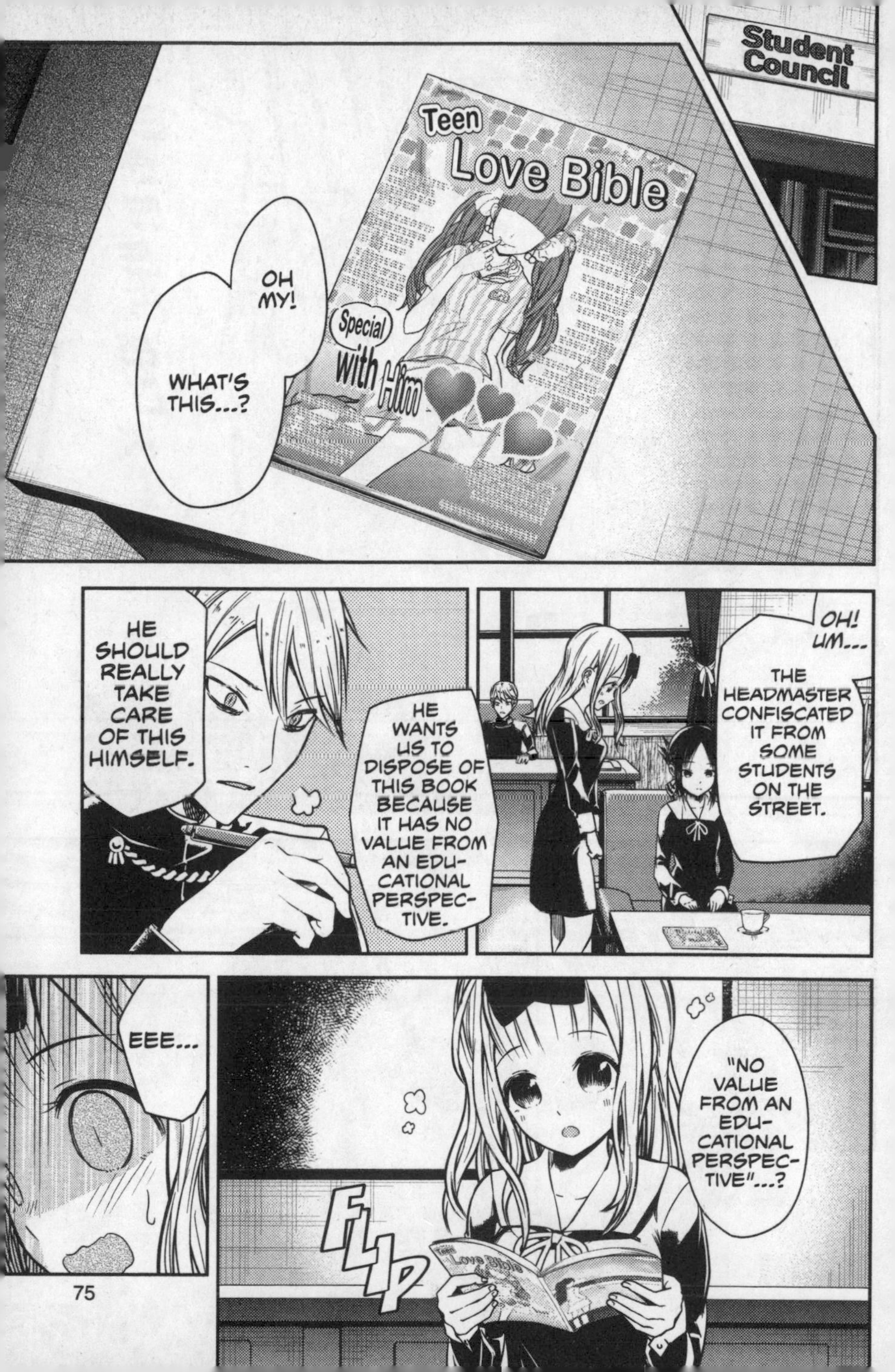
Student Council
Teen Love Bible
Special with Him
OH MY!
WHAT'S THIS...?
OH! UM...
THE HEADMASTER CONFISCATED IT FROM SOME STUDENTS ON THE STREET.
HE WANTS US TO DISPOSE OF THIS BOOK BECAUSE IT HAS NO VALUE FROM AN EDUCATIONAL PERSPECTIVE.
HE SHOULD REALLY TAKE CARE OF THIS HIMSELF.
"NO VALUE FROM AN EDUCATIONAL PERSPECTIVE"...?
FLIP
Teen Love Bible
EEE...

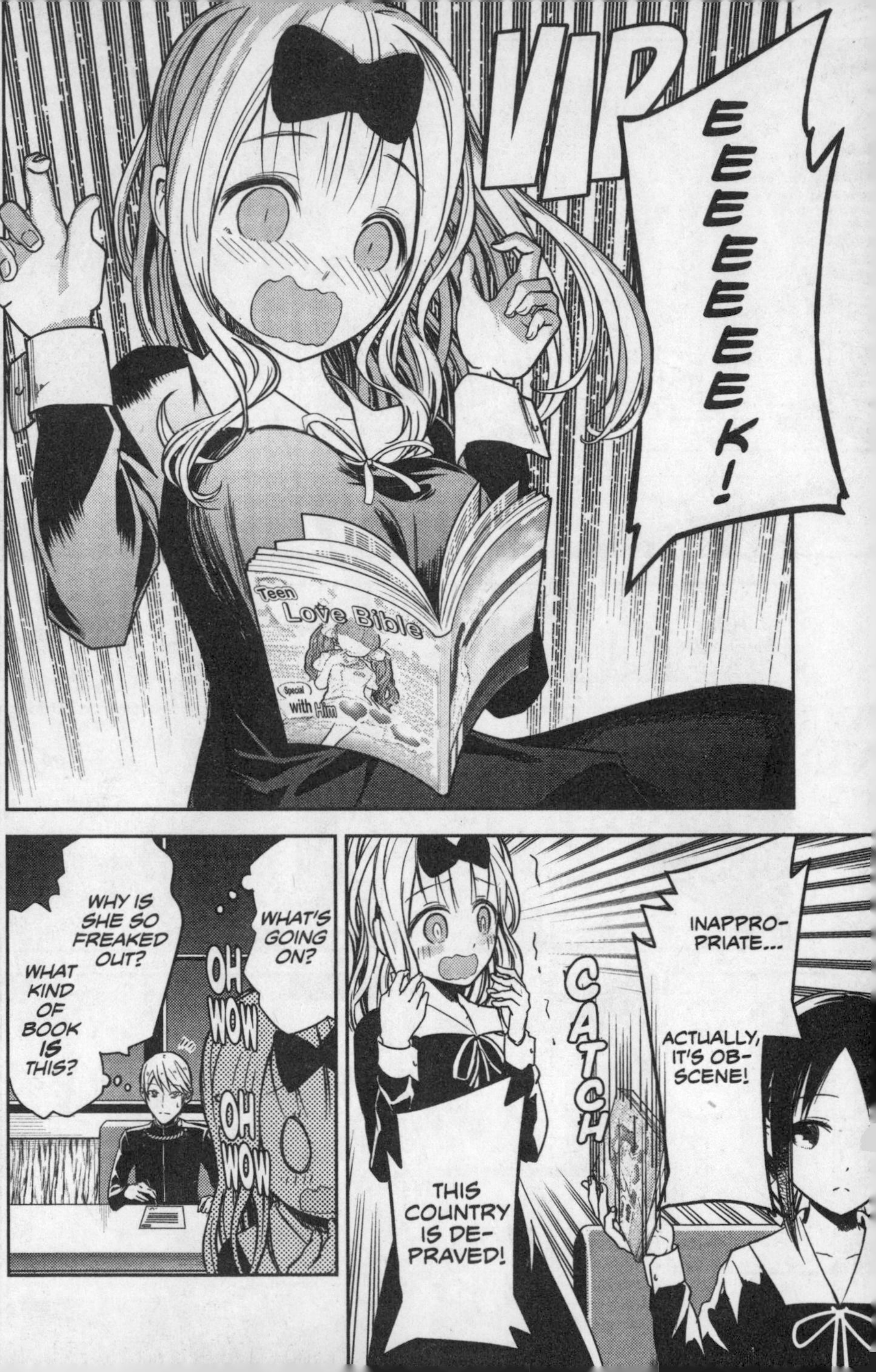
VIPEEEEEEEK!
Teen Love Bible
Special with Him
INAPPRO-PRIATE...
ACTUALLY, IT'S OB-SCENE!
CATCH
THIS COUNTRY IS DE-PRAVED!
WHAT'S GOING ON?
OH WOW OH WOW
WHY IS SHE SO FREAKED OUT?
WHAT KIND OF BOOK IS THIS?

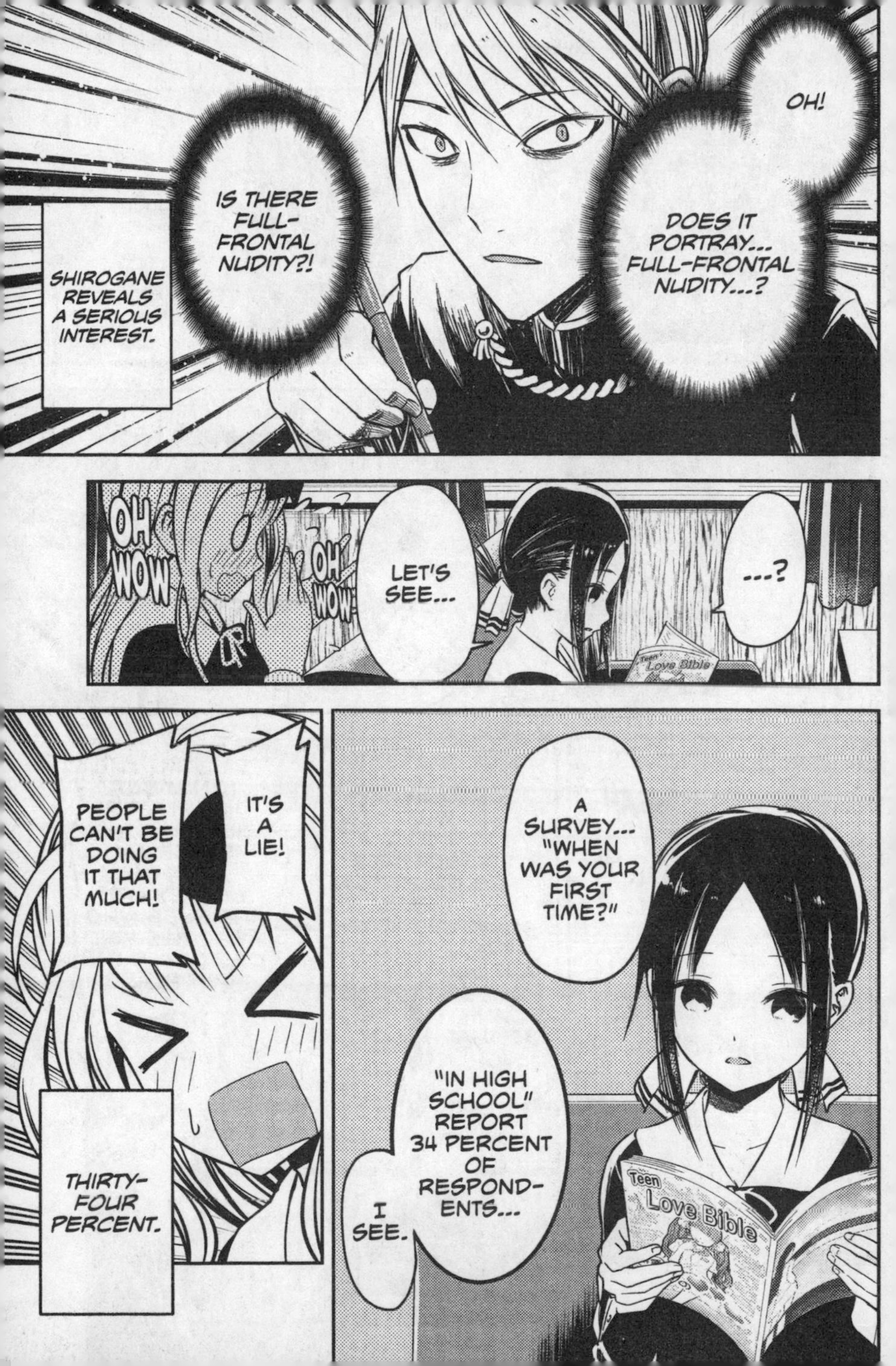
OH!
DOES IT PORTRAY... FULL-FRONTAL NUDITY...?
IS THERE FULL-FRONTAL NUDITY?!
SHIROGANE REVEALS A SERIOUS INTEREST.
...?
Teen Love Bible
LET'S SEE...
OH WOW
OH WOW
A SURVEY... "WHEN WAS YOUR FIRST TIME?"
"IN HIGH SCHOOL" REPORT 34 PERCENT OF RESPOND-ENTS...
I SEE.
Teen Love Bible
IT'S A LIE!
PEOPLE CAN'T BE DOING IT THAT MUCH!
THIRTY-FOUR PERCENT.

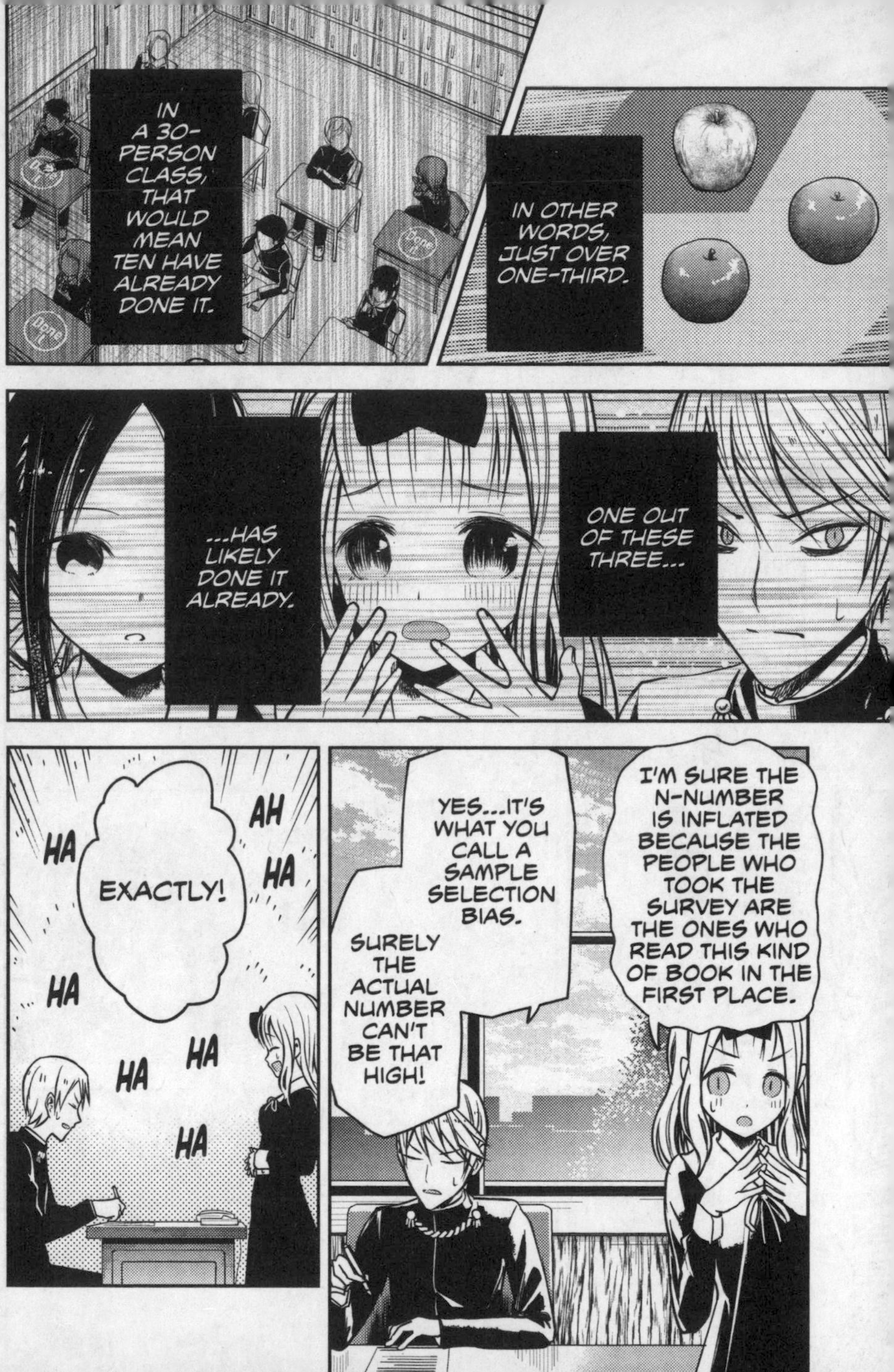
IN OTHER WORDS, JUST OVER ONE-THIRD.
IN A 30-PERSON CLASS, THAT WOULD MEAN TEN HAVE ALREADY DONE IT.
ONE OUT OF THESE THREE...
...HAS LIKELY DONE IT ALREADY.
I'M SURE THE N-NUMBER IS INFLATED BECAUSE THE PEOPLE WHO TOOK THE SURVEY ARE THE ONES WHO READ THIS KIND OF BOOK IN THE FIRST PLACE.
YES...IT'S WHAT YOU CALL A SAMPLE SELECTION BIAS.
SURELY THE ACTUAL NUMBER CAN'T BE THAT HIGH!
AH
HA
HA
EXACTLY!
HA
HA
HA
HA

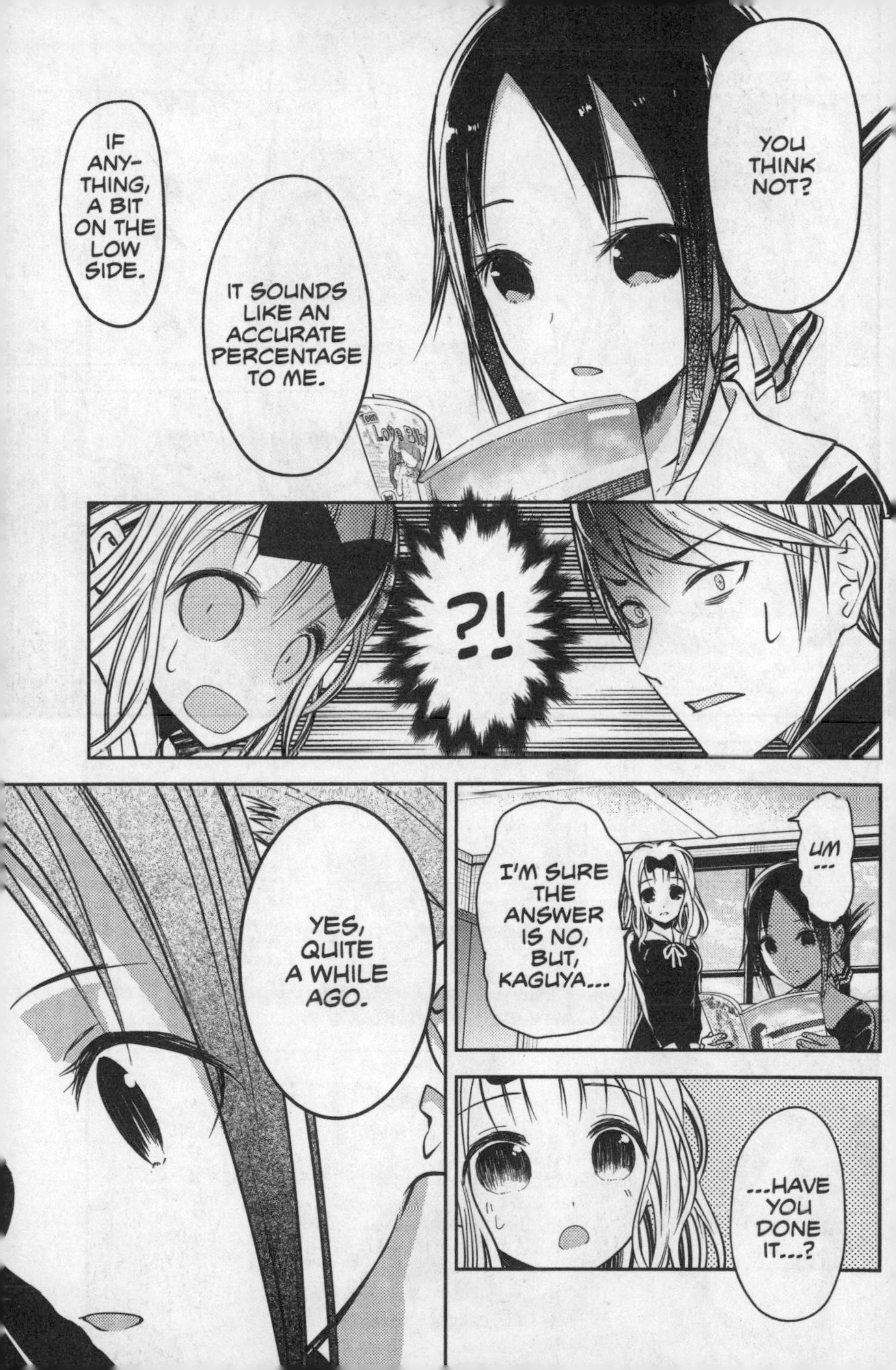
YOU THINK NOT?
IT SOUNDS LIKE AN ACCURATE PERCENTAGE TO ME.
IF ANY-THING, A BIT ON THE LOW SIDE.
?!
UM...
I'M SURE THE ANSWER IS NO, BUT, KAGUYA...
...HAVE YOU DONE IT...?
YES, QUITE A WHILE AGO.

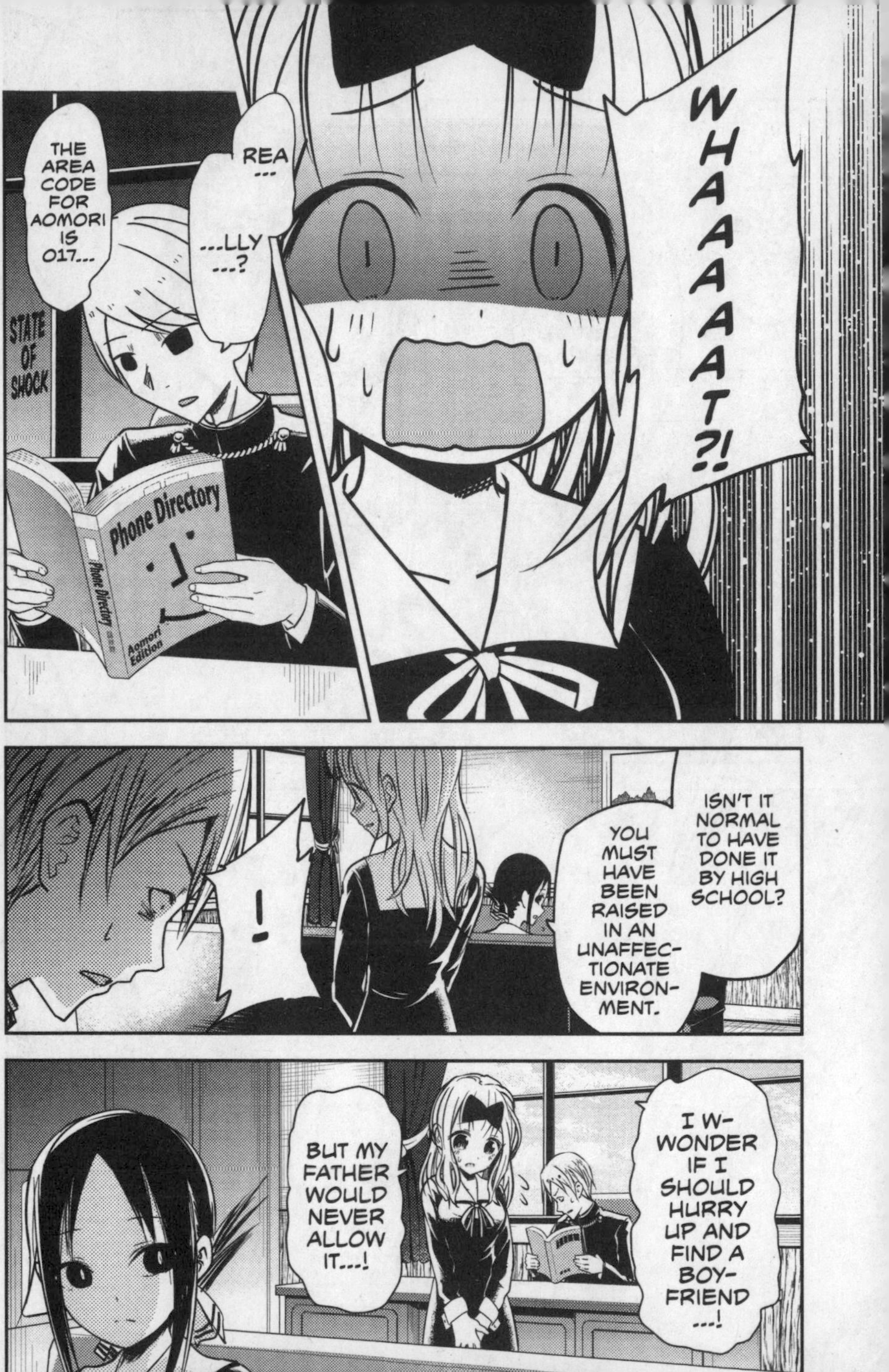
WHAAAAAT?!
REA... ...LLY...?
THE AREA CODE FOR AOMORI IS 017...
STATE OF SHOCK
Phone Directory
Aomori Edition
ISN'T IT NORMAL TO HAVE DONE IT BY HIGH SCHOOL?
YOU MUST HAVE BEEN RAISED IN AN UNAFFECTIONATE ENVIRONMENT.
!
I W-WONDER IF I SHOULD HURRY UP AND FIND A BOYFRIEND...!
BUT MY FATHER WOULD NEVER ALLOW IT...!

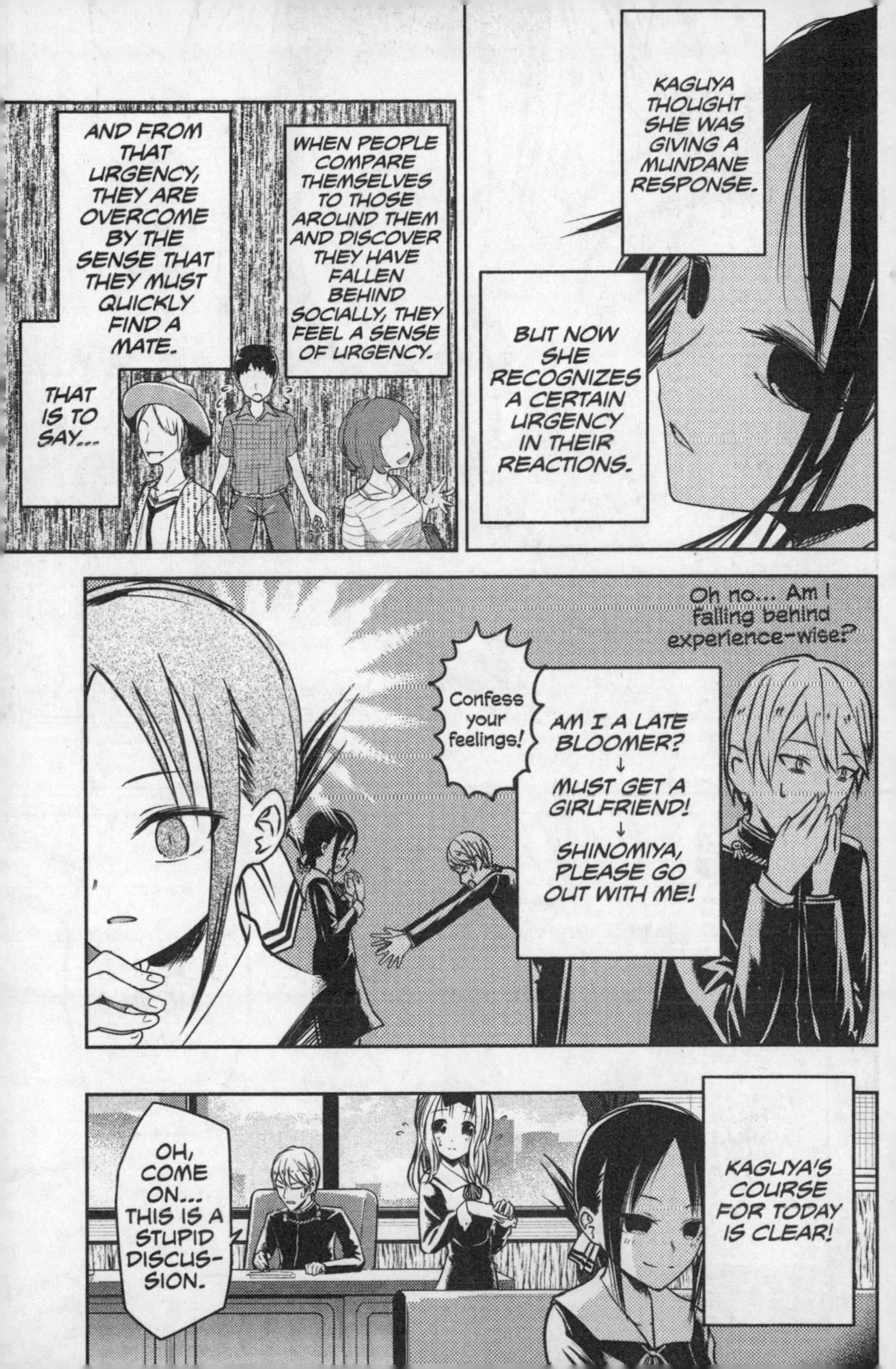
KAGUYA THOUGHT SHE WAS GIVING A MUNDANE RESPONSE.
BUT NOW SHE RECOGNIZES A CERTAIN URGENCY IN THEIR REACTIONS.
WHEN PEOPLE COMPARE THEMSELVES TO THOSE AROUND THEM AND DISCOVER THEY HAVE FALLEN BEHIND SOCIALLY, THEY FEEL A SENSE OF URGENCY.
AND FROM THAT URGENCY, THEY ARE OVERCOME BY THE SENSE THAT THEY MUST QUICKLY FIND A MATE.
THAT IS TO SAY...
Oh no... Am I falling behind experience-wise?
AM I A LATE BLOOMER? ↓ MUST GET A GIRLFRIEND! ↓ SHINOMIYA, PLEASE GO OUT WITH ME!
Confess your feelings!
KAGUYA'S COURSE FOR TODAY IS CLEAR!
OH, COME ON... THIS IS A STUPID DISCUSSION.

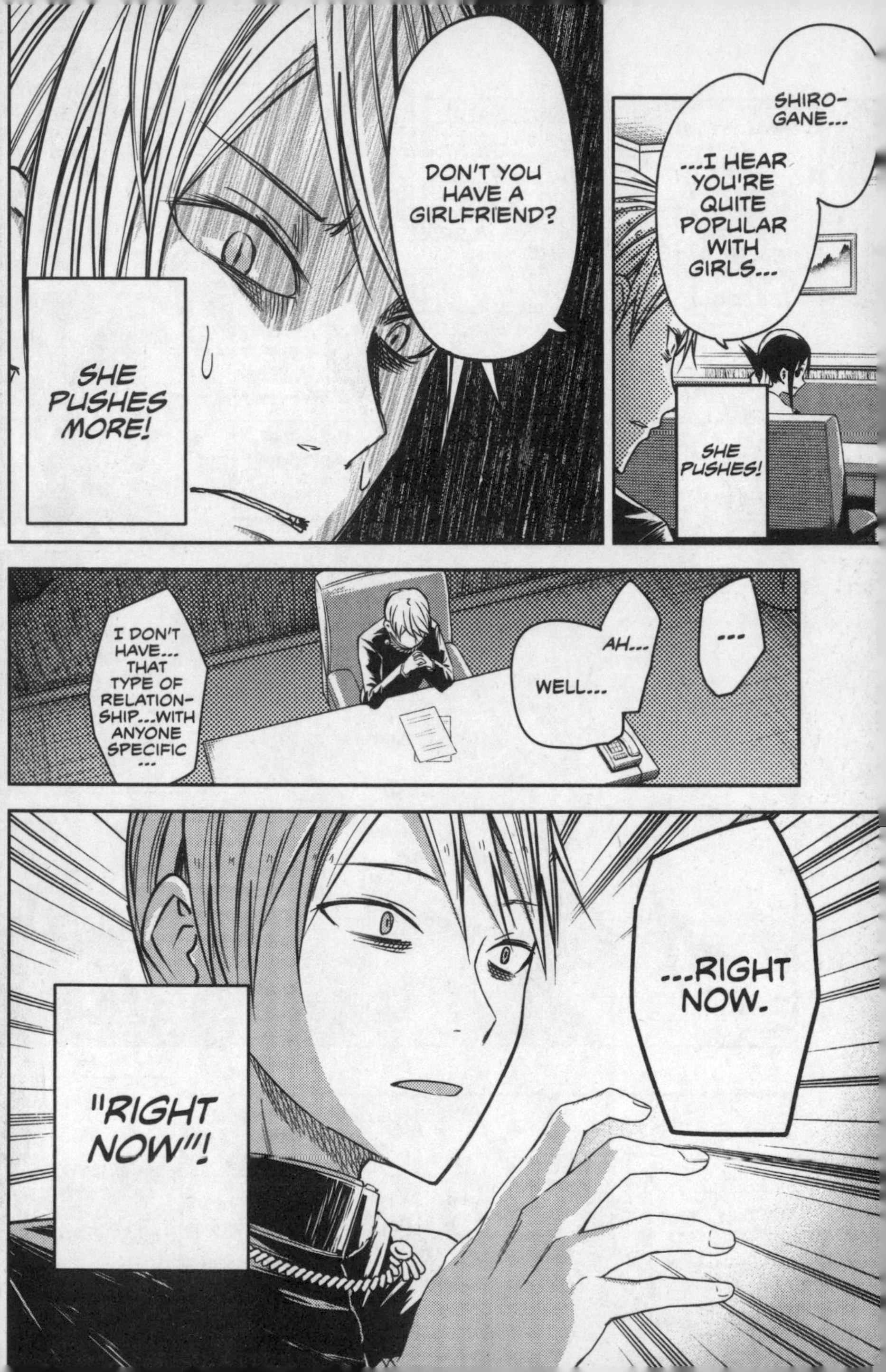
SHIRO-GANE...
...I HEAR YOU'RE QUITE POPULAR WITH GIRLS...
SHE PUSHES!
DON'T YOU HAVE A GIRLFRIEND?
SHE PUSHES MORE!
...
AH... WELL...
I DON'T HAVE... THAT TYPE OF RELATION-SHIP...WITH ANYONE SPECIFIC...
...RIGHT NOW.
"RIGHT NOW"!

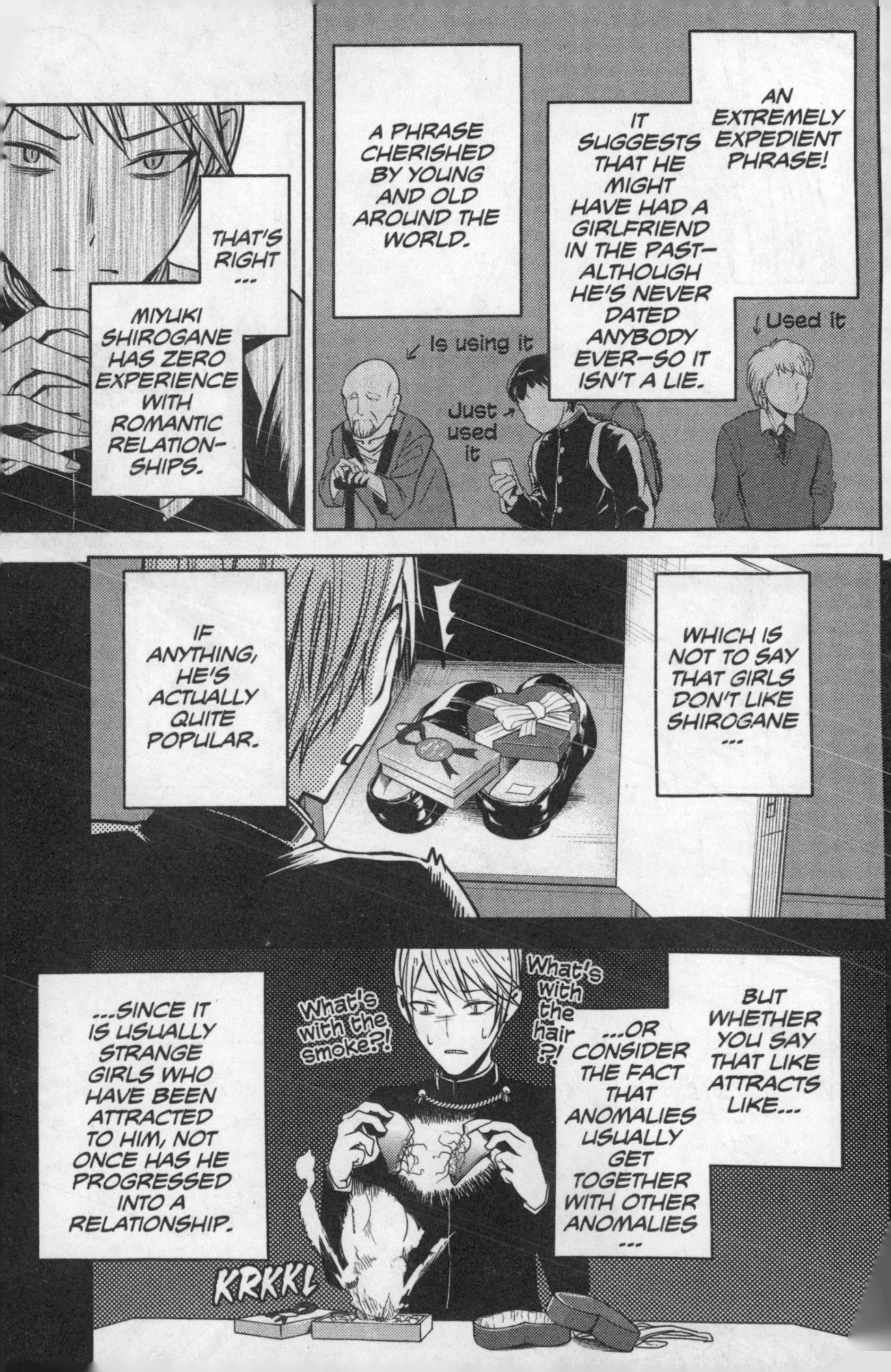

AN EXTREMELY EXPEDIENT PHRASE!
IT SUGGESTS THAT HE MIGHT HAVE HAD A GIRLFRIEND IN THE PAST—ALTHOUGH HE'S NEVER DATED ANYBODY EVER—SO IT ISN'T A LIE.
A PHRASE CHERISHED BY YOUNG AND OLD AROUND THE WORLD.
Used it
Just used it
Is using it
THAT'S RIGHT...
MIYUKI SHIROGANE HAS ZERO EXPERIENCE WITH ROMANTIC RELATIONSHIPS.
WHICH IS NOT TO SAY THAT GIRLS DON'T LIKE SHIROGANE...
IF ANYTHING, HE'S ACTUALLY QUITE POPULAR.
BUT WHETHER YOU SAY THAT LIKE ATTRACTS LIKE...
...OR CONSIDER THE FACT THAT ANOMALIES USUALLY GET TOGETHER WITH OTHER ANOMALIES...
What's with the hair?!
What's with the smoke?!
...SINCE IT IS USUALLY STRANGE GIRLS WHO HAVE BEEN ATTRACTED TO HIM, NOT ONCE HAS HE PROGRESSED INTO A RELATIONSHIP.
KRKKL

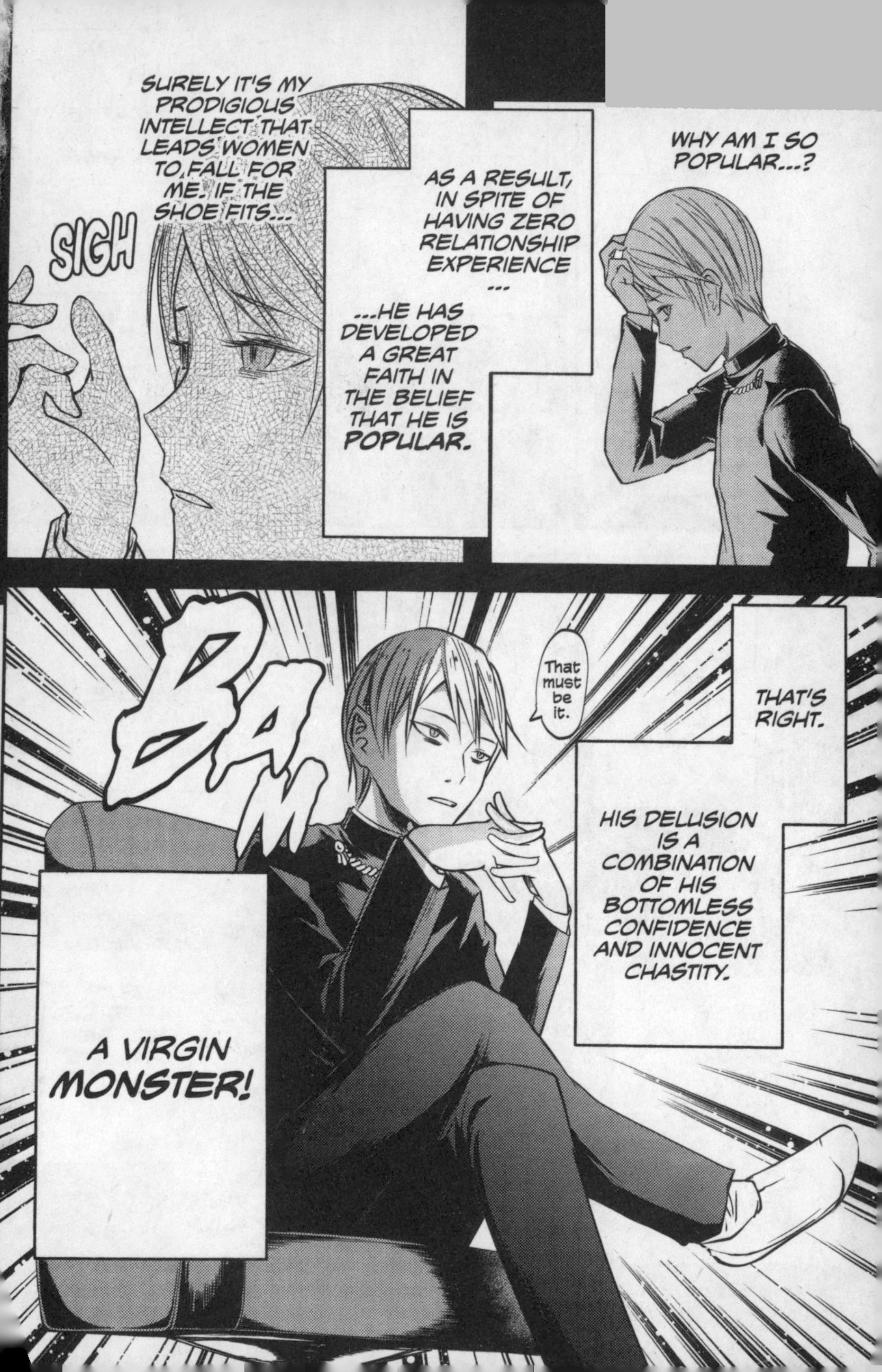
WHY AM I SO POPULAR...?
AS A RESULT, IN SPITE OF HAVING ZERO RELATIONSHIP EXPERIENCE...
...HE HAS DEVELOPED A GREAT FAITH IN THE BELIEF THAT HE IS POPULAR.
SURELY IT'S MY PRODIGIOUS INTELLECT THAT LEADS WOMEN TO FALL FOR ME. IF THE SHOE FITS...
SIGH
THAT'S RIGHT.
That must be it.
BAM
HIS DELUSION IS A COMBINATION OF HIS BOTTOMLESS CONFIDENCE AND INNOCENT CHASTITY.
A VIRGIN MONSTER!

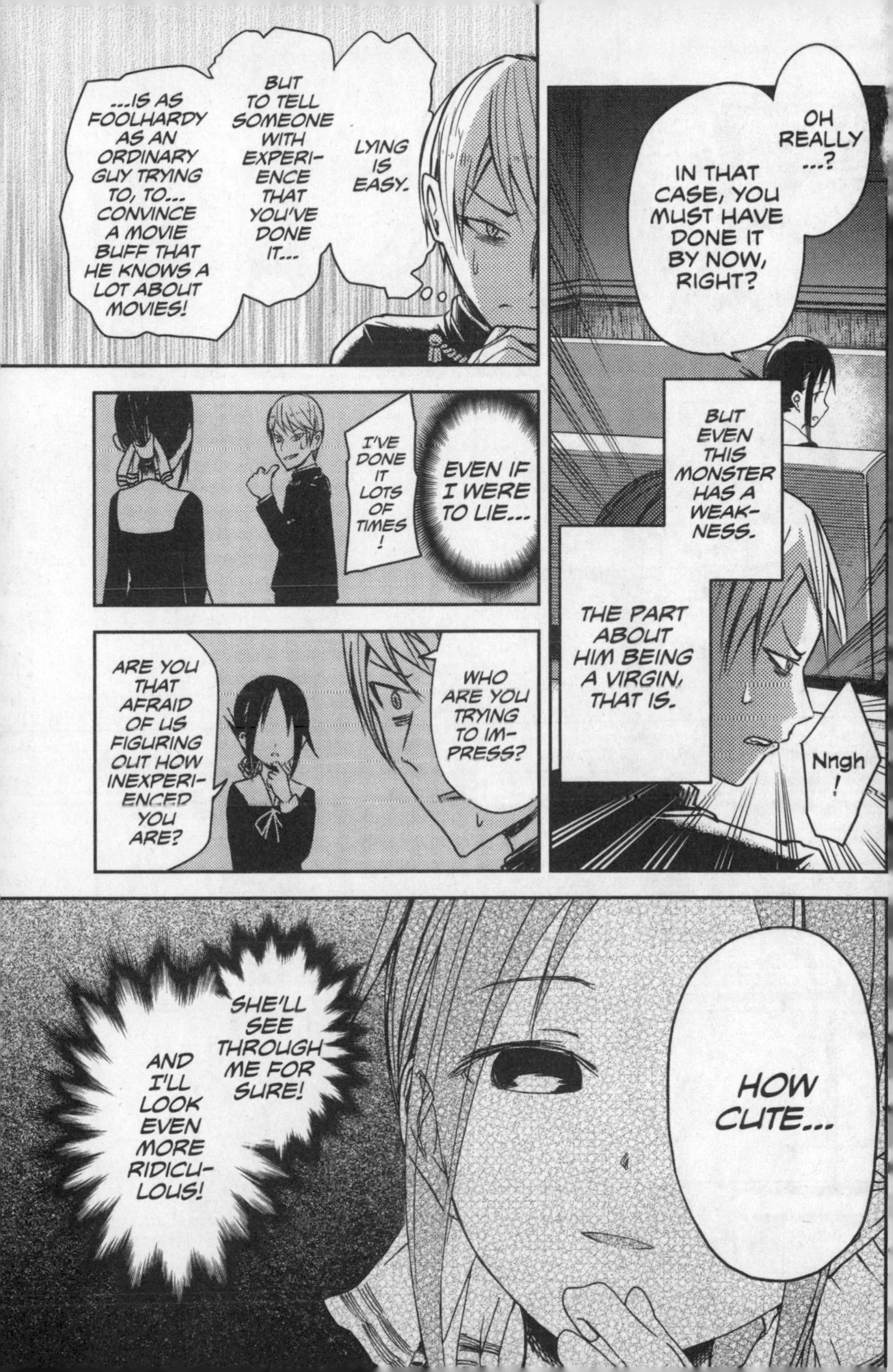
OH REALLY ...?
IN THAT CASE, YOU MUST HAVE DONE IT BY NOW, RIGHT?
BUT EVEN THIS MONSTER HAS A WEAK-NESS.
THE PART ABOUT HIM BEING A VIRGIN, THAT IS.
Nngh!
LYING IS EASY.
BUT TO TELL SOMEONE WITH EXPERI-ENCE THAT YOU'VE DONE IT...
...IS AS FOOLHARDY AS AN ORDINARY GUY TRYING TO, TO... CONVINCE A MOVIE BUFF THAT HE KNOWS A LOT ABOUT MOVIES!
EVEN IF I WERE TO LIE...
I'VE DONE IT LOTS OF TIMES!
WHO ARE YOU TRYING TO IM-PRESS?
ARE YOU THAT AFRAID OF US FIGURING OUT HOW INEXPERI-ENCED YOU ARE?
HOW CUTE...
SHE'LL SEE THROUGH ME FOR SURE!
AND I'LL LOOK EVEN MORE RIDICU-LOUS!

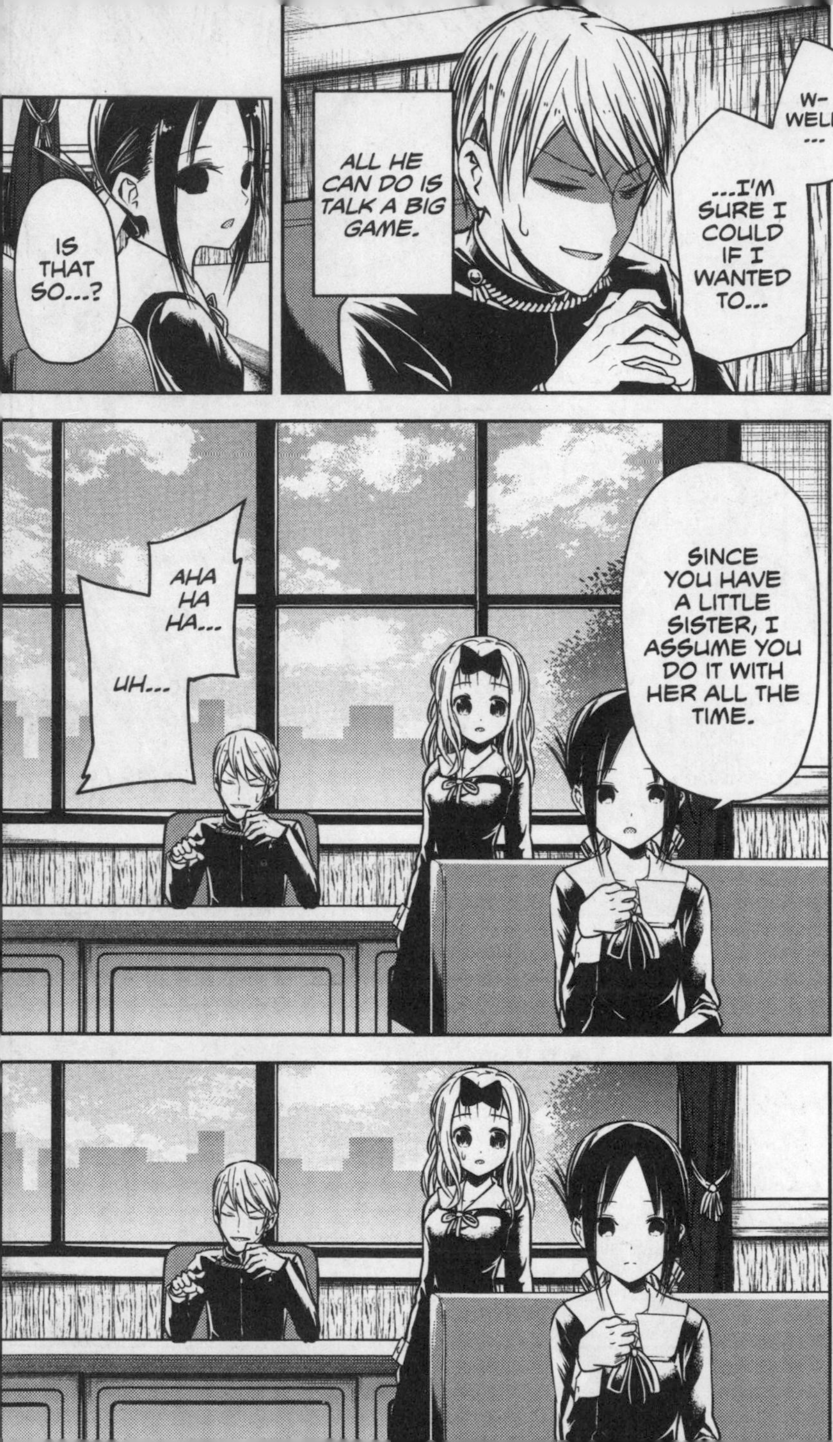
W-WELL...
...I'M SURE I COULD IF I WANTED TO...
ALL HE CAN DO IS TALK A BIG GAME.
IS THAT SO...?
SINCE YOU HAVE A LITTLE SISTER, I ASSUME YOU DO IT WITH HER ALL THE TIME.
AHA HA HA...
UH...

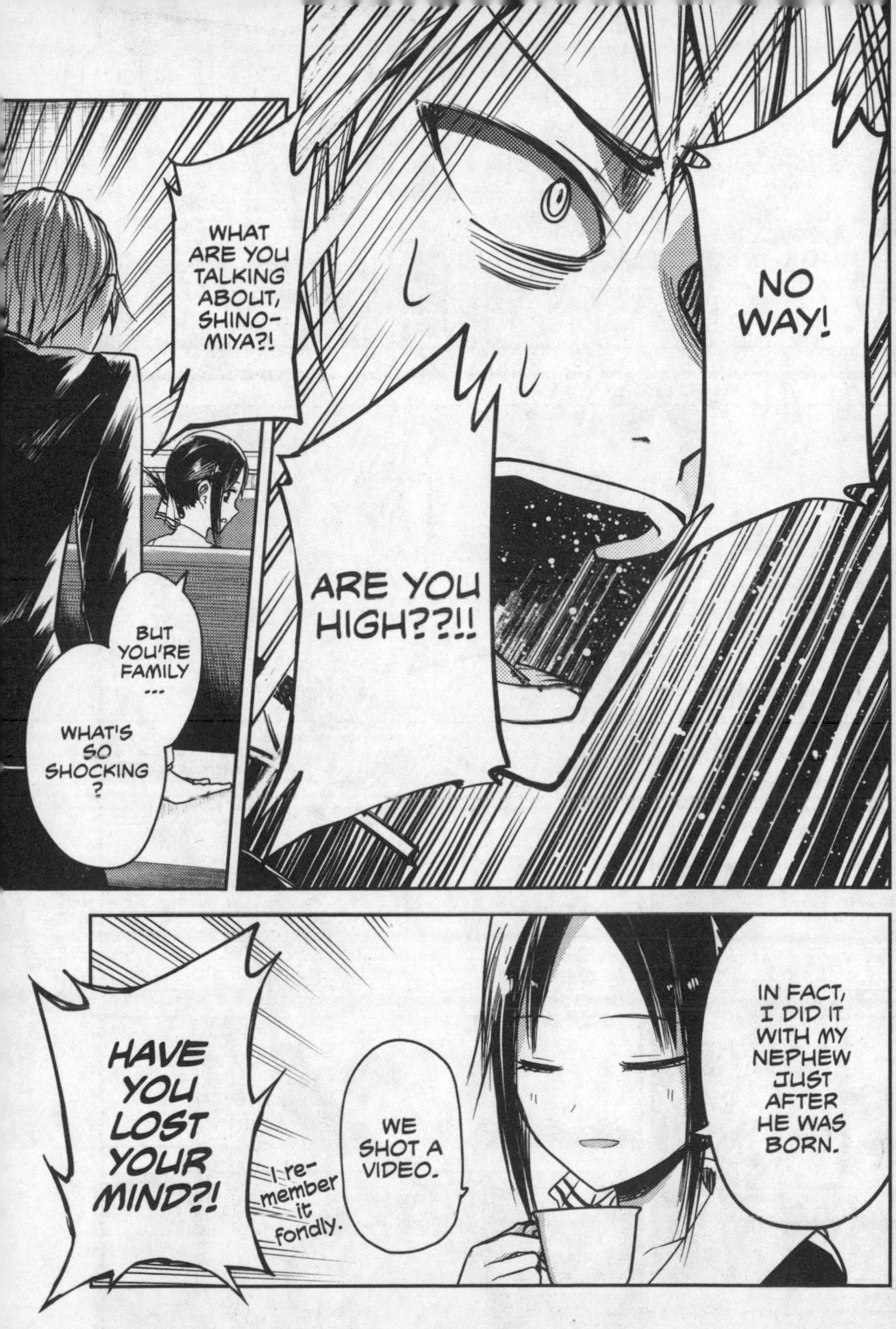
NO WAY!
WHAT ARE YOU TALKING ABOUT, SHINO-MIYA?!
ARE YOU HIGH??!!
BUT YOU'RE FAMILY...
WHAT'S SO SHOCKING?
IN FACT, I DID IT WITH MY NEPHEW JUST AFTER HE WAS BORN.
WE SHOT A VIDEO.
I re-member it fondly.
HAVE YOU LOST YOUR MIND?!

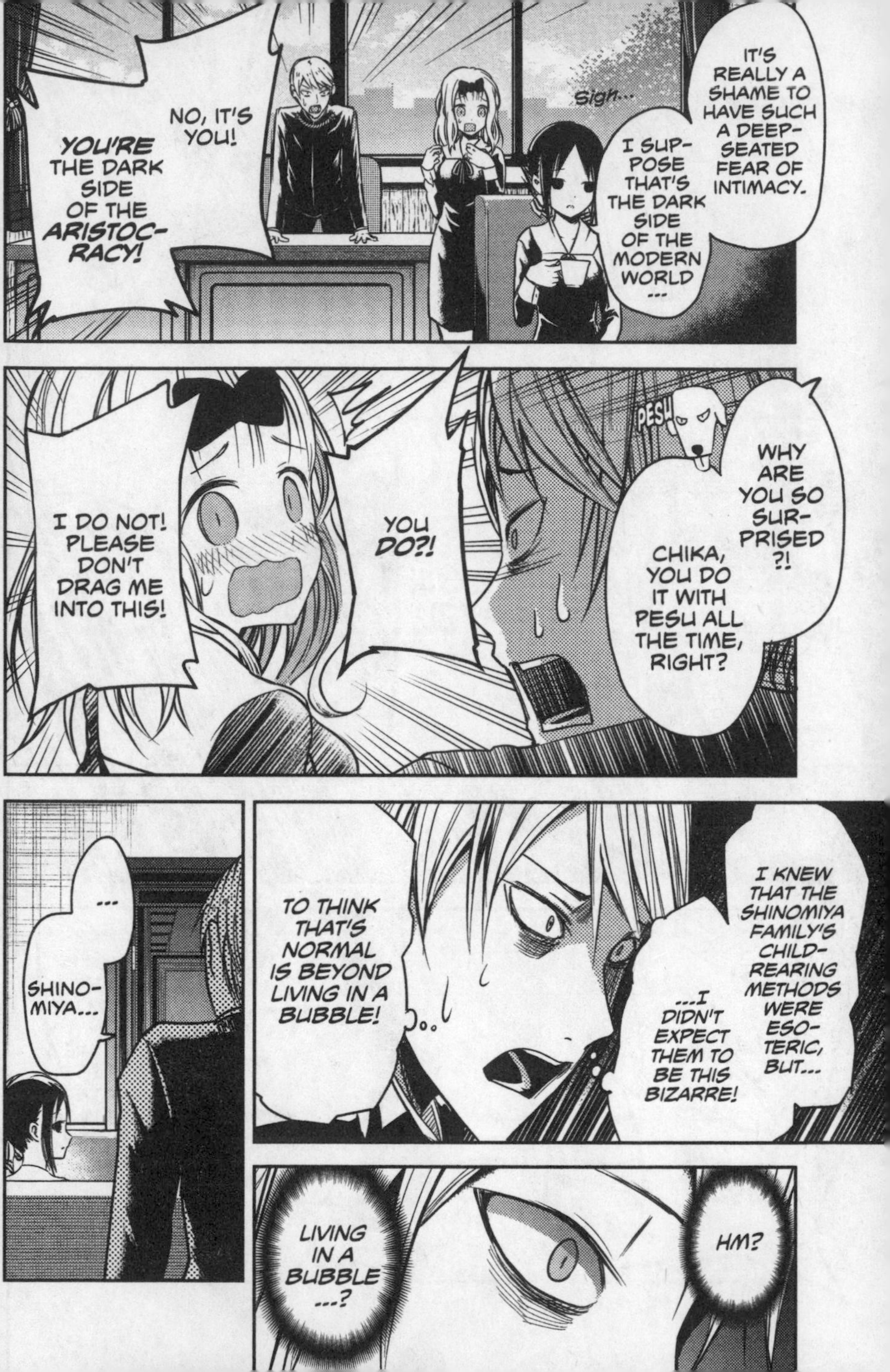
Sigh...
IT'S REALLY A SHAME TO HAVE SUCH A DEEP-SEATED FEAR OF INTIMACY.
I SUPPOSE THAT'S THE DARK SIDE OF THE MODERN WORLD...
NO, IT'S YOU!
YOU'RE THE DARK SIDE OF THE ARISTOCRACY!
PESU
WHY ARE YOU SO SURPRISED?!
CHIKA, YOU DO IT WITH PESU ALL THE TIME, RIGHT?
YOU DO?!
I DO NOT! PLEASE DON'T DRAG ME INTO THIS!
I KNEW THAT THE SHINOMIYA FAMILY'S CHILD-REARING METHODS WERE ESOTERIC, BUT...
...I DIDN'T EXPECT THEM TO BE THIS BIZARRE!
TO THINK THAT'S NORMAL IS BEYOND LIVING IN A BUBBLE!
HM?
LIVING IN A BUBBLE...?
...
SHINOMIYA...

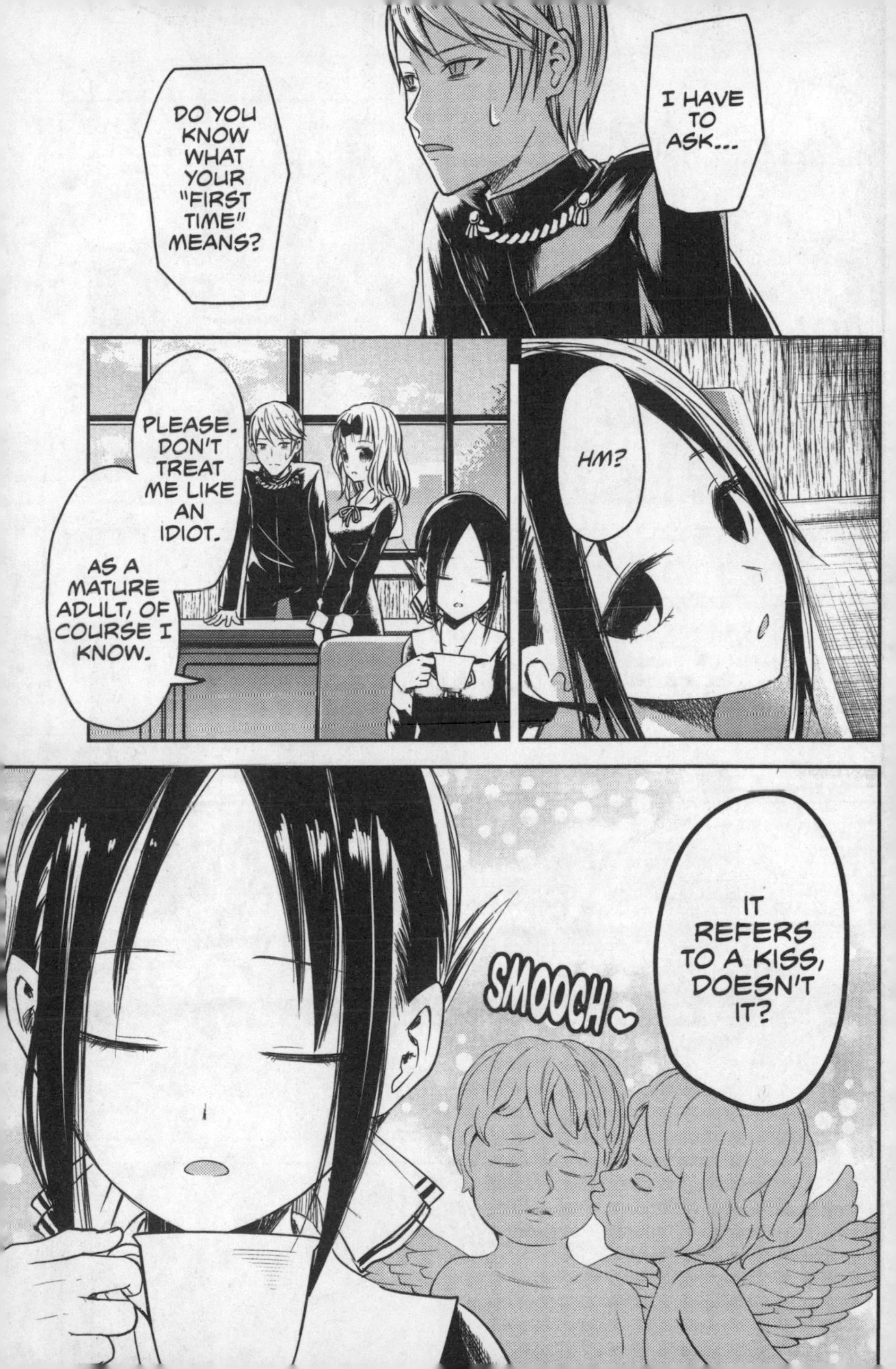
I HAVE TO ASK...
DO YOU KNOW WHAT YOUR "FIRST TIME" MEANS?
HM?
PLEASE. DON'T TREAT ME LIKE AN IDIOT.
AS A MATURE ADULT, OF COURSE I KNOW.
IT REFERS TO A KISS, DOESN'T IT?
SMOOCH

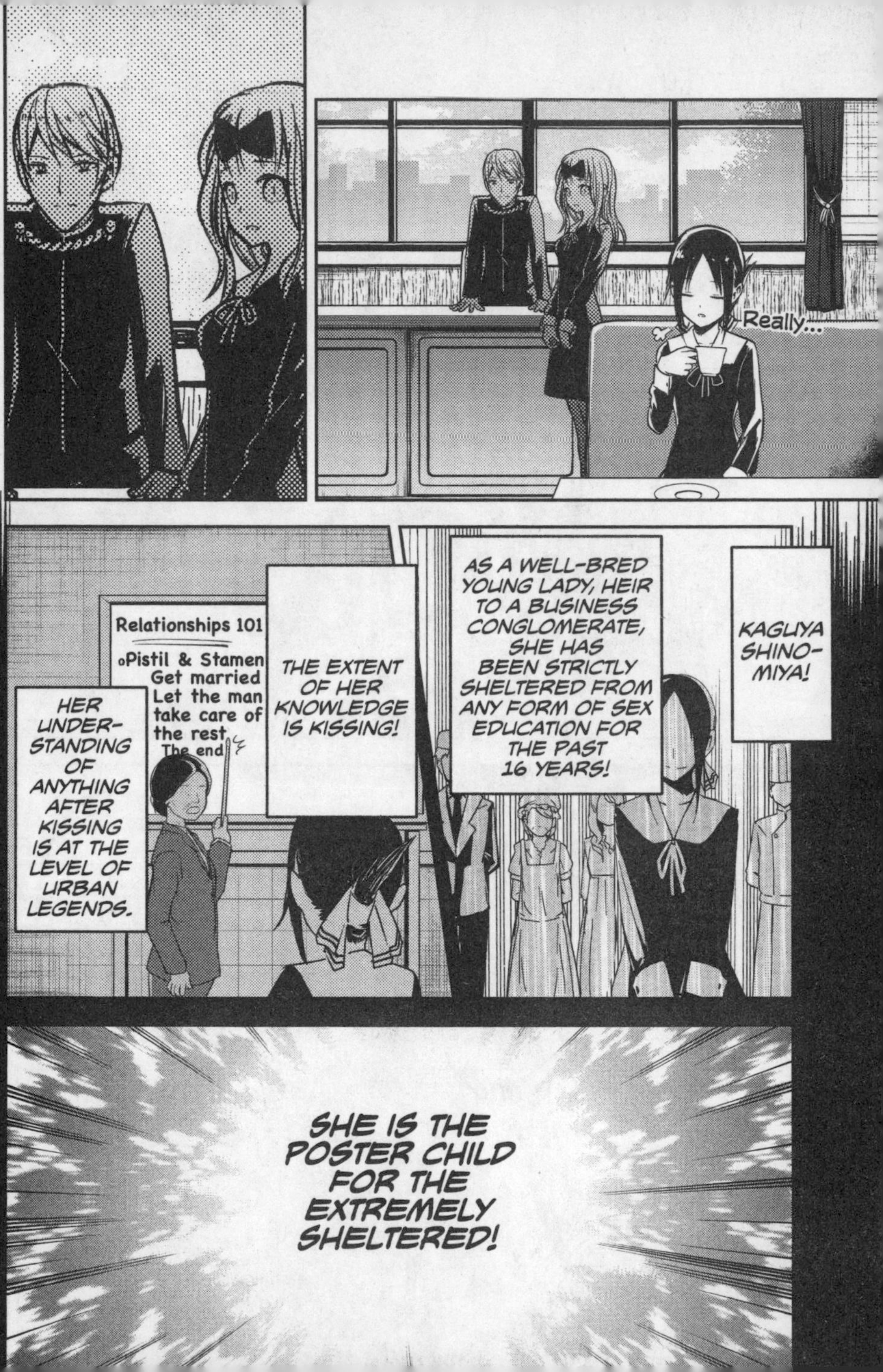
Really...
KAGUYA SHINOMIYA!
AS A WELL-BRED YOUNG LADY, HEIR TO A BUSINESS CONGLOMERATE, SHE HAS BEEN STRICTLY SHELTERED FROM ANY FORM OF SEX EDUCATION FOR THE PAST 16 YEARS!
THE EXTENT OF HER KNOWLEDGE IS KISSING!
Relationships 101
oPistil & Stamen
Get married
Let the man take care of the rest
The end
HER UNDERSTANDING OF ANYTHING AFTER KISSING IS AT THE LEVEL OF URBAN LEGENDS.
SHE IS THE POSTER CHILD FOR THE EXTREMELY SHELTERED!

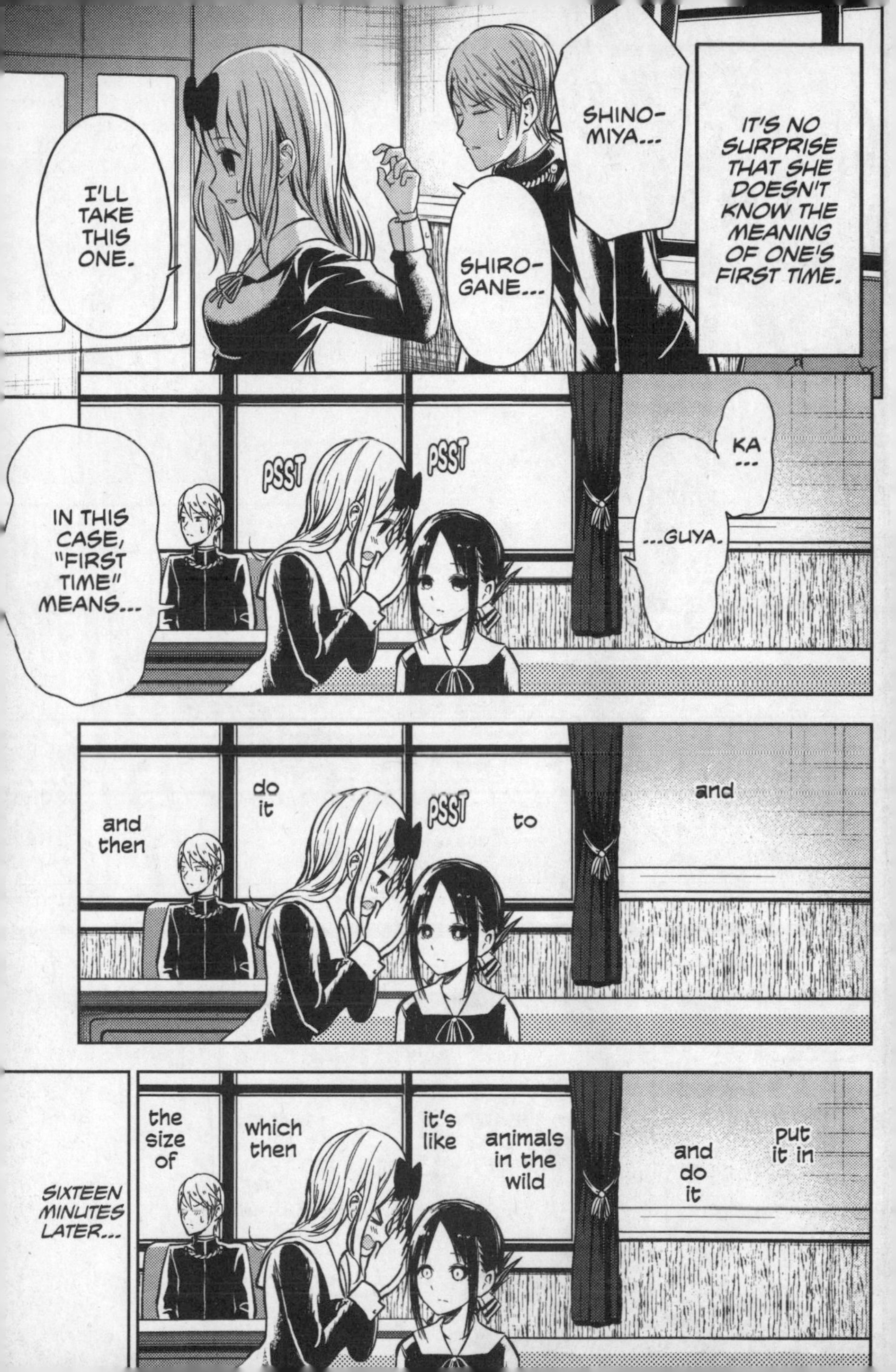
IT'S NO SURPRISE THAT SHE DOESN'T KNOW THE MEANING OF ONE'S FIRST TIME.
SHINO-MIYA...
SHIRO-GANE...
I'LL TAKE THIS ONE.
KA ...
...GUYA.
PSST
PSST
IN THIS CASE, "FIRST TIME" MEANS...
and
to
PSST
do it
and then
put it in
and do it
animals in the wild
it's like
which then
the size of
SIXTEEN MINUTES LATER...

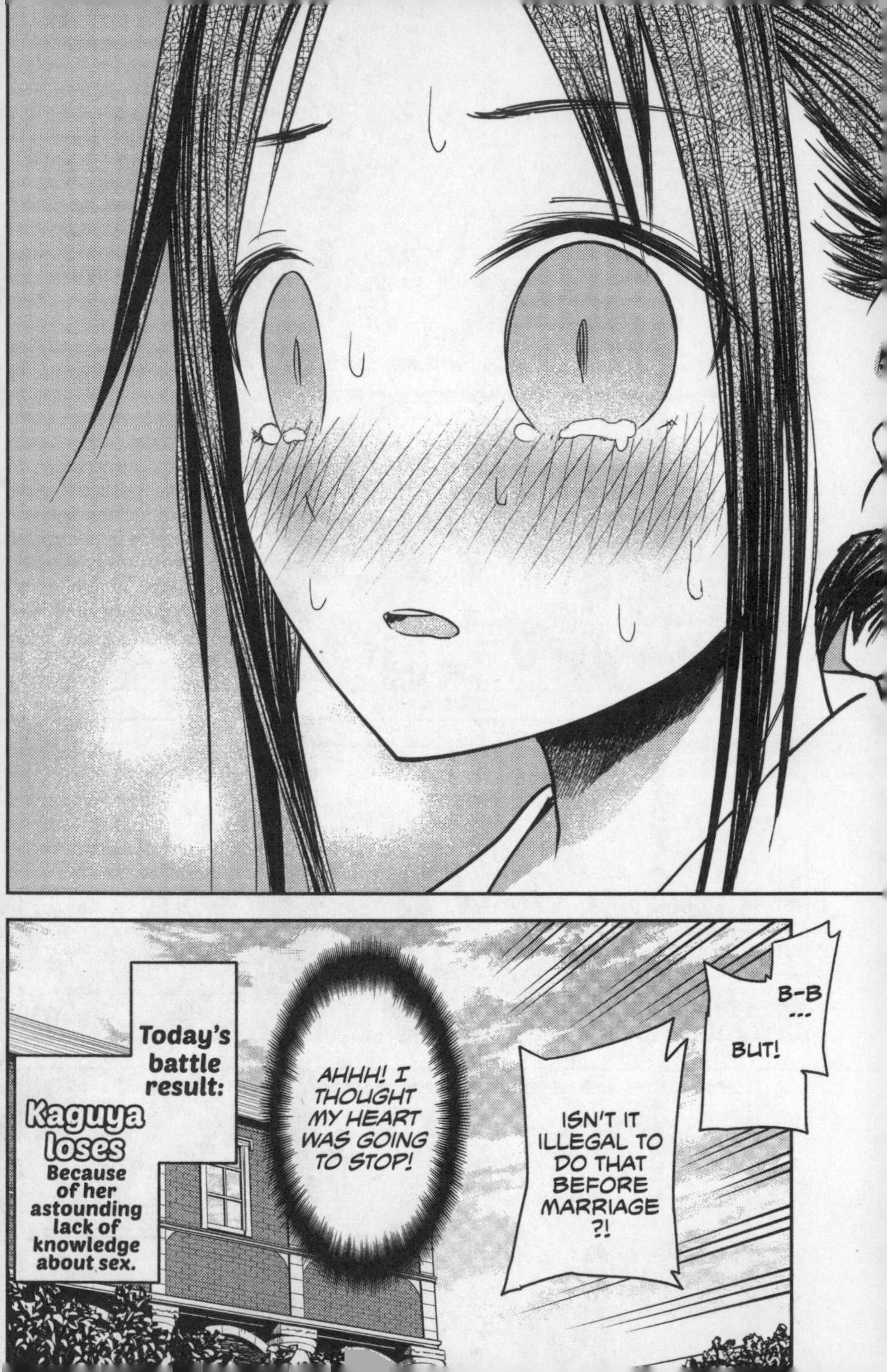
B-B... BUT!
ISN'T IT ILLEGAL TO DO THAT BEFORE MARRIAGE?!
AHHH! I THOUGHT MY HEART WAS GOING TO STOP!
Today's battle result:
Kaguya loses
Because of her astounding lack of knowledge about sex.

KAGUYA-SAMA
LOVE IS WAR

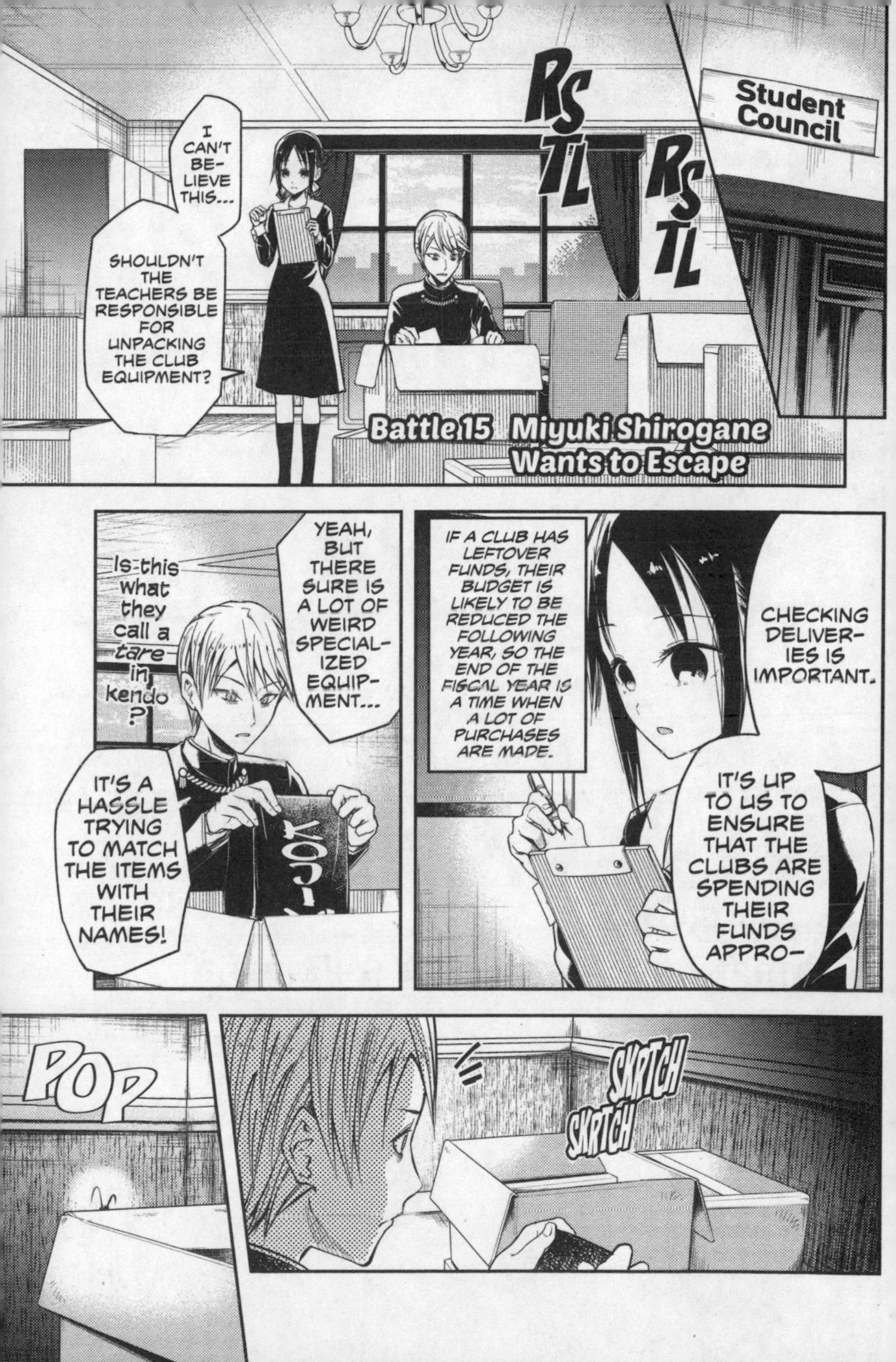
Student Council
RSTL
RSTL
I CAN'T BELIEVE THIS...
SHOULDN'T THE TEACHERS BE RESPONSIBLE FOR UNPACKING THE CLUB EQUIPMENT?
Battle 15 Miyuki Shirogane Wants to Escape
CHECKING DELIVERIES IS IMPORTANT.
IF A CLUB HAS LEFTOVER FUNDS, THEIR BUDGET IS LIKELY TO BE REDUCED THE FOLLOWING YEAR, SO THE END OF THE FISCAL YEAR IS A TIME WHEN A LOT OF PURCHASES ARE MADE.
IT'S UP TO US TO ENSURE THAT THE CLUBS ARE SPENDING THEIR FUNDS APPRO–
YEAH, BUT THERE SURE IS A LOT OF WEIRD SPECIALIZED EQUIPMENT...
Is this what they call a *tare* in kendo?
IT'S A HASSLE TRYING TO MATCH THE ITEMS WITH THEIR NAMES!
SKRTCH
SKRTCH
POP

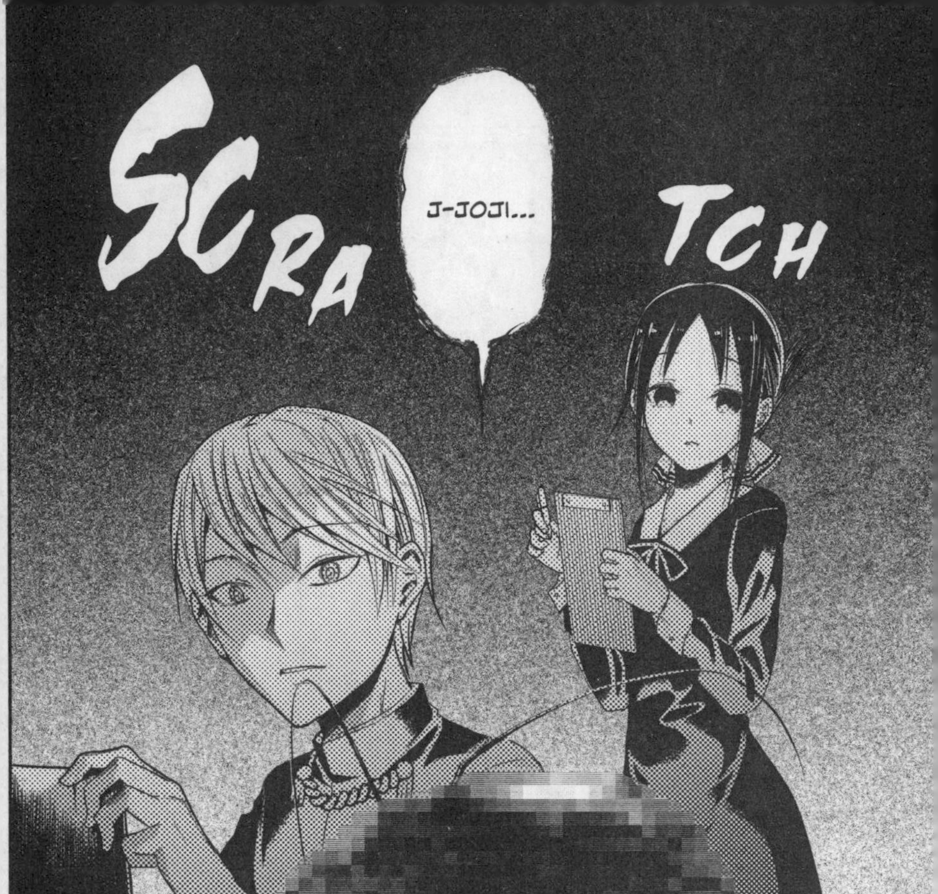
J-JOJI...
SCRA TCH

Battle 15
Miyuki Shirogane Wants to Escape

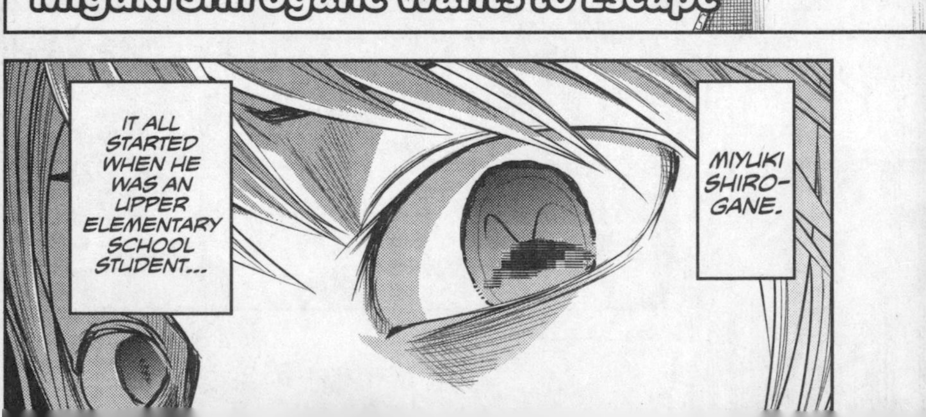
MIYUKI SHIRO-GANE.
IT ALL STARTED WHEN HE WAS AN UPPER ELEMENTARY SCHOOL STUDENT...

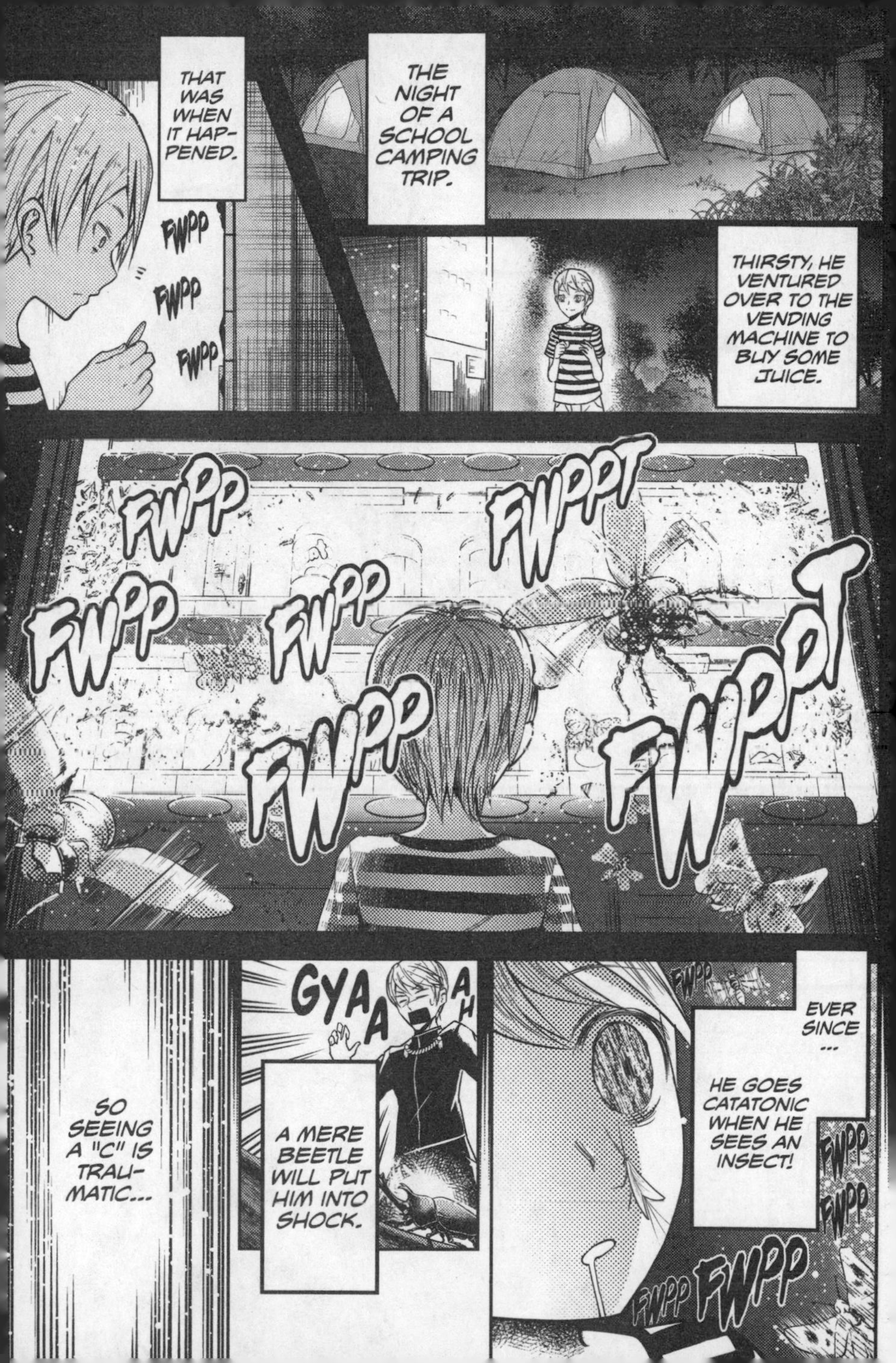
THE NIGHT OF A SCHOOL CAMPING TRIP.
THIRSTY, HE VENTURED OVER TO THE VENDING MACHINE TO BUY SOME JUICE.
THAT WAS WHEN IT HAPPENED.
FWPP
FWPP
FWPP
FWPPT
FWPP
FWPP
FWPP
FWPPT
FWPP
FWPP
FWPP
FWPP
EVER SINCE...
HE GOES CATATONIC WHEN HE SEES AN INSECT!
FWPP
FWPP
FWPP
FWPP
GYAAAH
A MERE BEETLE WILL PUT HIM INTO SHOCK.
SO SEEING A "C" IS TRAUMATIC...

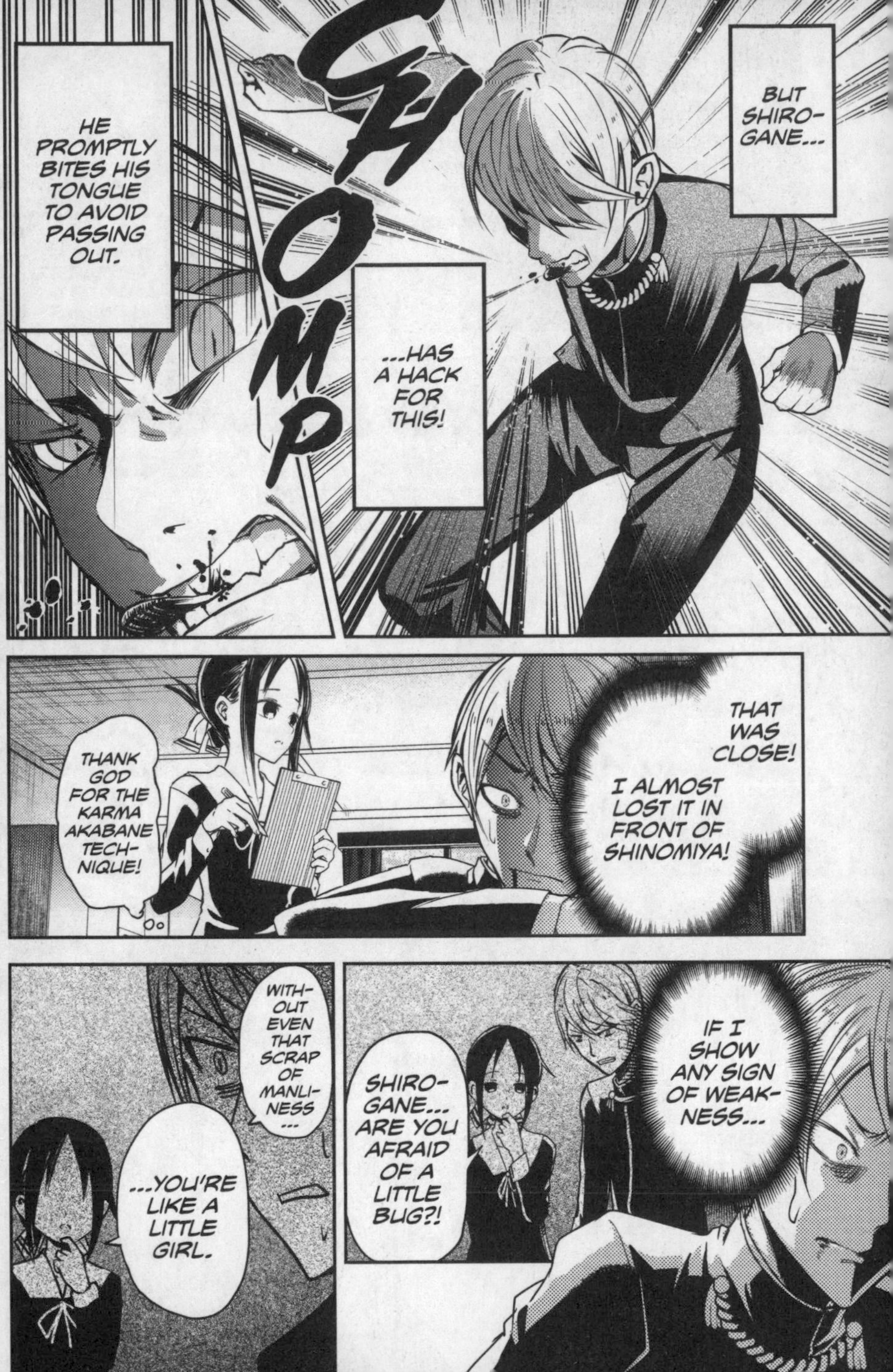
BUT SHIRO-GANE...
...HAS A HACK FOR THIS!
CHOMP
HE PROMPTLY BITES HIS TONGUE TO AVOID PASSING OUT.
THAT WAS CLOSE!
I ALMOST LOST IT IN FRONT OF SHINOMIYA!
THANK GOD FOR THE KARMA AKABANE TECH-NIQUE!
IF I SHOW ANY SIGN OF WEAK-NESS...
SHIRO-GANE... ARE YOU AFRAID OF A LITTLE BUG?!
WITH-OUT EVEN THAT SCRAP OF MANLI-NESS...
...YOU'RE LIKE A LITTLE GIRL.

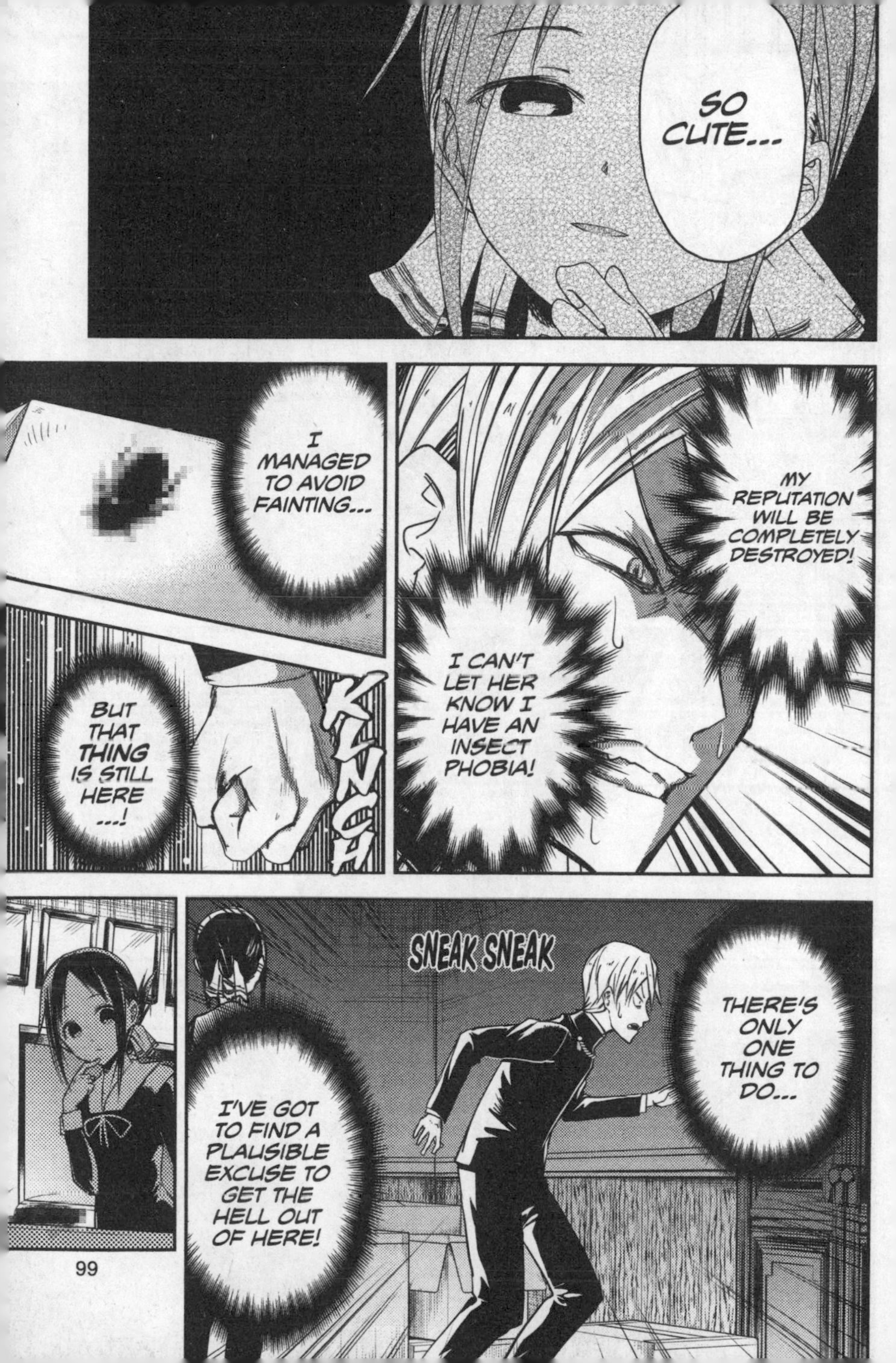
SO CUTE...
MY REPUTATION WILL BE COMPLETELY DESTROYED!
I CAN'T LET HER KNOW I HAVE AN INSECT PHOBIA!
I MANAGED TO AVOID FAINTING...
BUT THAT THING IS STILL HERE...!
KLUNCH
SNEAK SNEAK
THERE'S ONLY ONE THING TO DO...
I'VE GOT TO FIND A PLAUSIBLE EXCUSE TO GET THE HELL OUT OF HERE!

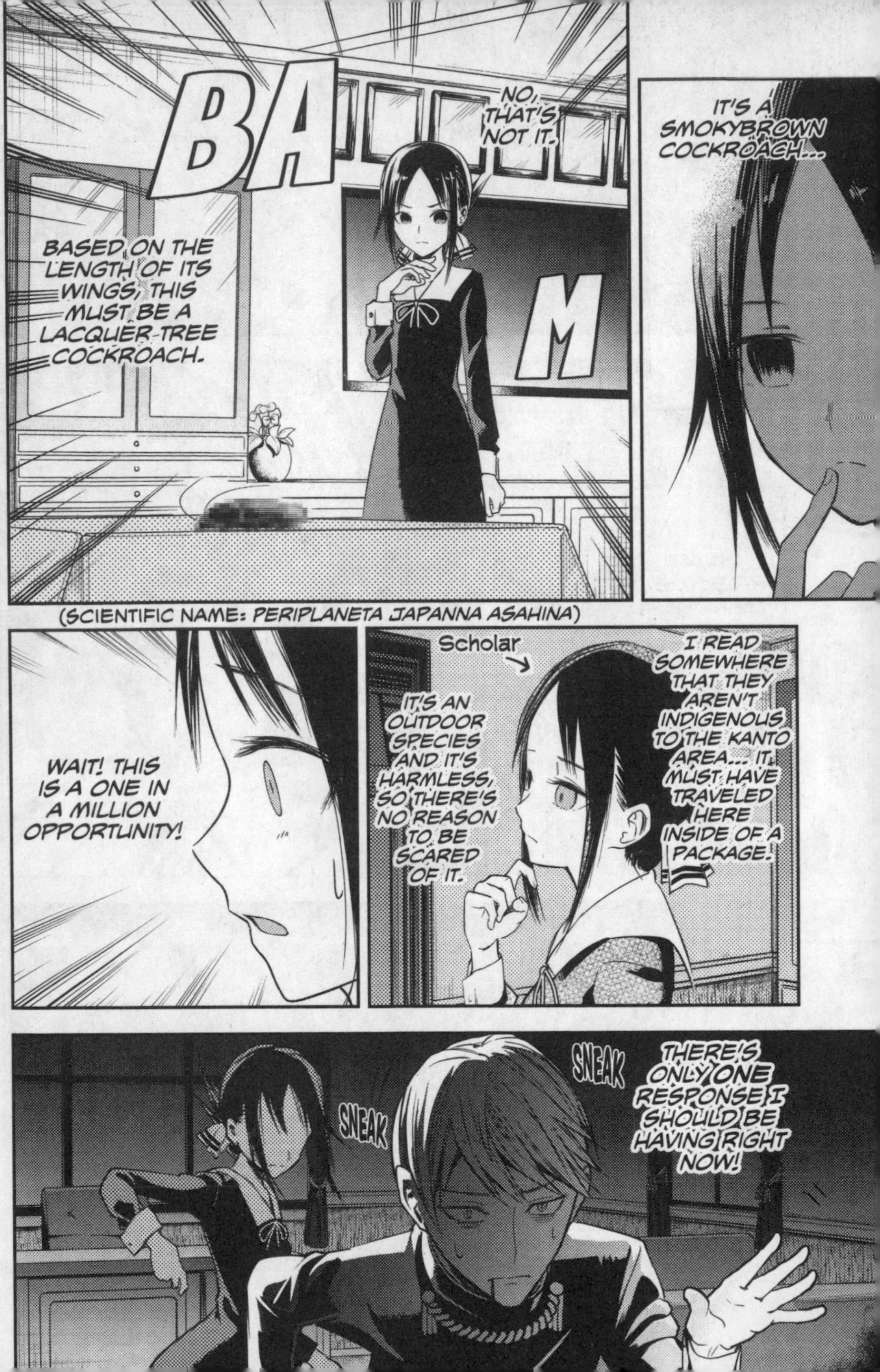
IT'S A SMOKYBROWN COCKROACH...
BA
NO, THAT'S NOT IT.
M
BASED ON THE LENGTH OF ITS WINGS, THIS MUST BE A LACQUER-TREE COCKROACH.
(SCIENTIFIC NAME: PERIPLANETA JAPANNA ASAHINA)
Scholar
I READ SOMEWHERE THAT THEY AREN'T INDIGENOUS TO THE KANTO AREA... IT MUST HAVE TRAVELED HERE INSIDE OF A PACKAGE.
IT'S AN OUTDOOR SPECIES AND IT'S HARMLESS, SO THERE'S NO REASON TO BE SCARED OF IT.
WAIT! THIS IS A ONE IN A MILLION OPPORTUNITY!
SNEAK
THERE'S ONLY ONE RESPONSE I SHOULD BE HAVING RIGHT NOW!
SNEAK

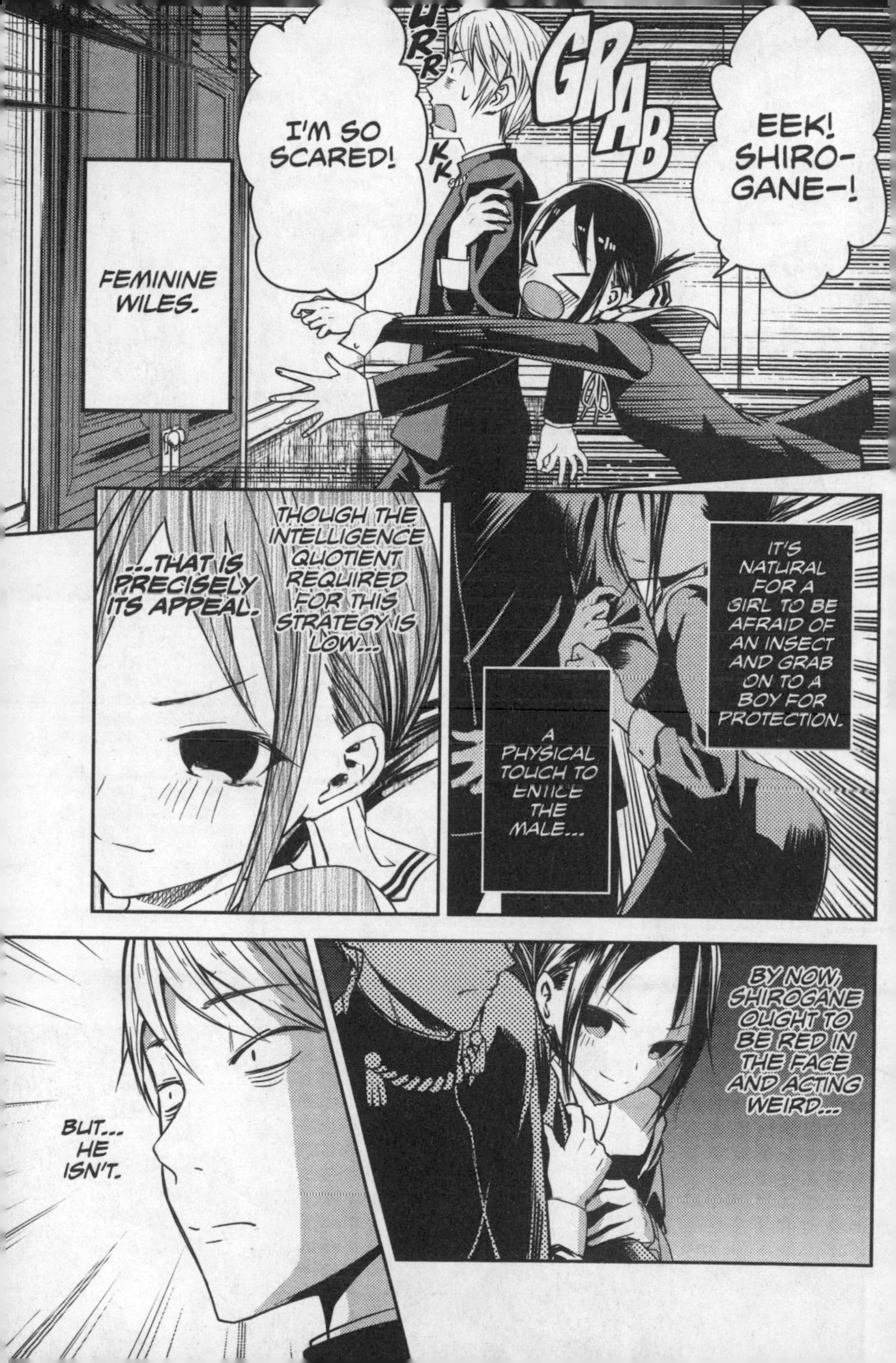
EEK! SHIRO-GANE—!
GRAB
I'M SO SCARED!
URRKK
FEMININE WILES.
IT'S NATURAL FOR A GIRL TO BE AFRAID OF AN INSECT AND GRAB ON TO A BOY FOR PROTECTION.
A PHYSICAL TOUCH TO ENTICE THE MALE...
THOUGH THE INTELLIGENCE QUOTIENT REQUIRED FOR THIS STRATEGY IS LOW...
...THAT IS PRECISELY ITS APPEAL.
BY NOW, SHIROGANE OUGHT TO BE RED IN THE FACE AND ACTING WEIRD...
BUT... HE ISN'T.

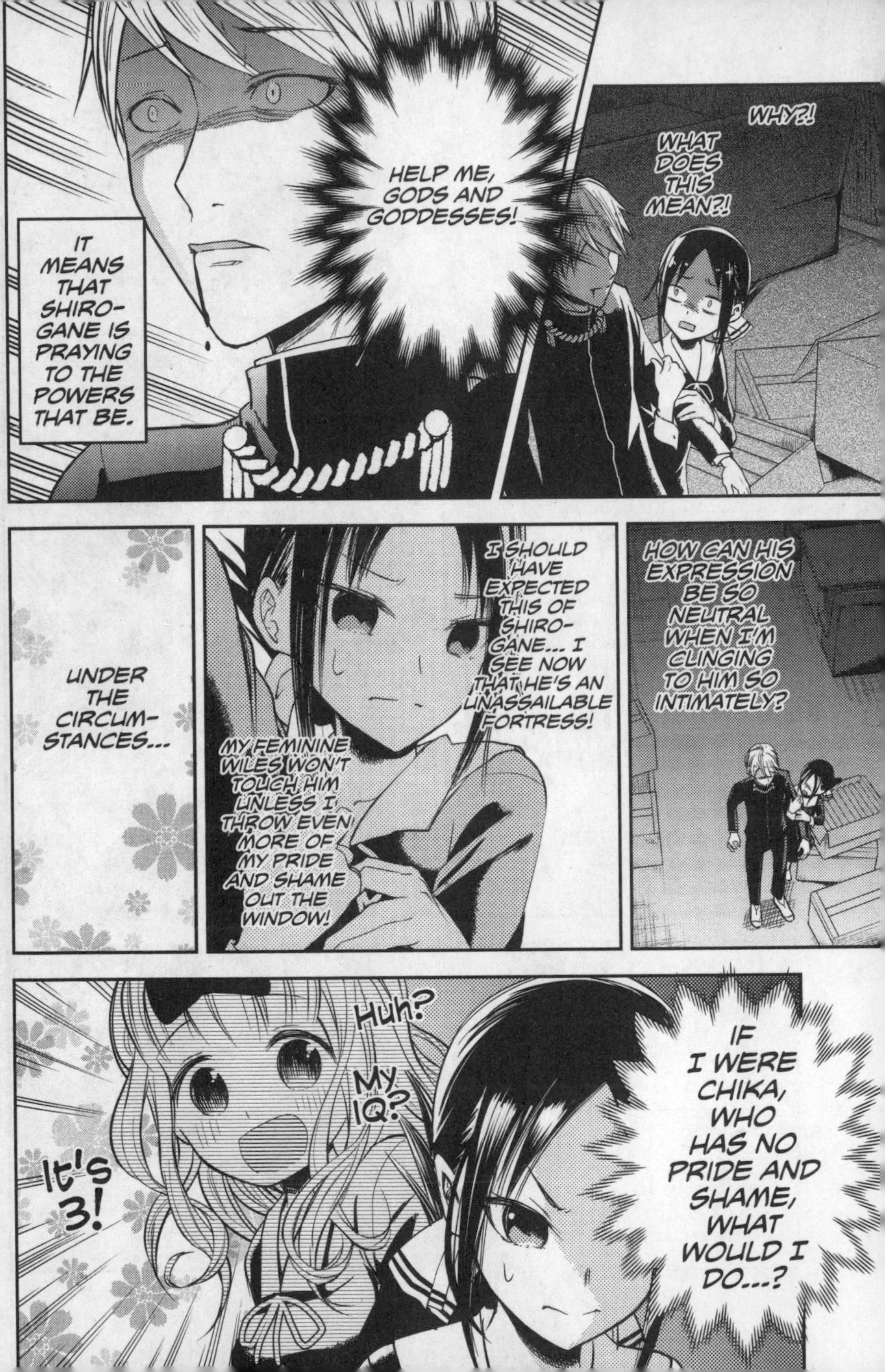
WHY?!
WHAT DOES THIS MEAN?!
HELP ME, GODS AND GODDESSES!
IT MEANS THAT SHIRO-GANE IS PRAYING TO THE POWERS THAT BE.
HOW CAN HIS EXPRESSION BE SO NEUTRAL WHEN I'M CLINGING TO HIM SO INTIMATELY?
I SHOULD HAVE EXPECTED THIS OF SHIRO-GANE... I SEE NOW THAT HE'S AN UNASSAILABLE FORTRESS!
MY FEMININE WILES WON'T TOUCH HIM UNLESS I THROW EVEN MORE OF MY PRIDE AND SHAME OUT THE WINDOW!
UNDER THE CIRCUM-STANCES...
IF I WERE CHIKA, WHO HAS NO PRIDE AND SHAME, WHAT WOULD I DO...?
Huh?
My IQ?
It's 3!

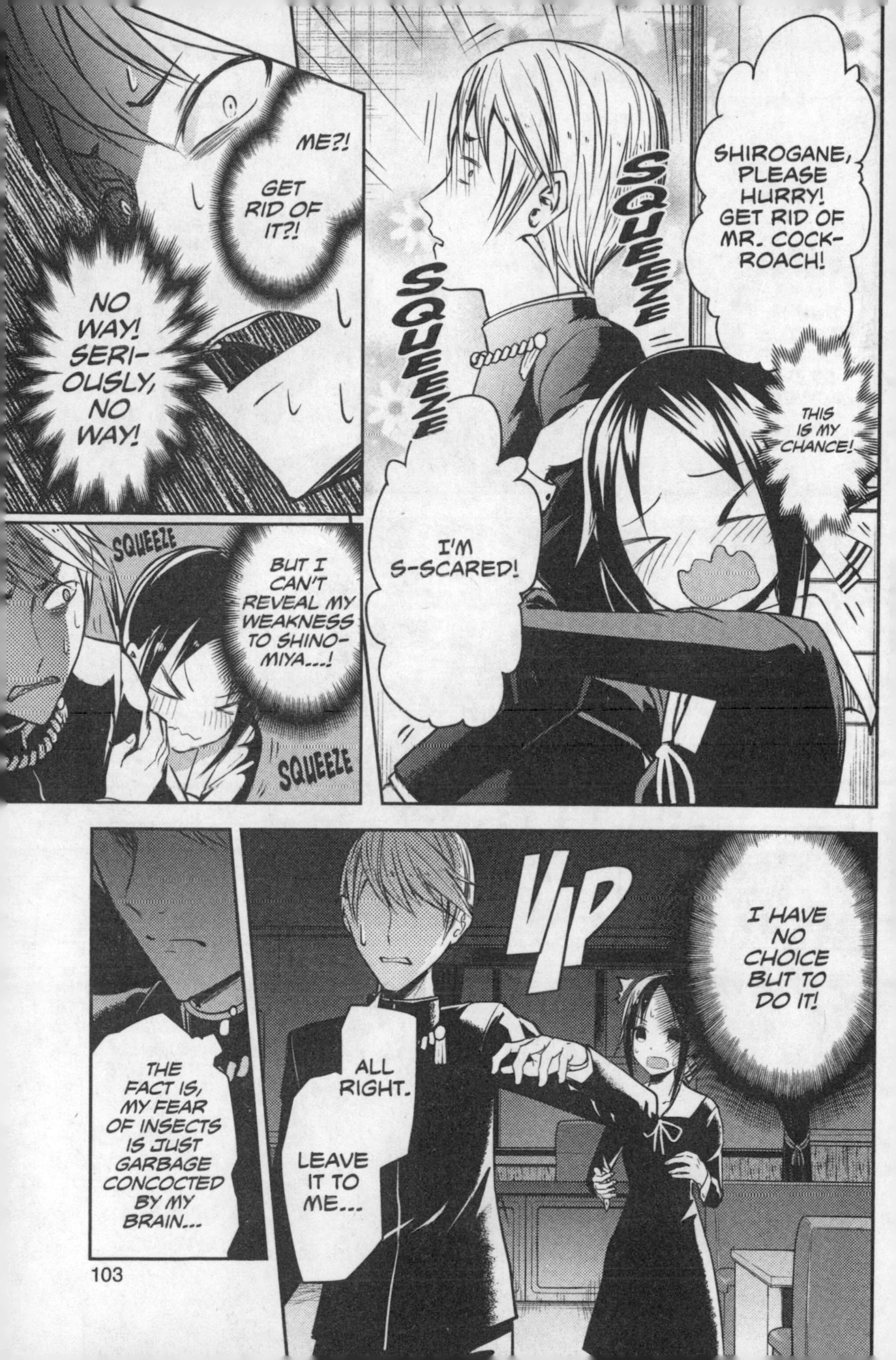
SHIROGANE, PLEASE HURRY! GET RID OF MR. COCK-ROACH!
SQUEEZE
SQUEEZE
THIS IS MY CHANCE!
I'M S-SCARED!
ME?!
GET RID OF IT?!
NO WAY! SERI-OUSLY, NO WAY!
SQUEEZE
BUT I CAN'T REVEAL MY WEAKNESS TO SHINO-MIYA...!
SQUEEZE
I HAVE NO CHOICE BUT TO DO IT!
VIP
ALL RIGHT.
LEAVE IT TO ME...
THE FACT IS, MY FEAR OF INSECTS IS JUST GARBAGE CONCOCTED BY MY BRAIN...

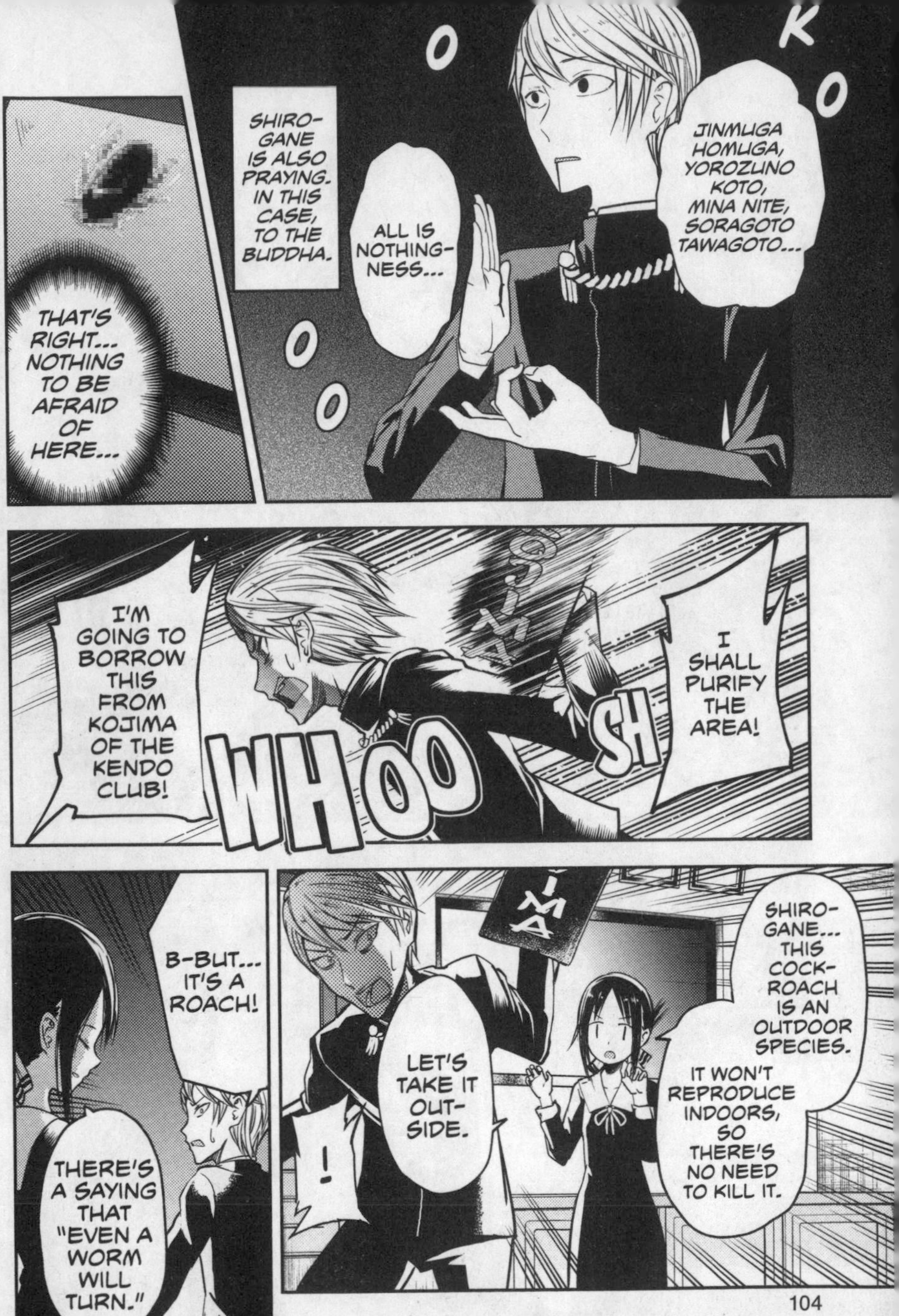
JINMUGA HOMUGA, YOROZUNO KOTO, MINA NITE, SORAGOTO TAWAGOTO...
ALL IS NOTHINGNESS...
SHIROGANE IS ALSO PRAYING. IN THIS CASE, TO THE BUDDHA.
THAT'S RIGHT... NOTHING TO BE AFRAID OF HERE...
I SHALL PURIFY THE AREA!
WHOOSH
I'M GOING TO BORROW THIS FROM KOJIMA OF THE KENDO CLUB!
SHIROGANE... THIS COCKROACH IS AN OUTDOOR SPECIES.
IT WON'T REPRODUCE INDOORS, SO THERE'S NO NEED TO KILL IT.
LET'S TAKE IT OUTSIDE.
!
B-BUT... IT'S A ROACH!
THERE'S A SAYING THAT "EVEN A WORM WILL TURN."

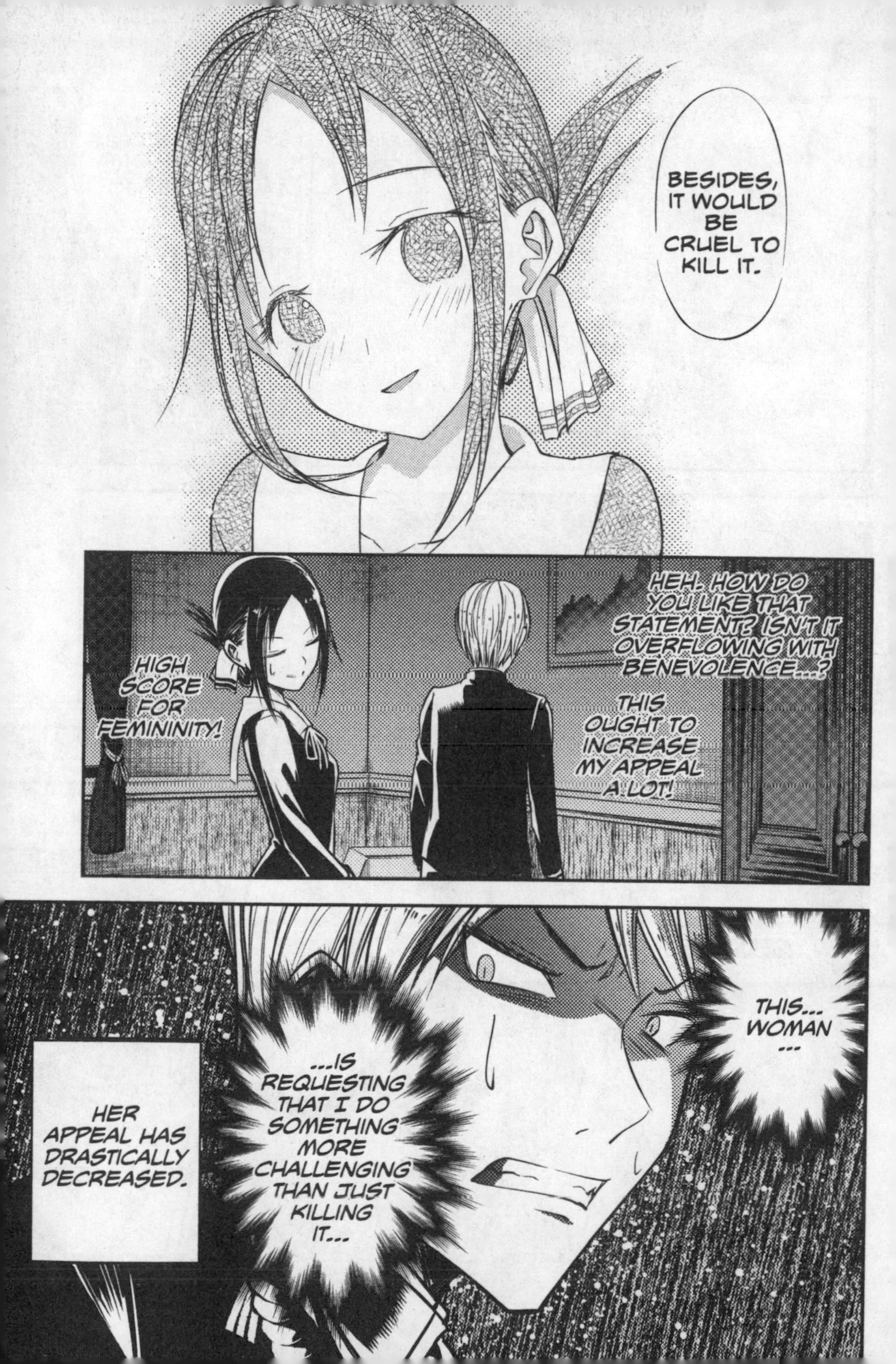
BESIDES, IT WOULD BE CRUEL TO KILL IT.
HEH. HOW DO YOU LIKE THAT STATEMENT? ISN'T IT OVERFLOWING WITH BENEVOLENCE...?
THIS OUGHT TO INCREASE MY APPEAL A LOT!
HIGH SCORE FOR FEMININITY!
THIS... WOMAN...
...IS REQUESTING THAT I DO SOMETHING MORE CHALLENGING THAN JUST KILLING IT...
HER APPEAL HAS DRASTICALLY DECREASED.

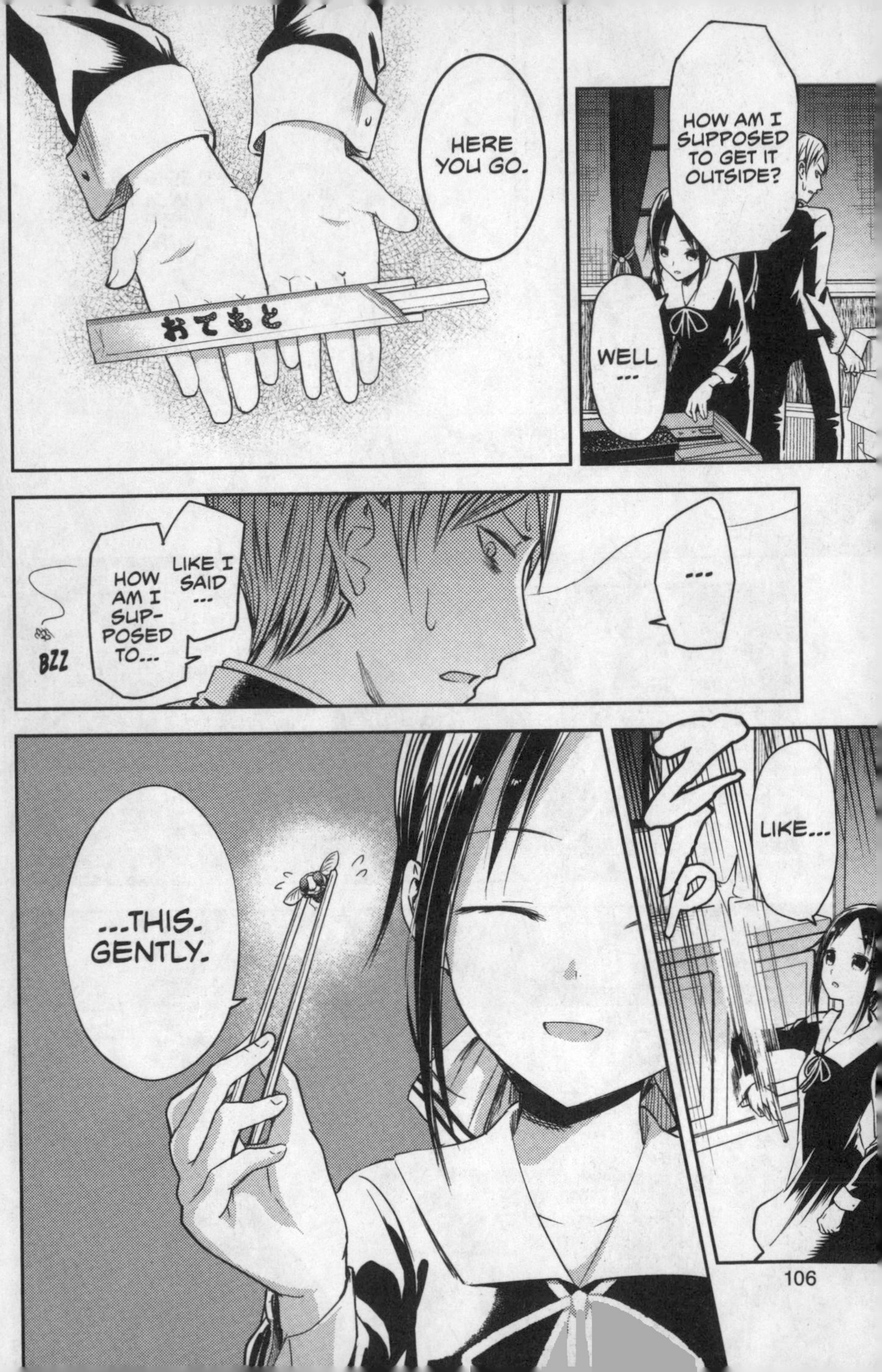
HOW AM I SUPPOSED TO GET IT OUTSIDE?
WELL...
HERE YOU GO.
おてもと
...
LIKE I SAID... HOW AM I SUPPOSED TO...
BZZ
LIKE...
ZIP
...THIS. GENTLY.

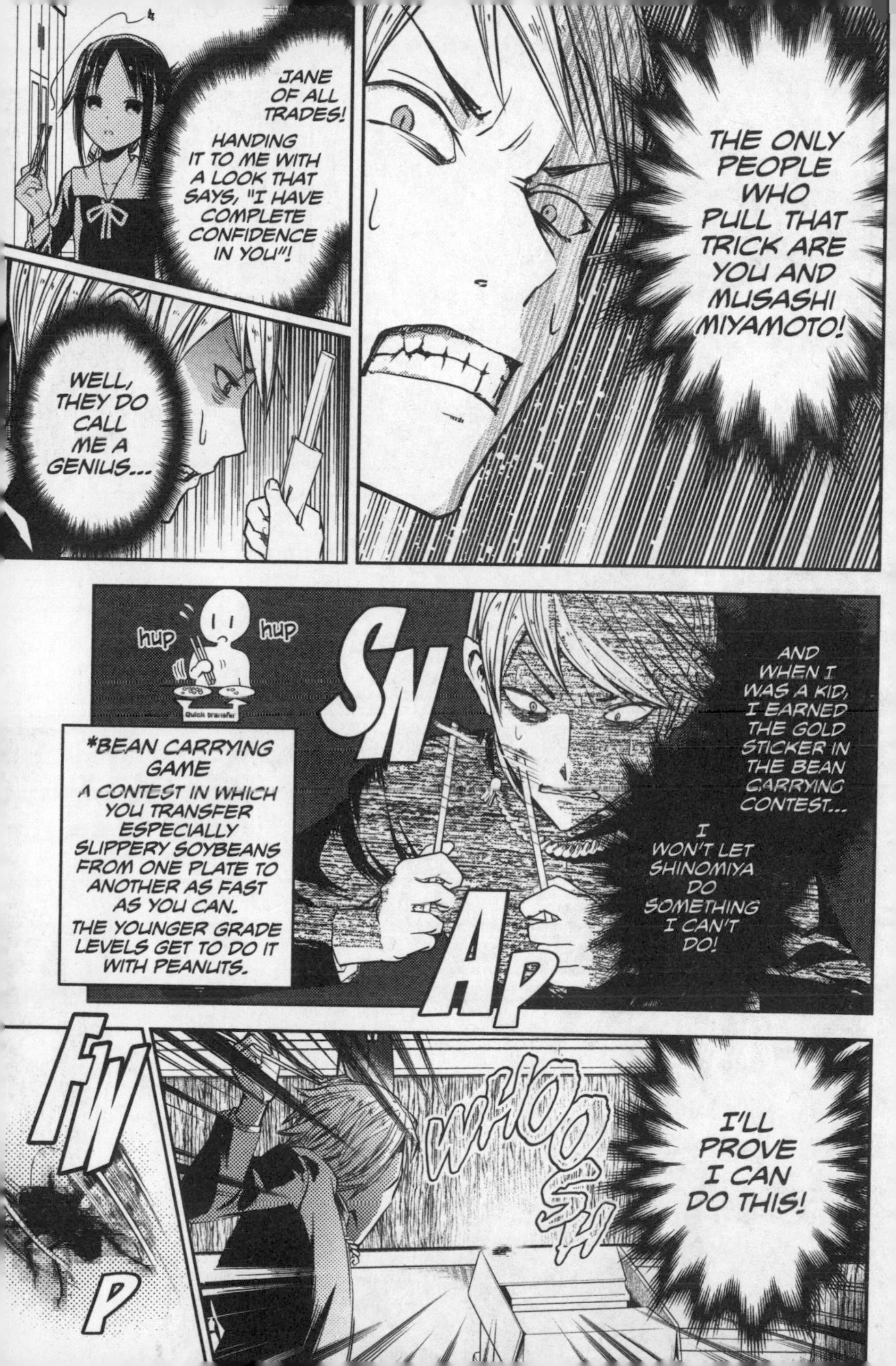
THE ONLY PEOPLE WHO PULL THAT TRICK ARE YOU AND MUSASHI MIYAMOTO!
JANE OF ALL TRADES!
HANDING IT TO ME WITH A LOOK THAT SAYS, "I HAVE COMPLETE CONFIDENCE IN YOU"!
WELL, THEY DO CALL ME A GENIUS...
AND WHEN I WAS A KID, I EARNED THE GOLD STICKER IN THE BEAN CARRYING CONTEST...
I WON'T LET SHINOMIYA DO SOMETHING I CAN'T DO!
SNAP
hup
hup
Quick transfer
*BEAN CARRYING GAME
A CONTEST IN WHICH YOU TRANSFER ESPECIALLY SLIPPERY SOYBEANS FROM ONE PLATE TO ANOTHER AS FAST AS YOU CAN.
THE YOUNGER GRADE LEVELS GET TO DO IT WITH PEANUTS.
I'LL PROVE I CAN DO THIS!
WHOOSH
FWP

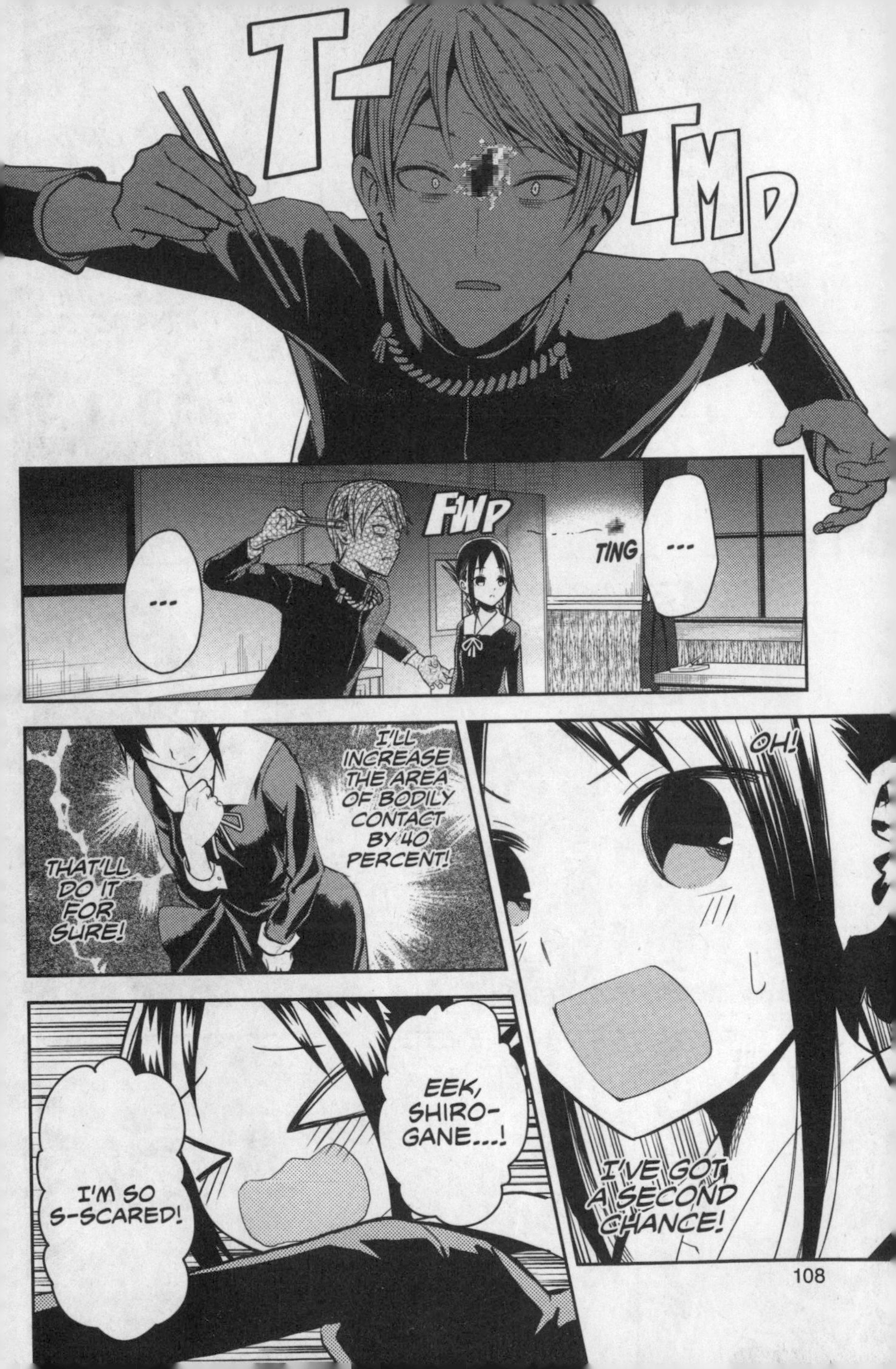
T-
TMP
...
TING
FWP
...
OH!
I'VE GOT A SECOND CHANCE!
I'LL INCREASE THE AREA OF BODILY CONTACT BY 40 PERCENT!
THAT'LL DO IT FOR SURE!
EEK, SHIRO-GANE...!
I'M SO S-SCARED!

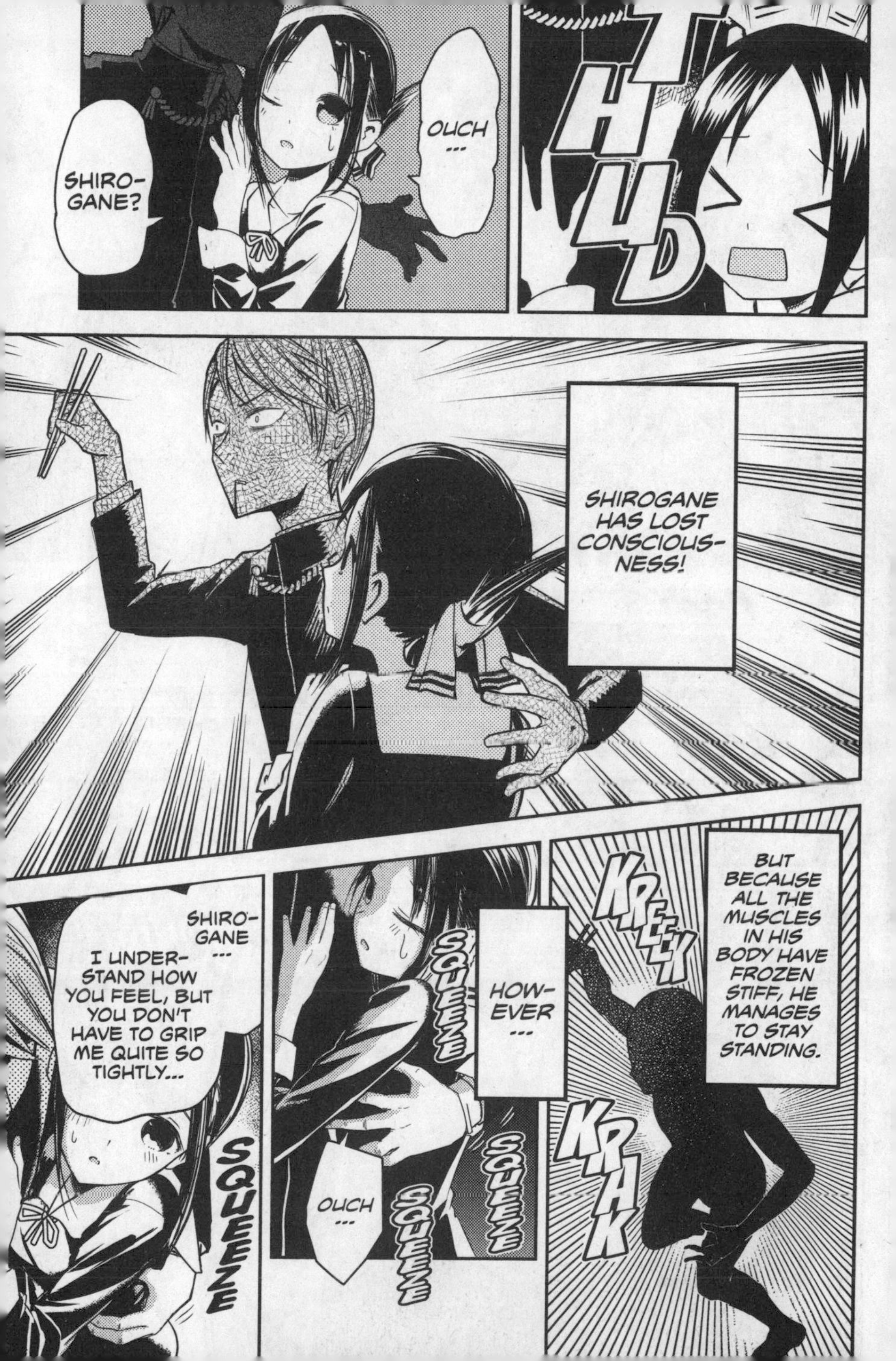
THUD
OUCH ...
SHIRO-GANE?
SHIROGANE HAS LOST CONSCIOUSNESS!
KREEK
BUT BECAUSE ALL THE MUSCLES IN HIS BODY HAVE FROZEN STIFF, HE MANAGES TO STAY STANDING.
KRAK
HOW-EVER ...
SQUEEZE
SQUEEZE
SQUEEZE
OUCH ...
SHIRO-GANE ...
I UNDER-STAND HOW YOU FEEL, BUT YOU DON'T HAVE TO GRIP ME QUITE SO TIGHTLY...
SQUEEZE

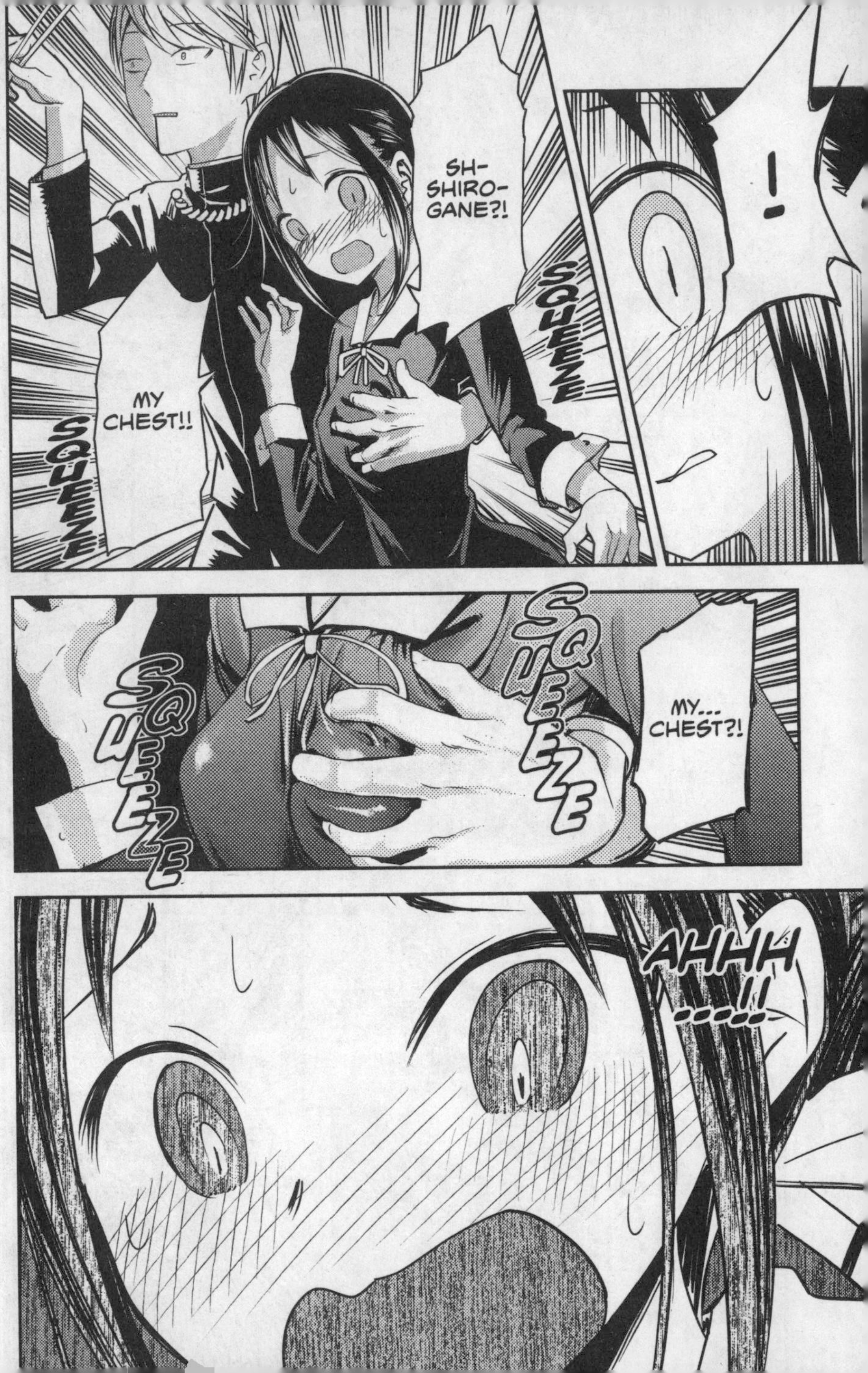
!
SH-SHIRO-GANE?!
SQUEEZE
MY CHEST!!
SQUEEZE
MY... CHEST?!
SQUEEZE
SQUEEZE
AHHH...!!

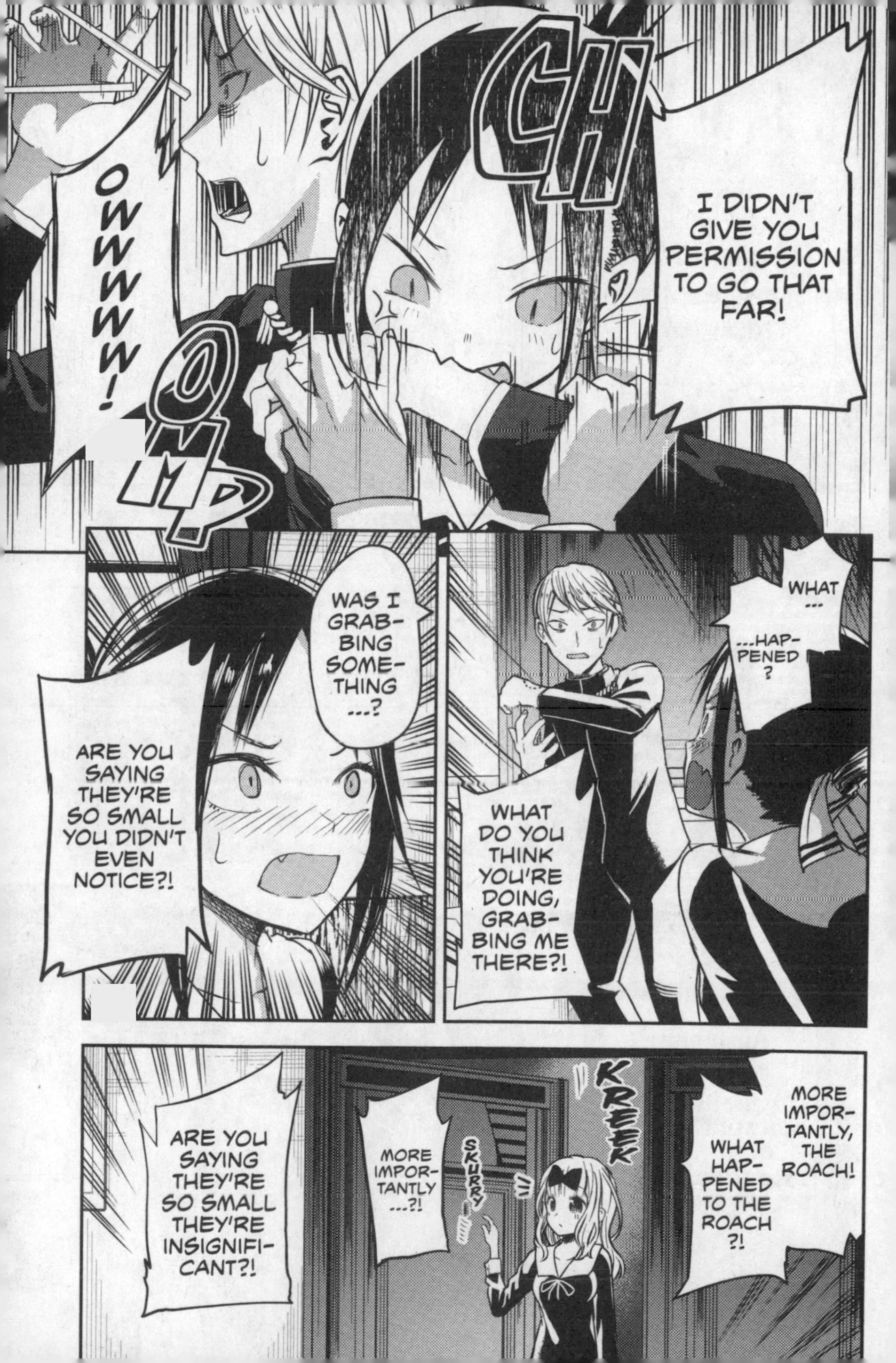
CH
I DIDN'T GIVE YOU PERMISSION TO GO THAT FAR!
OWWWWWW!
OMMP
WHAT... ...HAPPENED?
WHAT DO YOU THINK YOU'RE DOING, GRABBING ME THERE?!
WAS I GRABBING SOMETHING...?
ARE YOU SAYING THEY'RE SO SMALL YOU DIDN'T EVEN NOTICE?!
MORE IMPORTANTLY, THE ROACH!
WHAT HAPPENED TO THE ROACH?!
KREEK
SKURRY
MORE IMPORTANTLY...?!
ARE YOU SAYING THEY'RE SO SMALL THEY'RE INSIGNIFICANT?!

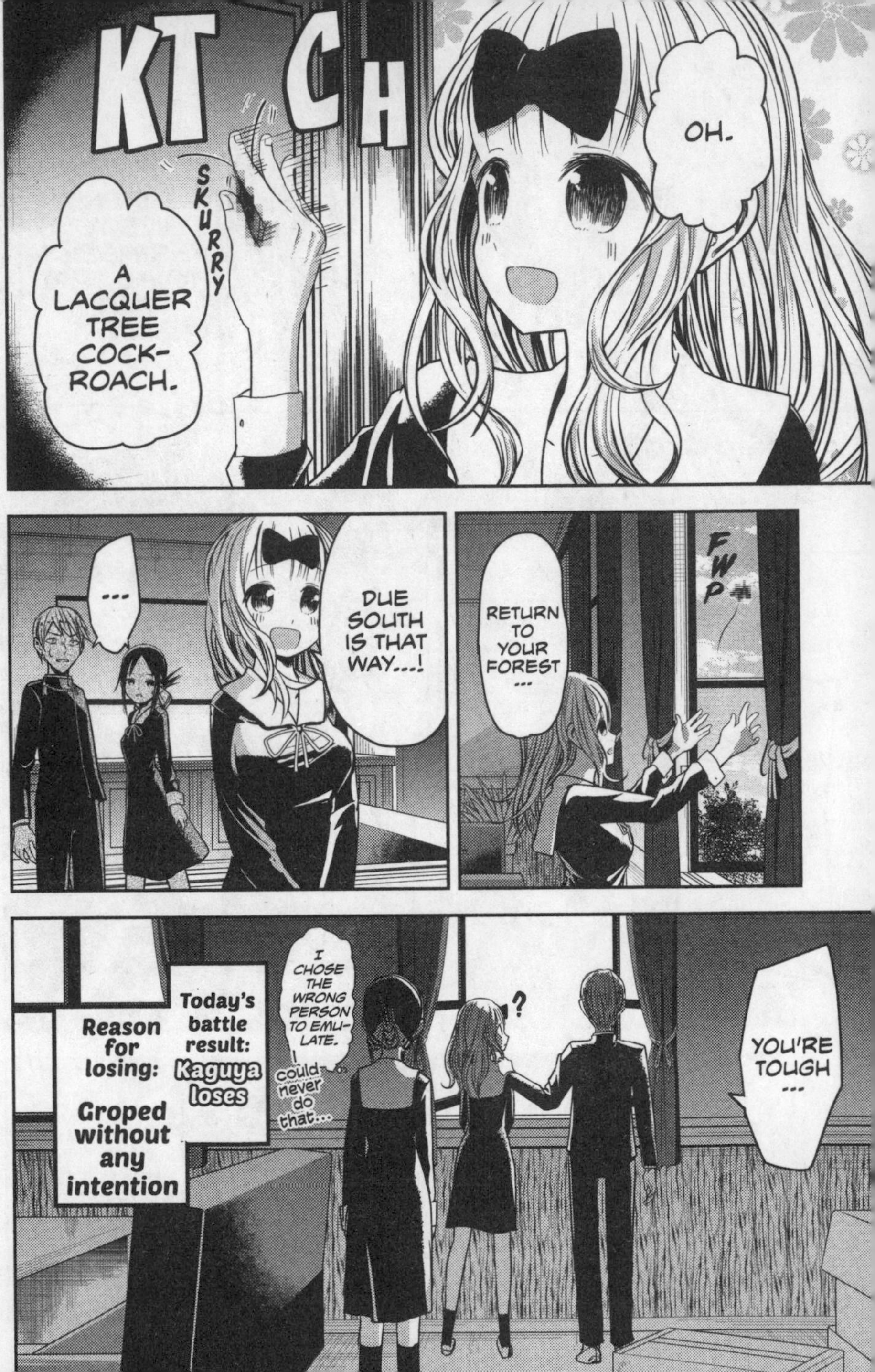
OH.
KTCH
SKURRY
A LACQUER TREE COCKROACH.
FWP
RETURN TO YOUR FOREST...
DUE SOUTH IS THAT WAY...!
...
YOU'RE TOUGH...
?
I CHOSE THE WRONG PERSON TO EMULATE.
I could never do that...
Today's battle result: Kaguya loses
Reason for losing:
Groped without any intention

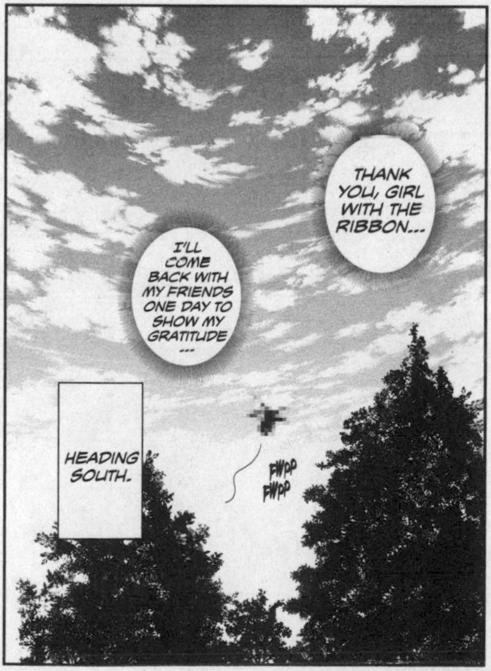
THANK YOU, GIRL WITH THE RIBBON...
I'LL COME BACK WITH MY FRIENDS ONE DAY TO SHOW MY GRATITUDE...
HEADING SOUTH.
FWPP FWPP

KAGUYA-SAMA
LOVE IS WAR

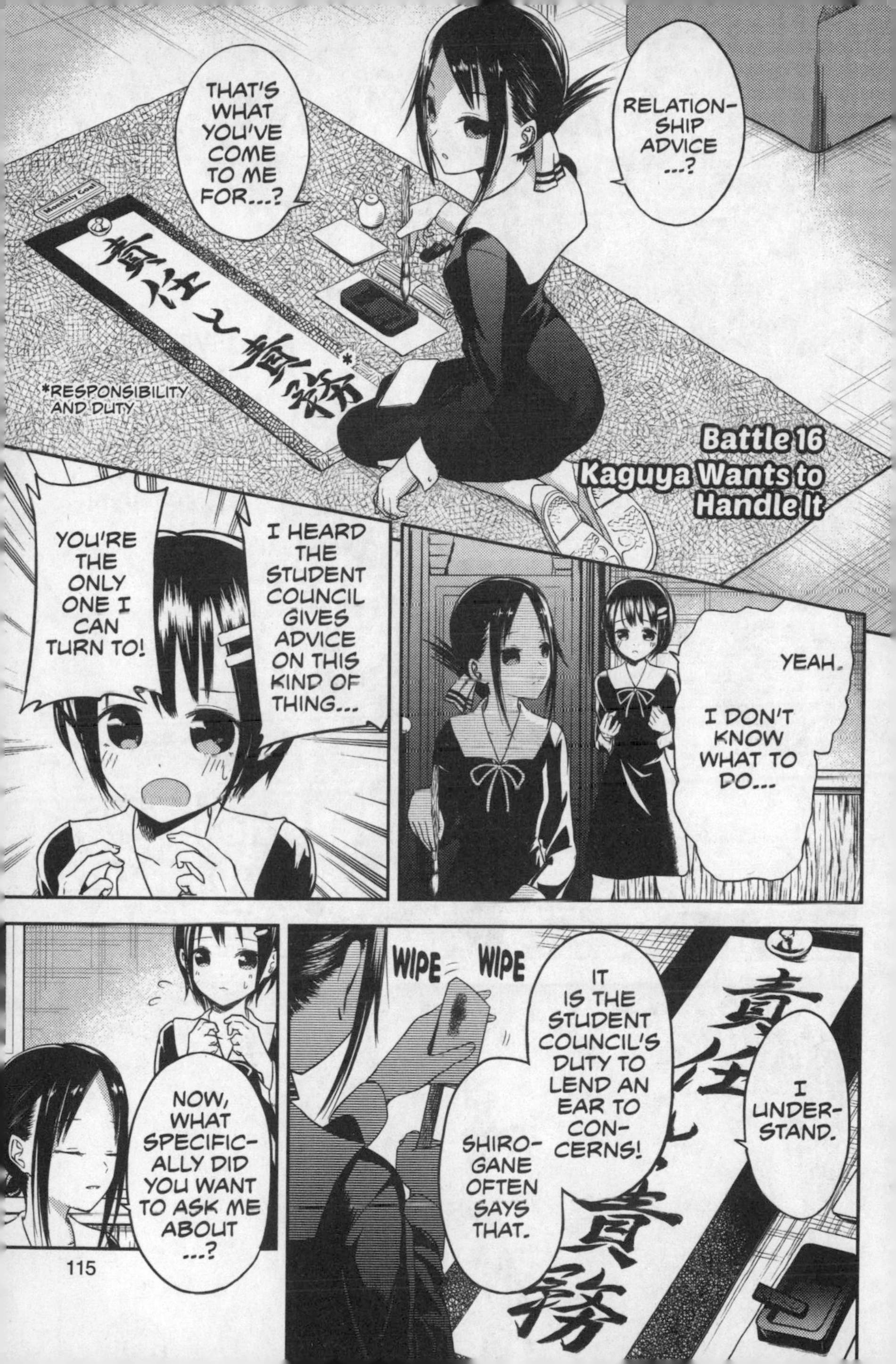
RELATIONSHIP ADVICE ...?
THAT'S WHAT YOU'VE COME TO ME FOR...?
Monthly Goal
責任と責務*
*RESPONSIBILITY AND DUTY
Battle 16 Kaguya Wants to Handle It
YEAH.
I DON'T KNOW WHAT TO DO...
I HEARD THE STUDENT COUNCIL GIVES ADVICE ON THIS KIND OF THING...
YOU'RE THE ONLY ONE I CAN TURN TO!
責任と責務
I UNDERSTAND.
IT IS THE STUDENT COUNCIL'S DUTY TO LEND AN EAR TO CONCERNS!
SHIROGANE OFTEN SAYS THAT.
WIPE WIPE
NOW, WHAT SPECIFICALLY DID YOU WANT TO ASK ME ABOUT ...?

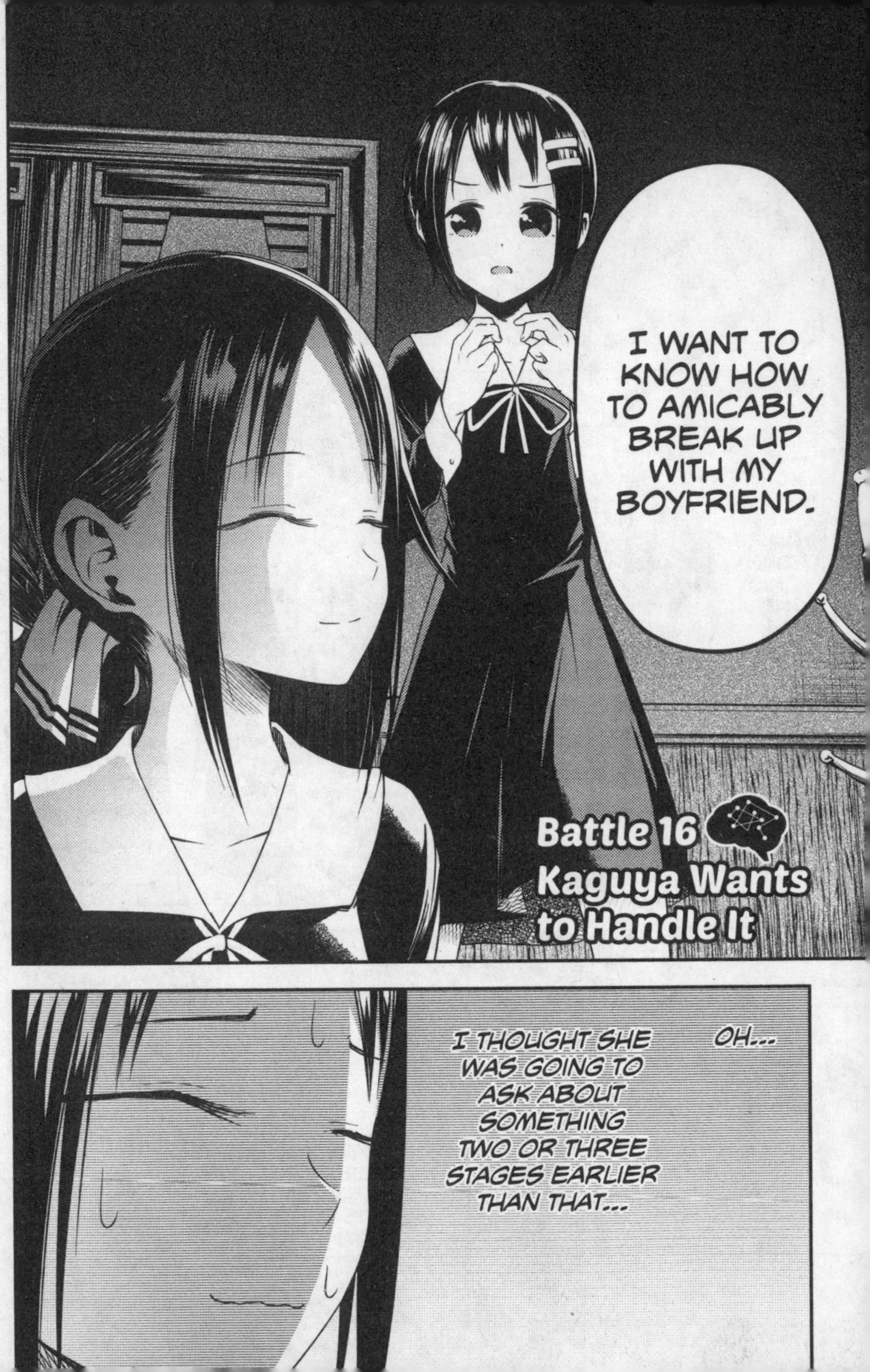
I WANT TO KNOW HOW TO AMICABLY BREAK UP WITH MY BOYFRIEND.
Battle 16
Kaguya Wants to Handle It
OH...
I THOUGHT SHE WAS GOING TO ASK ABOUT SOMETHING TWO OR THREE STAGES EARLIER THAN THAT...

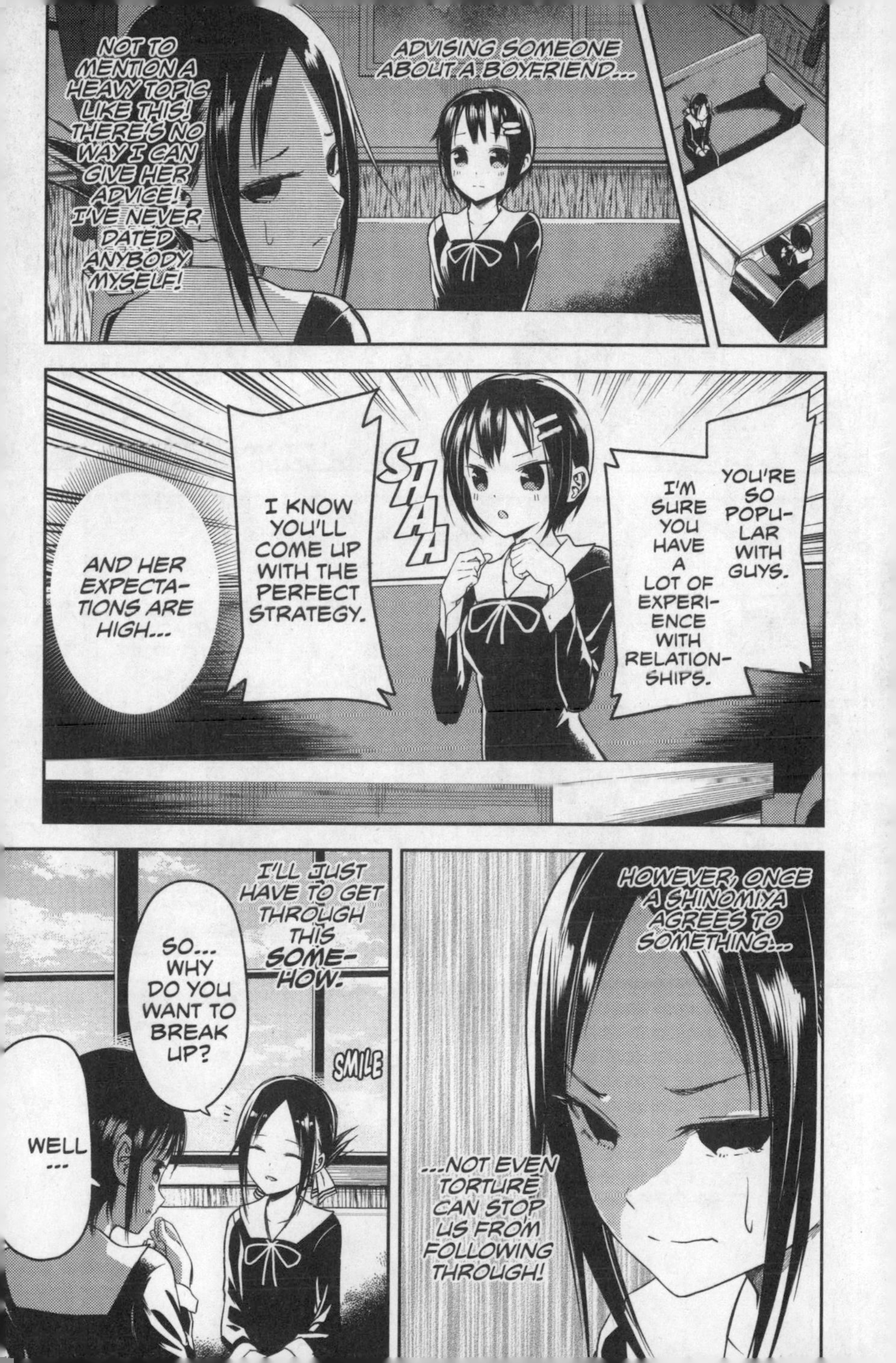

ADVISING SOMEONE ABOUT A BOYFRIEND...
NOT TO MENTION A HEAVY TOPIC LIKE THIS! THERE'S NO WAY I CAN GIVE HER ADVICE! I'VE NEVER DATED ANYBODY MYSELF!
YOU'RE SO POPULAR WITH GUYS.
I'M SURE YOU HAVE A LOT OF EXPERIENCE WITH RELATIONSHIPS.
SHAA
I KNOW YOU'LL COME UP WITH THE PERFECT STRATEGY.
AND HER EXPECTATIONS ARE HIGH...
HOWEVER, ONCE A SHINOMIYA AGREES TO SOMETHING...
...NOT EVEN TORTURE CAN STOP US FROM FOLLOWING THROUGH!
I'LL JUST HAVE TO GET THROUGH THIS SOMEHOW.
SO... WHY DO YOU WANT TO BREAK UP?
SMILE
WELL...

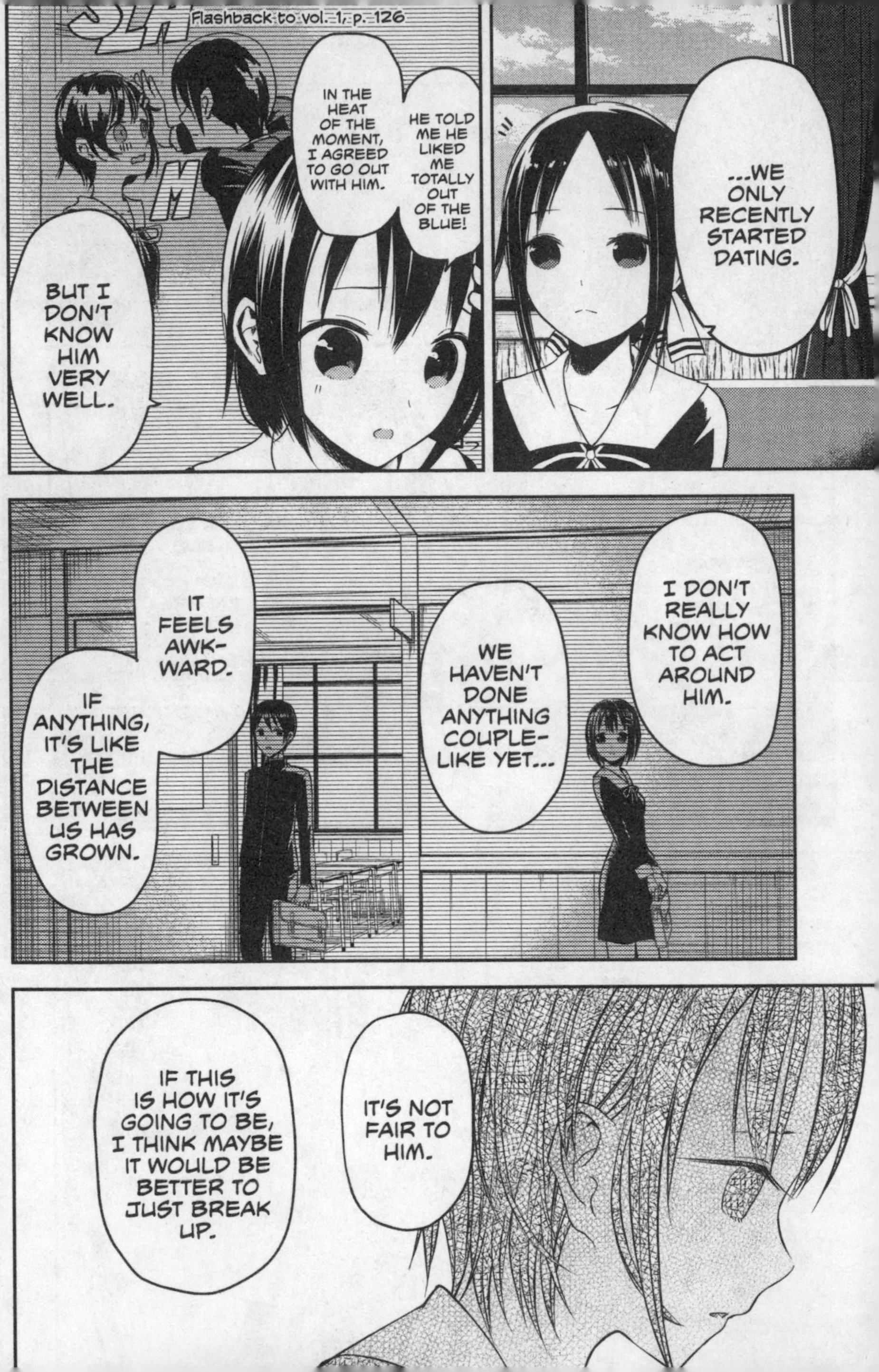
...WE ONLY RECENTLY STARTED DATING.
Flashback to vol. 1, p. 126
HE TOLD ME HE LIKED ME TOTALLY OUT OF THE BLUE!
IN THE HEAT OF THE MOMENT, I AGREED TO GO OUT WITH HIM.
BUT I DON'T KNOW HIM VERY WELL.
I DON'T REALLY KNOW HOW TO ACT AROUND HIM.
WE HAVEN'T DONE ANYTHING COUPLE-LIKE YET...
IT FEELS AWK-WARD.
IF ANYTHING, IT'S LIKE THE DISTANCE BETWEEN US HAS GROWN.
IT'S NOT FAIR TO HIM.
IF THIS IS HOW IT'S GOING TO BE, I THINK MAYBE IT WOULD BE BETTER TO JUST BREAK UP.

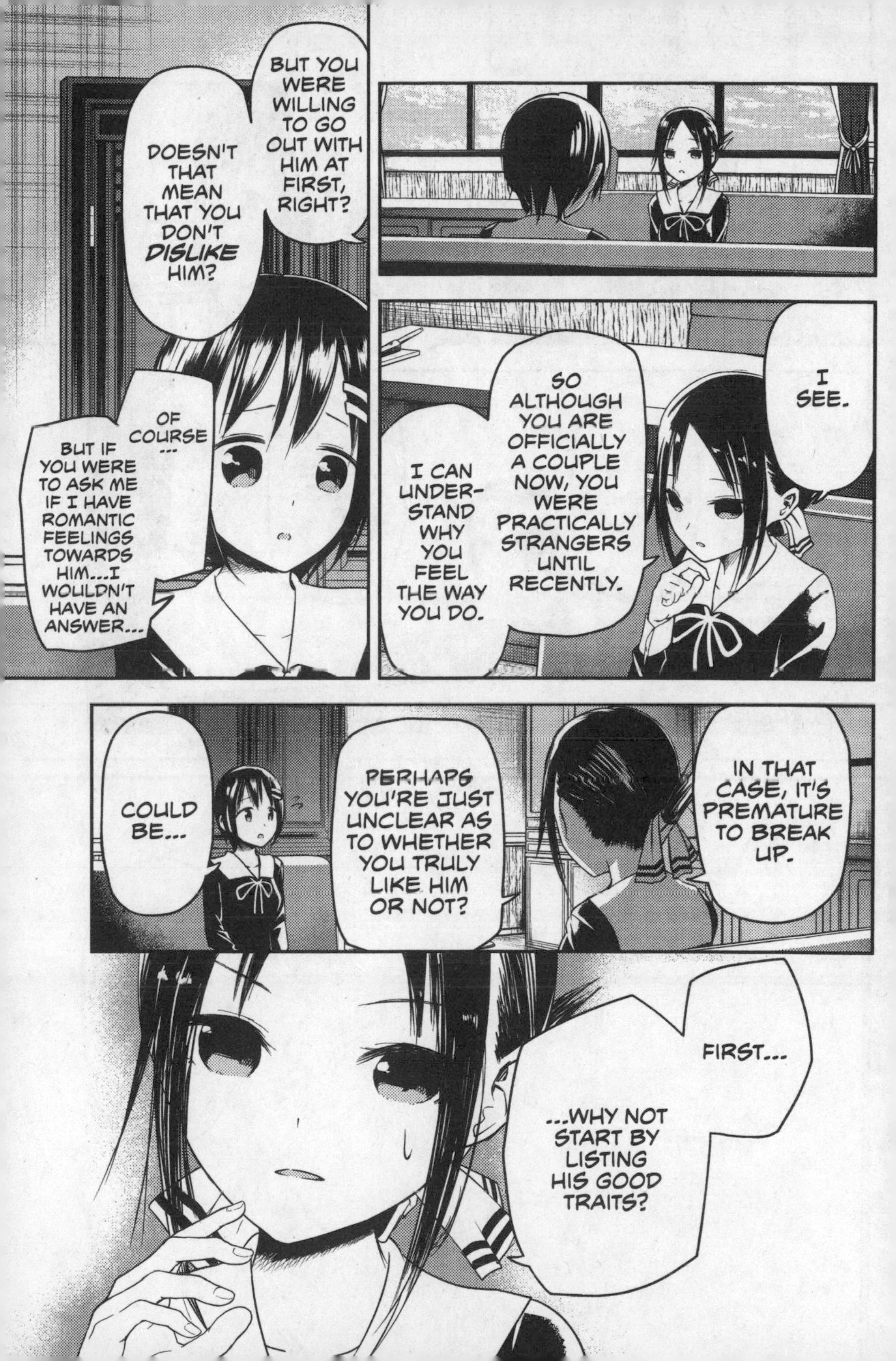
I SEE.
SO ALTHOUGH YOU ARE OFFICIALLY A COUPLE NOW, YOU WERE PRACTICALLY STRANGERS UNTIL RECENTLY.
I CAN UNDER-STAND WHY YOU FEEL THE WAY YOU DO.
BUT YOU WERE WILLING TO GO OUT WITH HIM AT FIRST, RIGHT?
DOESN'T THAT MEAN THAT YOU DON'T DISLIKE HIM?
OF COURSE ...
BUT IF YOU WERE TO ASK ME IF I HAVE ROMANTIC FEELINGS TOWARDS HIM...I WOULDN'T HAVE AN ANSWER...
IN THAT CASE, IT'S PREMATURE TO BREAK UP.
PERHAPS YOU'RE JUST UNCLEAR AS TO WHETHER YOU TRULY LIKE HIM OR NOT?
COULD BE...
FIRST...
...WHY NOT START BY LISTING HIS GOOD TRAITS?

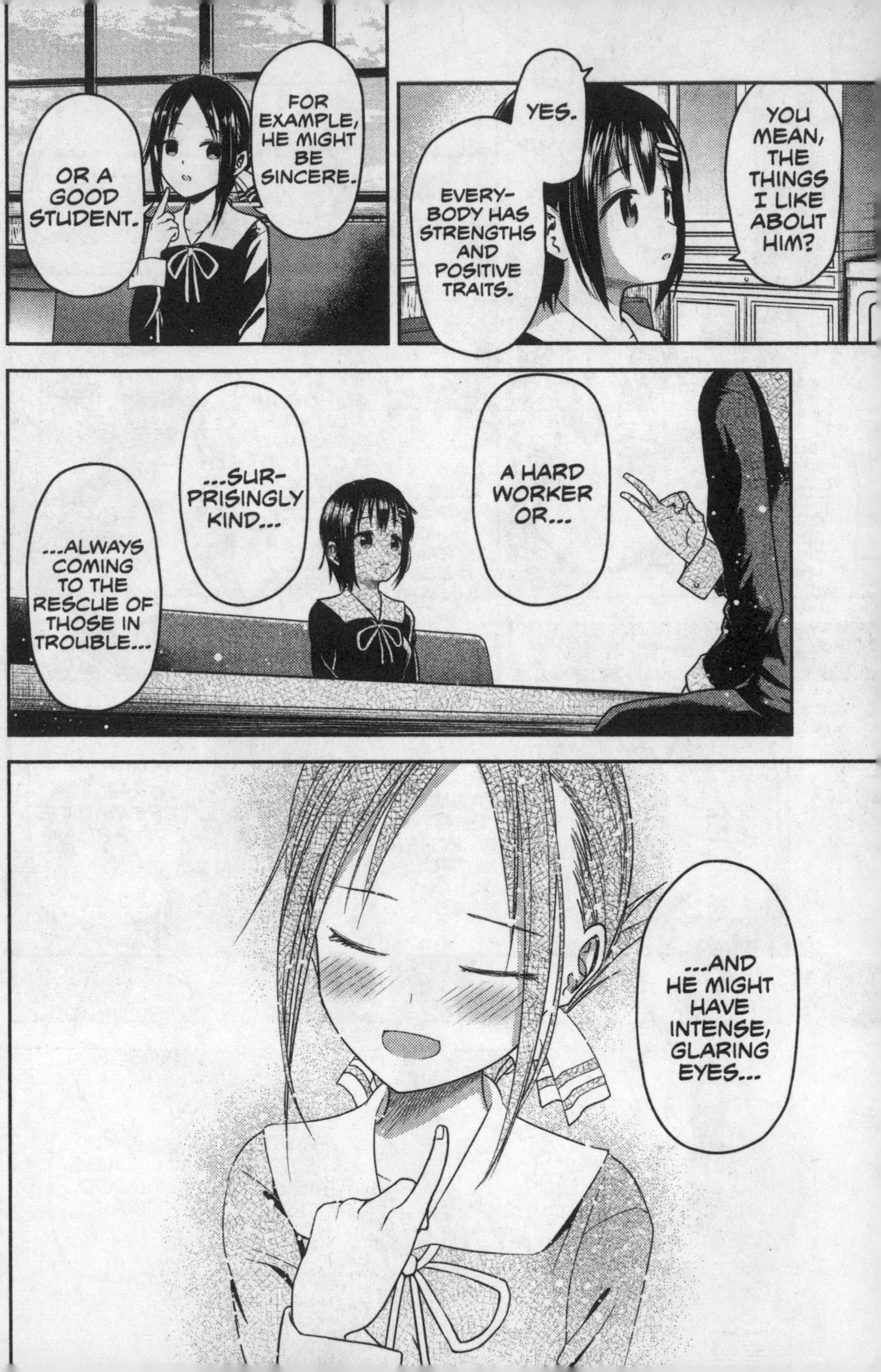
YOU MEAN, THE THINGS I LIKE ABOUT HIM?
YES.
EVERY-BODY HAS STRENGTHS AND POSITIVE TRAITS.
FOR EXAMPLE, HE MIGHT BE SINCERE.
OR A GOOD STUDENT.
A HARD WORKER OR...
...SUR-PRISINGLY KIND...
...ALWAYS COMING TO THE RESCUE OF THOSE IN TROUBLE...
...AND HE MIGHT HAVE INTENSE, GLARING EYES...

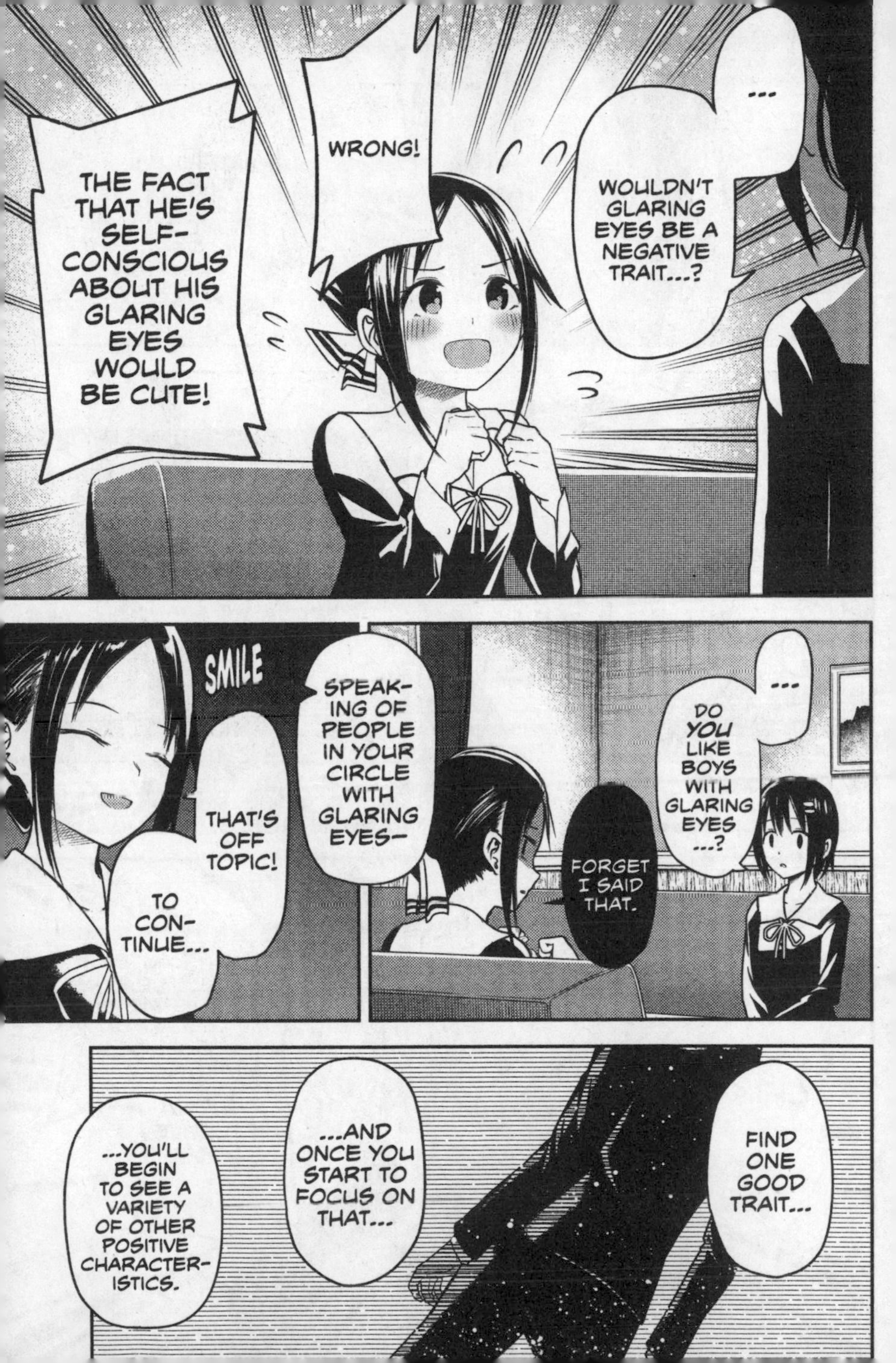
...
WOULDN'T GLARING EYES BE A NEGATIVE TRAIT...?
WRONG!
THE FACT THAT HE'S SELF-CONSCIOUS ABOUT HIS GLARING EYES WOULD BE CUTE!
...
DO YOU LIKE BOYS WITH GLARING EYES...?
FORGET I SAID THAT.
SPEAKING OF PEOPLE IN YOUR CIRCLE WITH GLARING EYES—
SMILE
THAT'S OFF TOPIC!
TO CONTINUE...
FIND ONE GOOD TRAIT...
...AND ONCE YOU START TO FOCUS ON THAT...
...YOU'LL BEGIN TO SEE A VARIETY OF OTHER POSITIVE CHARACTERISTICS.

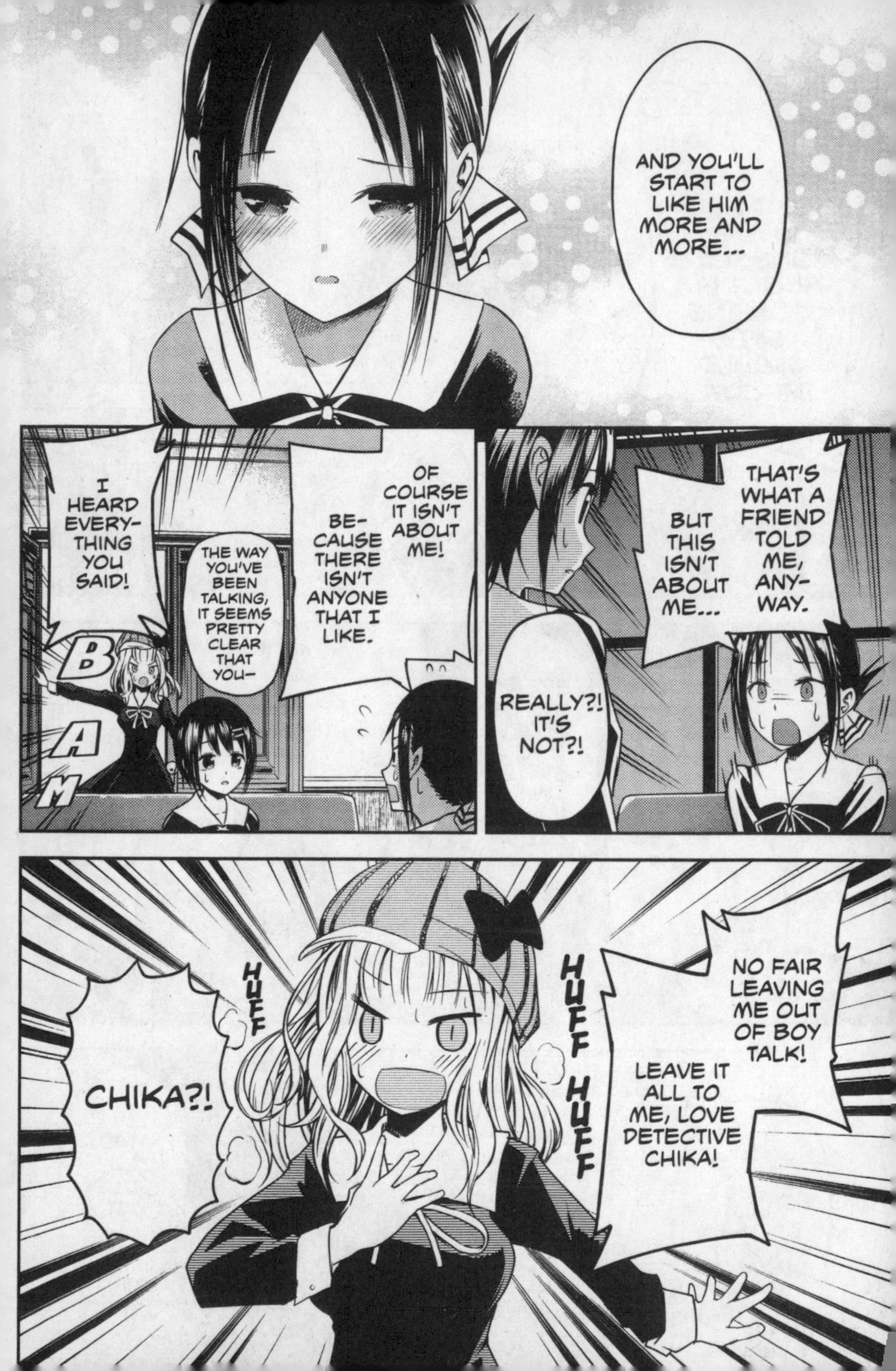
AND YOU'LL START TO LIKE HIM MORE AND MORE...
THAT'S WHAT A FRIEND TOLD ME, ANYWAY.
BUT THIS ISN'T ABOUT ME...
REALLY?! IT'S NOT?!
OF COURSE IT ISN'T ABOUT ME!
BECAUSE THERE ISN'T ANYONE THAT I LIKE.
THE WAY YOU'VE BEEN TALKING, IT SEEMS PRETTY CLEAR THAT YOU—
I HEARD EVERYTHING YOU SAID!
BAM
NO FAIR LEAVING ME OUT OF BOY TALK!
LEAVE IT ALL TO ME, LOVE DETECTIVE CHIKA!
HUFF HUFF
HUFF
CHIKA?!

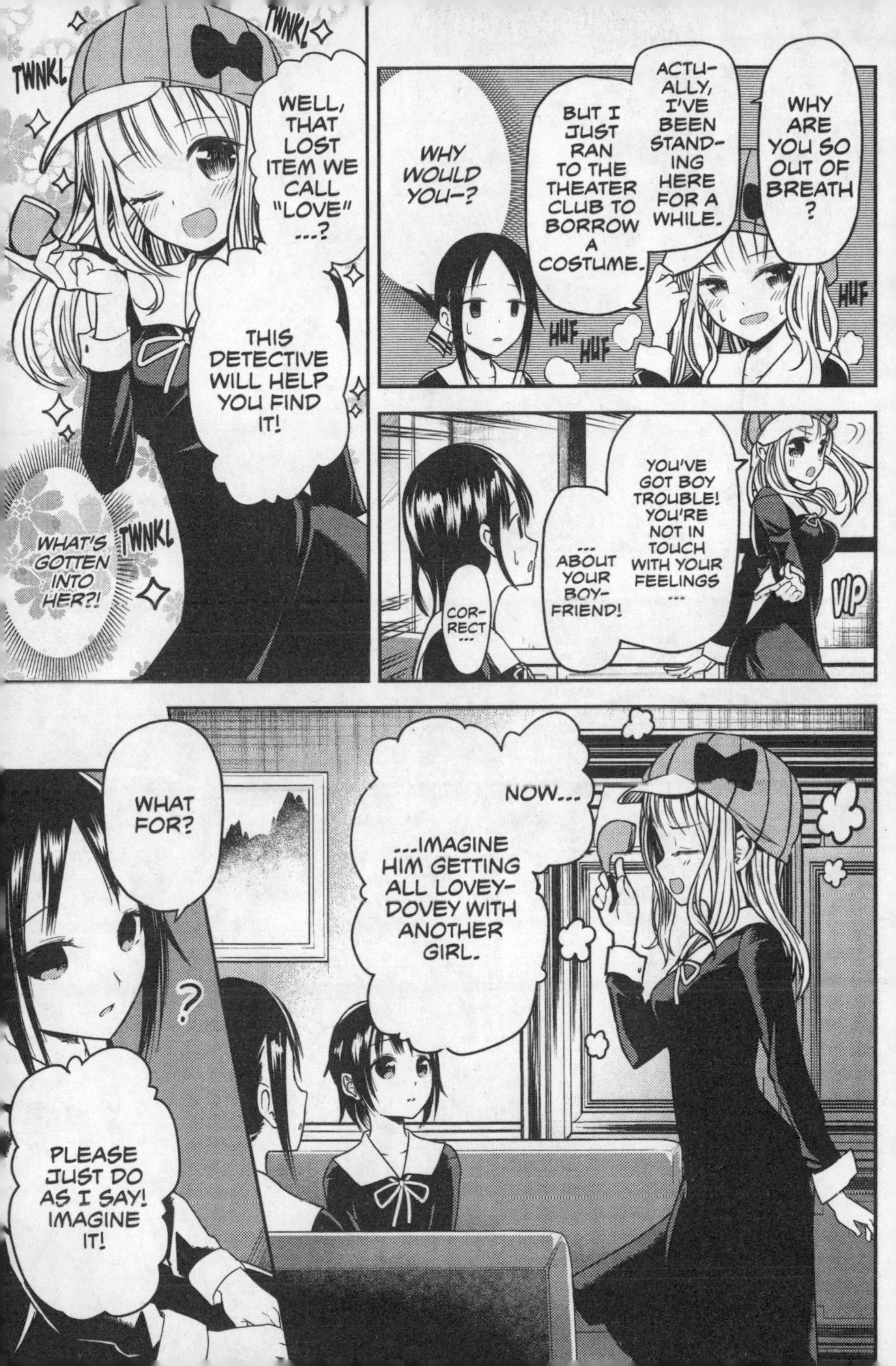
WHY ARE YOU SO OUT OF BREATH?
ACTUALLY, I'VE BEEN STANDING HERE FOR A WHILE.
BUT I JUST RAN TO THE THEATER CLUB TO BORROW A COSTUME.
HUF
HUF HUF
HUF
WHY WOULD YOU--?
YOU'VE GOT BOY TROUBLE! YOU'RE NOT IN TOUCH WITH YOUR FEELINGS...
...ABOUT YOUR BOYFRIEND!
VIP
CORRECT...
TWNKL
TWNKL
WELL, THAT LOST ITEM WE CALL "LOVE"...?
THIS DETECTIVE WILL HELP YOU FIND IT!
TWNKL
WHAT'S GOTTEN INTO HER?!
NOW...
...IMAGINE HIM GETTING ALL LOVEY-DOVEY WITH ANOTHER GIRL.
WHAT FOR?
?
PLEASE JUST DO AS I SAY! IMAGINE IT!

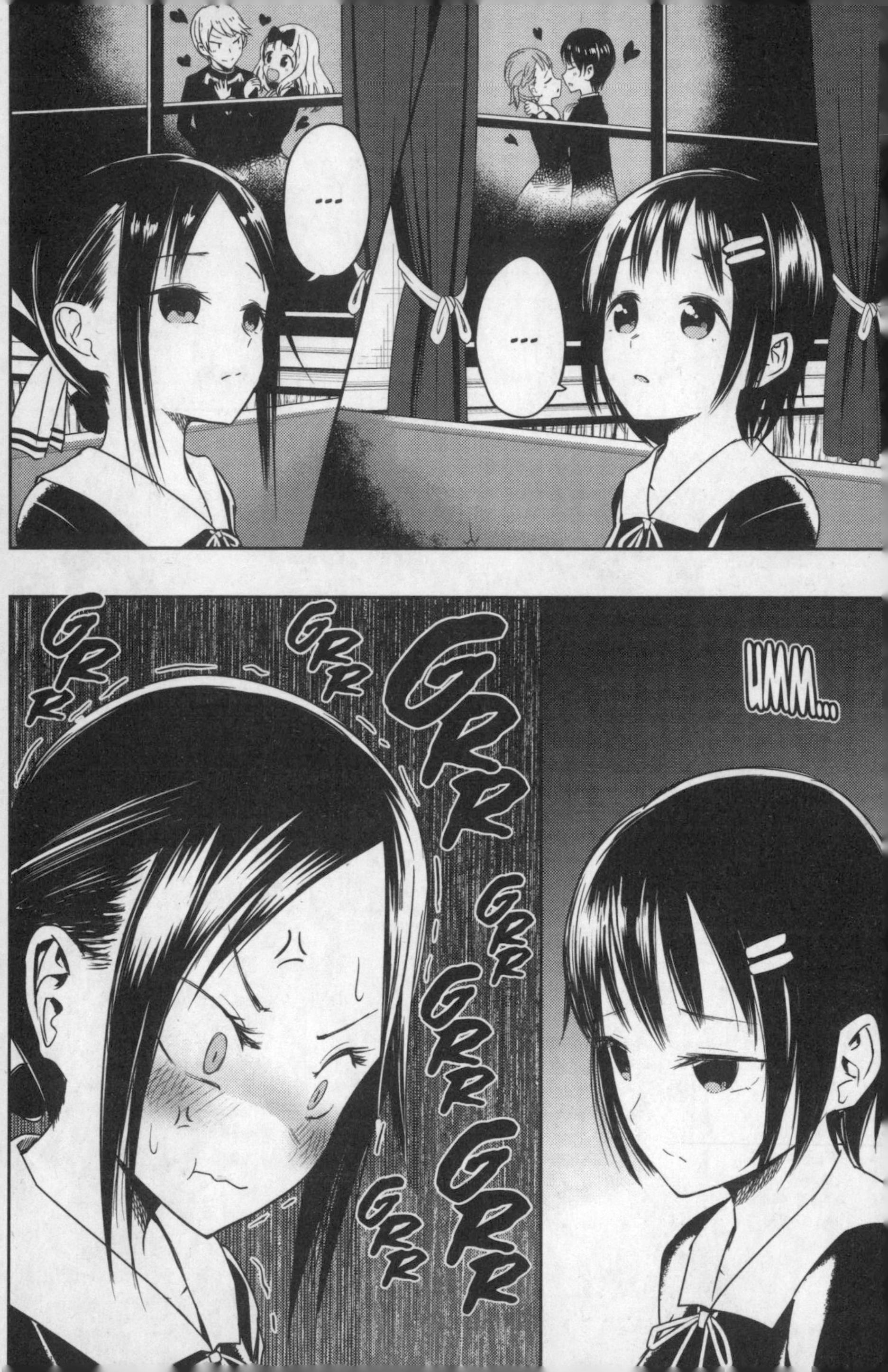
...
...
UMM...
GRR
GRR
GRR
GRR
GRR
GRR
GRR
GRR

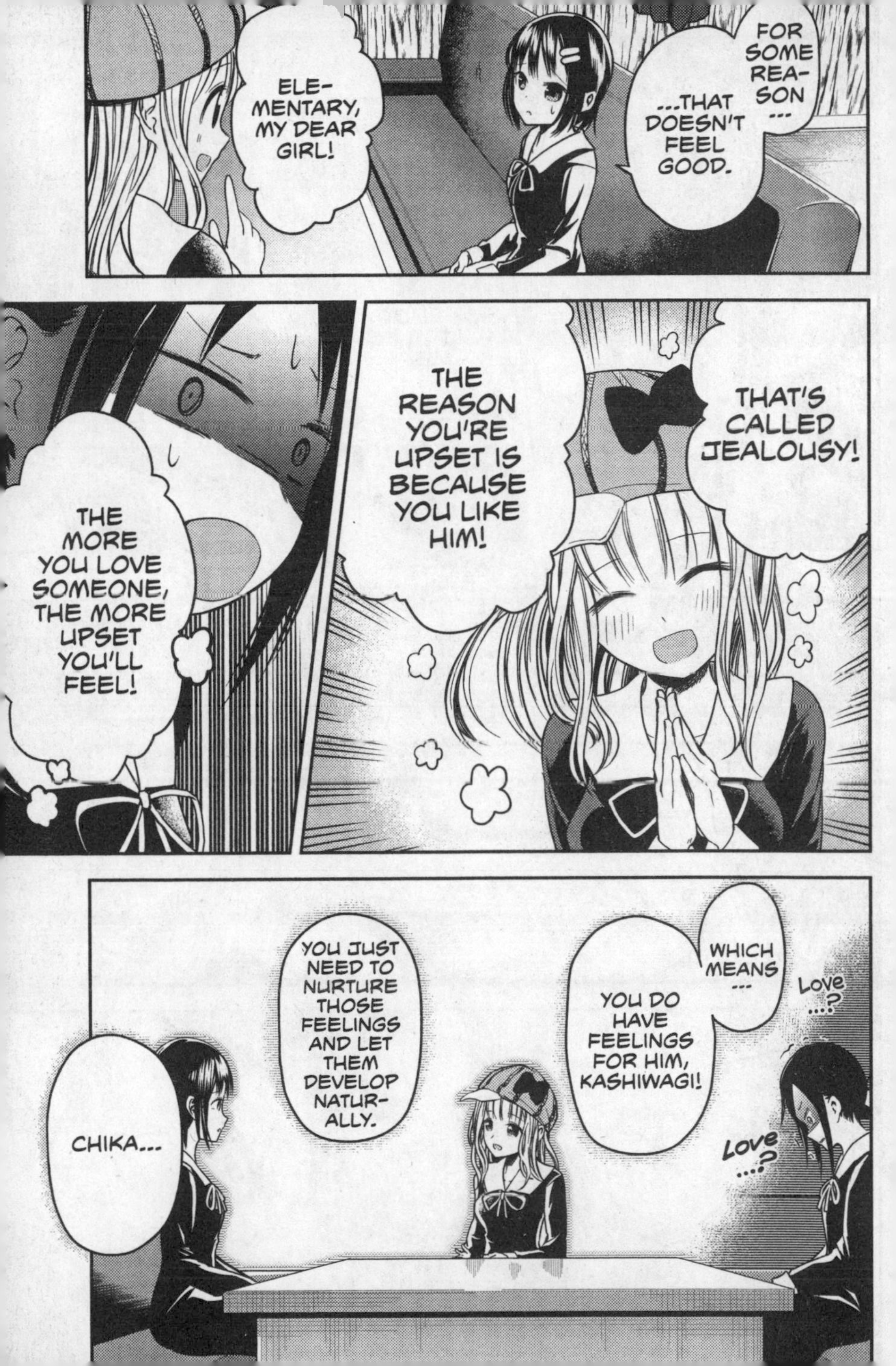
FOR SOME REASON ...
...THAT DOESN'T FEEL GOOD.
ELEMENTARY, MY DEAR GIRL!
THAT'S CALLED JEALOUSY!
THE REASON YOU'RE UPSET IS BECAUSE YOU LIKE HIM!
THE MORE YOU LOVE SOMEONE, THE MORE UPSET YOU'LL FEEL!
WHICH MEANS ...
YOU DO HAVE FEELINGS FOR HIM, KASHIWAGI!
Love ...?
Love ...?
YOU JUST NEED TO NURTURE THOSE FEELINGS AND LET THEM DEVELOP NATURALLY.
CHIKA...

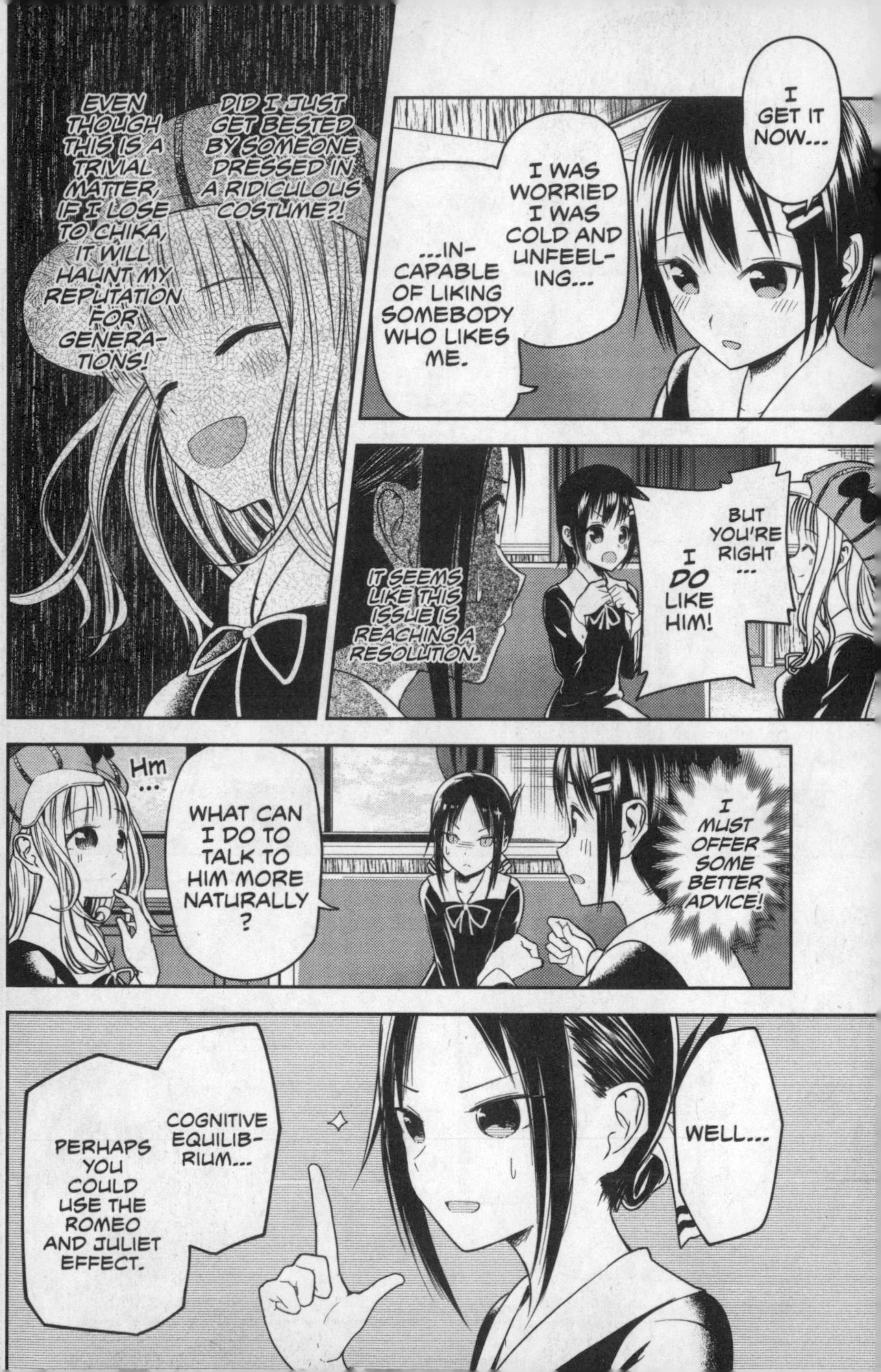
I GET IT NOW...
I WAS WORRIED I WAS COLD AND UNFEELING...
...INCAPABLE OF LIKING SOMEBODY WHO LIKES ME.
BUT YOU'RE RIGHT... I DO LIKE HIM!
IT SEEMS LIKE THIS ISSUE IS REACHING A RESOLUTION.
DID I JUST GET BESTED BY SOMEONE DRESSED IN A RIDICULOUS COSTUME?!
EVEN THOUGH THIS IS A TRIVIAL MATTER, IF I LOSE TO CHIKA, IT WILL HAUNT MY REPUTATION FOR GENERATIONS!
I MUST OFFER SOME BETTER ADVICE!
WHAT CAN I DO TO TALK TO HIM MORE NATURALLY?
Hm...
WELL...
COGNITIVE EQUILIBRIUM...
PERHAPS YOU COULD USE THE ROMEO AND JULIET EFFECT.

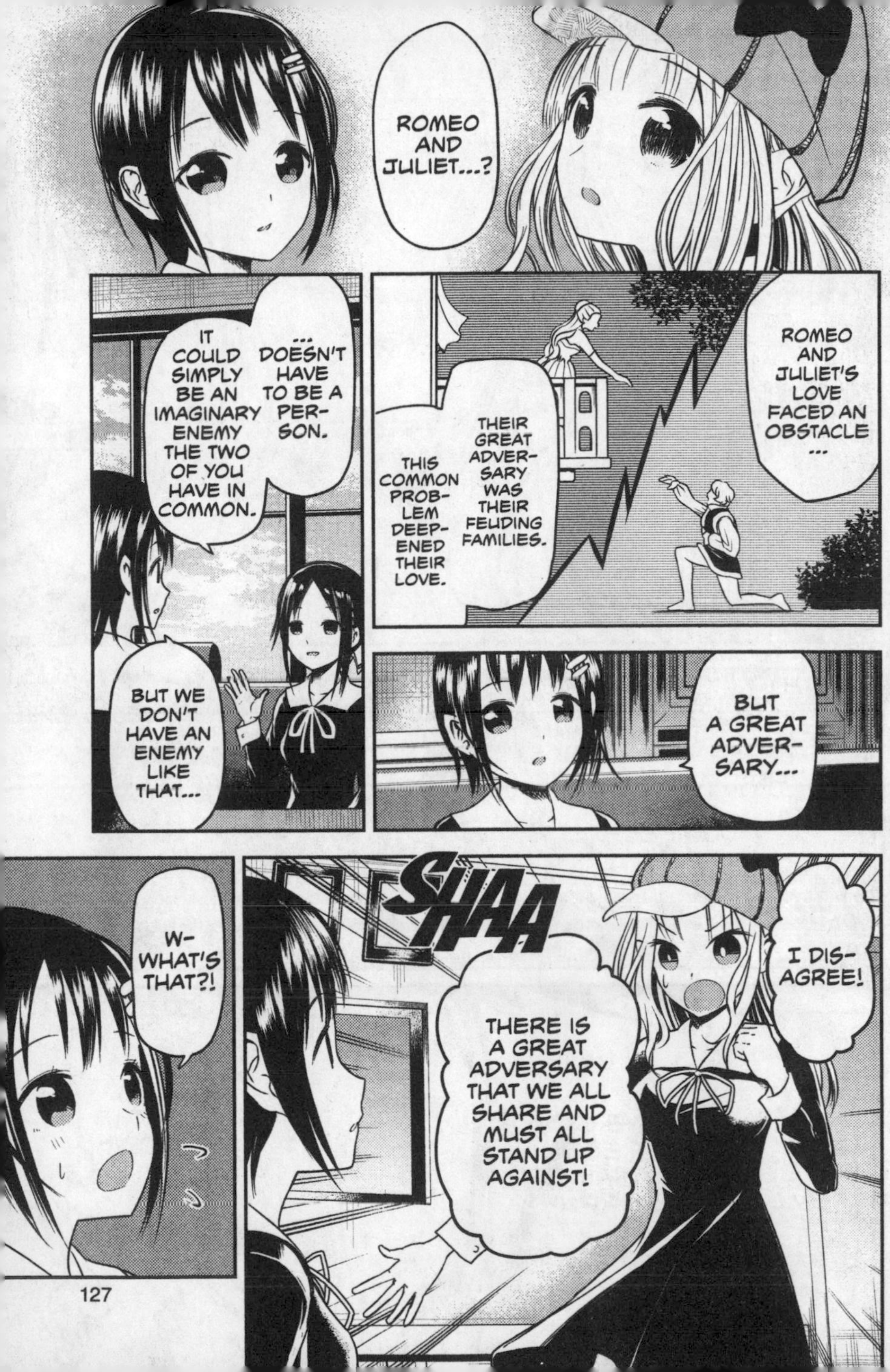
ROMEO AND JULIET...?
ROMEO AND JULIET'S LOVE FACED AN OBSTACLE...
THEIR GREAT ADVERSARY WAS THEIR FEUDING FAMILIES.
THIS COMMON PROBLEM DEEPENED THEIR LOVE.
BUT A GREAT ADVERSARY...
...DOESN'T HAVE TO BE A PERSON.
IT COULD SIMPLY BE AN IMAGINARY ENEMY THE TWO OF YOU HAVE IN COMMON.
BUT WE DON'T HAVE AN ENEMY LIKE THAT...
I DISAGREE!
SHAA
THERE IS A GREAT ADVERSARY THAT WE ALL SHARE AND MUST ALL STAND UP AGAINST!
W-WHAT'S THAT?!

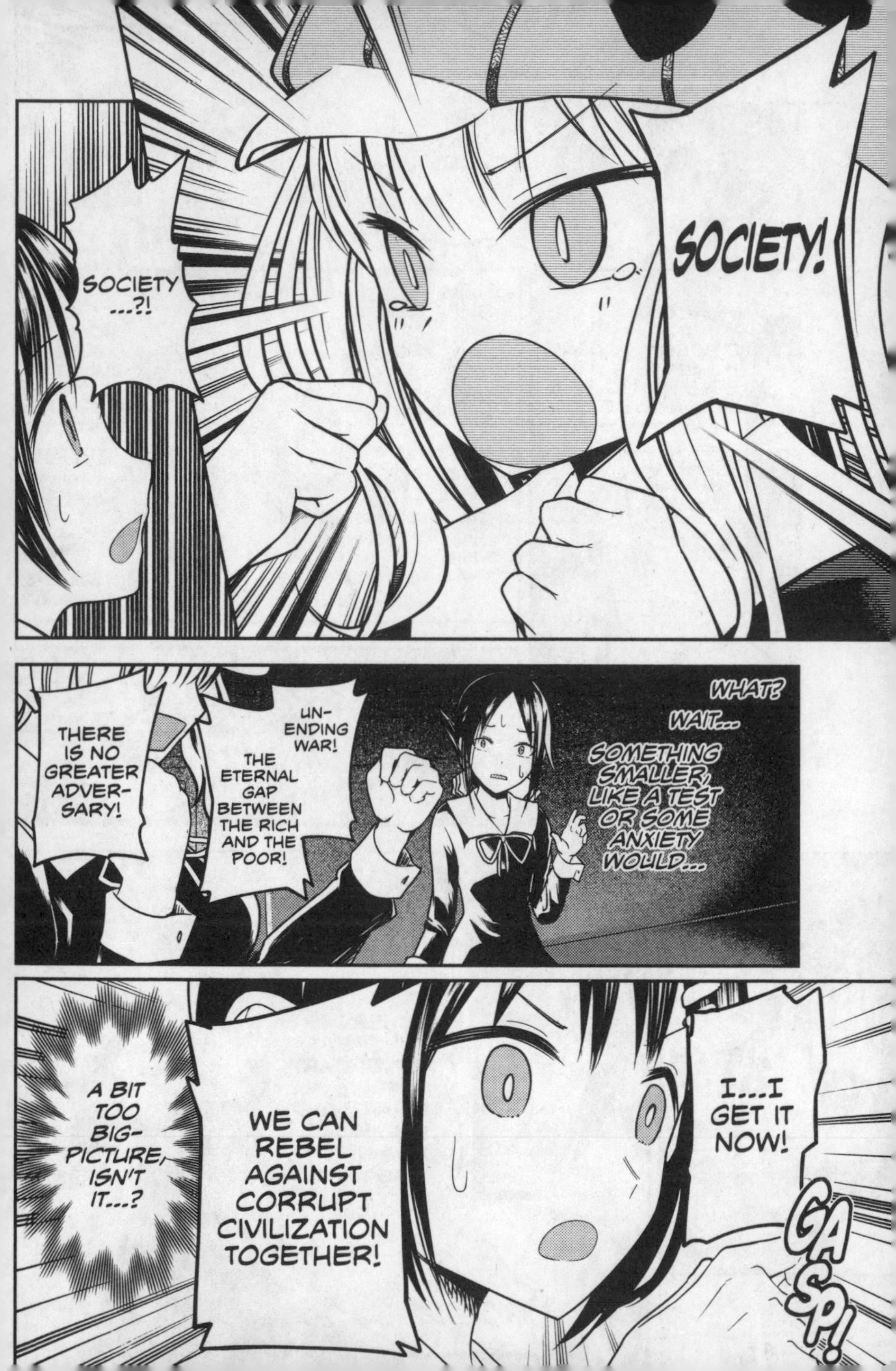
SOCIETY!
SOCIETY ...?!
WHAT?
WAIT...
SOMETHING SMALLER, LIKE A TEST OR SOME ANXIETY WOULD...
UN-ENDING WAR!
THE ETERNAL GAP BETWEEN THE RICH AND THE POOR!
THERE IS NO GREATER ADVER-SARY!
I...I GET IT NOW!
GASP!
WE CAN REBEL AGAINST CORRUPT CIVILIZATION TOGETHER!
A BIT TOO BIG-PICTURE, ISN'T IT...?

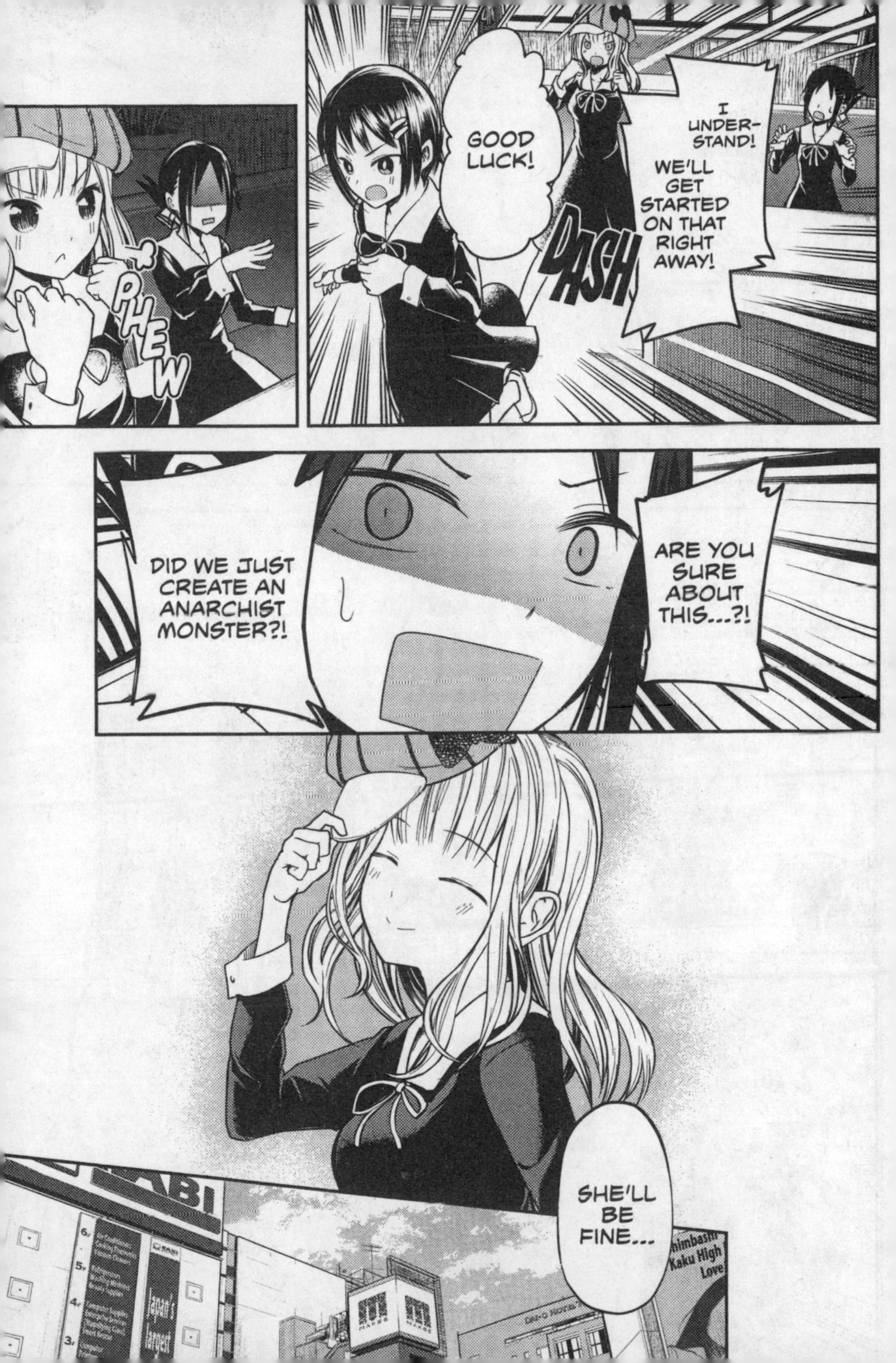
I UNDER-STAND! WE'LL GET STARTED ON THAT RIGHT AWAY!
DASH
GOOD LUCK!
PHEW
ARE YOU SURE ABOUT THIS...?!
DID WE JUST CREATE AN ANARCHIST MONSTER?!
SHE'LL BE FINE...

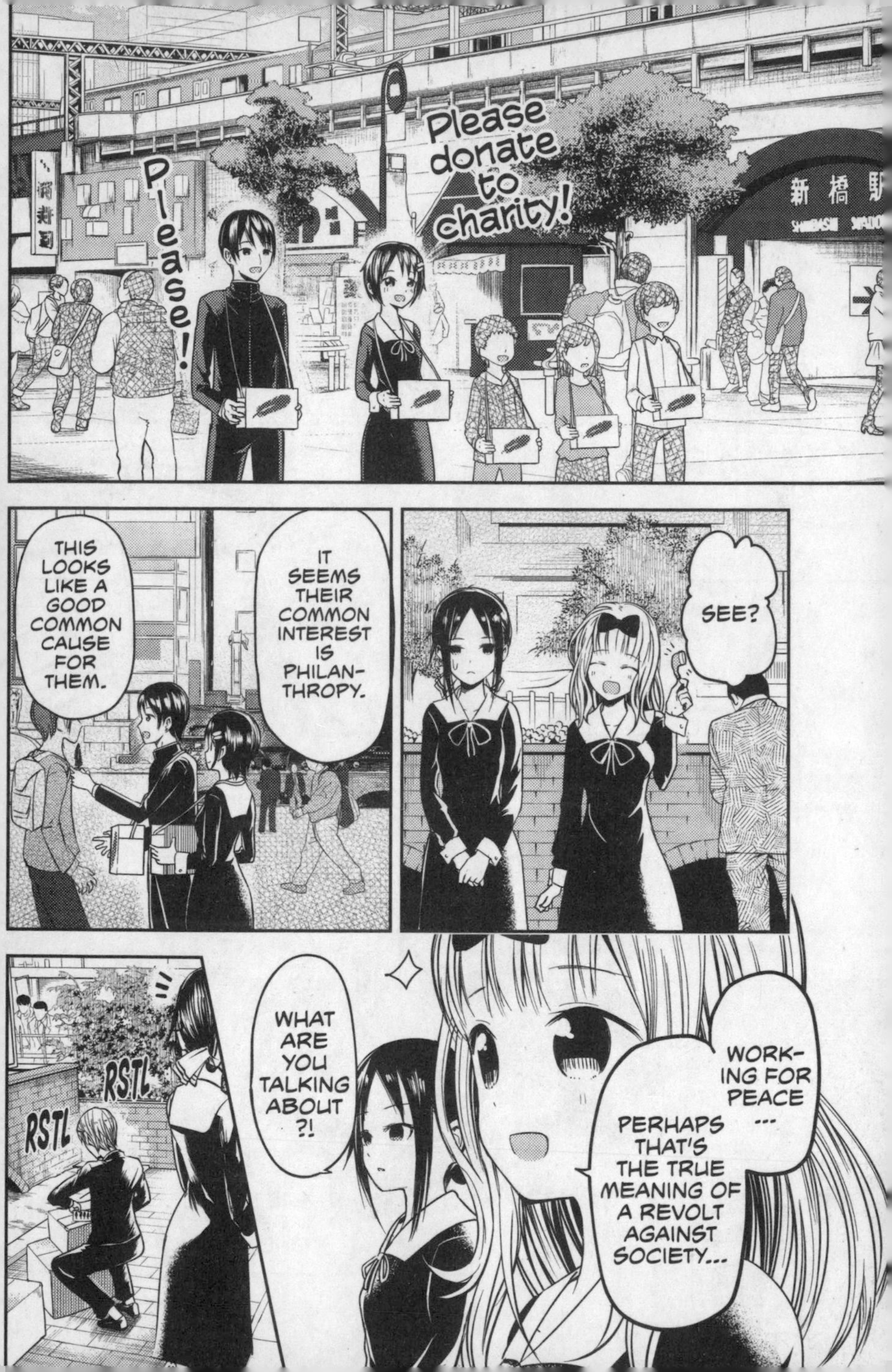
Please donate to charity!
Please!
新橋駅
SEE?
IT SEEMS THEIR COMMON INTEREST IS PHILANTHROPY.
THIS LOOKS LIKE A GOOD COMMON CAUSE FOR THEM.
WORKING FOR PEACE...
PERHAPS THAT'S THE TRUE MEANING OF A REVOLT AGAINST SOCIETY...
WHAT ARE YOU TALKING ABOUT?!
RSTL
RSTL

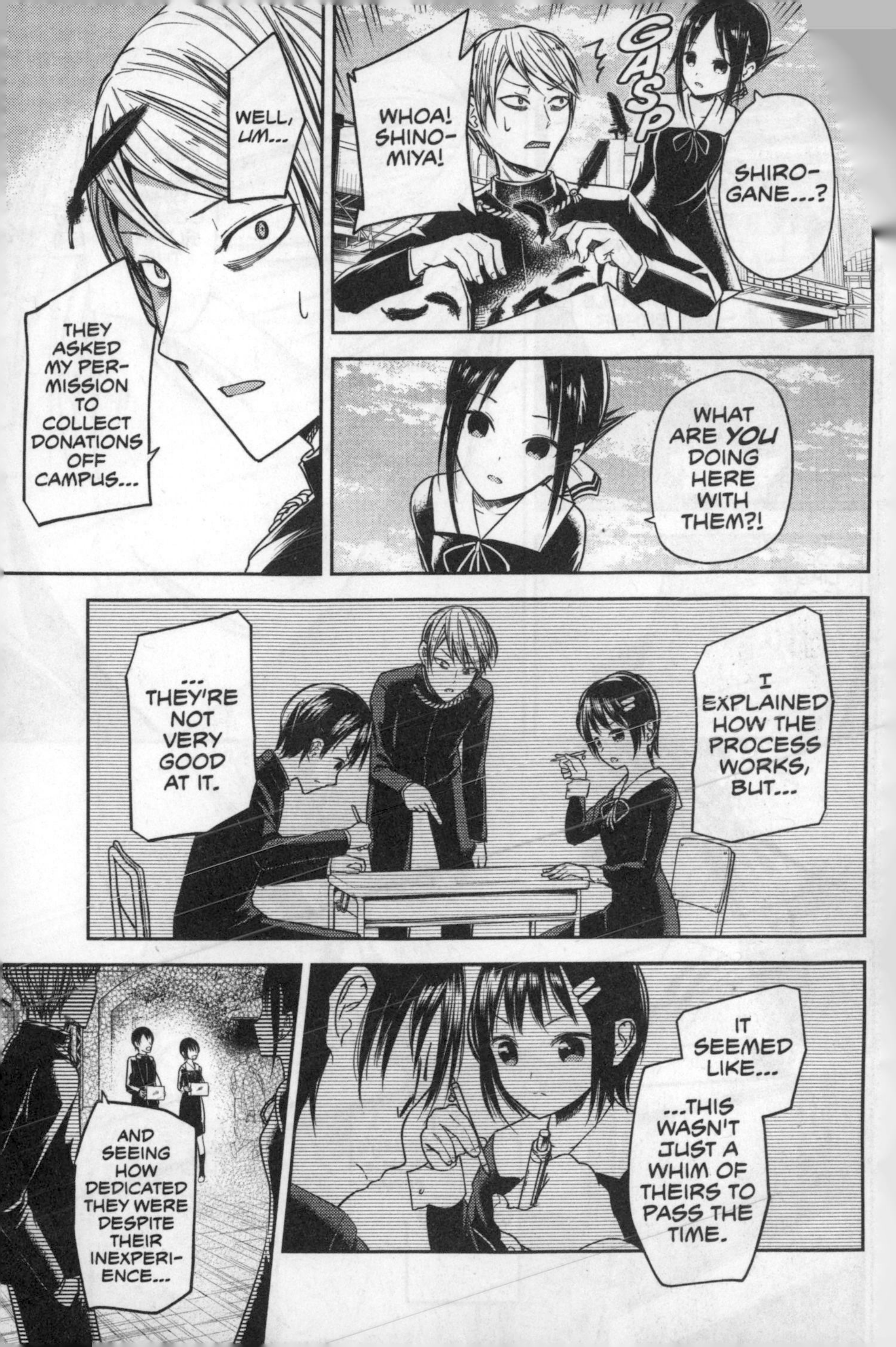
GASP
SHIRO-GANE...?
WHOA! SHINO-MIYA!
WHAT ARE *YOU* DOING HERE WITH THEM?!
WELL, UM...
THEY ASKED MY PER-MISSION TO COLLECT DONATIONS OFF CAMPUS...
I EXPLAINED HOW THE PROCESS WORKS, BUT...
...THEY'RE NOT VERY GOOD AT IT.
IT SEEMED LIKE...
...THIS WASN'T JUST A WHIM OF THEIRS TO PASS THE TIME.
AND SEEING HOW DEDICATED THEY WERE DESPITE THEIR INEXPERI-ENCE...

KAGUYA-SAMA
LOVE IS WAR

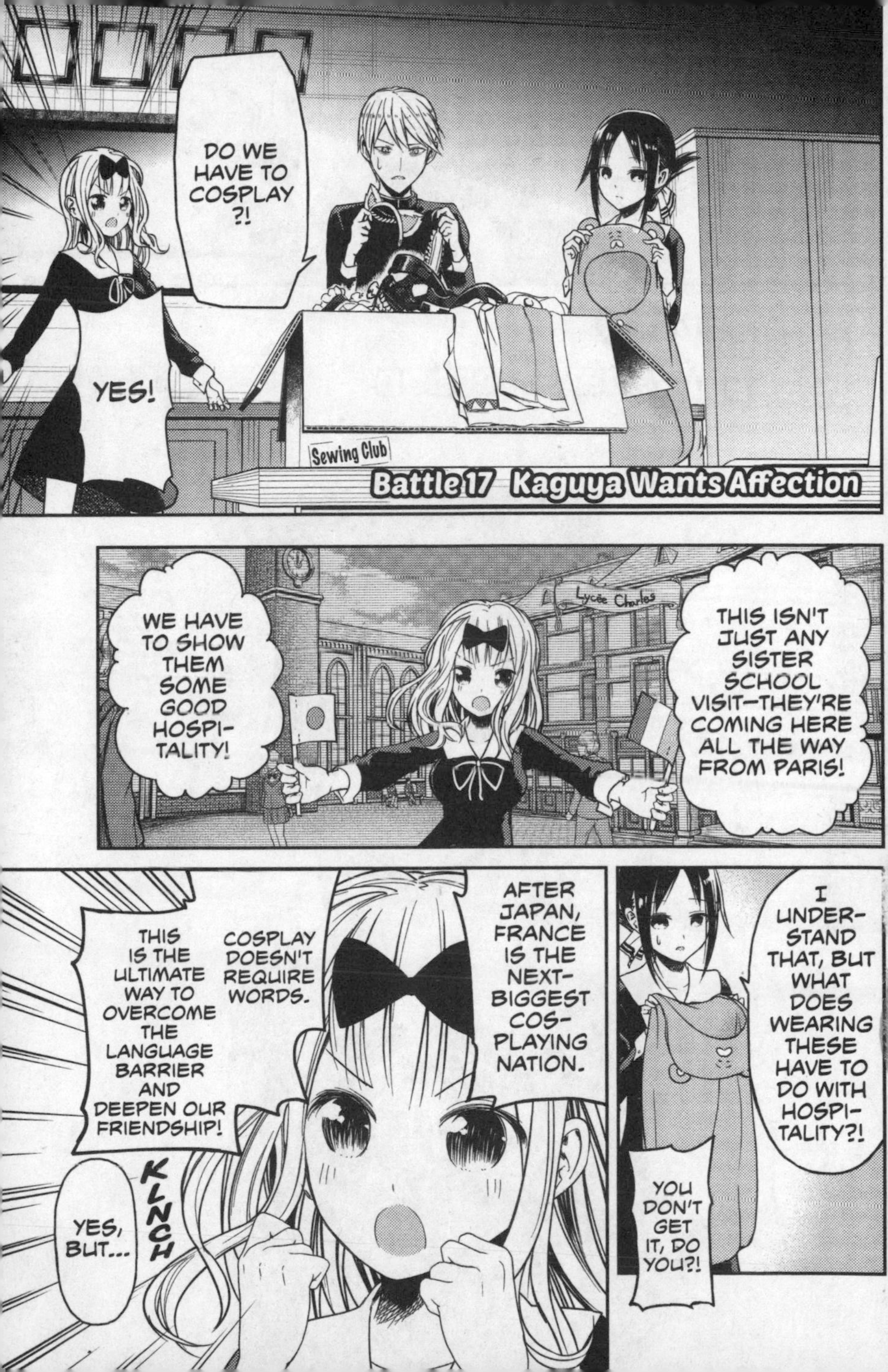
DO WE HAVE TO COSPLAY?!
YES!
Sewing Club
Battle 17 Kaguya Wants Affection
THIS ISN'T JUST ANY SISTER SCHOOL VISIT—THEY'RE COMING HERE ALL THE WAY FROM PARIS!
Lycée Charles
WE HAVE TO SHOW THEM SOME GOOD HOSPITALITY!
I UNDERSTAND THAT, BUT WHAT DOES WEARING THESE HAVE TO DO WITH HOSPITALITY?!
YOU DON'T GET IT, DO YOU?!
AFTER JAPAN, FRANCE IS THE NEXT-BIGGEST COSPLAYING NATION.
COSPLAY DOESN'T REQUIRE WORDS.
THIS IS THE ULTIMATE WAY TO OVERCOME THE LANGUAGE BARRIER AND DEEPEN OUR FRIENDSHIP!
KLNCH
YES, BUT...

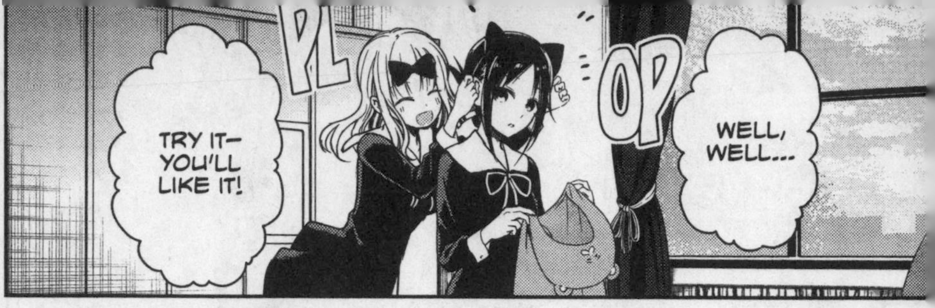
WELL, WELL...
PLOP
TRY IT— YOU'LL LIKE IT!

Battle 17 Kaguya Wants Affection

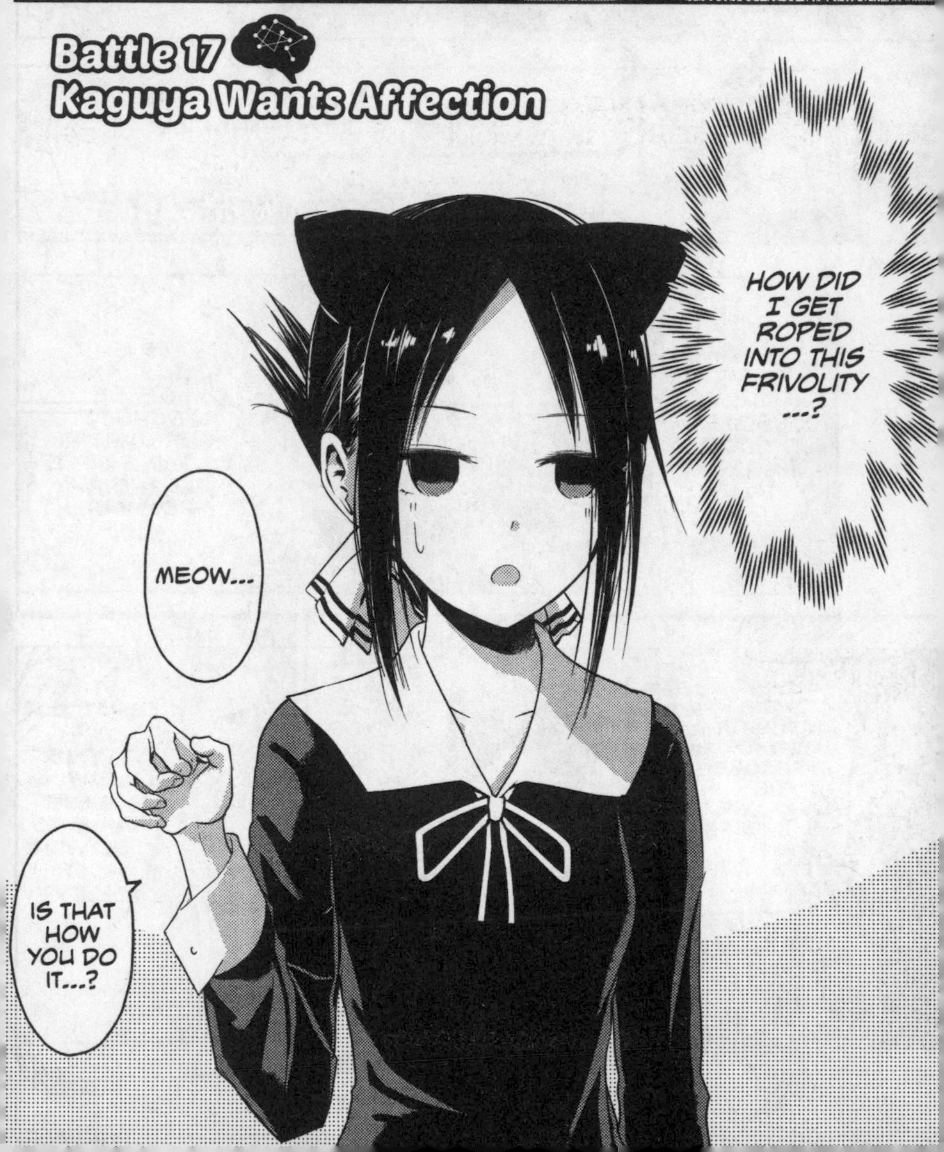
HOW DID I GET ROPED INTO THIS FRIVOLITY ...?
MEOW...
IS THAT HOW YOU DO IT...?

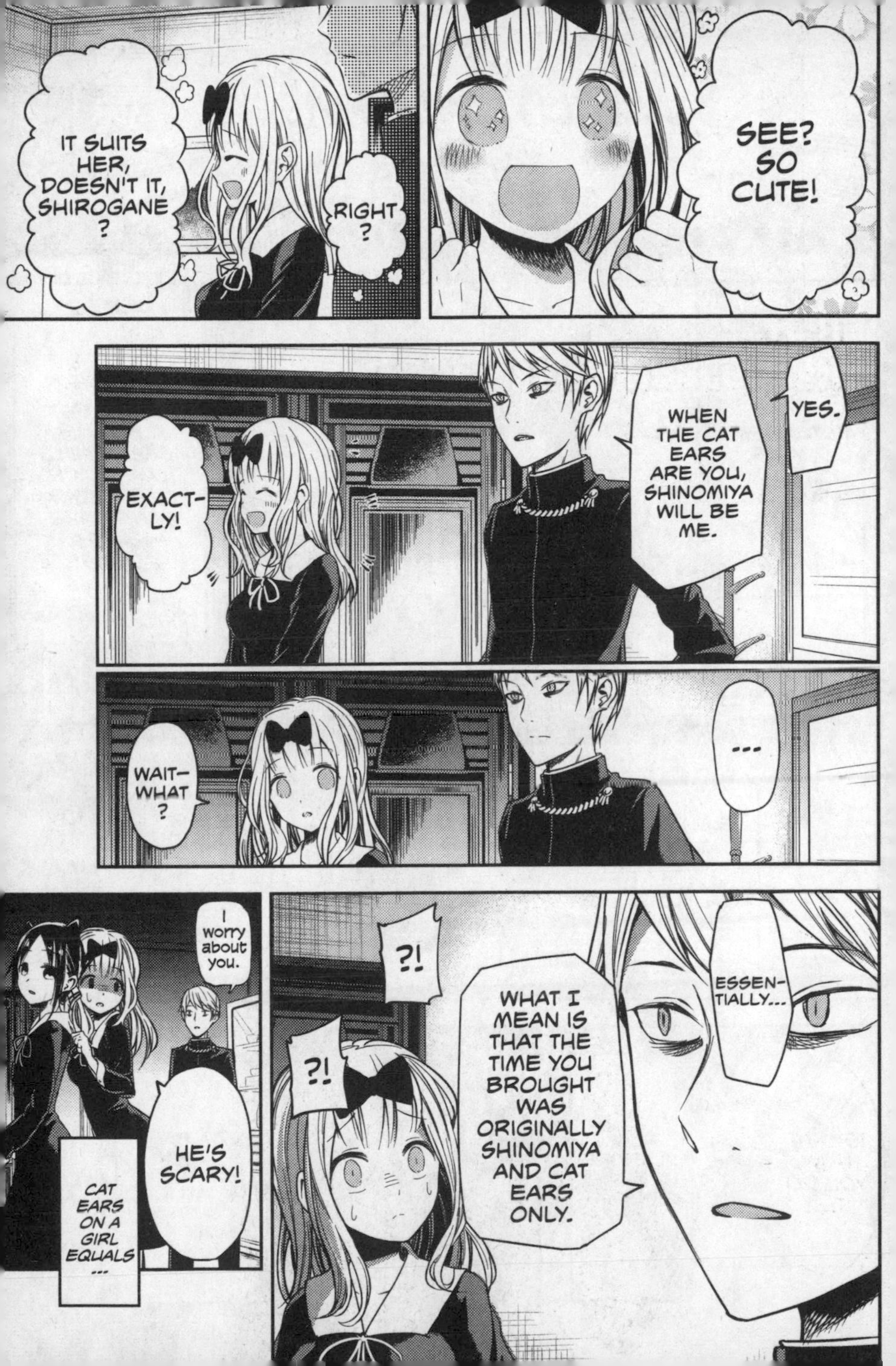
SEE? SO CUTE!
IT SUITS HER, DOESN'T IT, SHIROGANE?
RIGHT?
YES.
WHEN THE CAT EARS ARE YOU, SHINOMIYA WILL BE ME.
EXACTLY!
...
WAIT—WHAT?
ESSENTIALLY...
?!
WHAT I MEAN IS THAT THE TIME YOU BROUGHT WAS ORIGINALLY SHINOMIYA AND CAT EARS ONLY.
?!
I worry about you.
HE'S SCARY!
CAT EARS ON A GIRL EQUALS...

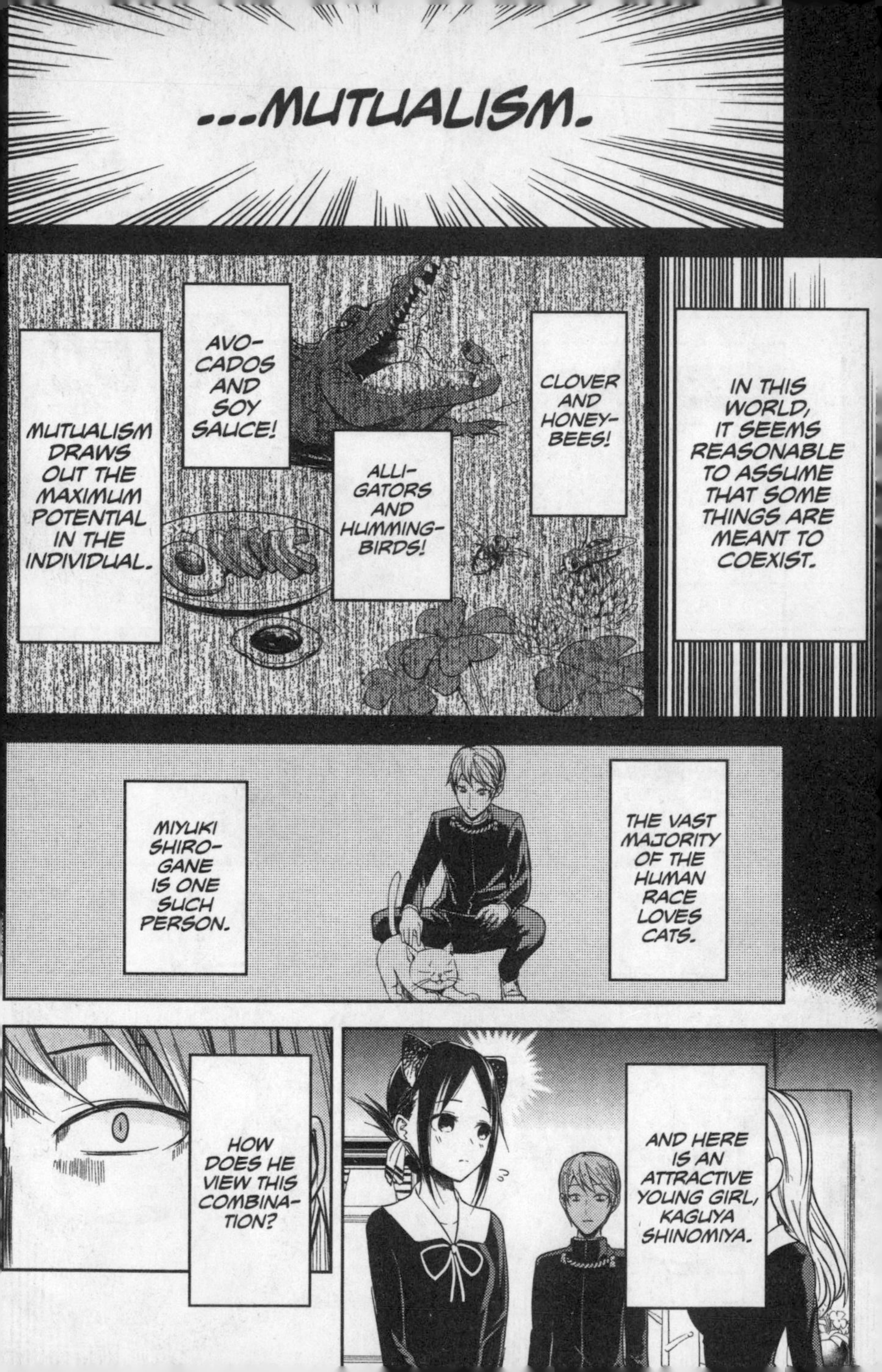
...MUTUALISM.
IN THIS WORLD, IT SEEMS REASONABLE TO ASSUME THAT SOME THINGS ARE MEANT TO COEXIST.
CLOVER AND HONEY-BEES!
ALLI-GATORS AND HUMMING-BIRDS!
AVO-CADOS AND SOY SAUCE!
MUTUALISM DRAWS OUT THE MAXIMUM POTENTIAL IN THE INDIVIDUAL.
THE VAST MAJORITY OF THE HUMAN RACE LOVES CATS.
MIYUKI SHIRO-GANE IS ONE SUCH PERSON.
AND HERE IS AN ATTRACTIVE YOUNG GIRL, KAGUYA SHINOMIYA.
HOW DOES HE VIEW THIS COMBINA-TION?

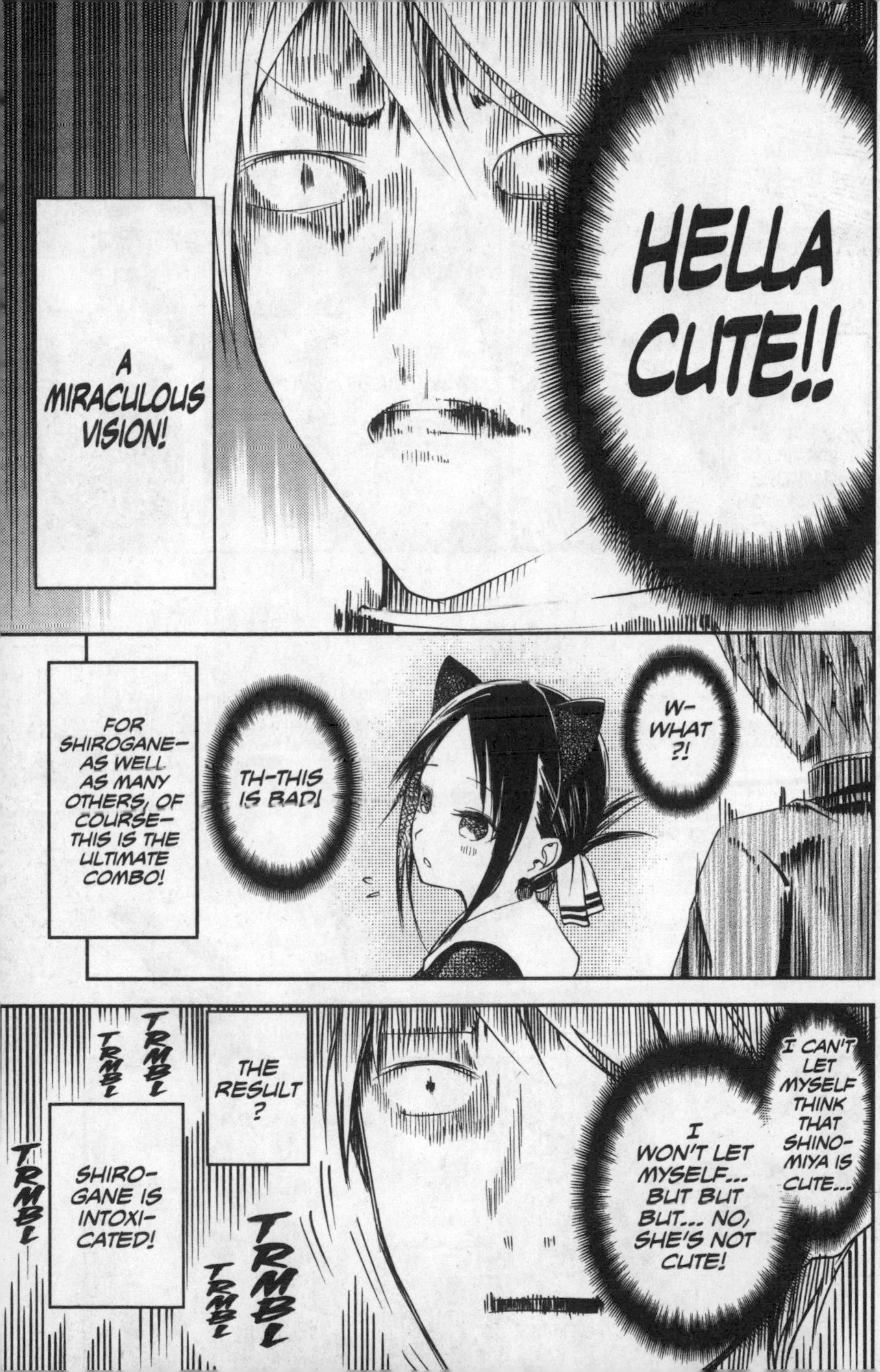
HELLA CUTE!!
A MIRACULOUS VISION!
W-WHAT?!
TH-THIS IS BAD!
FOR SHIROGANE—AS WELL AS MANY OTHERS, OF COURSE—THIS IS THE ULTIMATE COMBO!
I CAN'T LET MYSELF THINK THAT SHINOMIYA IS CUTE...
I WON'T LET MYSELF... BUT BUT BUT... NO, SHE'S NOT CUTE!
TRMBL TRMBL
THE RESULT?
TRMBL
TRMBL
TRMBL
TRMBL
SHIROGANE IS INTOXICATED!

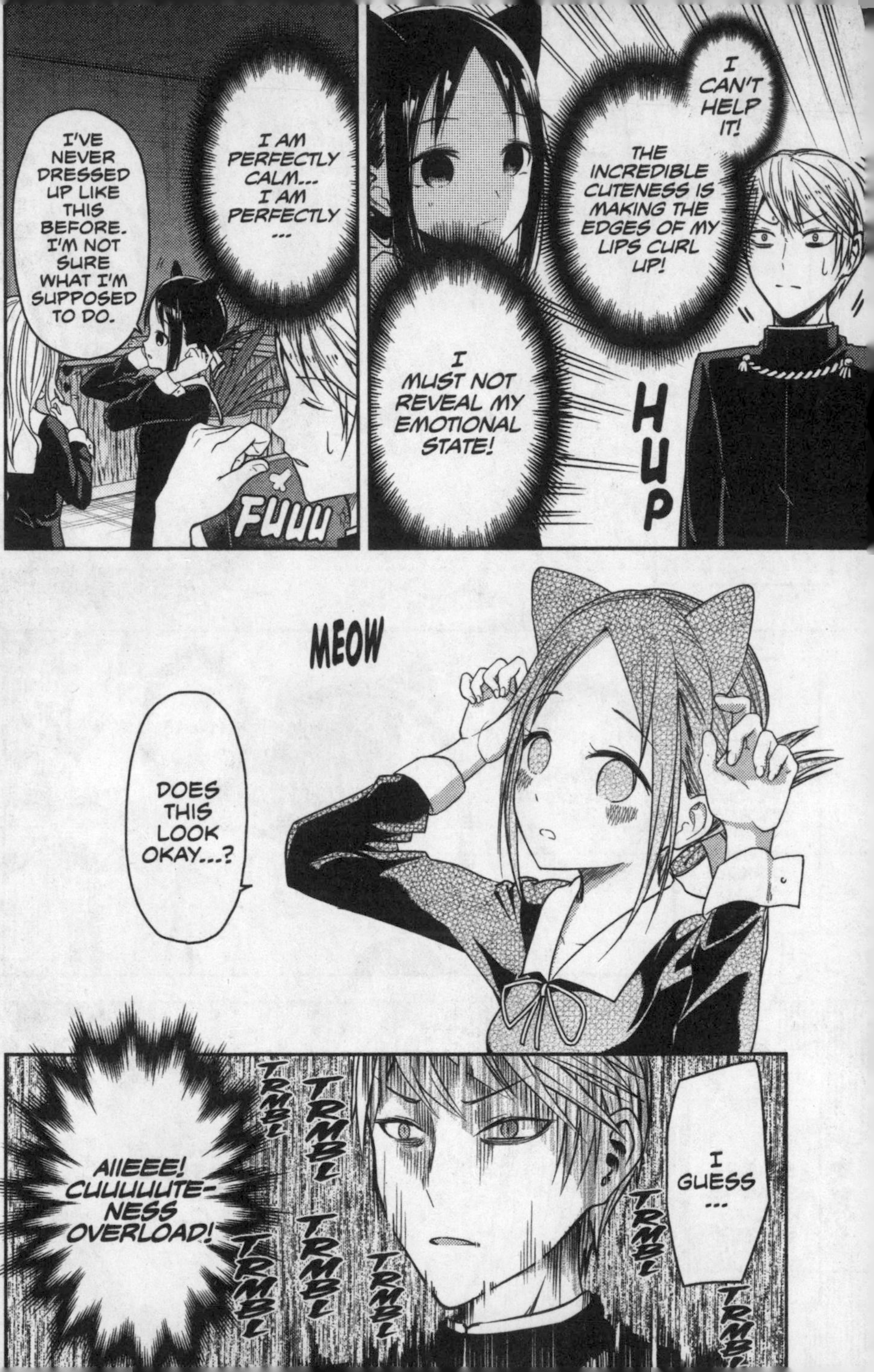
I CAN'T HELP IT!
THE INCREDIBLE CUTENESS IS MAKING THE EDGES OF MY LIPS CURL UP!
HUP HUP
I MUST NOT REVEAL MY EMOTIONAL STATE!
I AM PERFECTLY CALM... I AM PERFECTLY ...
I'VE NEVER DRESSED UP LIKE THIS BEFORE. I'M NOT SURE WHAT I'M SUPPOSED TO DO.
FUUU
MEOW
DOES THIS LOOK OKAY...?
I GUESS ...
TRMBL TRMBL TRMBL TRMBL TRMBL TRMBL TRMBL TRMBL
AIIEEE! CUUUUUTE-NESS OVERLOAD!

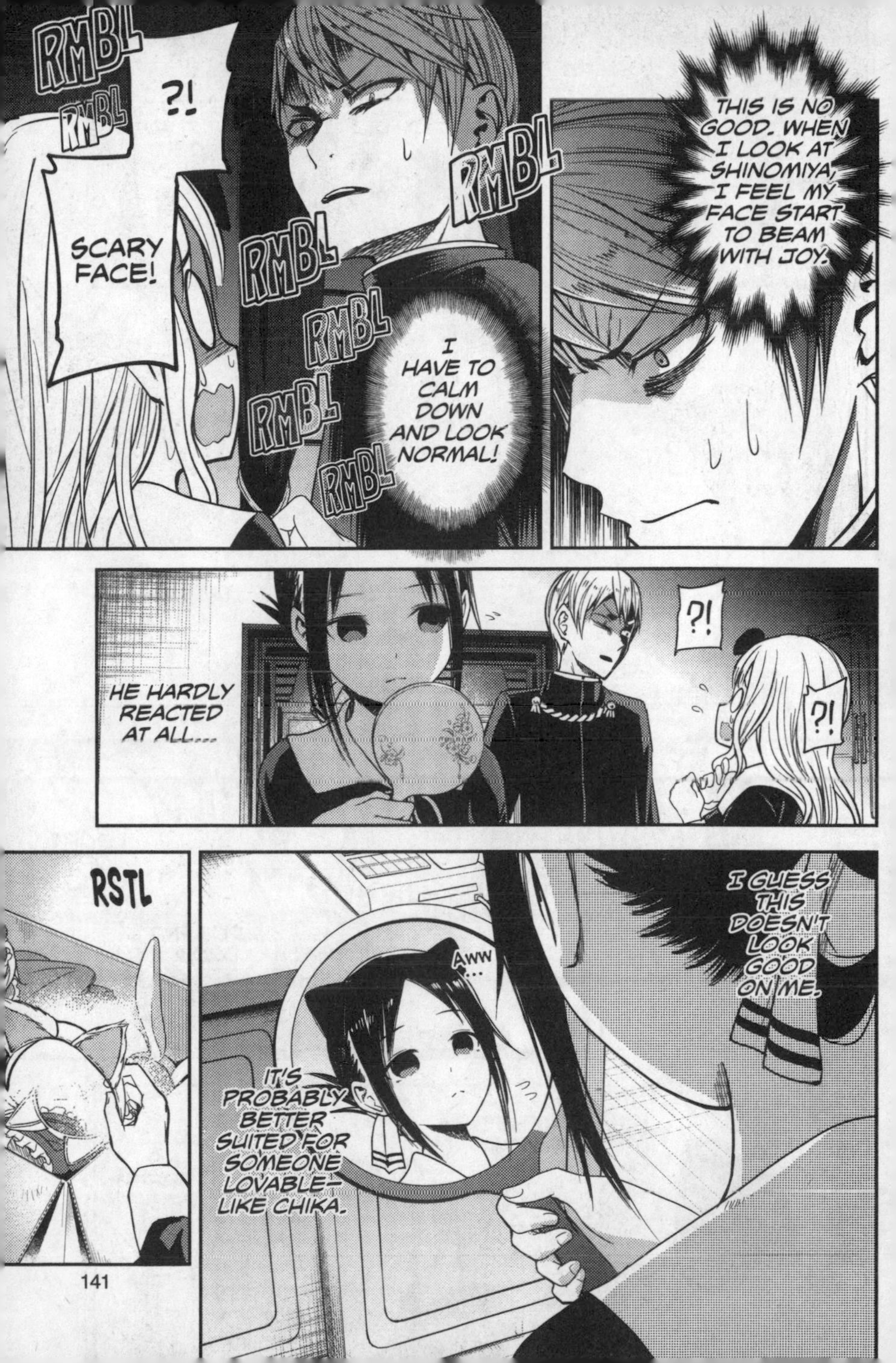
THIS IS NO GOOD. WHEN I LOOK AT SHINOMIYA, I FEEL MY FACE START TO BEAM WITH JOY.
RMBL
RMBL
I HAVE TO CALM DOWN AND LOOK NORMAL!
RMBL
RMBL
RMBL
RMBL
RMBL
?!
SCARY FACE!
?!
?!
HE HARDLY REACTED AT ALL...
I GUESS THIS DOESN'T LOOK GOOD ON ME.
AWW...
IT'S PROBABLY BETTER SUITED FOR SOMEONE LOVABLE— LIKE CHIKA.
RSTL

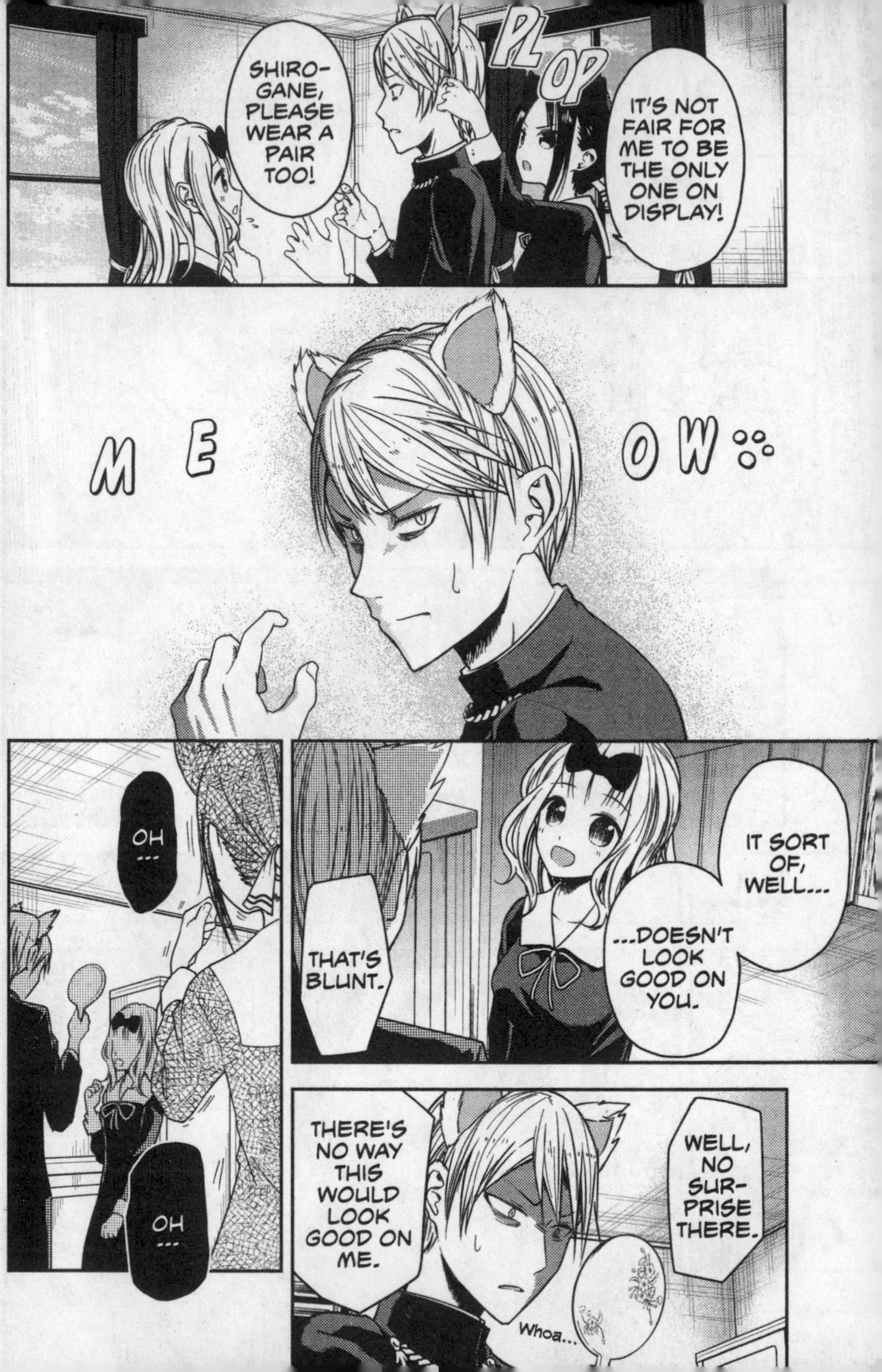
IT'S NOT FAIR FOR ME TO BE THE ONLY ONE ON DISPLAY!
PLOP
SHIRO-GANE, PLEASE WEAR A PAIR TOO!
M E OW
IT SORT OF, WELL...
...DOESN'T LOOK GOOD ON YOU.
THAT'S BLUNT.
WELL, NO SUR-PRISE THERE.
THERE'S NO WAY THIS WOULD LOOK GOOD ON ME.
Whoa...
OH...
OH...

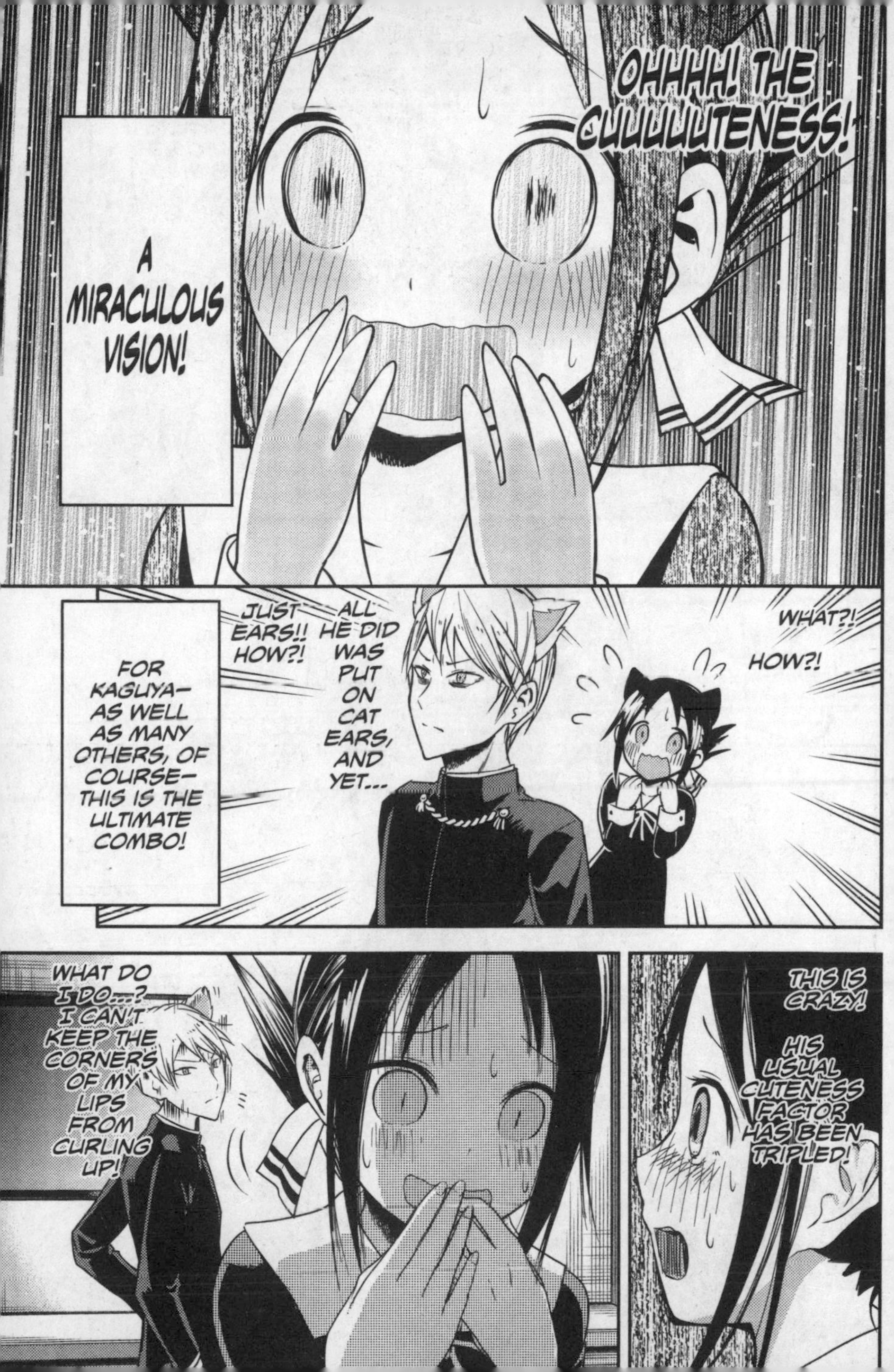
OHHHH! THE CUUUUUTENESS!
A MIRACULOUS VISION!
WHAT?!
HOW?!
ALL HE DID WAS PUT ON CAT EARS, AND YET...
JUST EARS!! HOW?!
FOR KAGUYA—AS WELL AS MANY OTHERS, OF COURSE—THIS IS THE ULTIMATE COMBO!
THIS IS CRAZY!
HIS USUAL CUTENESS FACTOR HAS BEEN TRIPLED!
WHAT DO I DO...? I CAN'T KEEP THE CORNERS OF MY LIPS FROM CURLING UP!

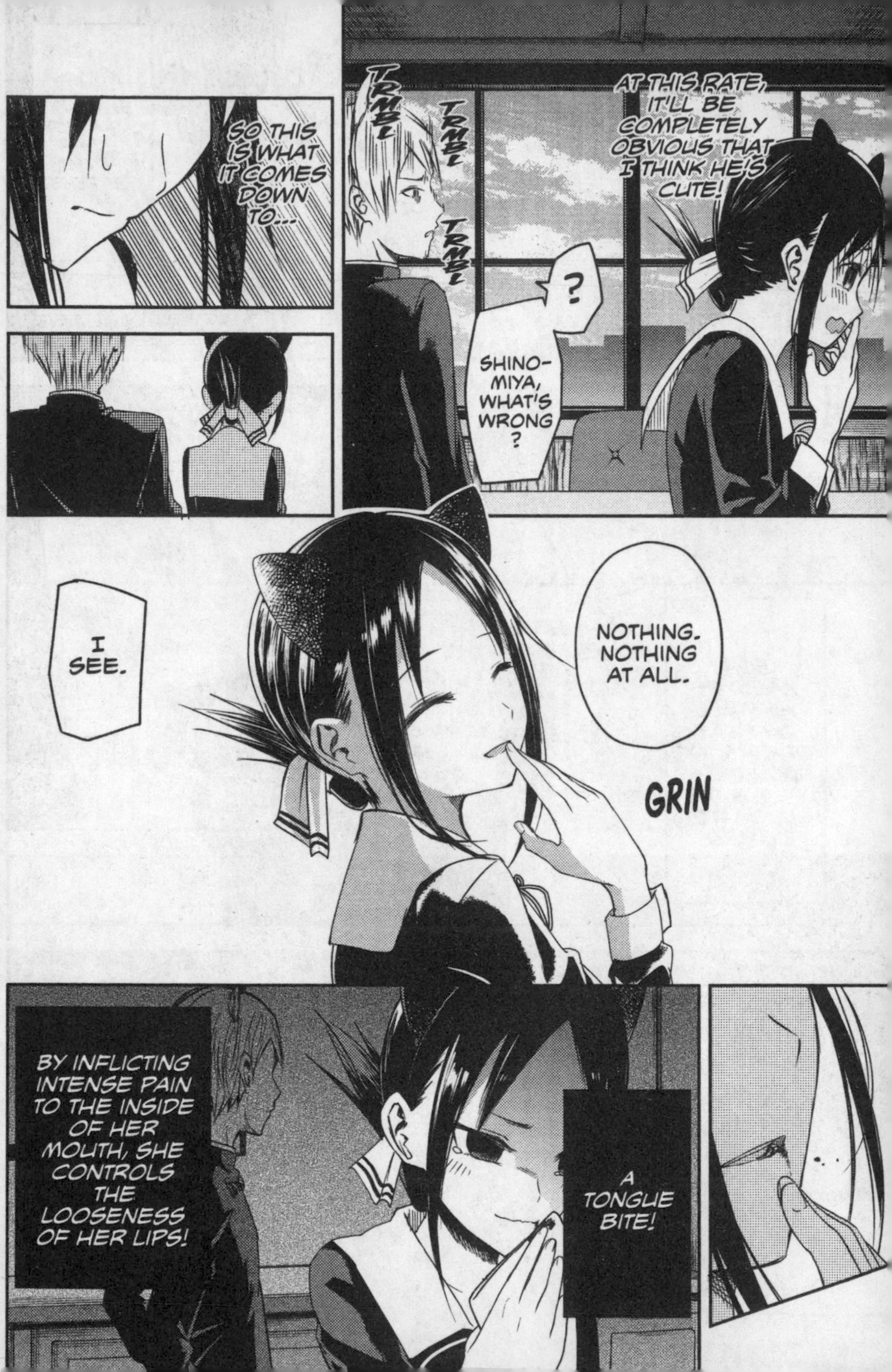
AT THIS RATE, IT'LL BE COMPLETELY OBVIOUS THAT I THINK HE'S CUTE!
TRMBL TRMBL TRMBL TRMBL
?
SHINO-MIYA, WHAT'S WRONG?
SO THIS IS WHAT IT COMES DOWN TO...
NOTHING. NOTHING AT ALL.
GRIN
I SEE.
BY INFLICTING INTENSE PAIN TO THE INSIDE OF HER MOUTH, SHE CONTROLS THE LOOSENESS OF HER LIPS!
A TONGUE BITE!

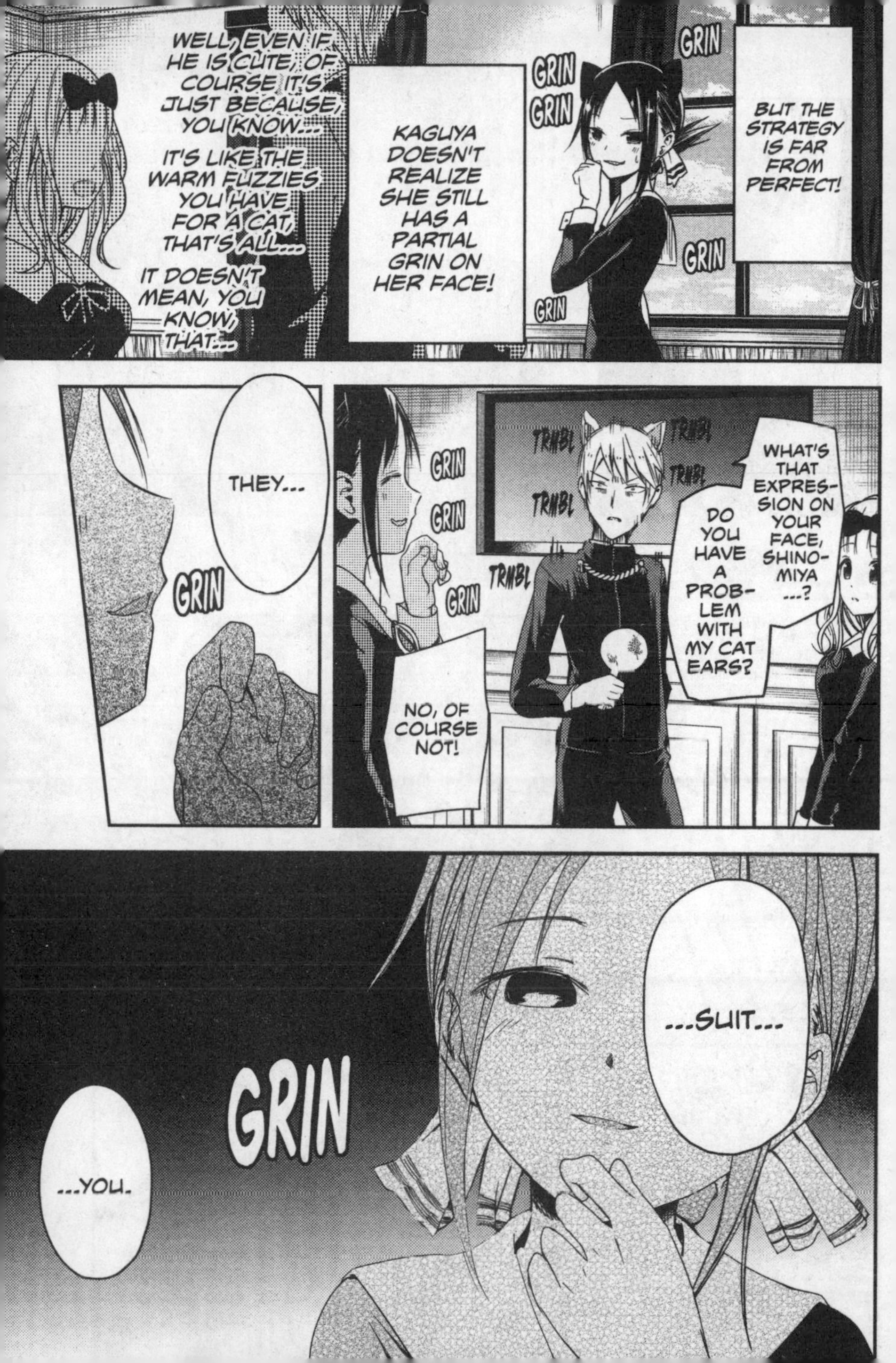
GRIN
BUT THE STRATEGY IS FAR FROM PERFECT!
GRIN
GRIN
GRIN
GRIN
KAGUYA DOESN'T REALIZE SHE STILL HAS A PARTIAL GRIN ON HER FACE!
WELL, EVEN IF HE IS CUTE, OF COURSE IT'S JUST BECAUSE, YOU KNOW...
IT'S LIKE THE WARM FUZZIES YOU HAVE FOR A CAT, THAT'S ALL...
IT DOESN'T MEAN, YOU KNOW, THAT...
WHAT'S THAT EXPRESSION ON YOUR FACE, SHINOMIYA...?
DO YOU HAVE A PROBLEM WITH MY CAT EARS?
TRMBL
TRMBL
TRMBL
TRMBL
TRMBL
GRIN
GRIN
GRIN
NO, OF COURSE NOT!
THEY...
GRIN
...SUIT...
GRIN
...YOU.

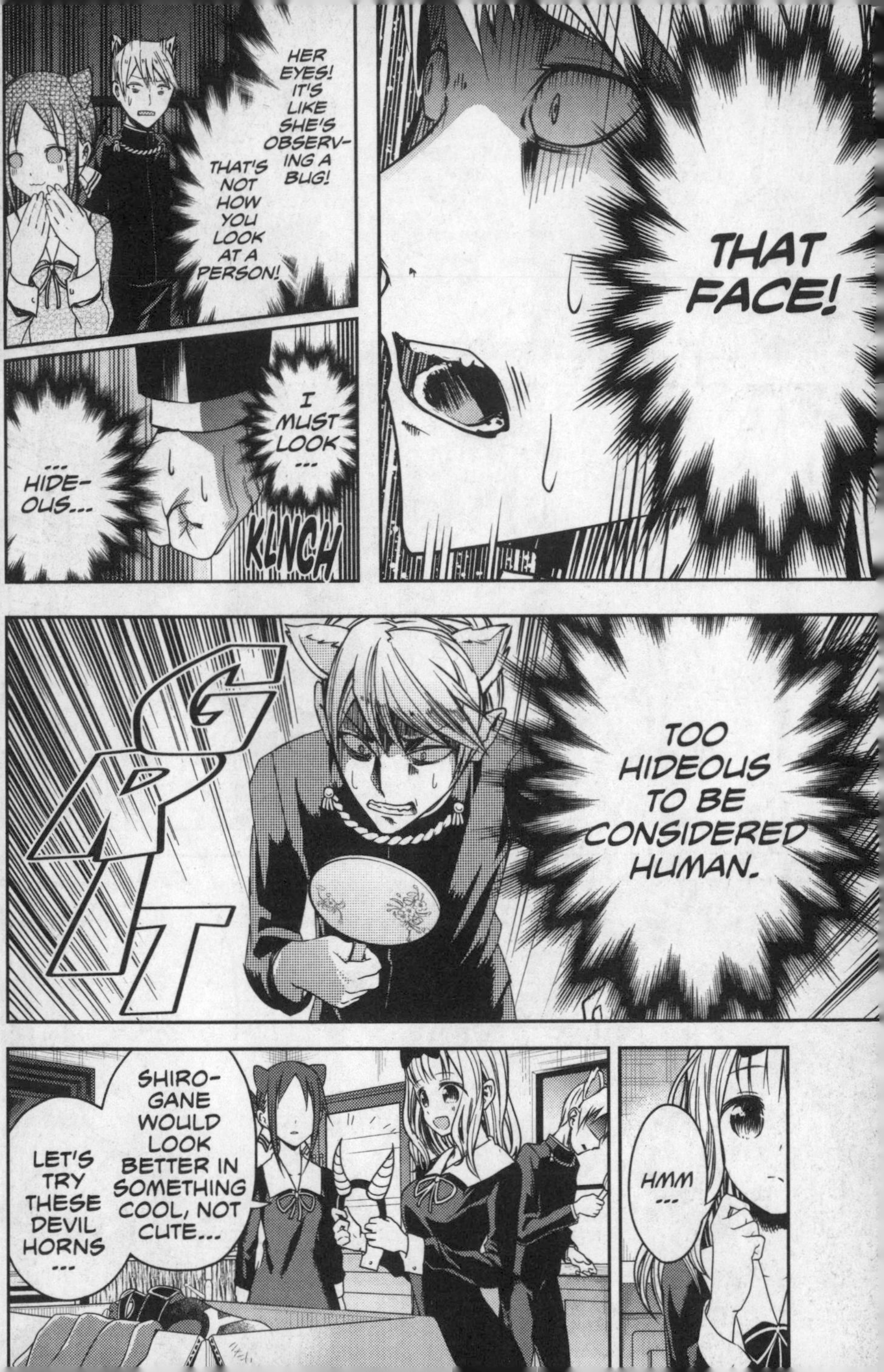
THAT FACE!
HER EYES! IT'S LIKE SHE'S OBSERV-ING A BUG!
THAT'S NOT HOW YOU LOOK AT A PERSON!
I MUST LOOK...
...HIDE-OUS...
KLNCH
TOO HIDEOUS TO BE CONSIDERED HUMAN.
HMM...
SHIRO-GANE WOULD LOOK BETTER IN SOMETHING COOL, NOT CUTE...
LET'S TRY THESE DEVIL HORNS...

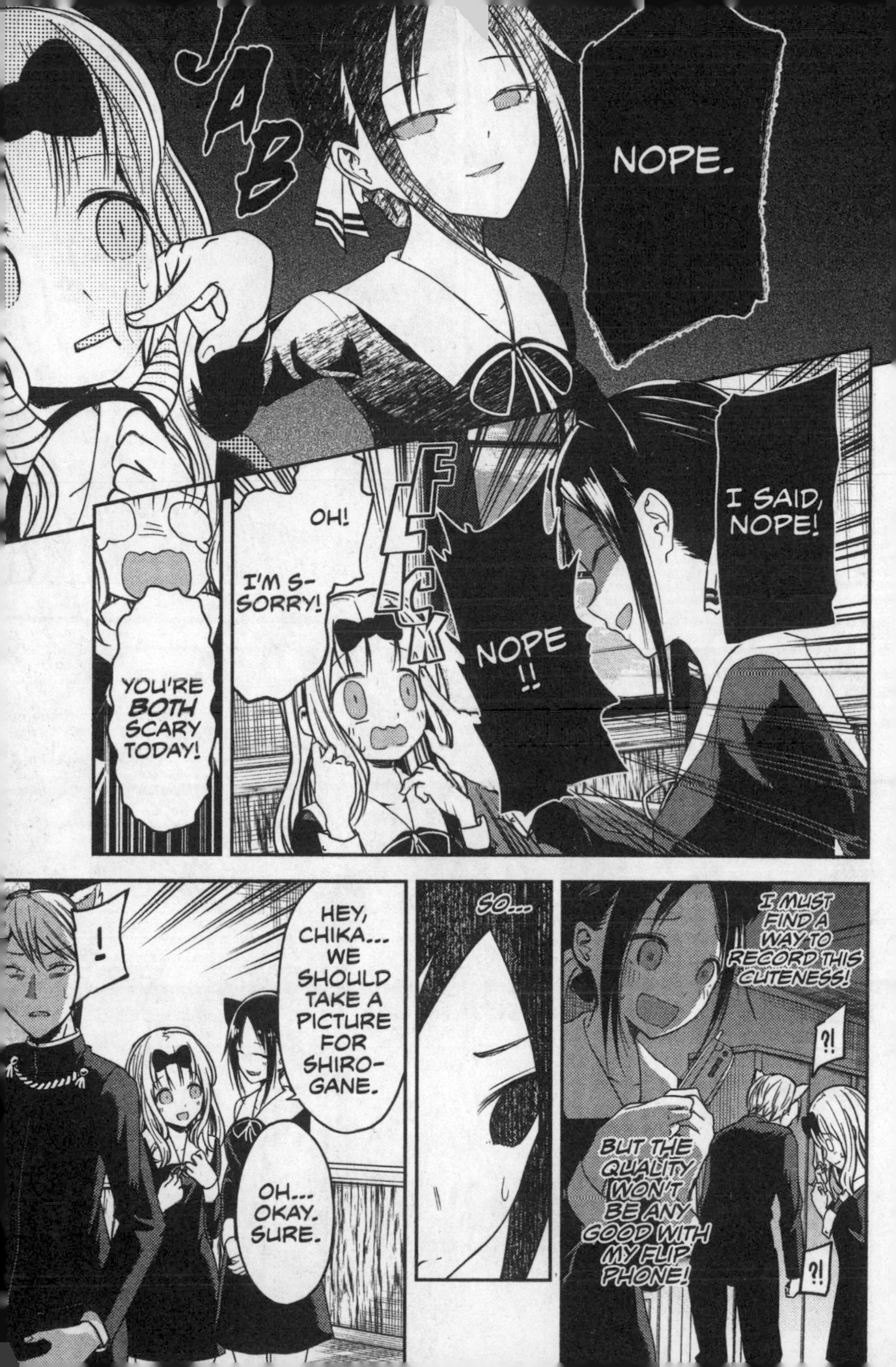
NOPE.
JAB
I SAID, NOPE!
NOPE !!
FLICK
OH!
I'M S-SORRY!
YOU'RE BOTH SCARY TODAY!
I MUST FIND A WAY TO RECORD THIS CUTENESS!
?!
BUT THE QUALITY WON'T BE ANY GOOD WITH MY FLIP PHONE!
?!
SO...
!
HEY, CHIKA... WE SHOULD TAKE A PICTURE FOR SHIRO-GANE.
OH... OKAY. SURE.

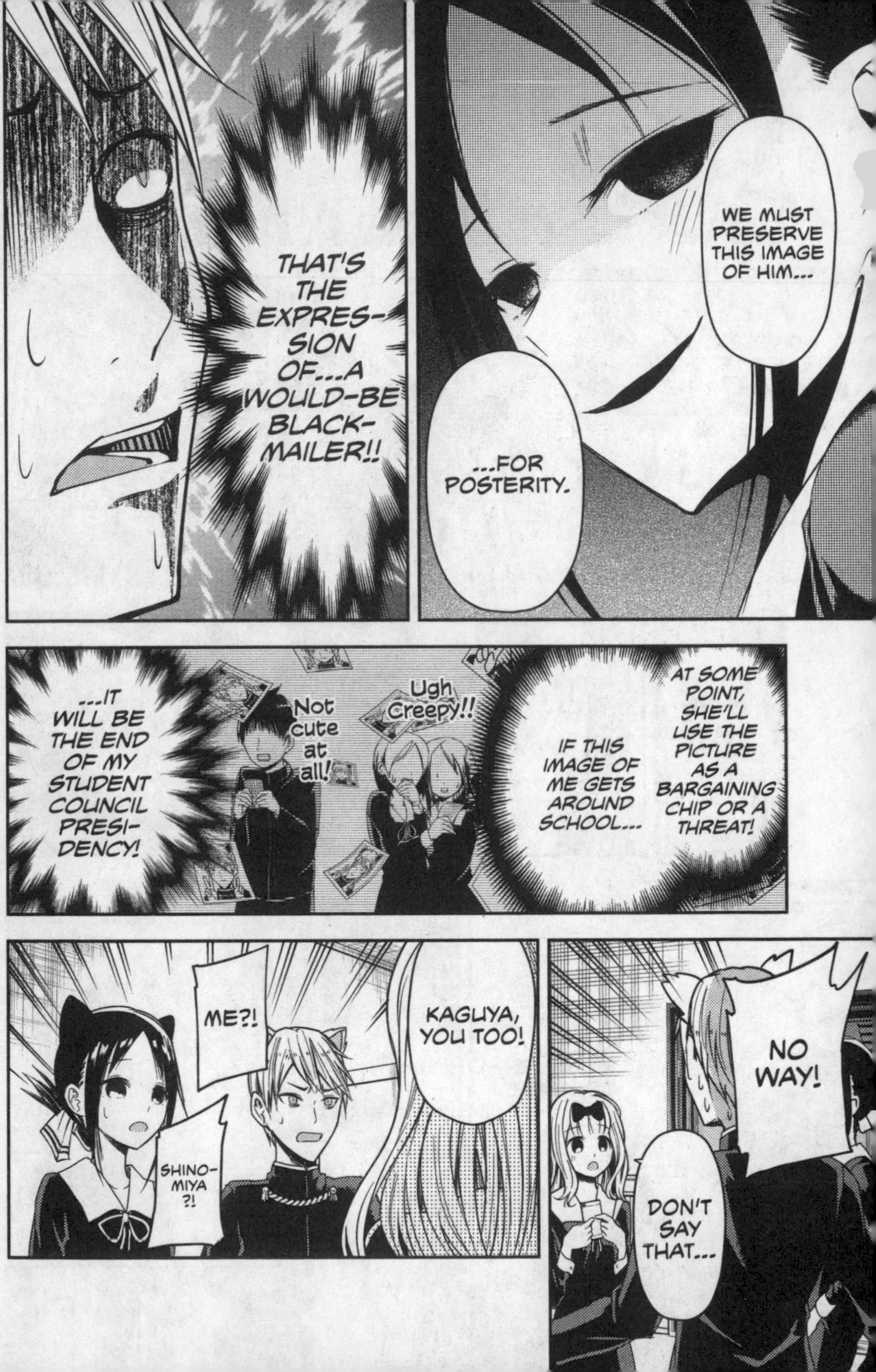
WE MUST PRESERVE THIS IMAGE OF HIM...
...FOR POSTERITY.
THAT'S THE EXPRESSION OF...A WOULD-BE BLACKMAILER!!
AT SOME POINT, SHE'LL USE THE PICTURE AS A BARGAINING CHIP OR A THREAT!
IF THIS IMAGE OF ME GETS AROUND SCHOOL...
Ugh Creepy!!
Not cute at all!
...IT WILL BE THE END OF MY STUDENT COUNCIL PRESIDENCY!
NO WAY!
DON'T SAY THAT...
KAGUYA, YOU TOO!
ME?!
SHINOMIYA?!

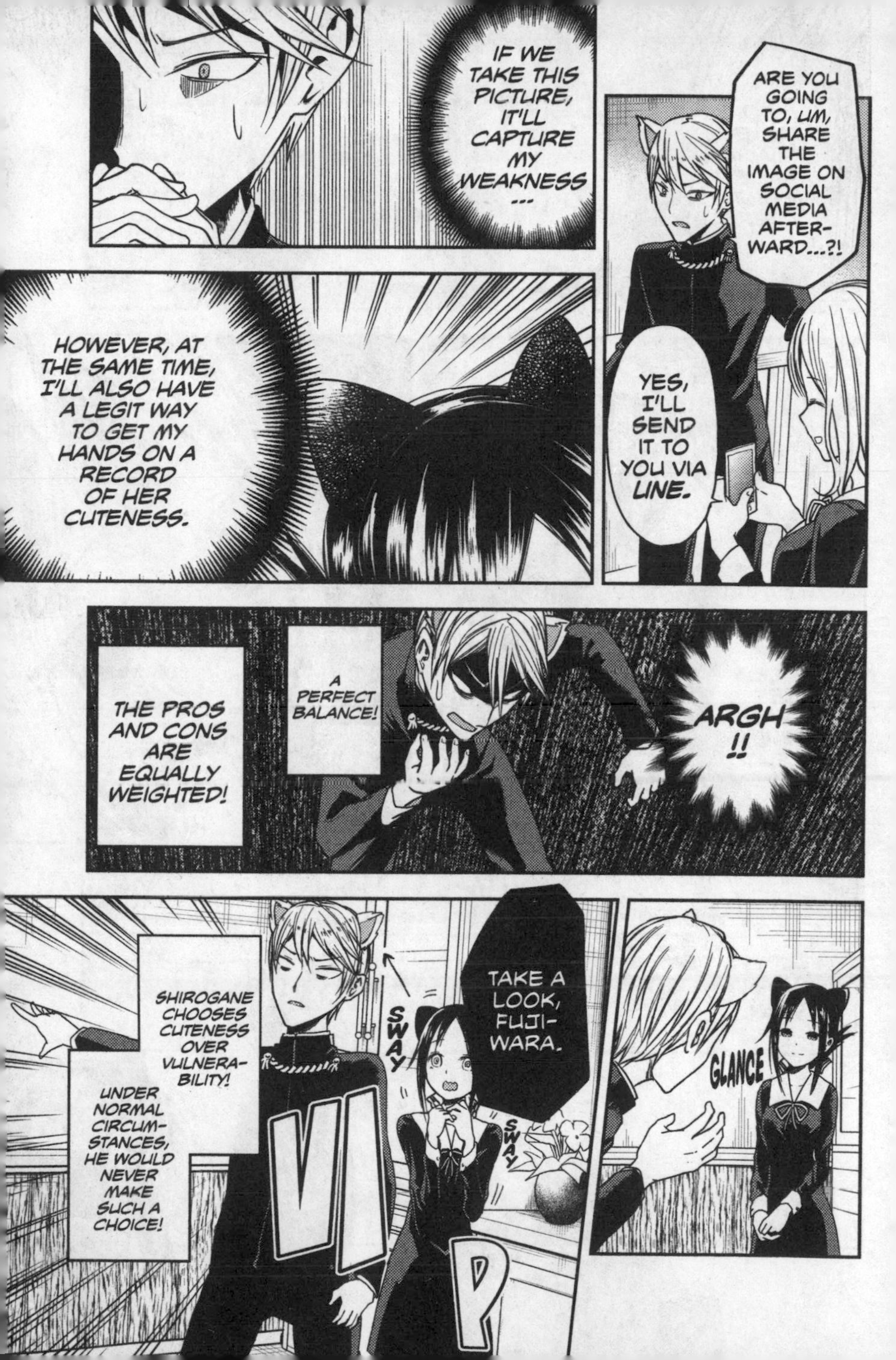
ARE YOU GOING TO, UM, SHARE THE IMAGE ON SOCIAL MEDIA AFTER-WARD...?!
YES, I'LL SEND IT TO YOU VIA LINE.
IF WE TAKE THIS PICTURE, IT'LL CAPTURE MY WEAKNESS...
HOWEVER, AT THE SAME TIME, I'LL ALSO HAVE A LEGIT WAY TO GET MY HANDS ON A RECORD OF HER CUTENESS.
ARGH!!
A PERFECT BALANCE!
THE PROS AND CONS ARE EQUALLY WEIGHTED!
GLANCE
TAKE A LOOK, FUJI-WARA.
SWAY
SWAY
SHIROGANE CHOOSES CUTENESS OVER VULNERA-BILITY!
UNDER NORMAL CIRCUM-STANCES, HE WOULD NEVER MAKE SUCH A CHOICE!
VIP

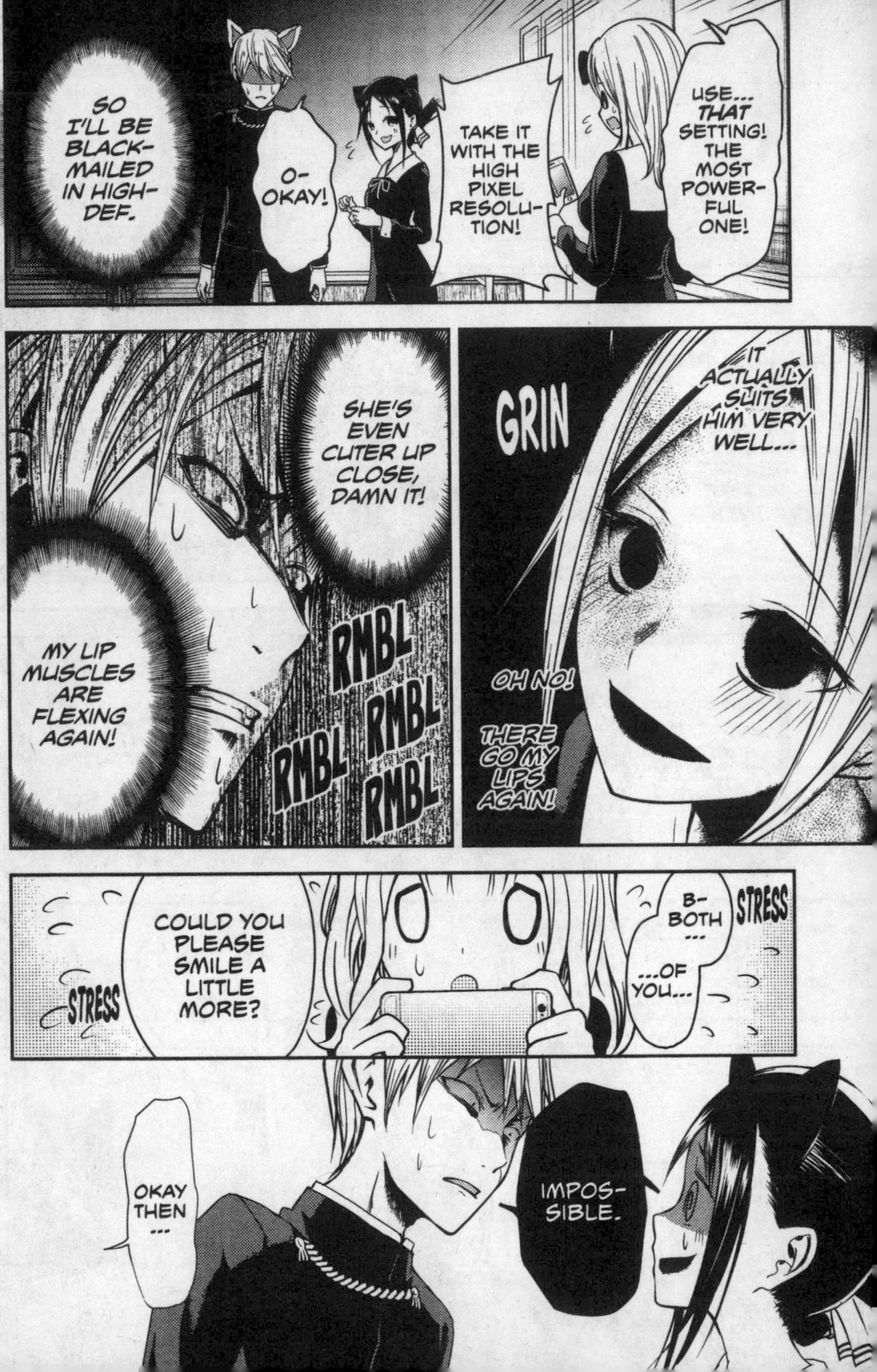
USE... THAT SETTING! THE MOST POWERFUL ONE!
TAKE IT WITH THE HIGH PIXEL RESOLUTION!
O-OKAY!
SO I'LL BE BLACKMAILED IN HIGH-DEF.
IT ACTUALLY SUITS HIM VERY WELL...
GRIN
OH NO! THERE GO MY LIPS AGAIN!
SHE'S EVEN CUTER UP CLOSE, DAMN IT!
RMBL RMBL RMBL RMBL
MY LIP MUSCLES ARE FLEXING AGAIN!
STRESS
B-BOTH... ...OF YOU...
COULD YOU PLEASE SMILE A LITTLE MORE?
STRESS
IMPOSSIBLE.
OKAY THEN...

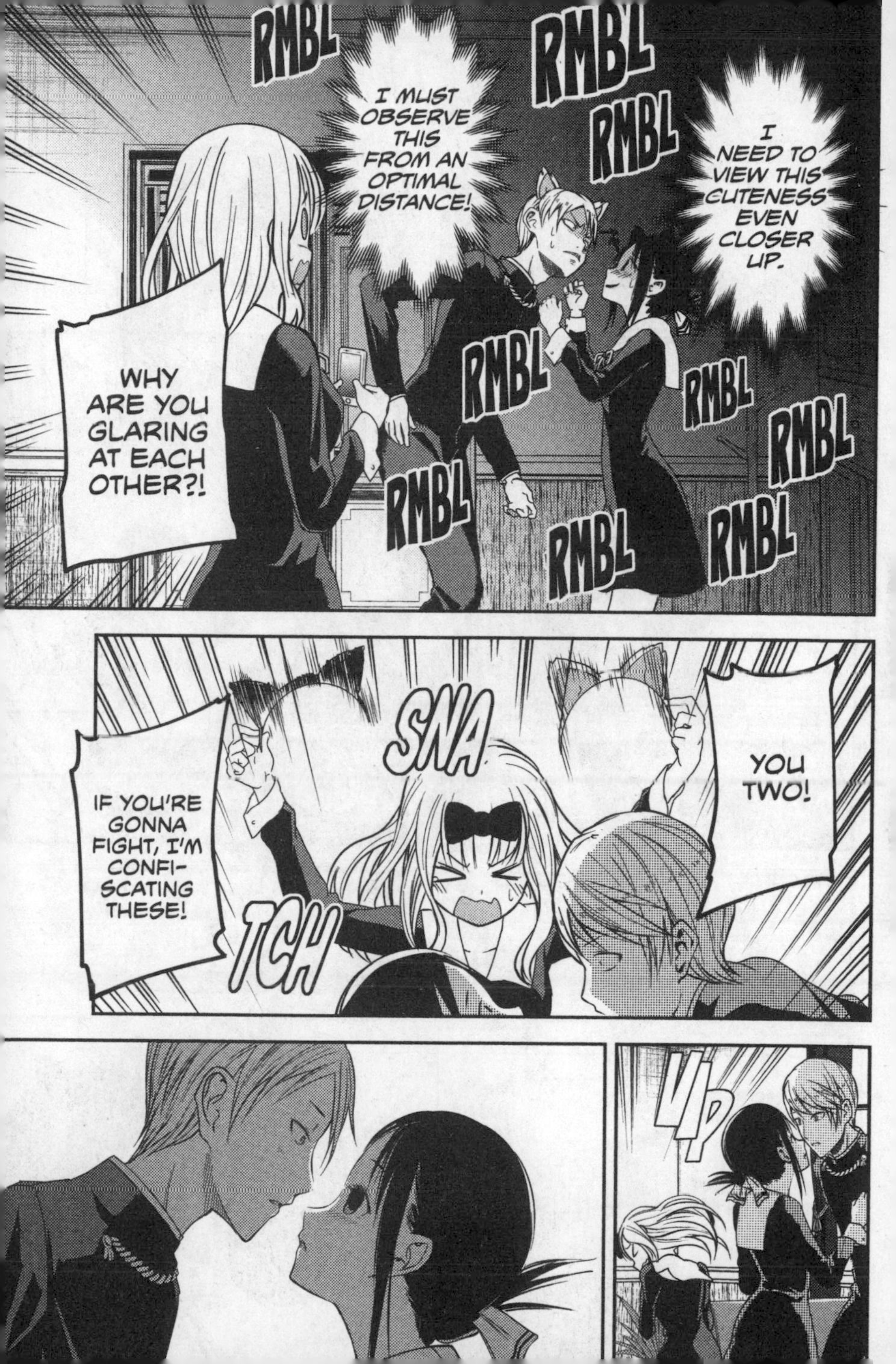
RMBL
RMBL
I NEED TO VIEW THIS CUTENESS EVEN CLOSER UP.
RMBL
I MUST OBSERVE THIS FROM AN OPTIMAL DISTANCE!
RMBL
RMBL
RMBL
RMBL
RMBL
RMBL
WHY ARE YOU GLARING AT EACH OTHER?!
YOU TWO!
SNA
TCH
IF YOU'RE GONNA FIGHT, I'M CONFI-SCATING THESE!
VIP

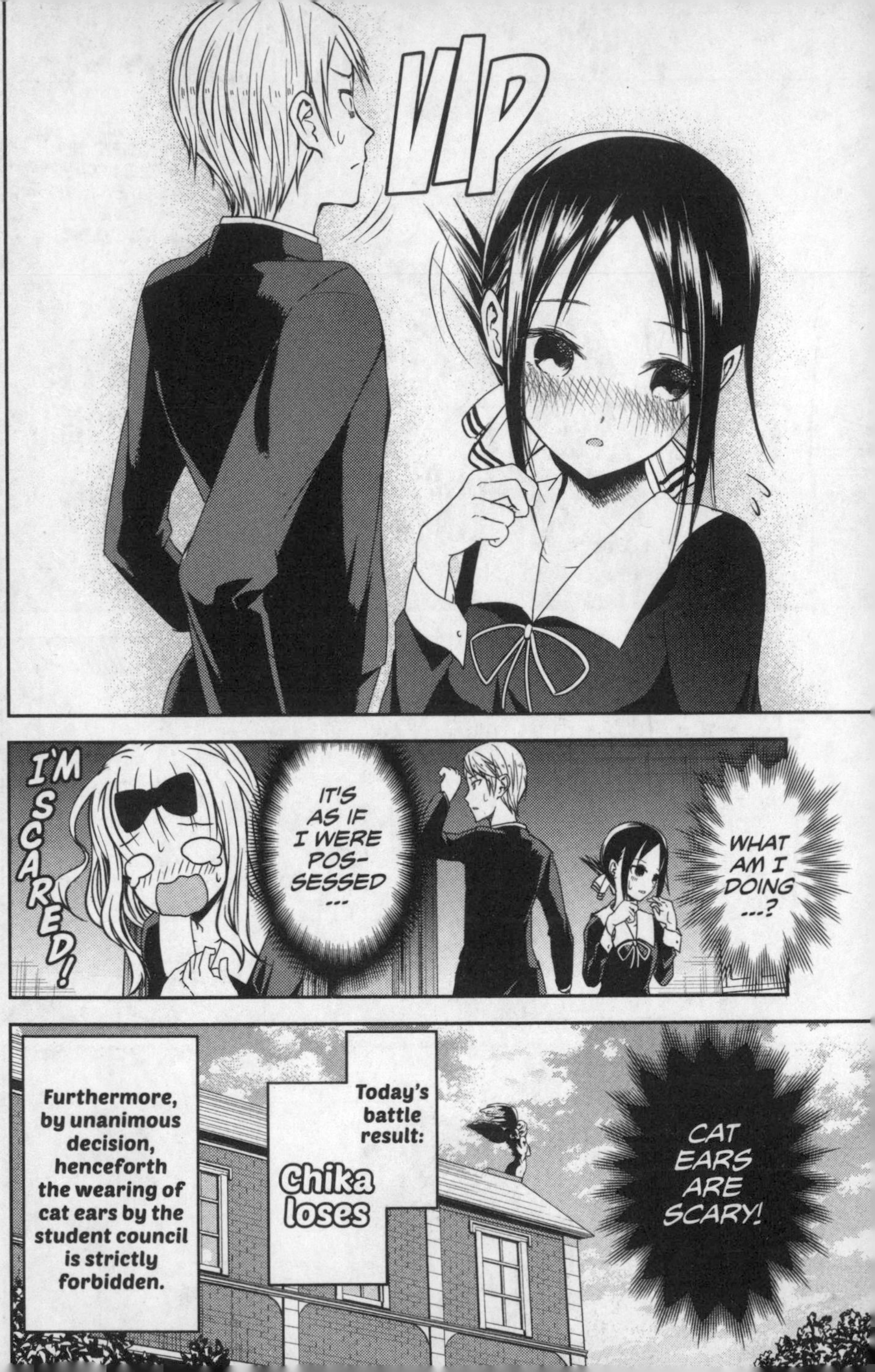
VIP
WHAT AM I DOING ---?
IT'S AS IF I WERE POS- SESSED ---
I'M SCARED!
CAT EARS ARE SCARY!
Today's battle result:
Chika loses
Furthermore, by unanimous decision, henceforth the wearing of cat ears by the student council is strictly forbidden.

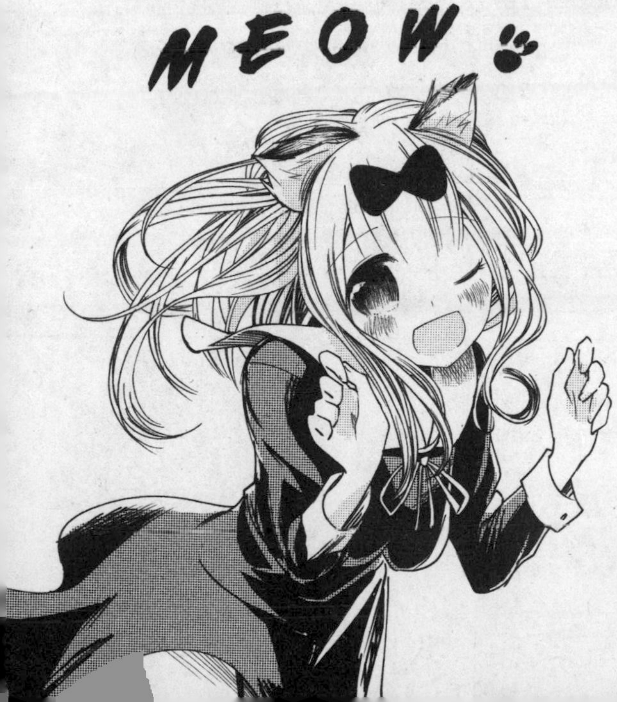
MEOW

KAGUYA-SAMA
LOVE IS WAR

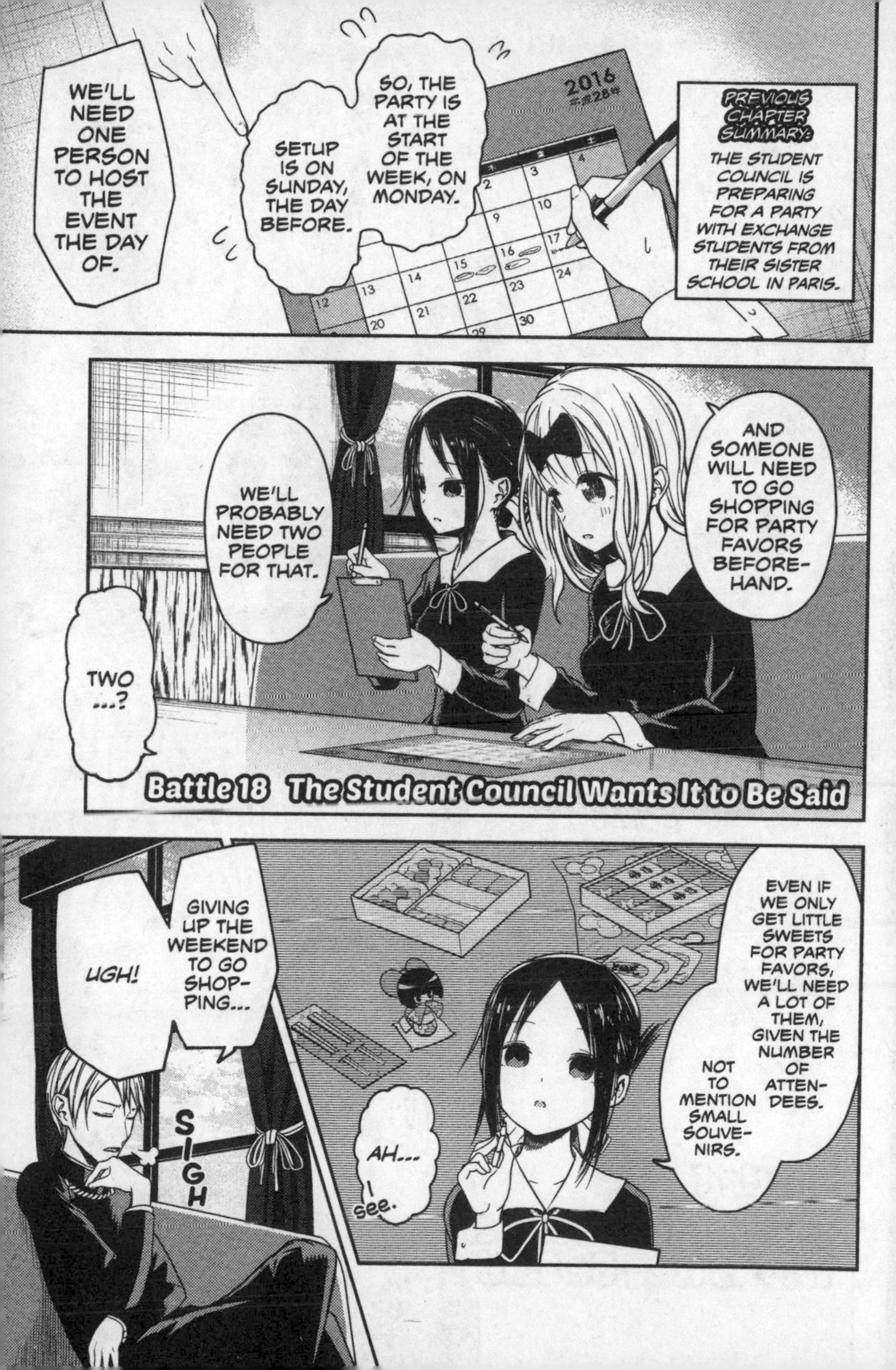
PREVIOUS CHAPTER SUMMARY: THE STUDENT COUNCIL IS PREPARING FOR A PARTY WITH EXCHANGE STUDENTS FROM THEIR SISTER SCHOOL IN PARIS.
2016
SO, THE PARTY IS AT THE START OF THE WEEK, ON MONDAY.
SETUP IS ON SUNDAY, THE DAY BEFORE.
WE'LL NEED ONE PERSON TO HOST THE EVENT THE DAY OF.
AND SOMEONE WILL NEED TO GO SHOPPING FOR PARTY FAVORS BEFORE-HAND.
WE'LL PROBABLY NEED TWO PEOPLE FOR THAT.
TWO ...?
Battle 18 The Student Council Wants It to Be Said
EVEN IF WE ONLY GET LITTLE SWEETS FOR PARTY FAVORS, WE'LL NEED A LOT OF THEM, GIVEN THE NUMBER OF ATTEN-DEES.
NOT TO MENTION SMALL SOUVE-NIRS.
AH... I see.
GIVING UP THE WEEKEND TO GO SHOP-PING...
UGH!
SIGH

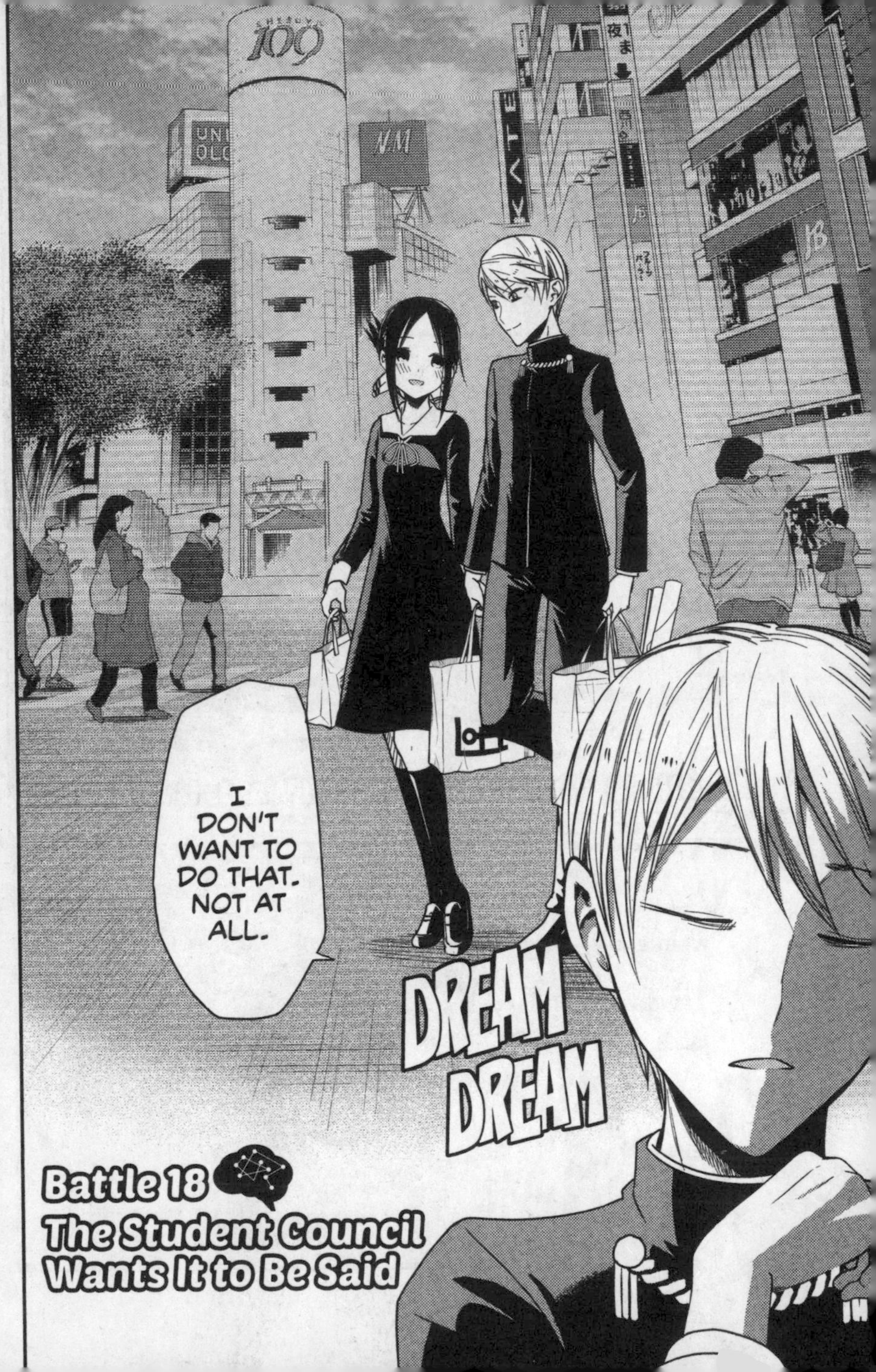
I DON'T WANT TO DO THAT. NOT AT ALL.
DREAM
DREAM

Battle 18 The Student Council Wants It to Be Said

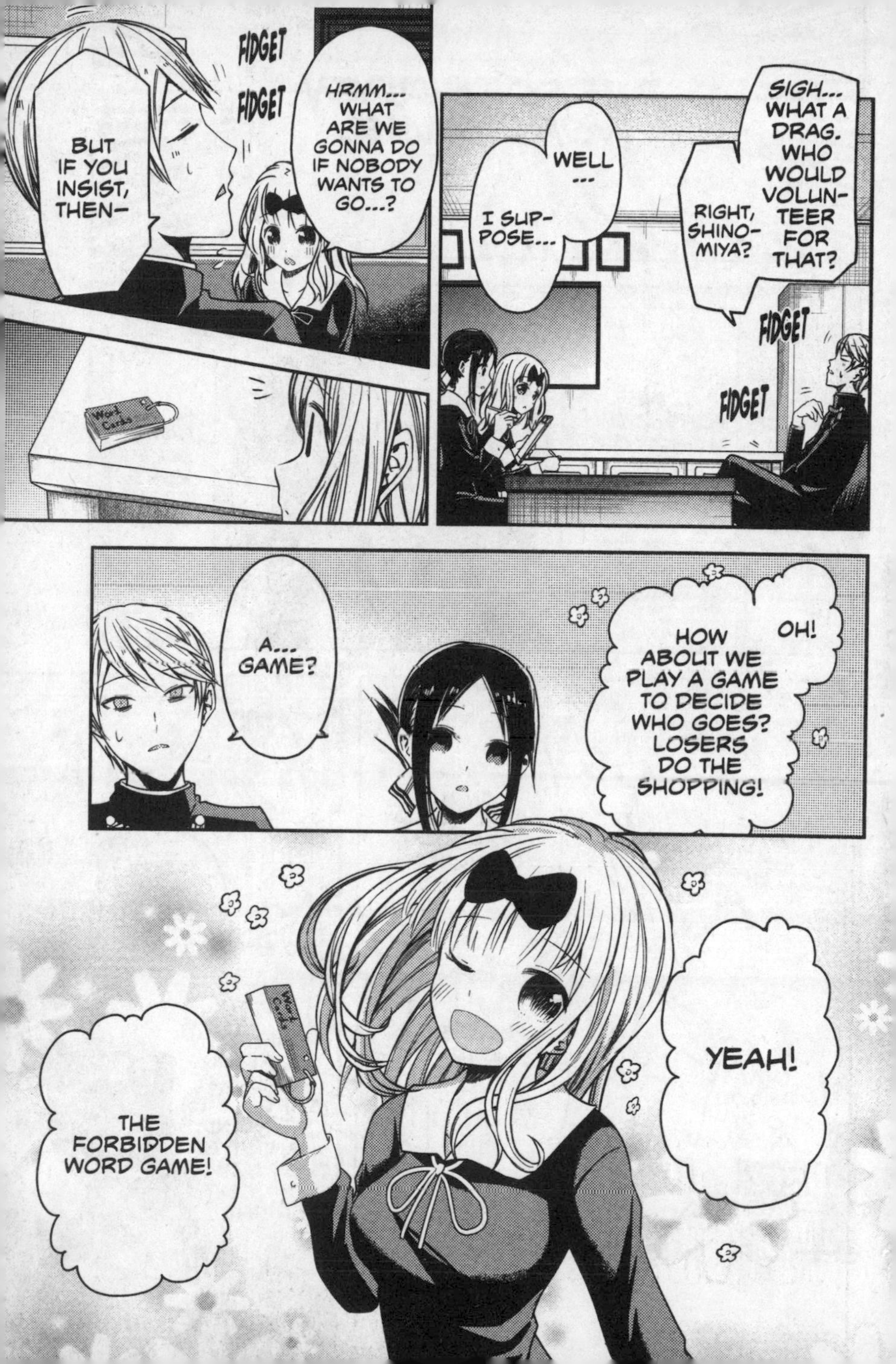
SIGH... WHAT A DRAG. WHO WOULD VOLUNTEER FOR THAT?
RIGHT, SHINOMIYA?
WELL...
I SUPPOSE...
FIDGET
FIDGET
HRMM... WHAT ARE WE GONNA DO IF NOBODY WANTS TO GO...?
FIDGET
FIDGET
BUT IF YOU INSIST, THEN—
Word Cards
OH!
HOW ABOUT WE PLAY A GAME TO DECIDE WHO GOES? LOSERS DO THE SHOPPING!
A... GAME?
YEAH!
Word Cards
THE FORBIDDEN WORD GAME!

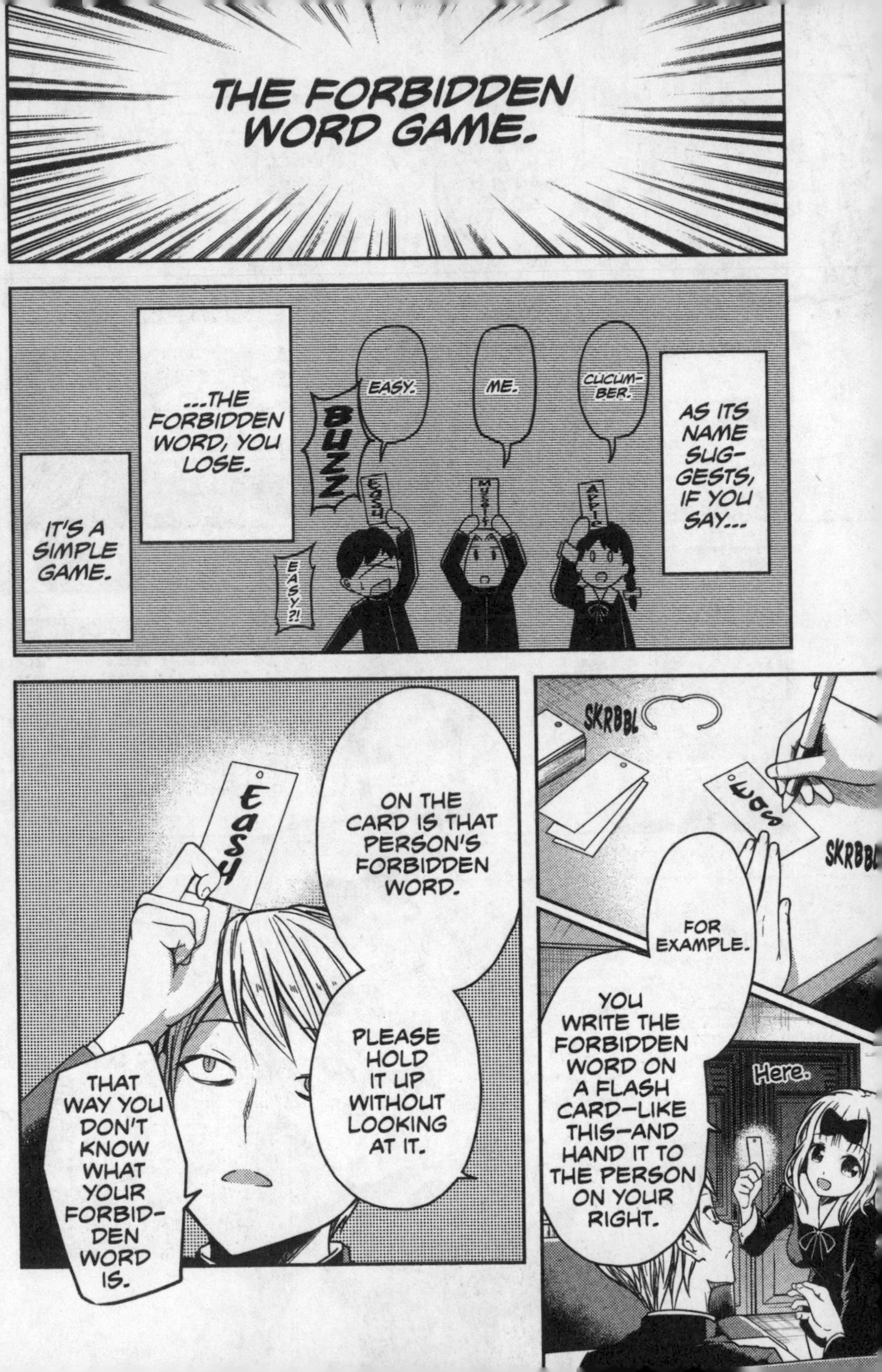

THE FORBIDDEN WORD GAME.
AS ITS NAME SUGGESTS, IF YOU SAY...
CUCUMBER.
ME.
EASY.
BUZZ
...THE FORBIDDEN WORD, YOU LOSE.
EASY?!
IT'S A SIMPLE GAME.
SKRBBL
SKRBBL
FOR EXAMPLE.
YOU WRITE THE FORBIDDEN WORD ON A FLASH CARD—LIKE THIS—AND HAND IT TO THE PERSON ON YOUR RIGHT.
Here.
Easy
ON THE CARD IS THAT PERSON'S FORBIDDEN WORD.
PLEASE HOLD IT UP WITHOUT LOOKING AT IT.
THAT WAY YOU DON'T KNOW WHAT YOUR FORBIDDEN WORD IS.

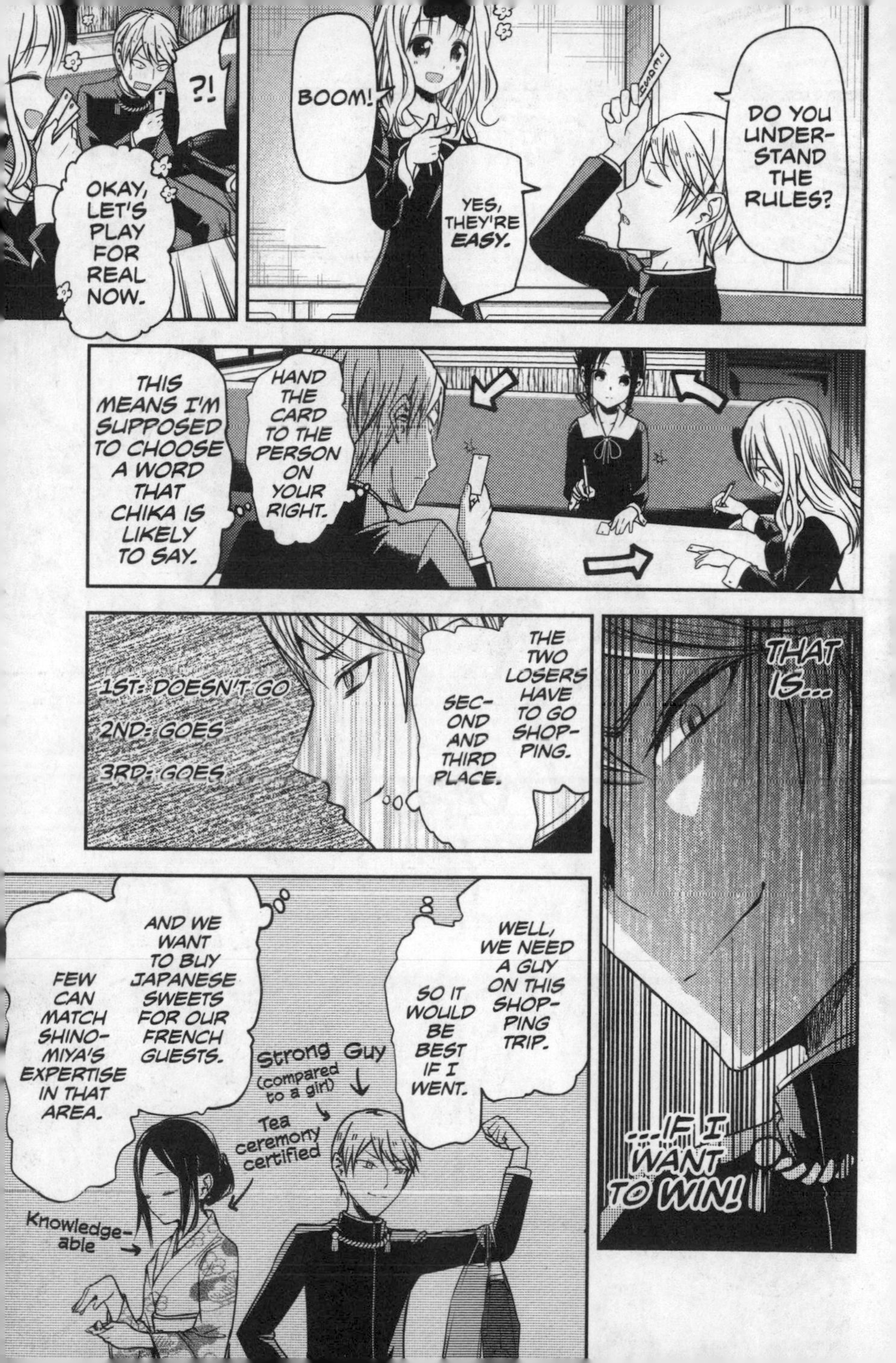
DO YOU UNDERSTAND THE RULES?
YES, THEY'RE EASY.
BOOM!
?!
OKAY, LET'S PLAY FOR REAL NOW.
HAND THE CARD TO THE PERSON ON YOUR RIGHT.
THIS MEANS I'M SUPPOSED TO CHOOSE A WORD THAT CHIKA IS LIKELY TO SAY.
THAT IS...
...IF I WANT TO WIN!
THE TWO LOSERS HAVE TO GO SHOPPING.
SECOND AND THIRD PLACE.
1ST: DOESN'T GO
2ND: GOES
3RD: GOES
WELL, WE NEED A GUY ON THIS SHOPPING TRIP.
SO IT WOULD BE BEST IF I WENT.
AND WE WANT TO BUY JAPANESE SWEETS FOR OUR FRENCH GUESTS.
FEW CAN MATCH SHINOMIYA'S EXPERTISE IN THAT AREA.
Strong Guy
(compared to a girl)
Tea ceremony certified
Knowledgeable

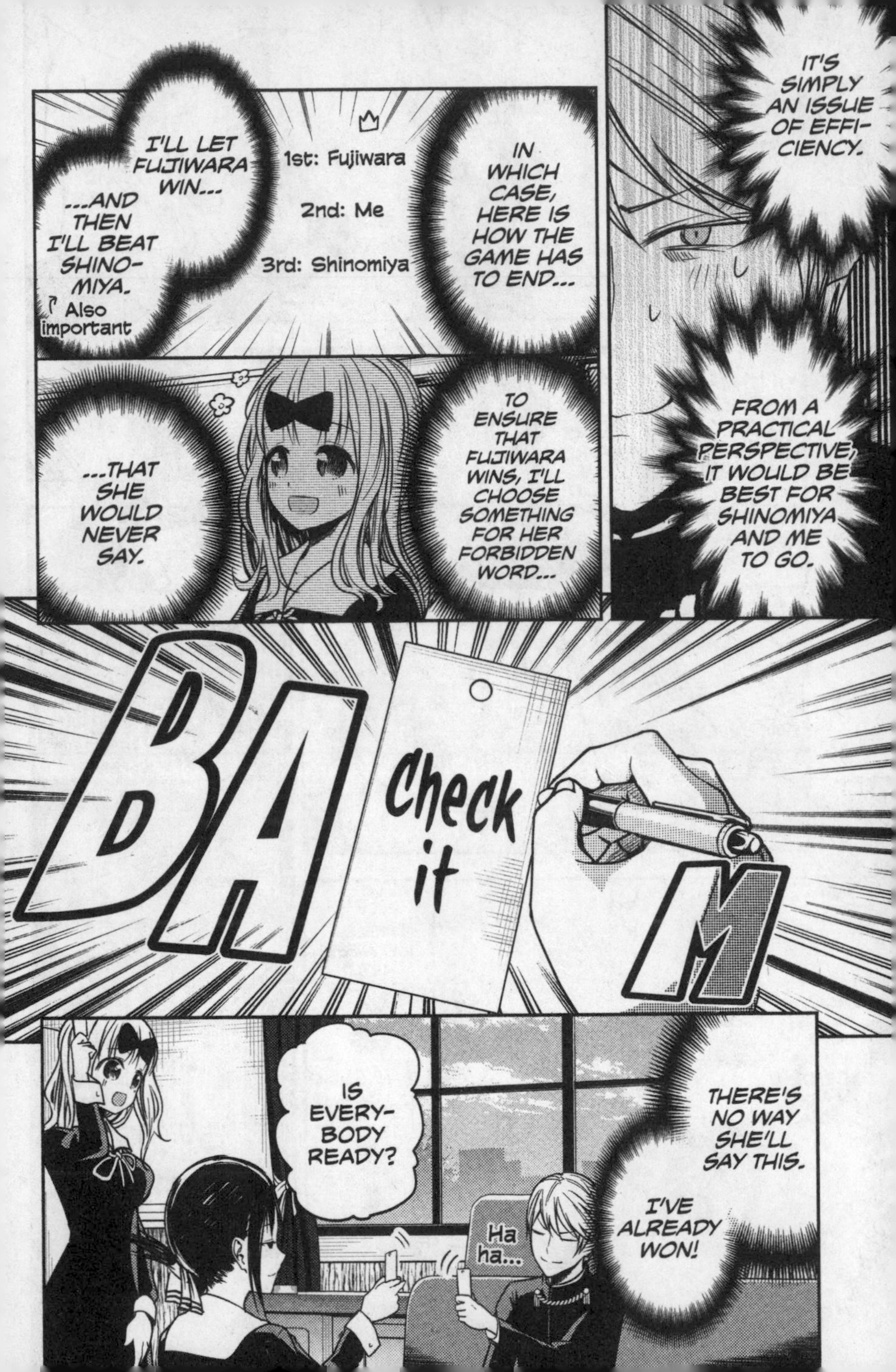
IT'S SIMPLY AN ISSUE OF EFFICIENCY.
FROM A PRACTICAL PERSPECTIVE, IT WOULD BE BEST FOR SHINOMIYA AND ME TO GO.
IN WHICH CASE, HERE IS HOW THE GAME HAS TO END...
1st: Fujiwara
2nd: Me
3rd: Shinomiya
I'LL LET FUJIWARA WIN...
...AND THEN I'LL BEAT SHINOMIYA.
Also important
TO ENSURE THAT FUJIWARA WINS, I'LL CHOOSE SOMETHING FOR HER FORBIDDEN WORD...
...THAT SHE WOULD NEVER SAY.
BAM
Check it
THERE'S NO WAY SHE'LL SAY THIS.
I'VE ALREADY WON!
Ha ha...
IS EVERYBODY READY?

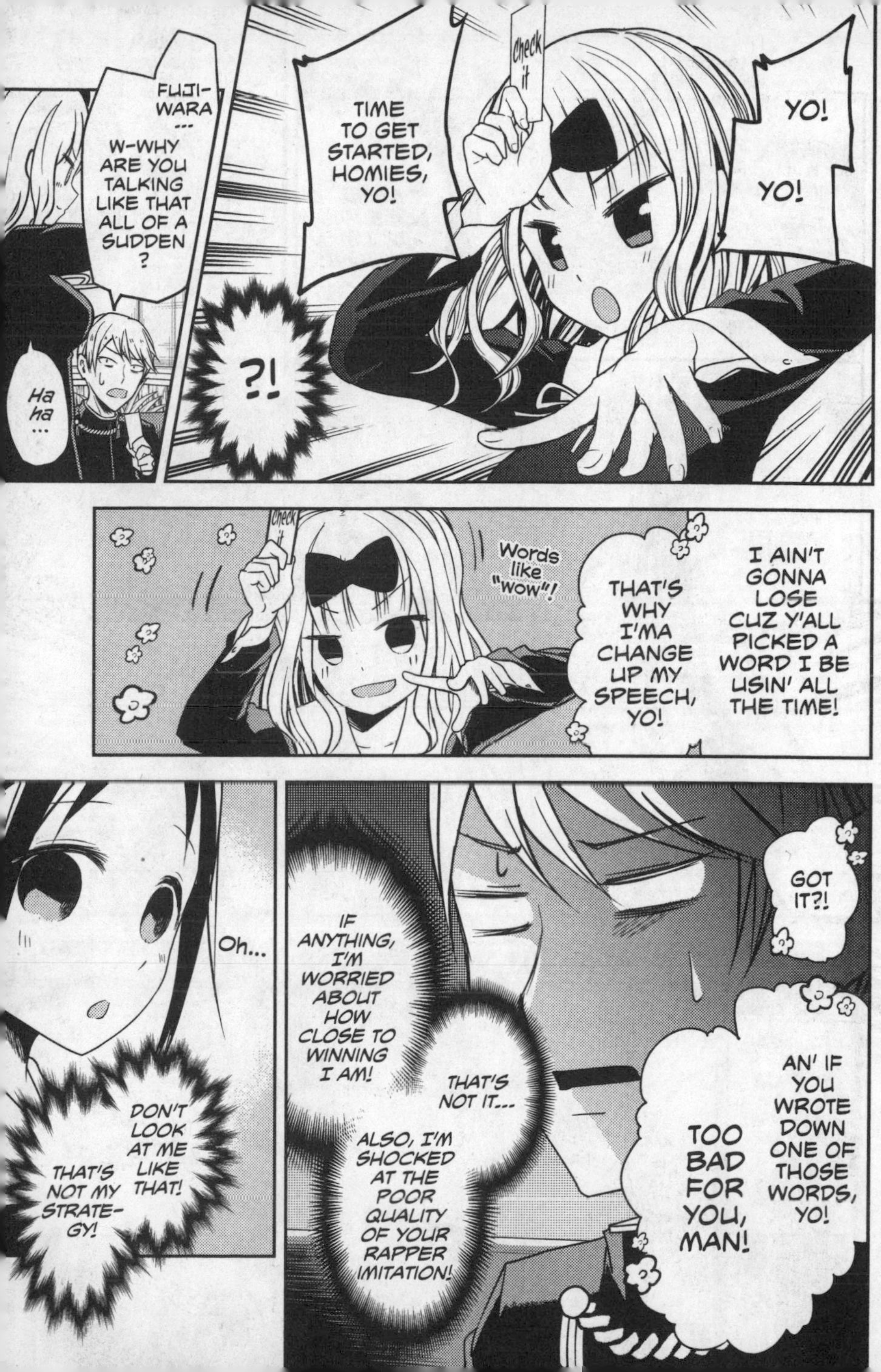
YO!
YO!
Check it
TIME TO GET STARTED, HOMIES, YO!
?!
FUJI-WARA... W-WHY ARE YOU TALKING LIKE THAT ALL OF A SUDDEN?
Ha ha...
I AIN'T GONNA LOSE CUZ Y'ALL PICKED A WORD I BE USIN' ALL THE TIME!
THAT'S WHY I'MA CHANGE UP MY SPEECH, YO!
Words like "wow"!
Check it
GOT IT?!
AN' IF YOU WROTE DOWN ONE OF THOSE WORDS, YO!
TOO BAD FOR YOU, MAN!
IF ANYTHING, I'M WORRIED ABOUT HOW CLOSE TO WINNING I AM!
THAT'S NOT IT...
ALSO, I'M SHOCKED AT THE POOR QUALITY OF YOUR RAPPER IMITATION!
Oh...
DON'T LOOK AT ME LIKE THAT!
THAT'S NOT MY STRATEGY!

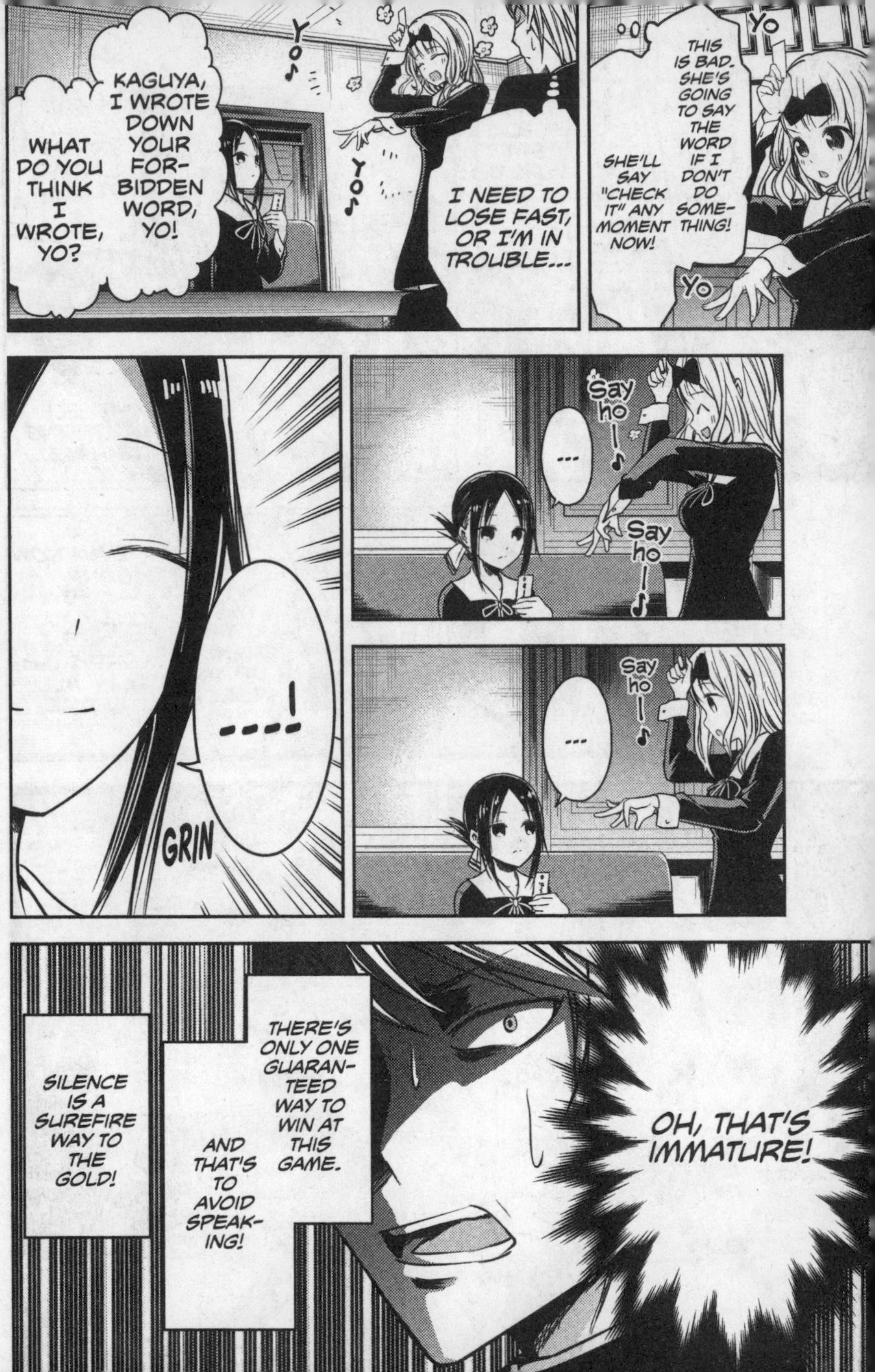

YO
THIS IS BAD. SHE'S GOING TO SAY THE WORD IF I DON'T DO SOME-THING!
SHE'LL SAY "CHECK IT" ANY MOMENT NOW!
YO
YO♪
I NEED TO LOSE FAST, OR I'M IN TROUBLE...
KAGUYA, I WROTE DOWN YOUR FOR-BIDDEN WORD, YO!
WHAT DO YOU THINK I WROTE, YO?
YO♪
Say ho-♪
...
Say ho-♪
Say ho-♪
...
...!
GRIN
OH, THAT'S IMMATURE!
THERE'S ONLY ONE GUARAN-TEED WAY TO WIN AT THIS GAME.
AND THAT'S TO AVOID SPEAK-ING!
SILENCE IS A SUREFIRE WAY TO THE GOLD!

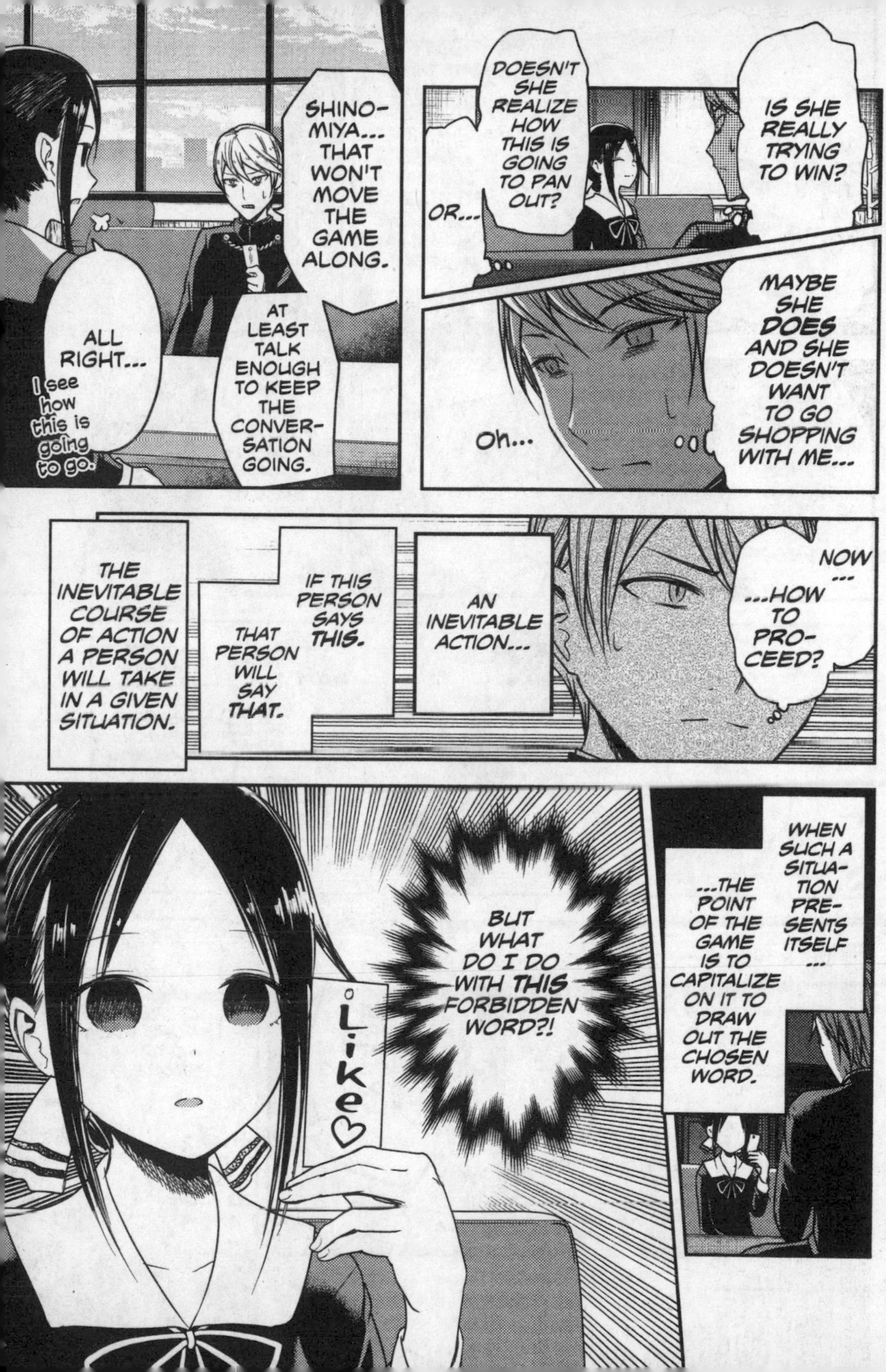
IS SHE REALLY TRYING TO WIN?
DOESN'T SHE REALIZE HOW THIS IS GOING TO PAN OUT?
OR...
MAYBE SHE DOES AND SHE DOESN'T WANT TO GO SHOPPING WITH ME...
Oh...
SHINO-MIYA... THAT WON'T MOVE THE GAME ALONG.
AT LEAST TALK ENOUGH TO KEEP THE CONVER-SATION GOING.
ALL RIGHT...
I see how this is going to go.
NOW... ...HOW TO PRO-CEED?
AN INEVITABLE ACTION...
IF THIS PERSON SAYS THIS.
THAT PERSON WILL SAY THAT.
THE INEVITABLE COURSE OF ACTION A PERSON WILL TAKE IN A GIVEN SITUATION.
WHEN SUCH A SITUA-TION PRE-SENTS ITSELF...
...THE POINT OF THE GAME IS TO CAPITALIZE ON IT TO DRAW OUT THE CHOSEN WORD.
BUT WHAT DO I DO WITH THIS FORBIDDEN WORD?!
Like♡

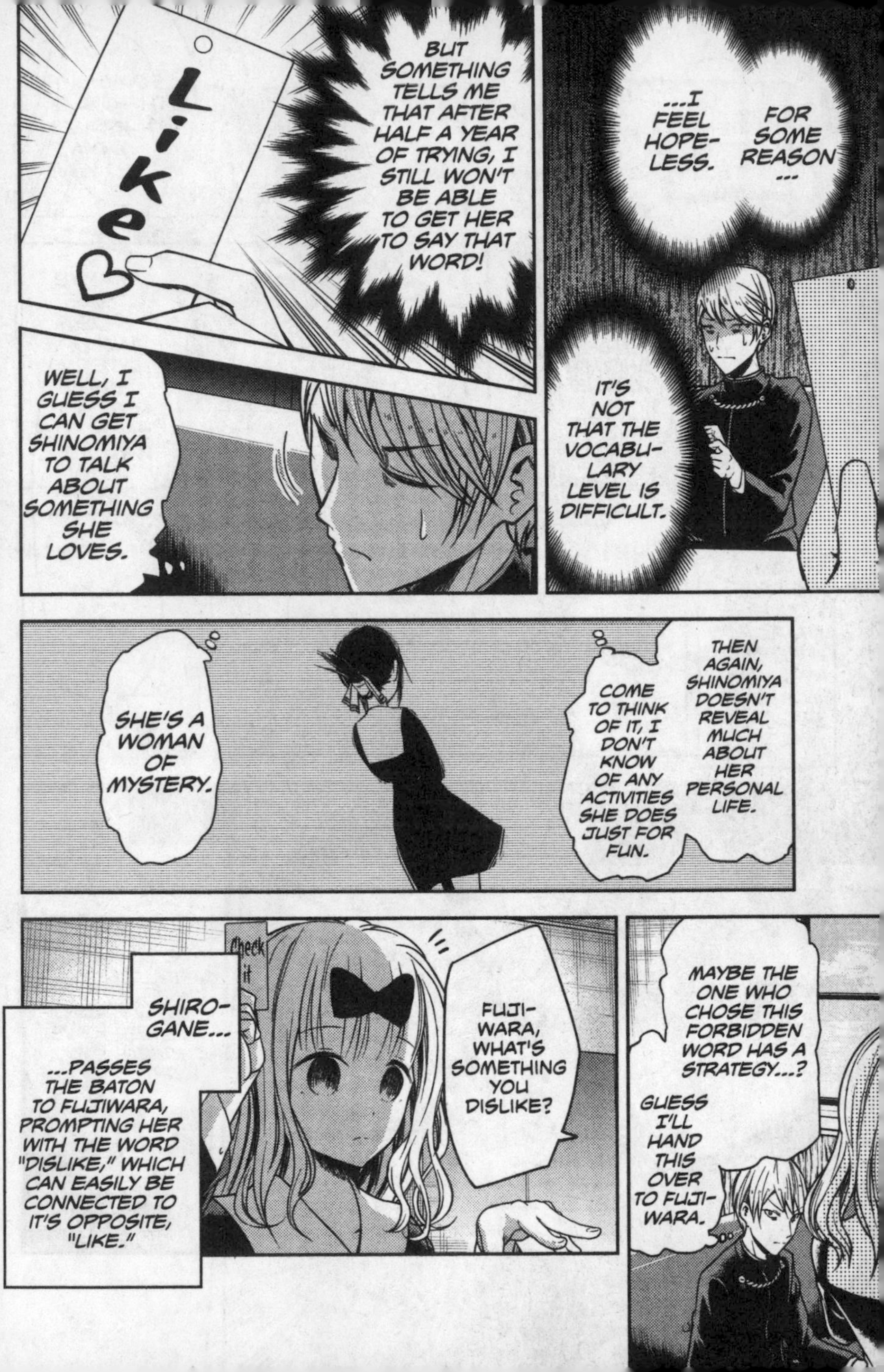

FOR SOME REASON ...
...I FEEL HOPE-LESS.
IT'S NOT THAT THE VOCABU-LARY LEVEL IS DIFFICULT.
BUT SOMETHING TELLS ME THAT AFTER HALF A YEAR OF TRYING, I STILL WON'T BE ABLE TO GET HER TO SAY THAT WORD!
Like
WELL, I GUESS I CAN GET SHINOMIYA TO TALK ABOUT SOMETHING SHE LOVES.
THEN AGAIN, SHINOMIYA DOESN'T REVEAL MUCH ABOUT HER PERSONAL LIFE.
COME TO THINK OF IT, I DON'T KNOW OF ANY ACTIVITIES SHE DOES JUST FOR FUN.
SHE'S A WOMAN OF MYSTERY.
MAYBE THE ONE WHO CHOSE THIS FORBIDDEN WORD HAS A STRATEGY...?
GUESS I'LL HAND THIS OVER TO FUJI-WARA.
FUJI-WARA, WHAT'S SOMETHING YOU DISLIKE?
Check it
SHIRO-GANE...
...PASSES THE BATON TO FUJIWARA, PROMPTING HER WITH THE WORD "DISLIKE," WHICH CAN EASILY BE CONNECTED TO IT'S OPPOSITE, "LIKE."

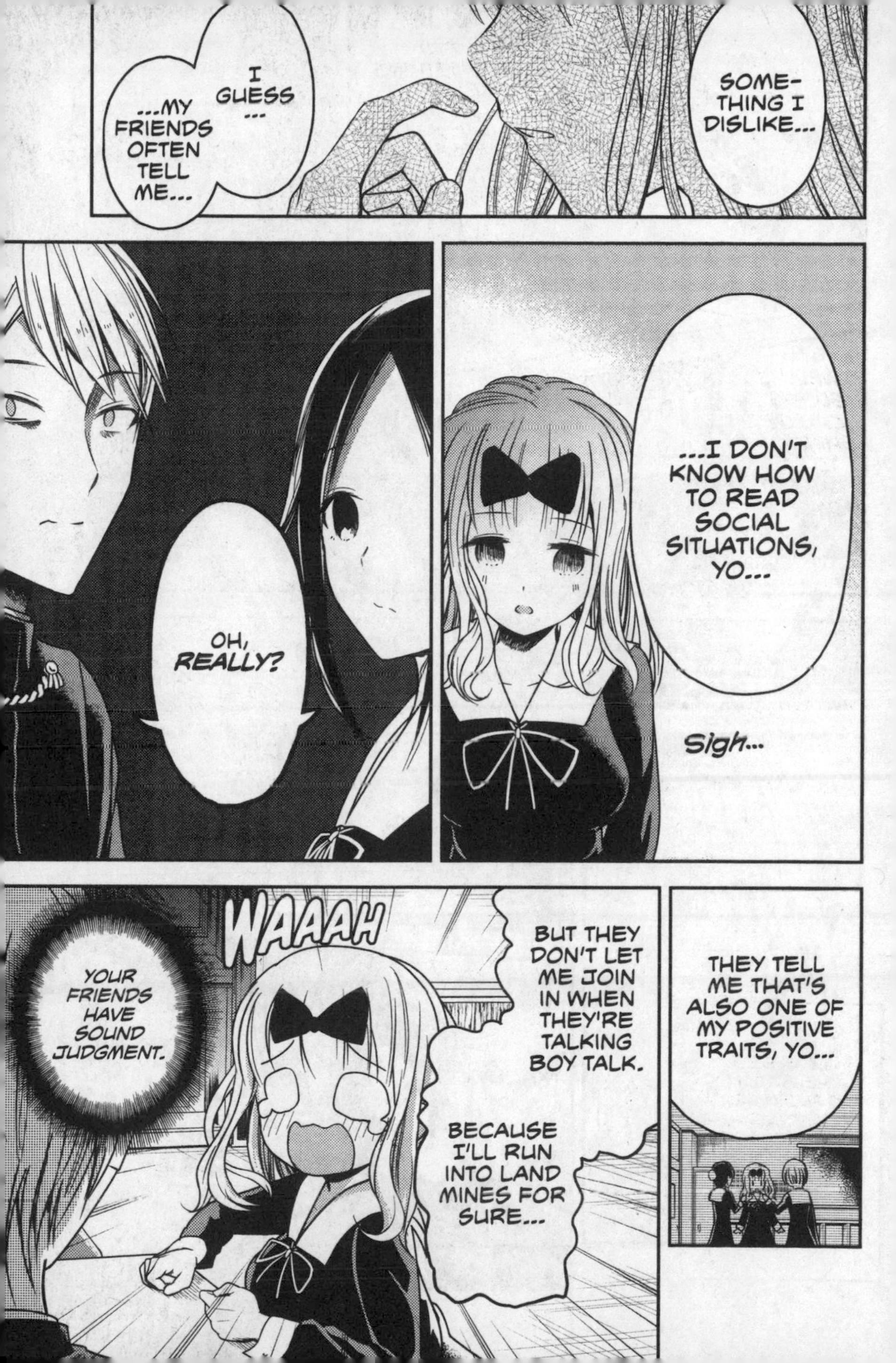
SOME-THING I DISLIKE...
I GUESS... ...MY FRIENDS OFTEN TELL ME...
...I DON'T KNOW HOW TO READ SOCIAL SITUATIONS, YO...
Sigh...
OH, REALLY?
THEY TELL ME THAT'S ALSO ONE OF MY POSITIVE TRAITS, YO...
BUT THEY DON'T LET ME JOIN IN WHEN THEY'RE TALKING BOY TALK.
WAAAH
BECAUSE I'LL RUN INTO LAND MINES FOR SURE...
YOUR FRIENDS HAVE SOUND JUDGMENT.

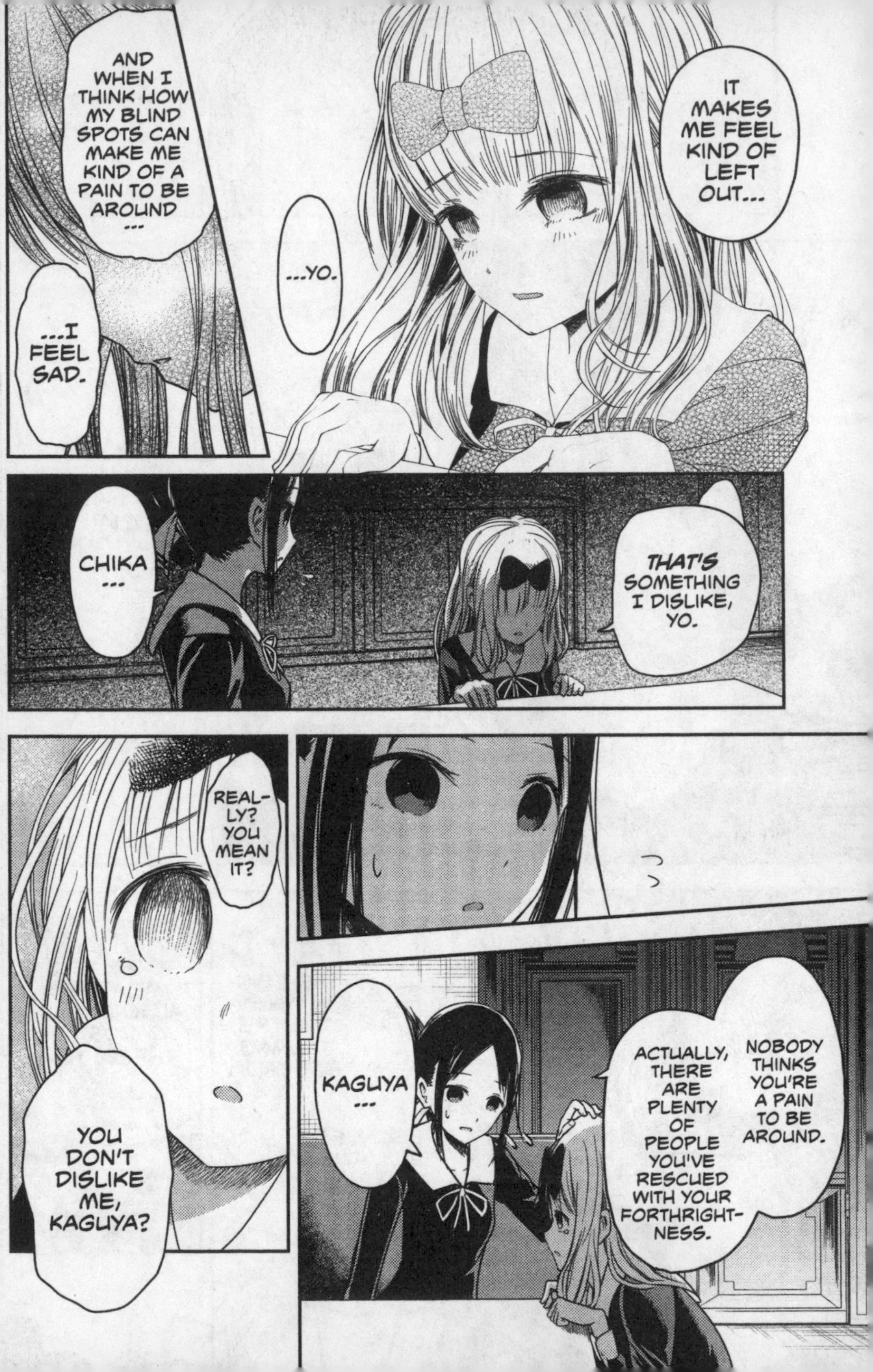

IT MAKES ME FEEL KIND OF LEFT OUT...
...YO.
AND WHEN I THINK HOW MY BLIND SPOTS CAN MAKE ME KIND OF A PAIN TO BE AROUND...
...I FEEL SAD.
THAT'S SOMETHING I DISLIKE, YO.
CHIKA...
NOBODY THINKS YOU'RE A PAIN TO BE AROUND.
ACTUALLY, THERE ARE PLENTY OF PEOPLE YOU'VE RESCUED WITH YOUR FORTHRIGHTNESS.
KAGUYA...
REALLY? YOU MEAN IT?
YOU DON'T DISLIKE ME, KAGUYA?

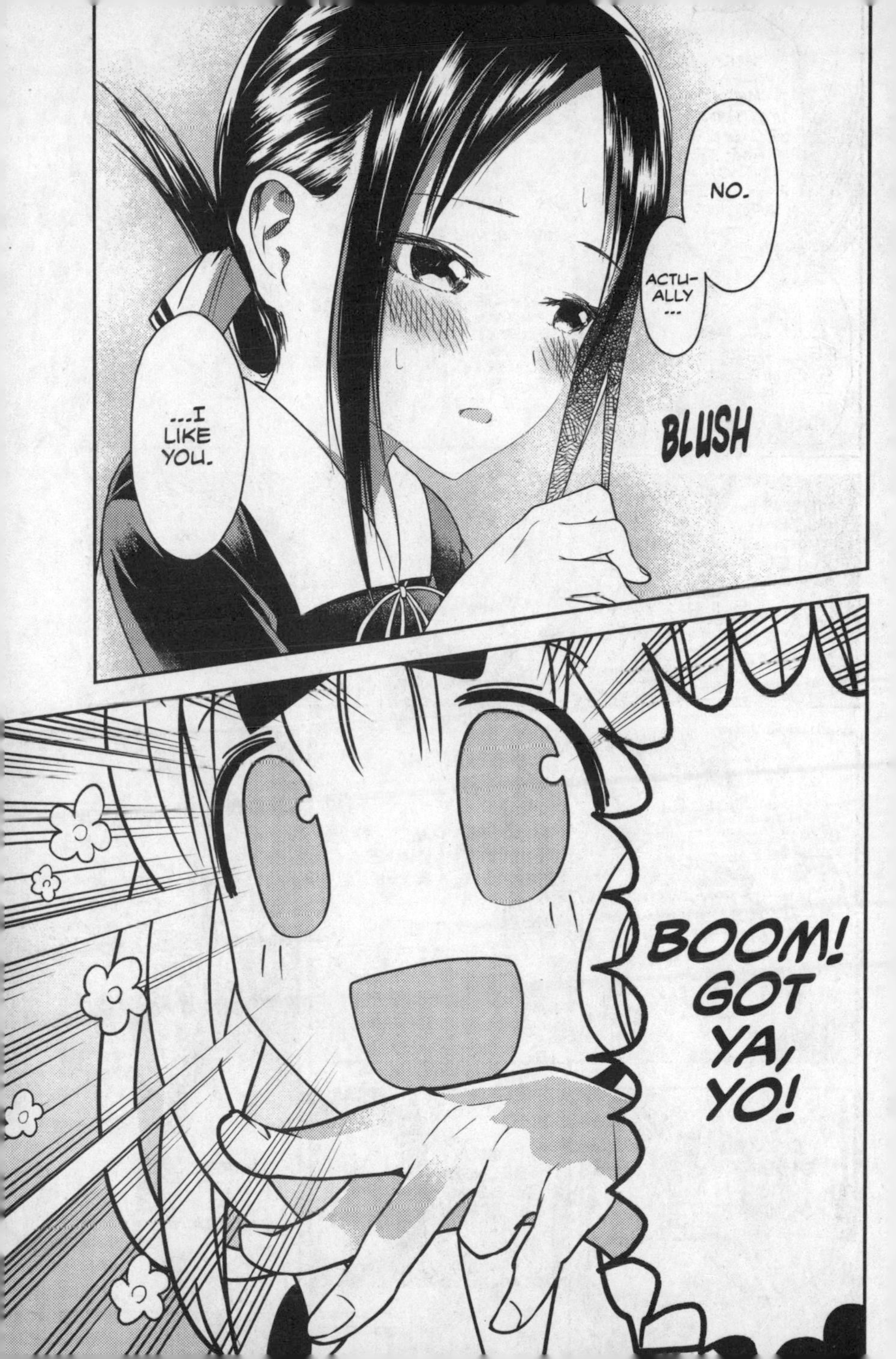
NO.
ACTU-
ALLY
...
BLUSH
...I
LIKE
YOU.
BOOM!
GOT
YA,
YO!

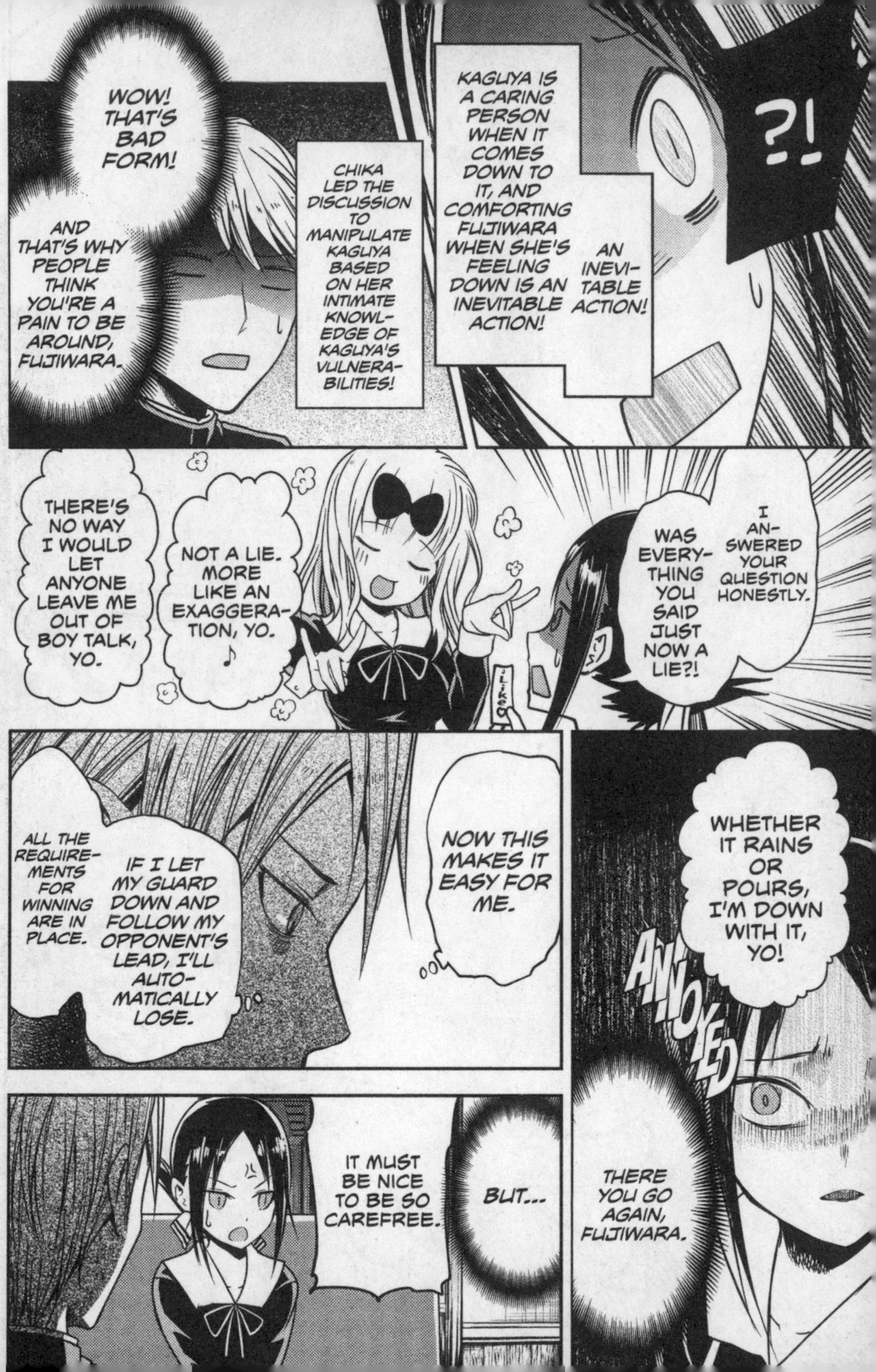
?!
KAGUYA IS A CARING PERSON WHEN IT COMES DOWN TO IT, AND COMFORTING FUJIWARA WHEN SHE'S FEELING DOWN IS AN INEVITABLE ACTION!
AN INEVI-TABLE ACTION!
CHIKA LED THE DISCUSSION TO MANIPULATE KAGUYA BASED ON HER INTIMATE KNOWL-EDGE OF KAGUYA'S VULNERA-BILITIES!
WOW! THAT'S BAD FORM!
AND THAT'S WHY PEOPLE THINK YOU'RE A PAIN TO BE AROUND, FUJIWARA.
I AN-SWERED YOUR QUESTION HONESTLY.
WAS EVERY-THING YOU SAID JUST NOW A LIE?!
NOT A LIE. MORE LIKE AN EXAGGERA-TION, YO. ♪
THERE'S NO WAY I WOULD LET ANYONE LEAVE ME OUT OF BOY TALK, YO.
WHETHER IT RAINS OR POURS, I'M DOWN WITH IT, YO!
ANNOYED
THERE YOU GO AGAIN, FUJIWARA.
NOW THIS MAKES IT EASY FOR ME.
IF I LET MY GUARD DOWN AND FOLLOW MY OPPONENT'S LEAD, I'LL AUTO-MATICALLY LOSE.
ALL THE REQUIRE-MENTS FOR WINNING ARE IN PLACE.
BUT...
IT MUST BE NICE TO BE SO CAREFREE.

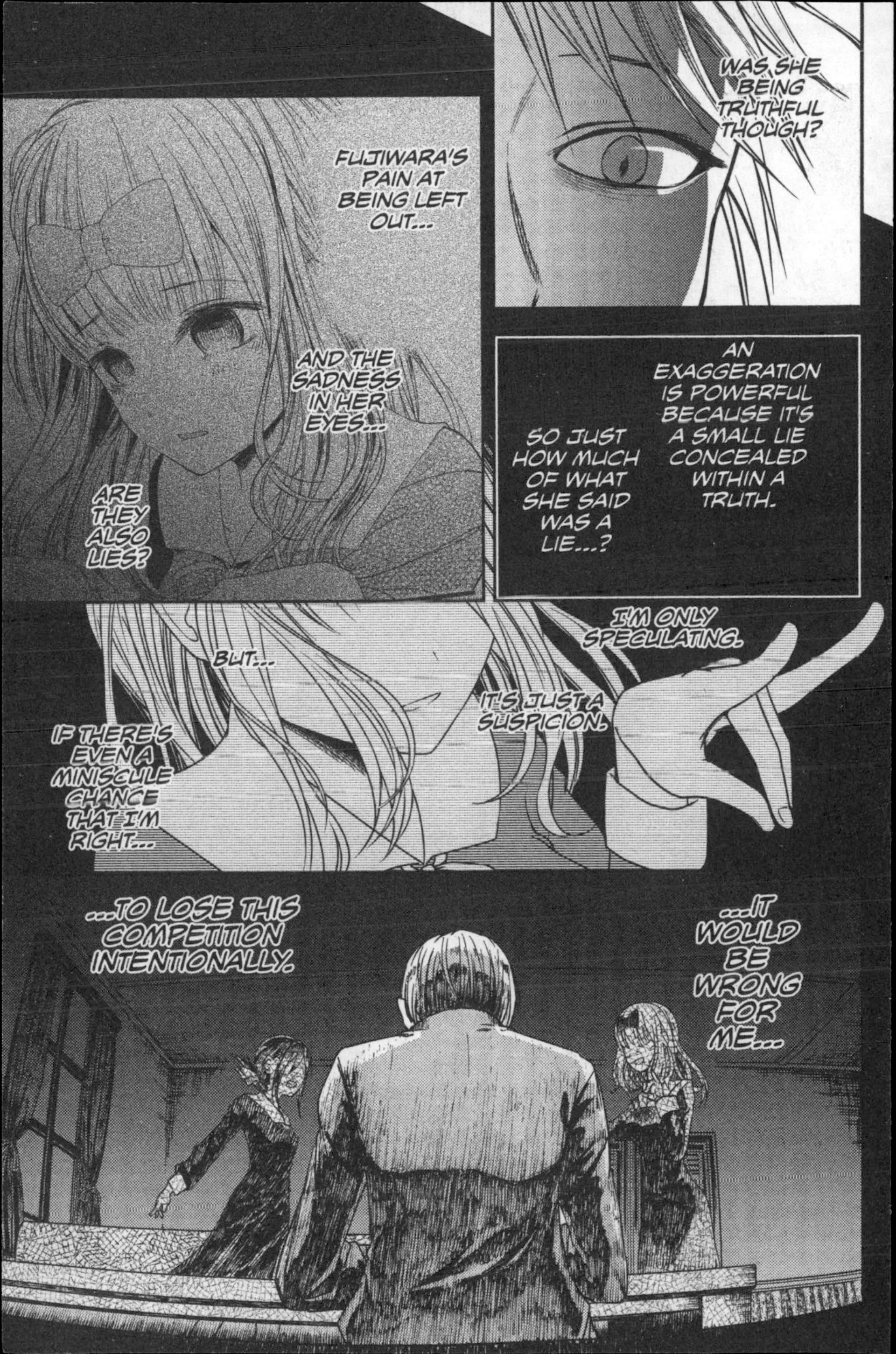
WAS SHE BEING TRUTHFUL THOUGH?
AN EXAGGERATION IS POWERFUL BECAUSE IT'S A SMALL LIE CONCEALED WITHIN A TRUTH.
SO JUST HOW MUCH OF WHAT SHE SAID WAS A LIE...?
FUJIWARA'S PAIN AT BEING LEFT OUT...
AND THE SADNESS IN HER EYES...
ARE THEY ALSO LIES?
I'M ONLY SPECULATING.
IT'S JUST A SUSPICION.
BUT...
IF THERE'S EVEN A MINISCULE CHANCE THAT I'M RIGHT...
...IT WOULD BE WRONG FOR ME...
...TO LOSE THIS COMPETITION INTENTIONALLY.

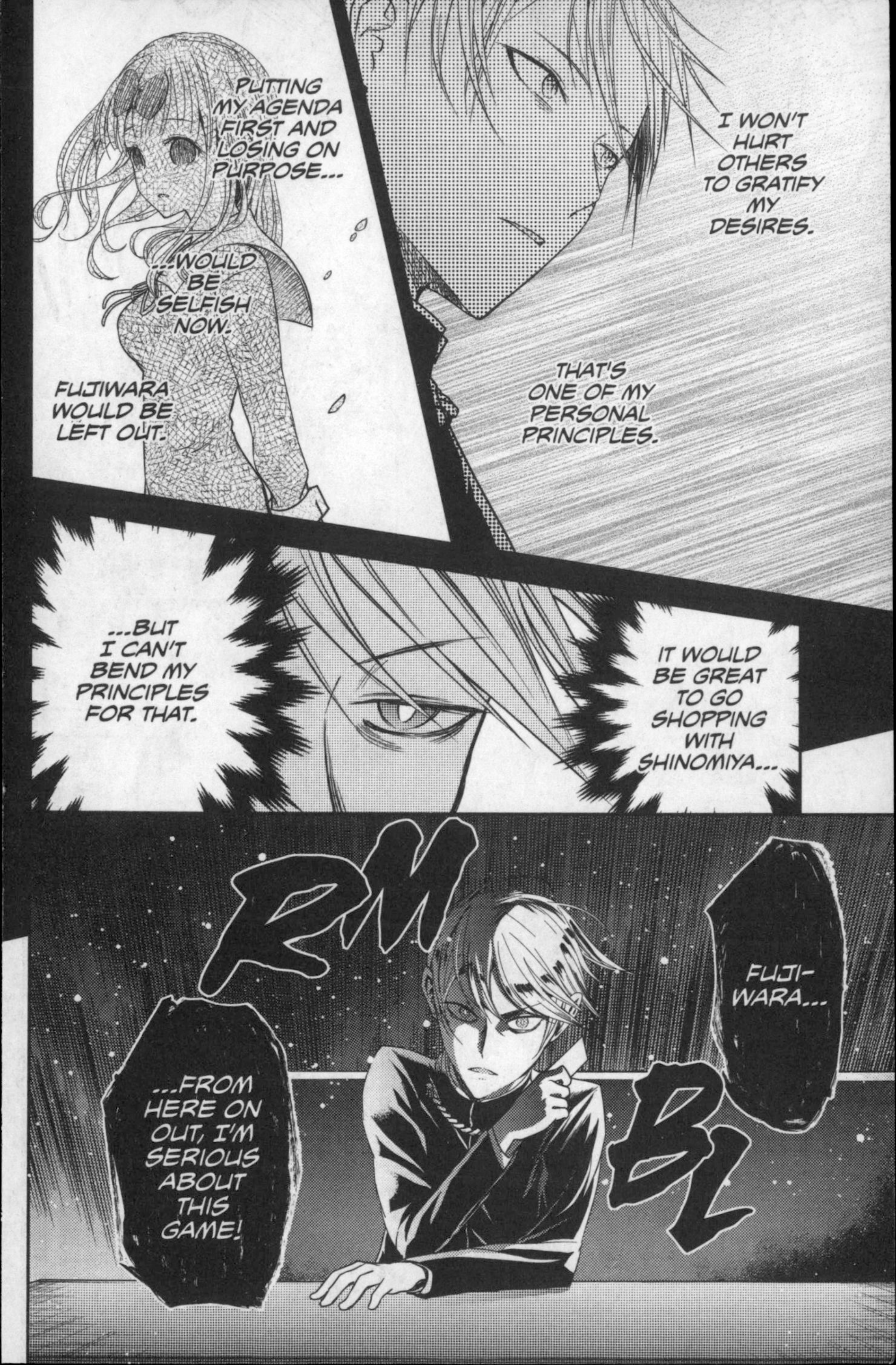
I WON'T HURT OTHERS TO GRATIFY MY DESIRES.
THAT'S ONE OF MY PERSONAL PRINCIPLES.
PUTTING MY AGENDA FIRST AND LOSING ON PURPOSE...
...WOULD BE SELFISH NOW.
FUJIWARA WOULD BE LEFT OUT.
IT WOULD BE GREAT TO GO SHOPPING WITH SHINOMIYA...
...BUT I CAN'T BEND MY PRINCIPLES FOR THAT.
FUJI-WARA...
RMBL
...FROM HERE ON OUT, I'M SERIOUS ABOUT THIS GAME!

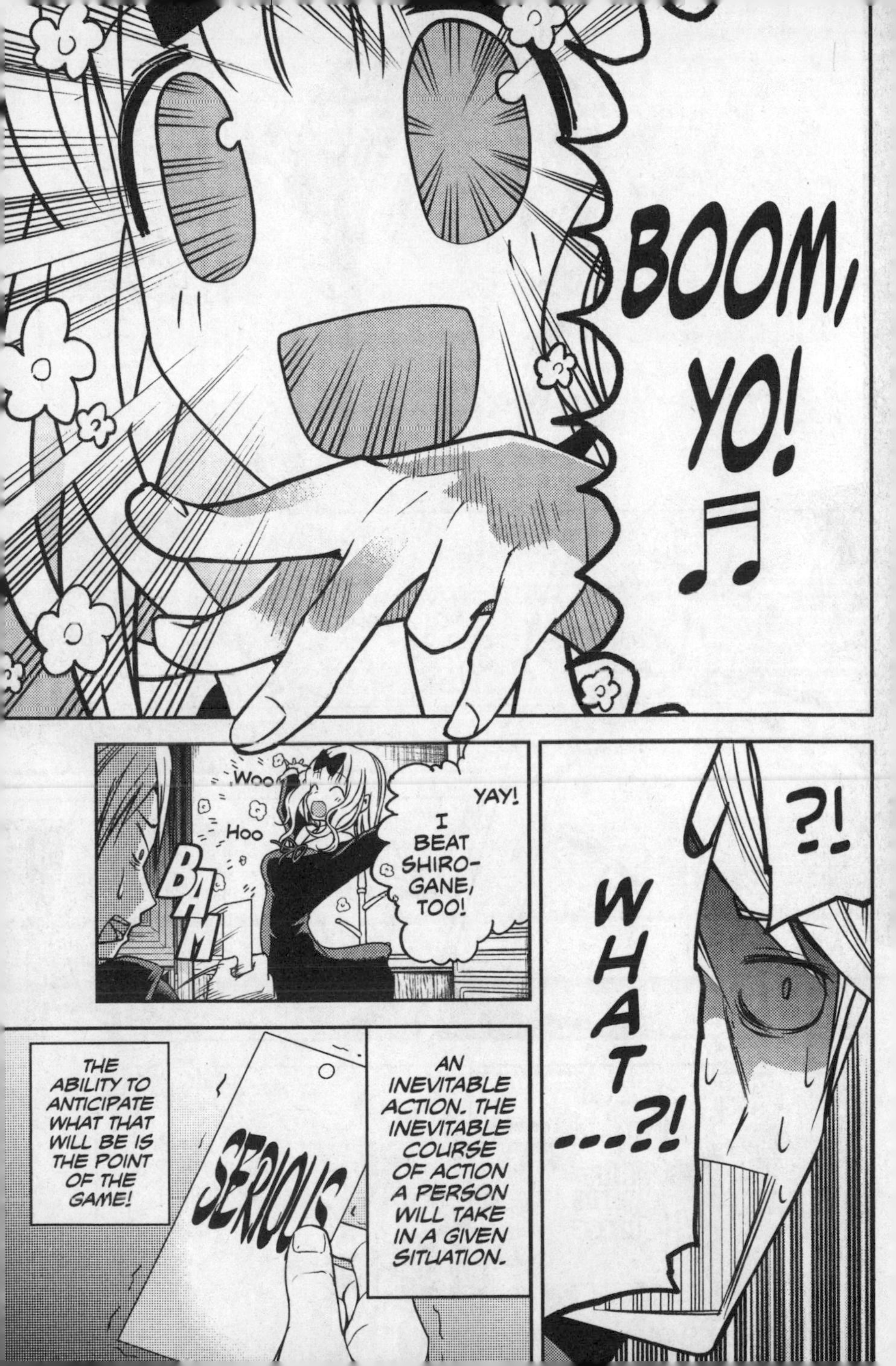
BOOM, YO! ♫
?!
WHAT...?!
YAY! I BEAT SHIROGANE, TOO!
Woo
Hoo
BAM
AN INEVITABLE ACTION. THE INEVITABLE COURSE OF ACTION A PERSON WILL TAKE IN A GIVEN SITUATION.
SERIOUS
THE ABILITY TO ANTICIPATE WHAT THAT WILL BE IS THE POINT OF THE GAME!

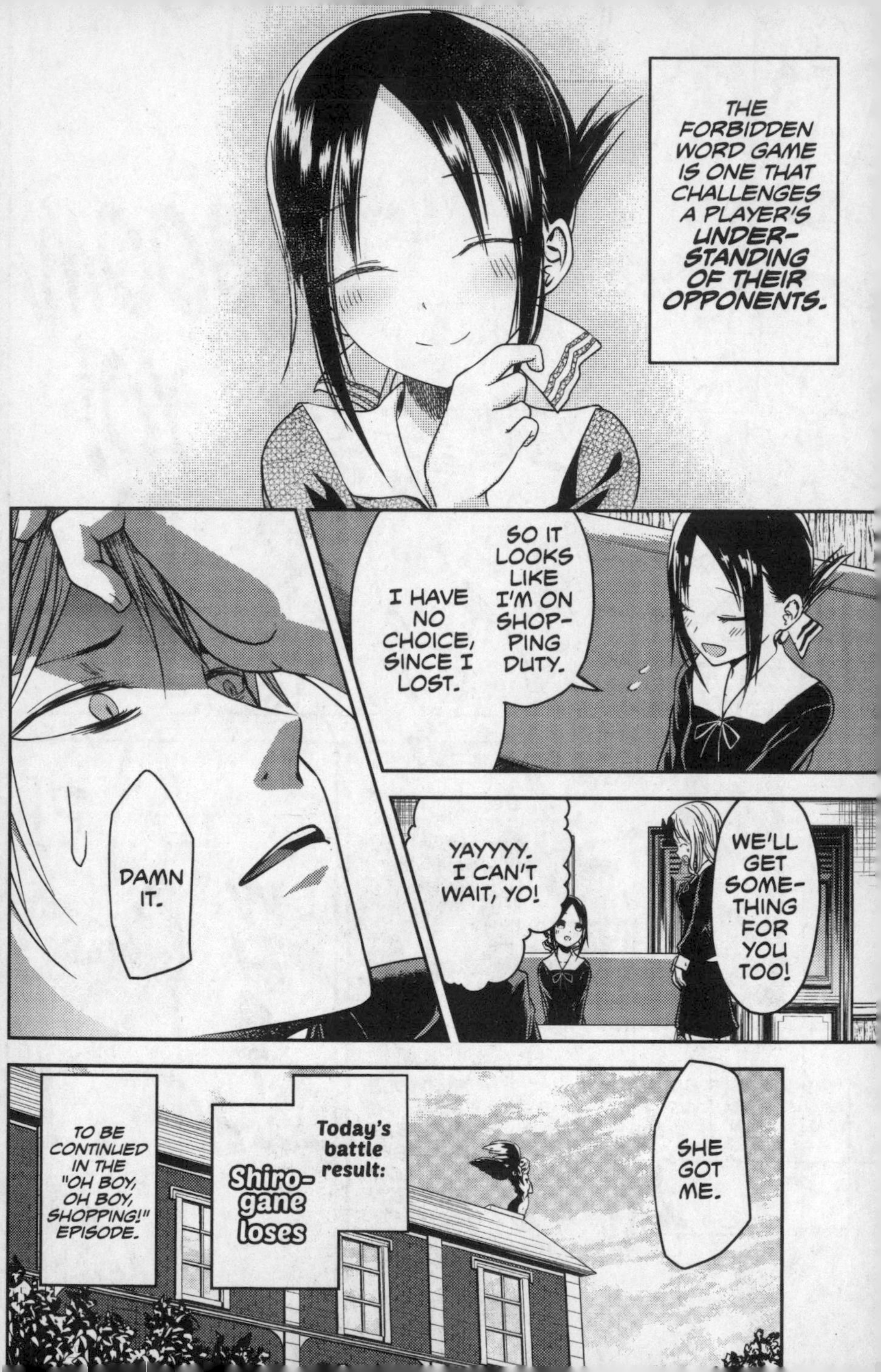
THE FORBIDDEN WORD GAME IS ONE THAT CHALLENGES A PLAYER'S UNDER-STANDING OF THEIR OPPONENTS.
SO IT LOOKS LIKE I'M ON SHOP-PING DUTY.
I HAVE NO CHOICE, SINCE I LOST.
WE'LL GET SOME-THING FOR YOU TOO!
YAYYYY. I CAN'T WAIT, YO!
DAMN IT.
SHE GOT ME.
Today's battle result:
Shiro-gane loses
TO BE CONTINUED IN THE "OH BOY, OH BOY, SHOPPING!" EPISODE.

A
CONFLICTED
FACIAL
EXPRESSION
DUE TO
HAVING BOTH
WON AND
LOST AT THE
SAME TIME →

KAGUYA-SAMA
LOVE IS WAR

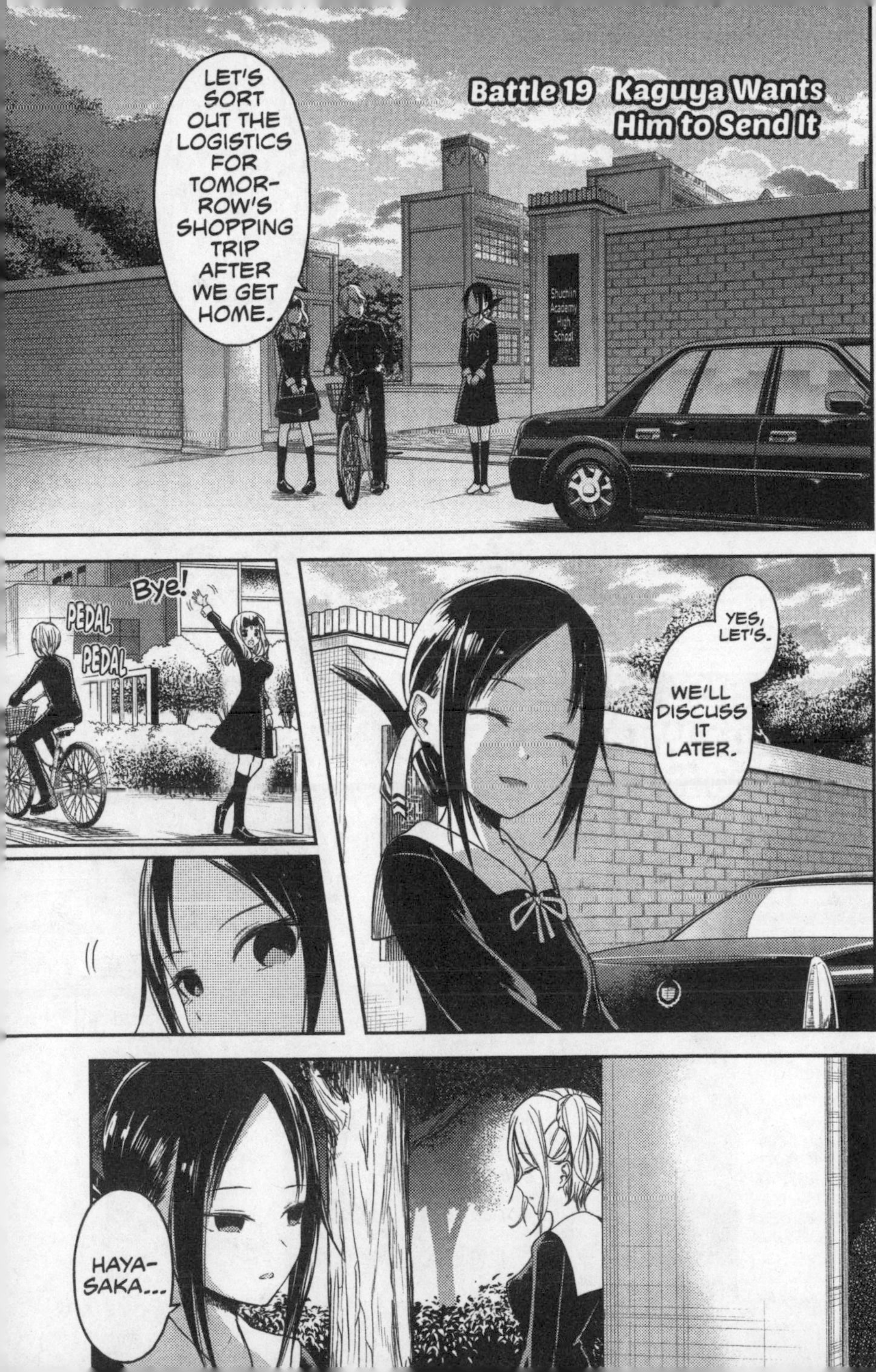
Battle 19 Kaguya Wants Him to Send It
LET'S SORT OUT THE LOGISTICS FOR TOMORROW'S SHOPPING TRIP AFTER WE GET HOME.
Shuchiin Academy High School
YES, LET'S.
WE'LL DISCUSS IT LATER.
Bye!
PEDAL
PEDAL
HAYA-SAKA...

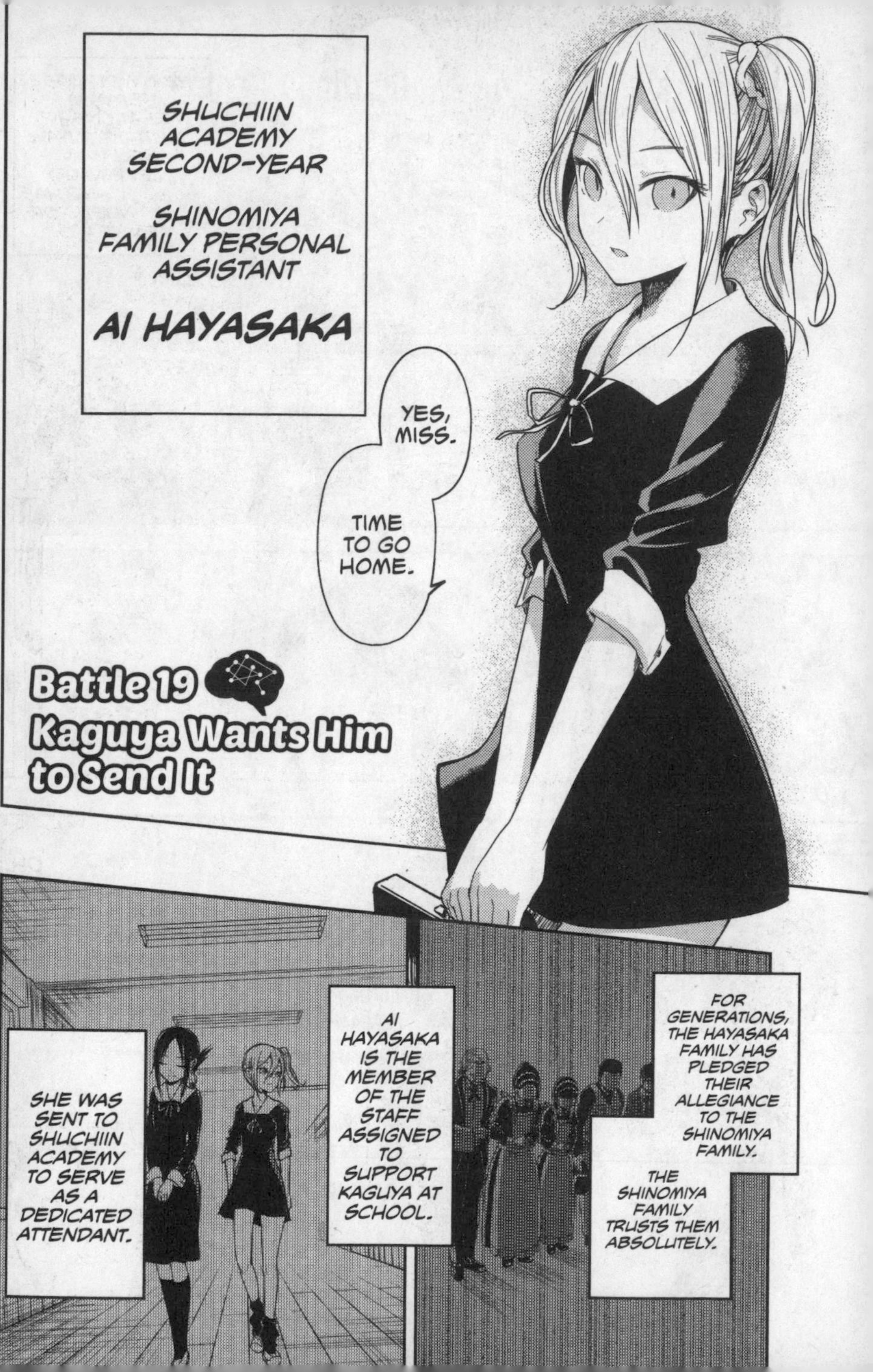
SHUCHIIN ACADEMY SECOND-YEAR
SHINOMIYA FAMILY PERSONAL ASSISTANT
AI HAYASAKA
YES, MISS.
TIME TO GO HOME.
Battle 19 Kaguya Wants Him to Send It
FOR GENERATIONS, THE HAYASAKA FAMILY HAS PLEDGED THEIR ALLEGIANCE TO THE SHINOMIYA FAMILY.
THE SHINOMIYA FAMILY TRUSTS THEM ABSOLUTELY.
AI HAYASAKA IS THE MEMBER OF THE STAFF ASSIGNED TO SUPPORT KAGUYA AT SCHOOL.
SHE WAS SENT TO SHUCHIIN ACADEMY TO SERVE AS A DEDICATED ATTENDANT.

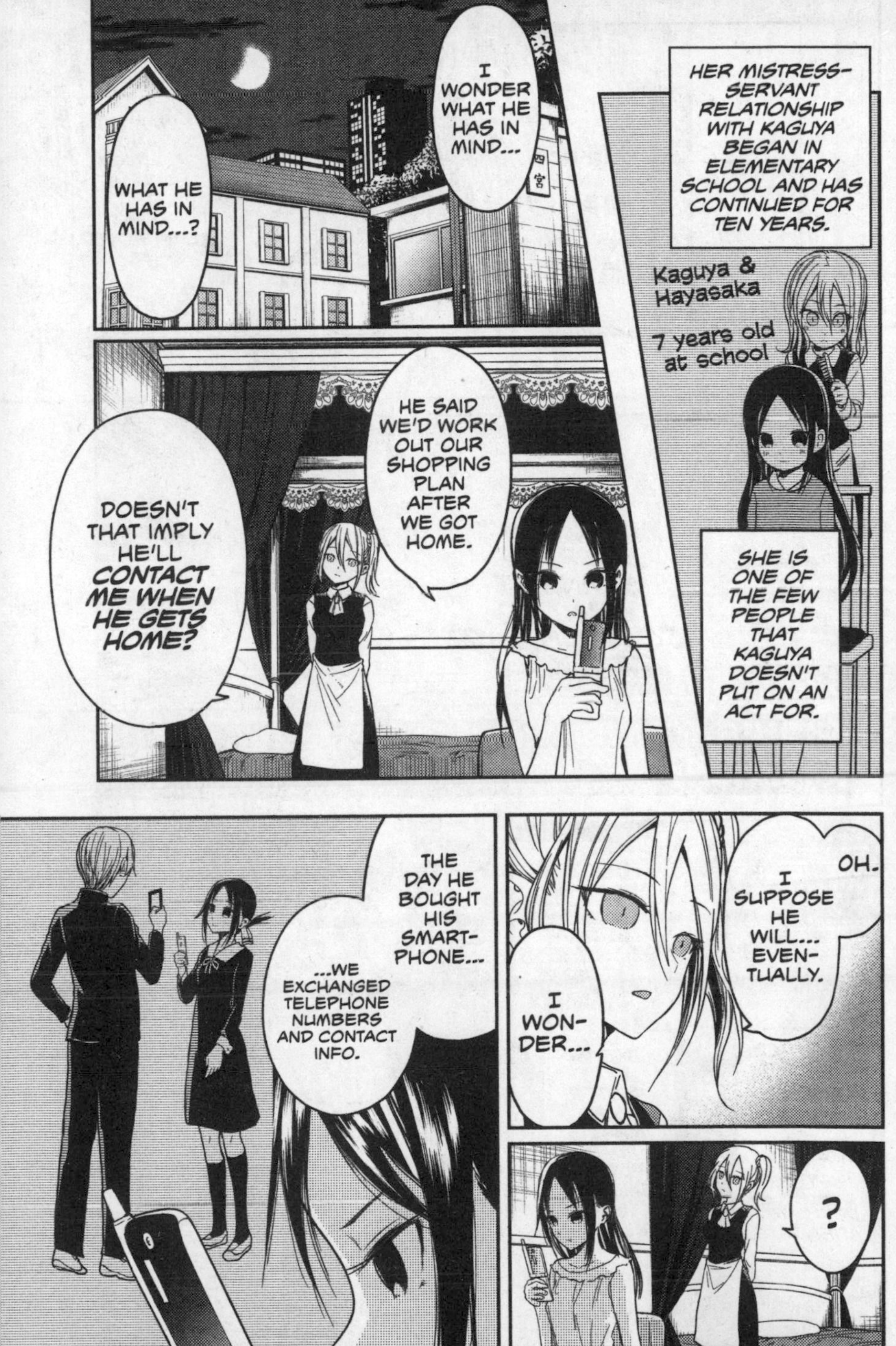
HER MISTRESS-SERVANT RELATIONSHIP WITH KAGUYA BEGAN IN ELEMENTARY SCHOOL AND HAS CONTINUED FOR TEN YEARS.
Kaguya & Hayasaka
7 years old at school
SHE IS ONE OF THE FEW PEOPLE THAT KAGUYA DOESN'T PUT ON AN ACT FOR.
I WONDER WHAT HE HAS IN MIND...
WHAT HE HAS IN MIND...?
HE SAID WE'D WORK OUT OUR SHOPPING PLAN AFTER WE GOT HOME.
DOESN'T THAT IMPLY HE'LL CONTACT ME WHEN HE GETS HOME?
OH.
I SUPPOSE HE WILL... EVENTUALLY.
I WONDER...
?
THE DAY HE BOUGHT HIS SMARTPHONE...
...WE EXCHANGED TELEPHONE NUMBERS AND CONTACT INFO.

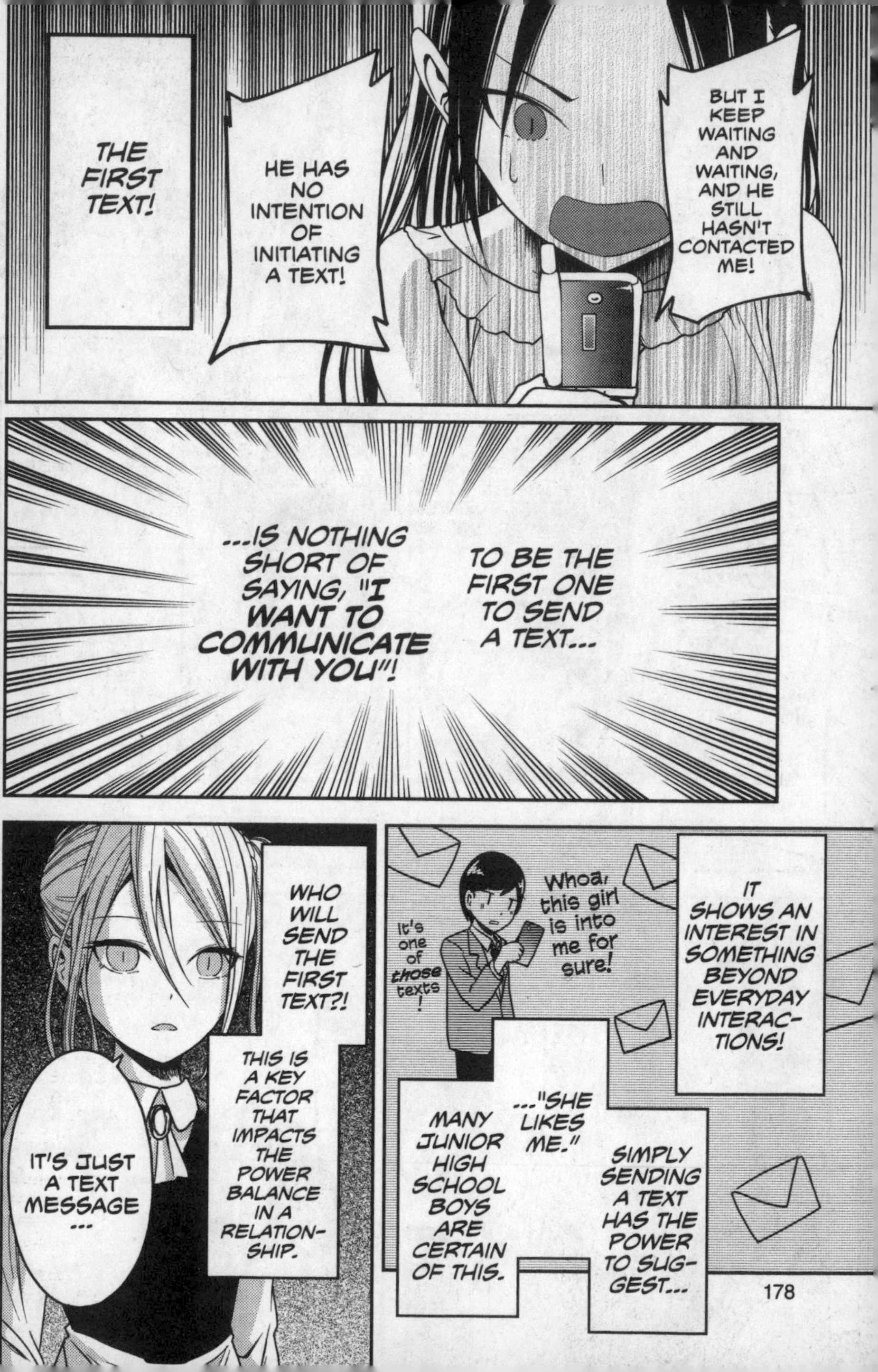
BUT I KEEP WAITING AND WAITING, AND HE STILL HASN'T CONTACTED ME!
HE HAS NO INTENTION OF INITIATING A TEXT!
THE FIRST TEXT!
TO BE THE FIRST ONE TO SEND A TEXT...
...IS NOTHING SHORT OF SAYING, "I WANT TO COMMUNICATE WITH YOU"!
IT SHOWS AN INTEREST IN SOMETHING BEYOND EVERYDAY INTERACTIONS!
Whoa, this girl is into me for sure!
It's one of *those* texts!
SIMPLY SENDING A TEXT HAS THE POWER TO SUGGEST...
..."SHE LIKES ME."
MANY JUNIOR HIGH SCHOOL BOYS ARE CERTAIN OF THIS.
WHO WILL SEND THE FIRST TEXT?!
THIS IS A KEY FACTOR THAT IMPACTS THE POWER BALANCE IN A RELATIONSHIP.
IT'S JUST A TEXT MESSAGE...

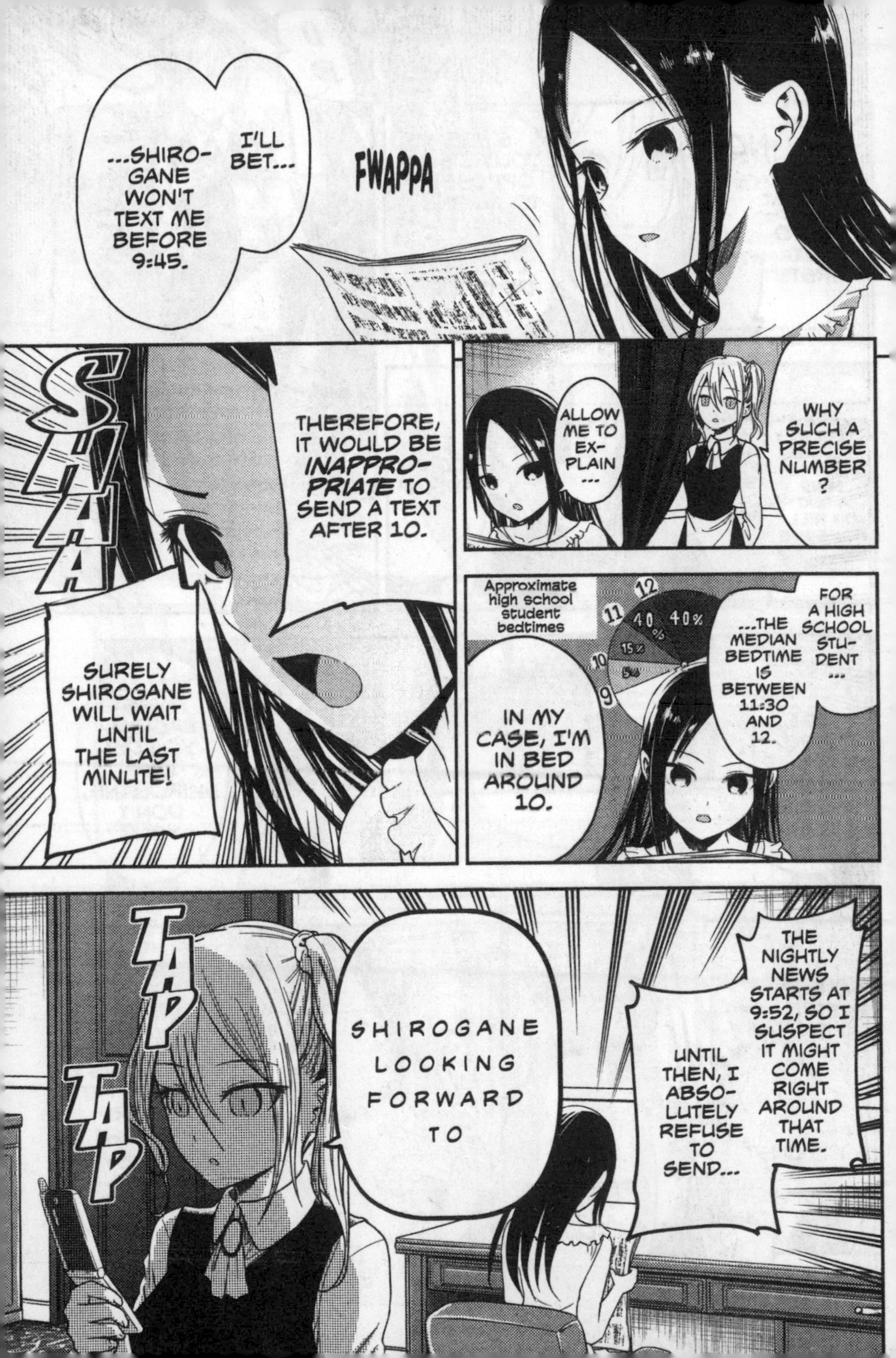
FWAPPA
I'LL BET...
...SHIROGANE WON'T TEXT ME BEFORE 9:45.
WHY SUCH A PRECISE NUMBER?
ALLOW ME TO EXPLAIN...
FOR A HIGH SCHOOL STUDENT...
...THE MEDIAN BEDTIME IS BETWEEN 11:30 AND 12.
Approximate high school student bedtimes
12
11
10
9
40%
40%
15%
5%
IN MY CASE, I'M IN BED AROUND 10.
THEREFORE, IT WOULD BE *INAPPROPRIATE* TO SEND A TEXT AFTER 10.
SHAAA
SURELY SHIROGANE WILL WAIT UNTIL THE LAST MINUTE!
THE NIGHTLY NEWS STARTS AT 9:52, SO I SUSPECT IT MIGHT COME RIGHT AROUND THAT TIME.
UNTIL THEN, I ABSOLUTELY REFUSE TO SEND...
SHIROGANE LOOKING FORWARD TO
TAP
TAP

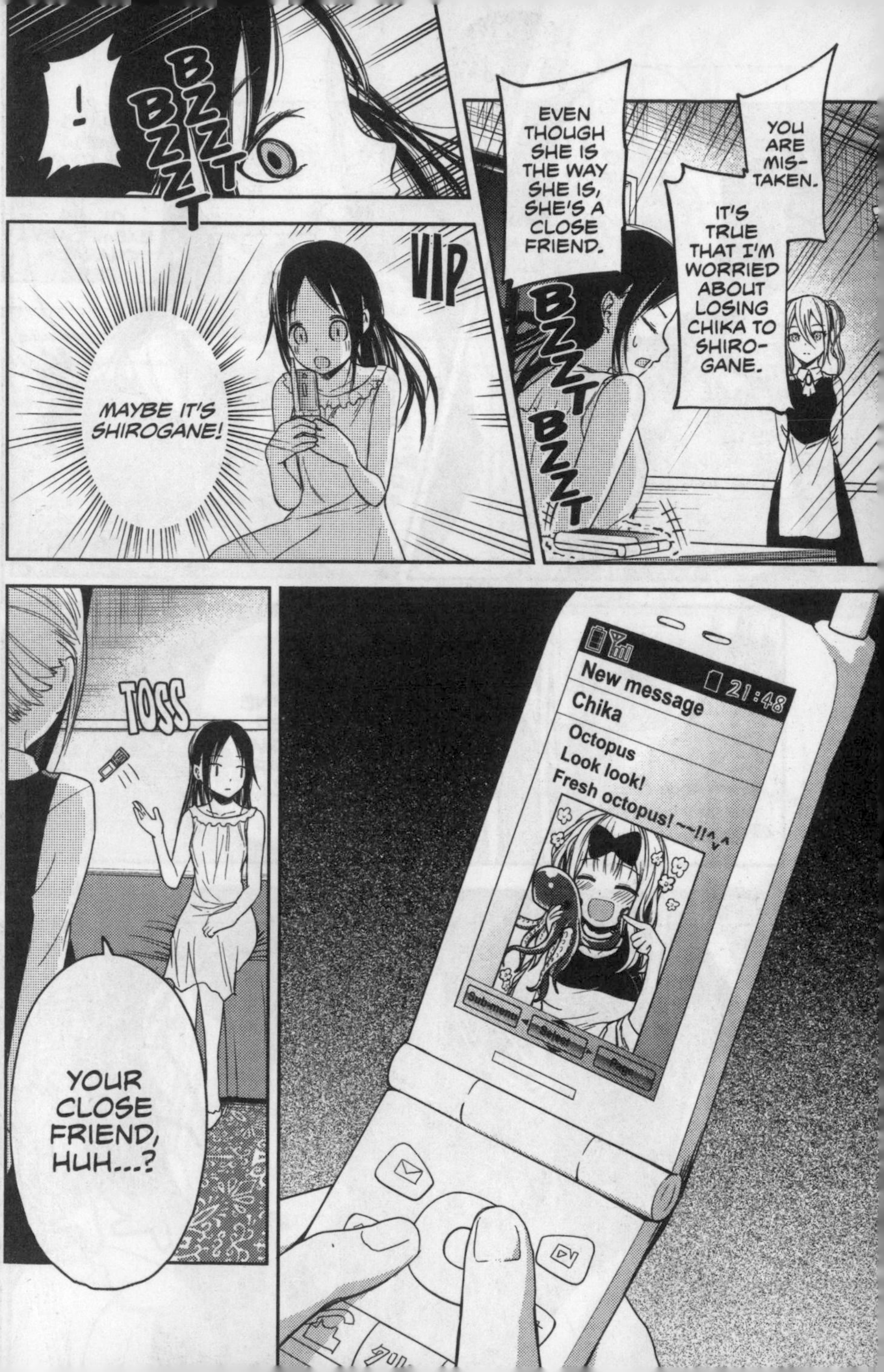
YOU ARE MIS-TAKEN.
IT'S TRUE THAT I'M WORRIED ABOUT LOSING CHIKA TO SHIRO-GANE.
EVEN THOUGH SHE IS THE WAY SHE IS, SHE'S A CLOSE FRIEND.
BZZZT
BZZZT
!
BZZZT
BZZZT
VIP
MAYBE IT'S SHIROGANE!
New message
21:48
Chika
Octopus
Look look!
Fresh octopus! ~~!!^_^
TOSS
YOUR CLOSE FRIEND, HUH...?

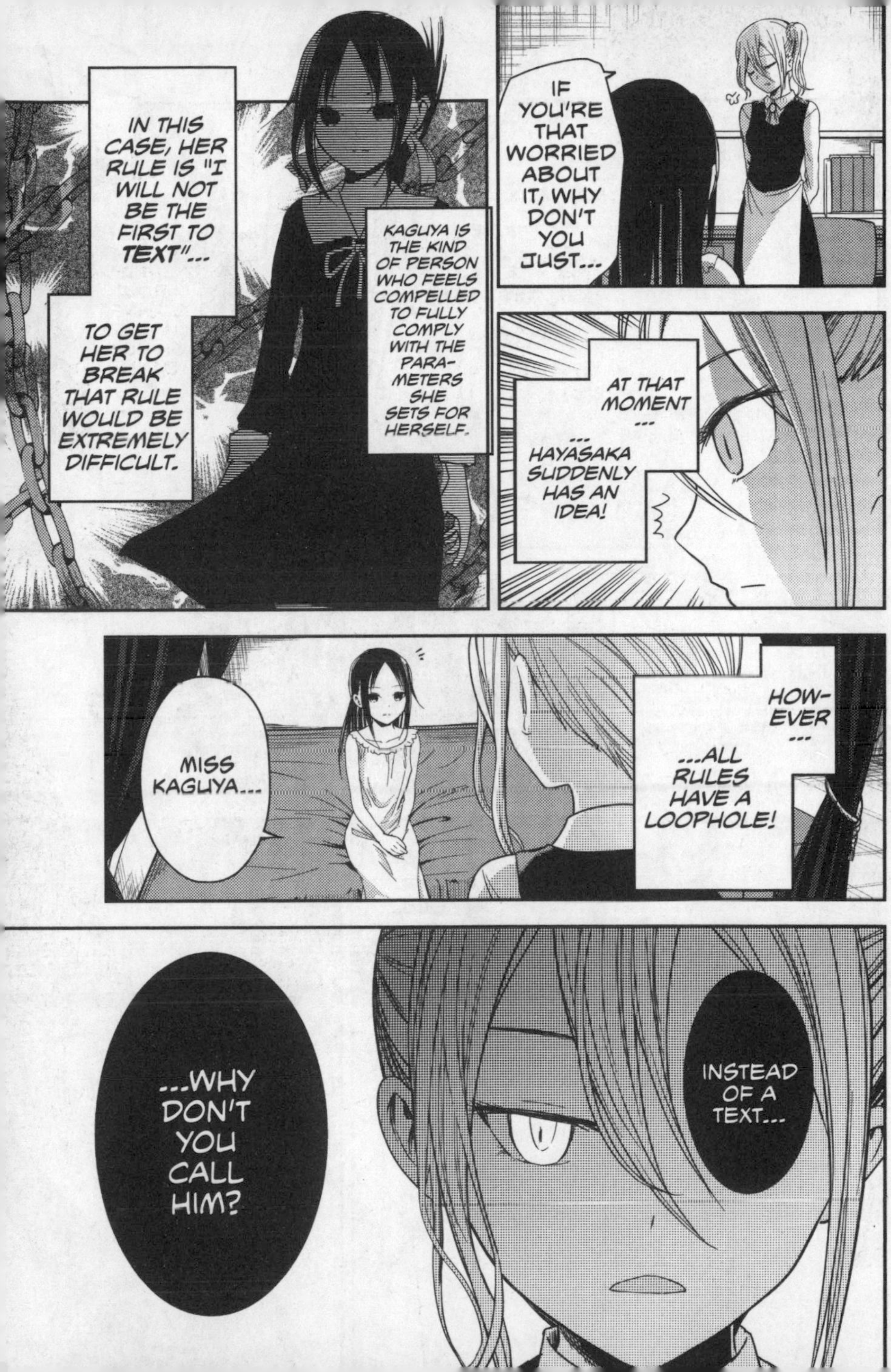
IF YOU'RE THAT WORRIED ABOUT IT, WHY DON'T YOU JUST...
AT THAT MOMENT ...
... HAYASAKA SUDDENLY HAS AN IDEA!
IN THIS CASE, HER RULE IS "I WILL NOT BE THE FIRST TO TEXT"...
KAGUYA IS THE KIND OF PERSON WHO FEELS COMPELLED TO FULLY COMPLY WITH THE PARA-METERS SHE SETS FOR HERSELF.
TO GET HER TO BREAK THAT RULE WOULD BE EXTREMELY DIFFICULT.
HOW-EVER ...
...ALL RULES HAVE A LOOPHOLE!
MISS KAGUYA...
INSTEAD OF A TEXT...
...WHY DON'T YOU CALL HIM?

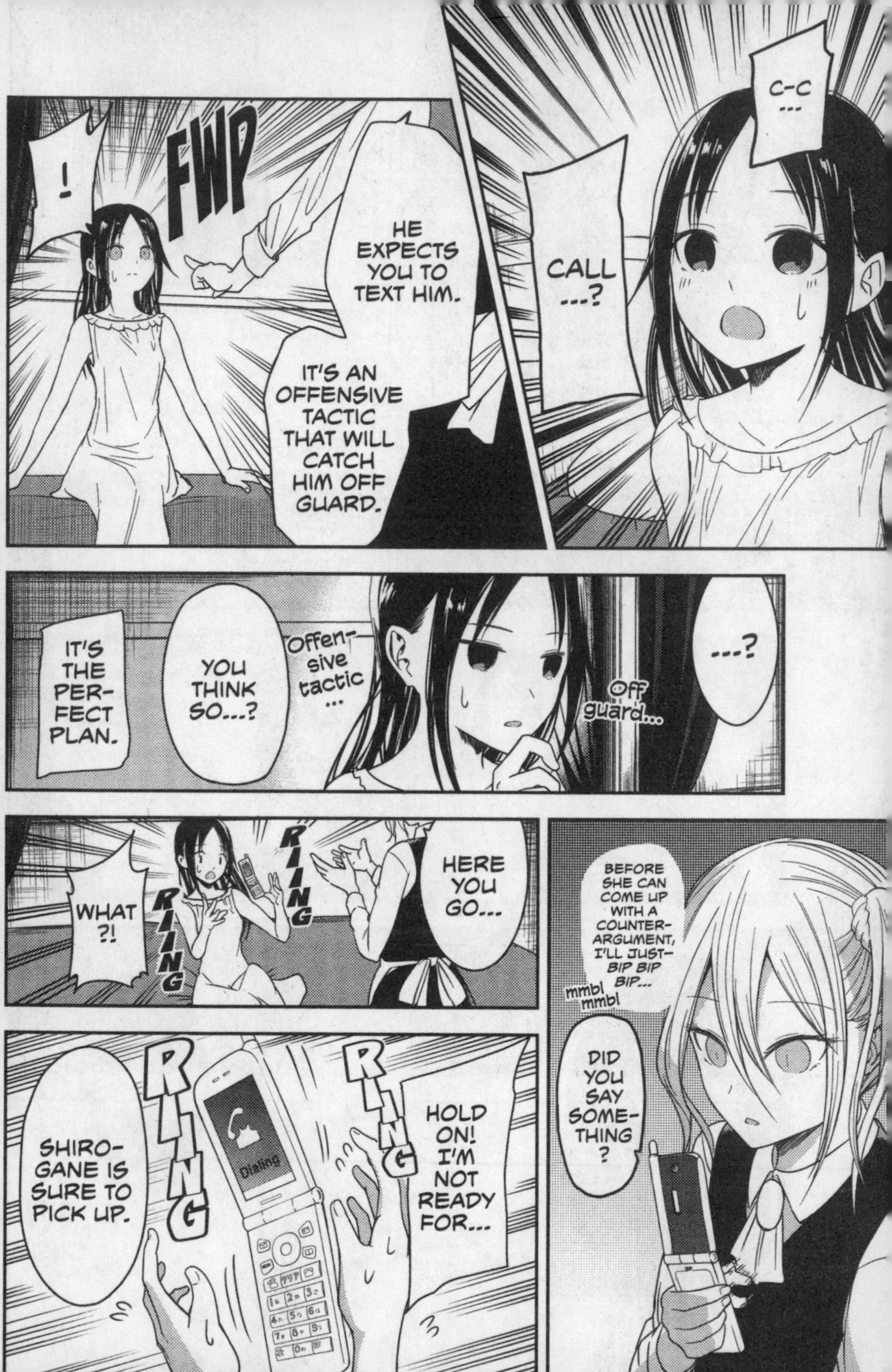
C-C...
CALL...?
HE EXPECTS YOU TO TEXT HIM.
IT'S AN OFFENSIVE TACTIC THAT WILL CATCH HIM OFF GUARD.
FWP
!
...?
Off guard...
Offensive tactic...
YOU THINK SO...?
IT'S THE PERFECT PLAN.
BEFORE SHE CAN COME UP WITH A COUNTERARGUMENT, I'LL JUST BIP BIP BIP...
mmbl mmbl
DID YOU SAY SOMETHING?
HERE YOU GO...
RING
WHAT?!
RING
HOLD ON! I'M NOT READY FOR...
RING
Dialing
RING
SHIROGANE IS SURE TO PICK UP.

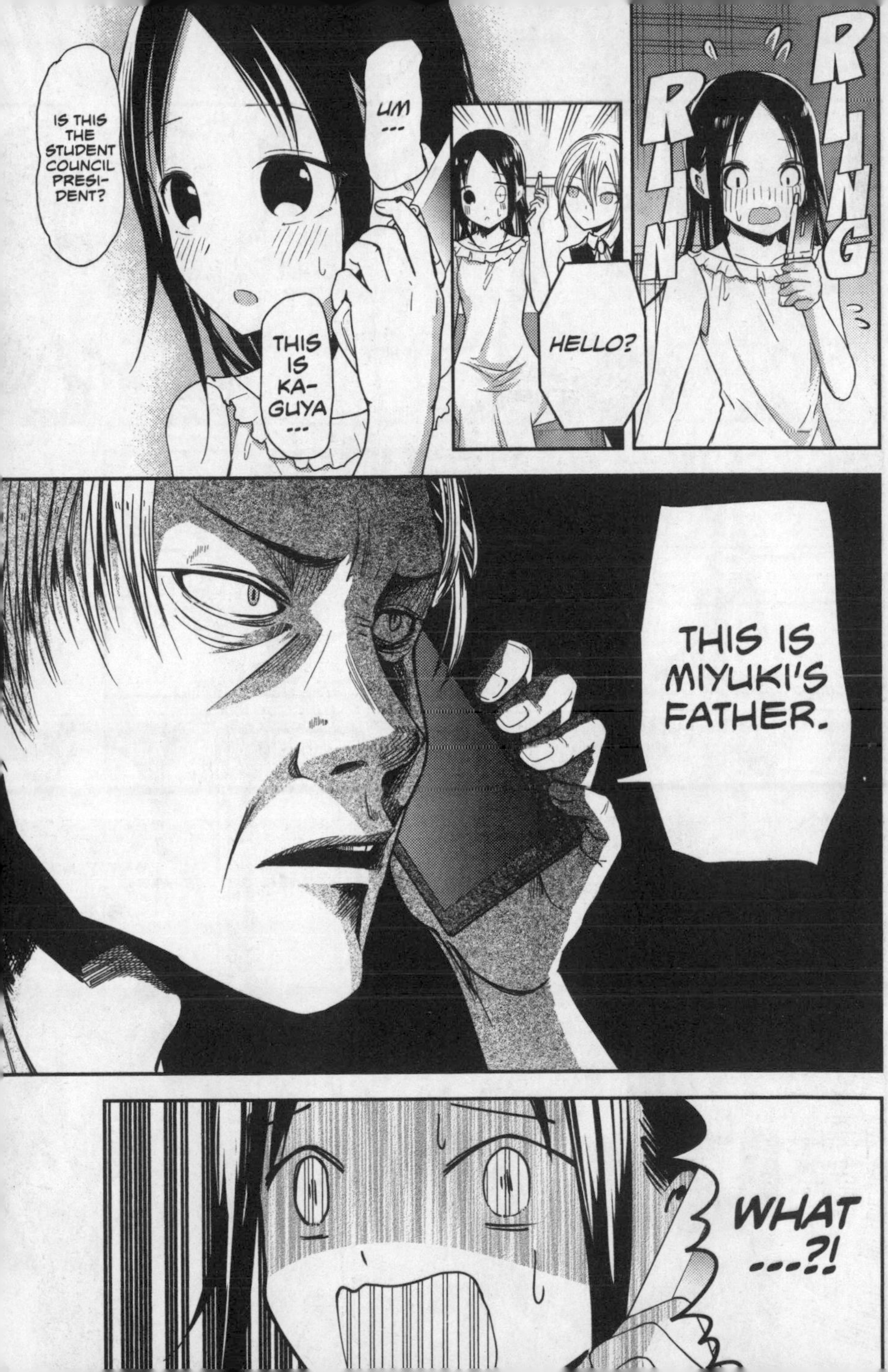
RING
RIN
HELLO?
UM ---
THIS IS KA-GUYA ---
IS THIS THE STUDENT COUNCIL PRESI-DENT?
THIS IS MIYUKI'S FATHER.
WHAT ---?!

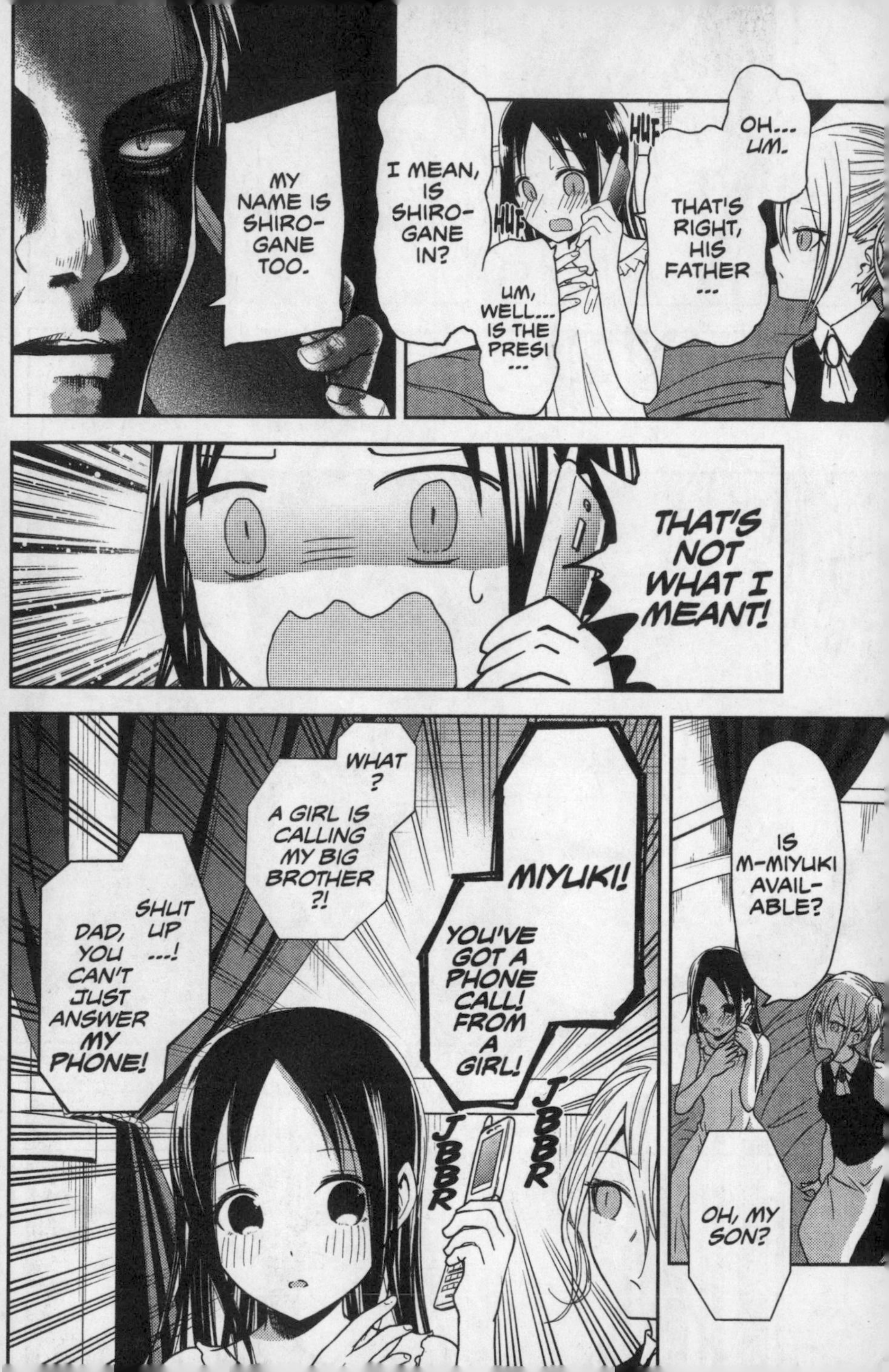
OH... UM.
THAT'S RIGHT, HIS FATHER ...
HUF
HUF
UM, WELL... IS THE PRESI ...
I MEAN, IS SHIROGANE IN?
MY NAME IS SHIROGANE TOO.
THAT'S NOT WHAT I MEANT!
IS M-MIYUKI AVAILABLE?
OH, MY SON?
MIYUKI!
YOU'VE GOT A PHONE CALL! FROM A GIRL!
WHAT? A GIRL IS CALLING MY BIG BROTHER?!
SHUT UP ...!
DAD, YOU CAN'T JUST ANSWER MY PHONE!
JBBR
JBBR

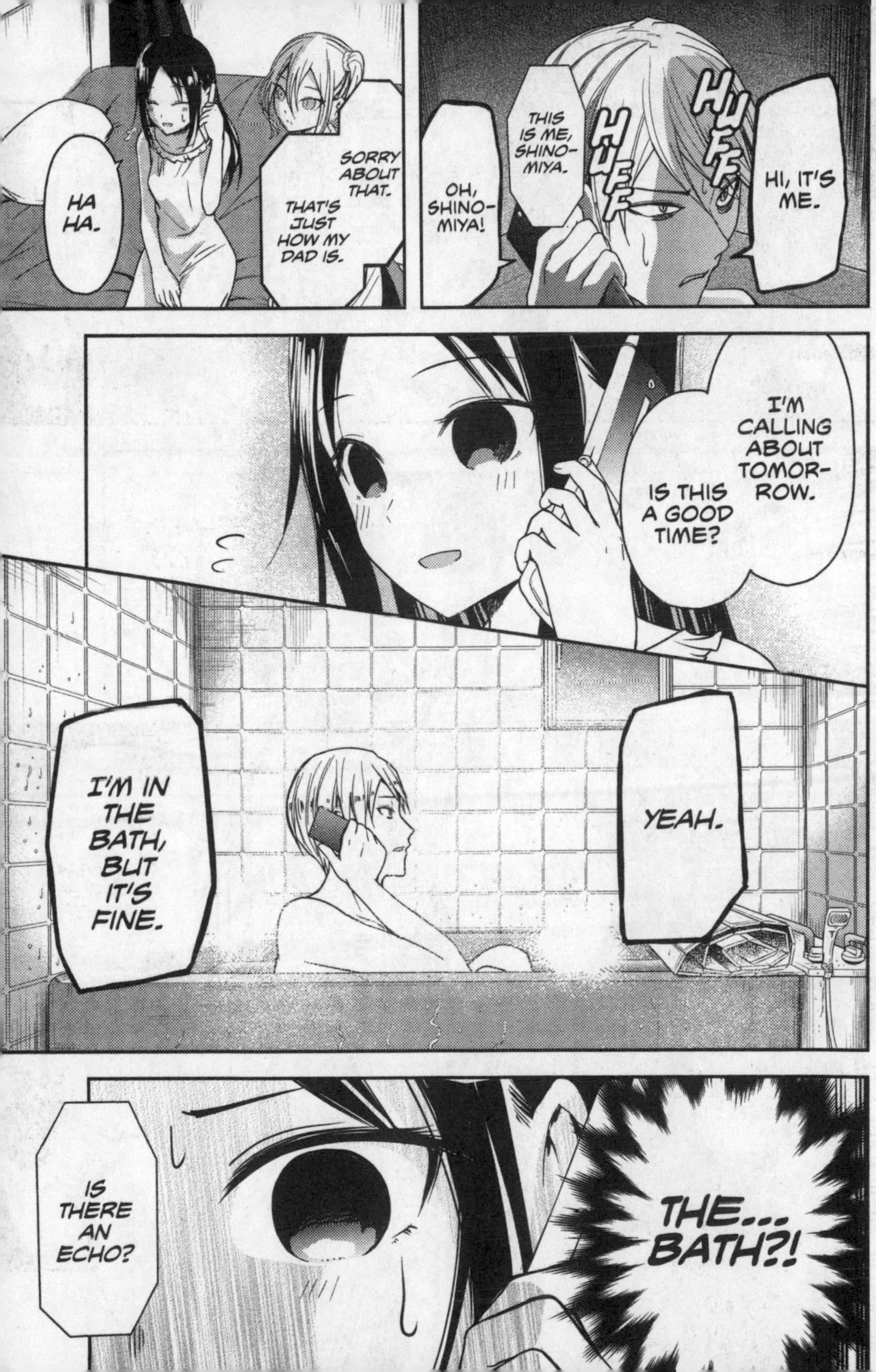
HI, IT'S ME.
HUFF HUFF
THIS IS ME, SHINO-MIYA.
OH, SHINO-MIYA!
SORRY ABOUT THAT.
THAT'S JUST HOW MY DAD IS.
HA HA.
I'M CALLING ABOUT TOMOR-ROW.
IS THIS A GOOD TIME?
YEAH.
I'M IN THE BATH, BUT IT'S FINE.
THE... BATH?!
IS THERE AN ECHO?

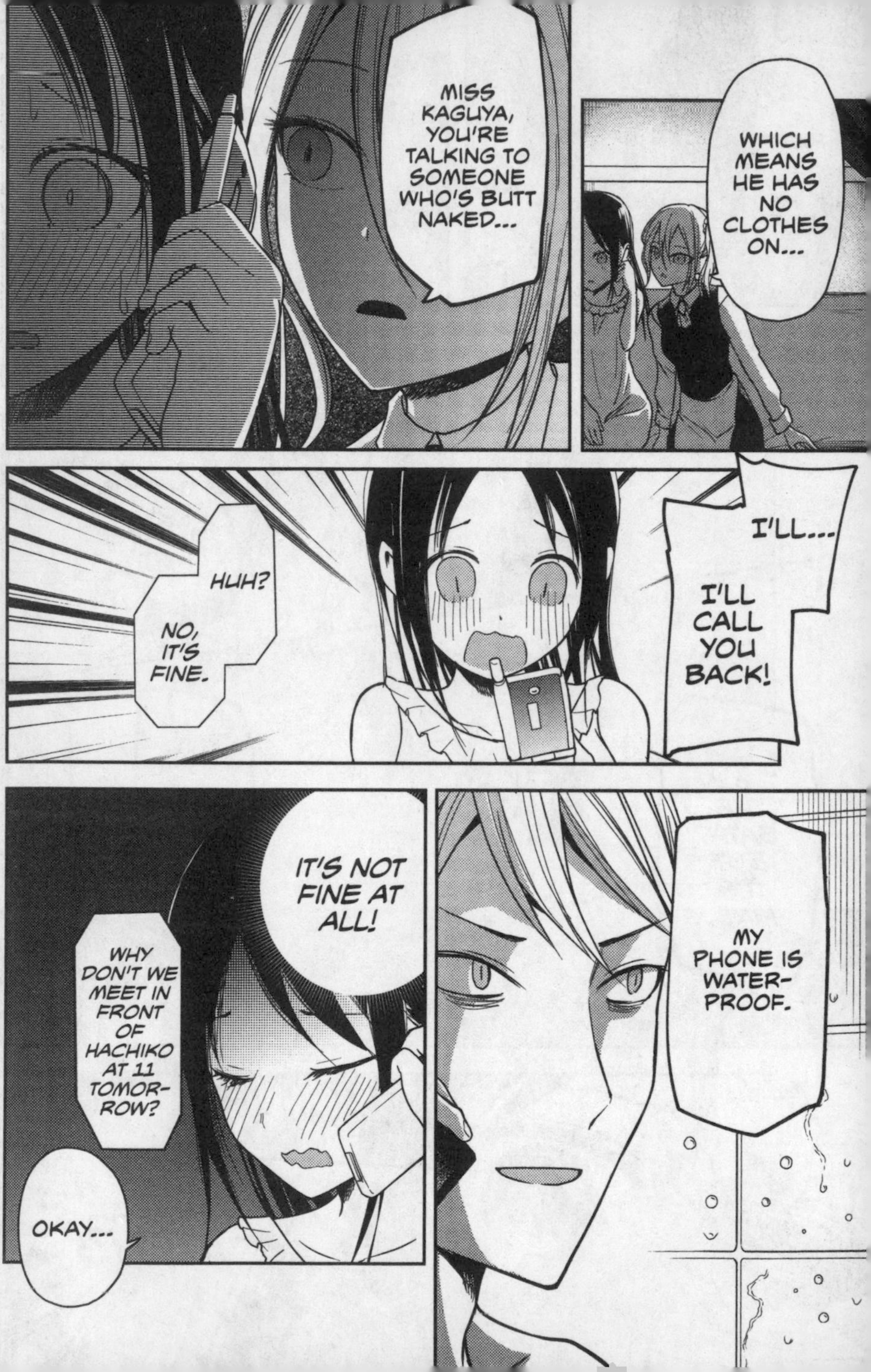
WHICH MEANS HE HAS NO CLOTHES ON...
MISS KAGUYA, YOU'RE TALKING TO SOMEONE WHO'S BUTT NAKED...
I'LL...
I'LL CALL YOU BACK!
HUH?
NO, IT'S FINE.
MY PHONE IS WATER-PROOF.
IT'S NOT FINE AT ALL!
WHY DON'T WE MEET IN FRONT OF HACHIKO AT 11 TOMOR-ROW?
OKAY...

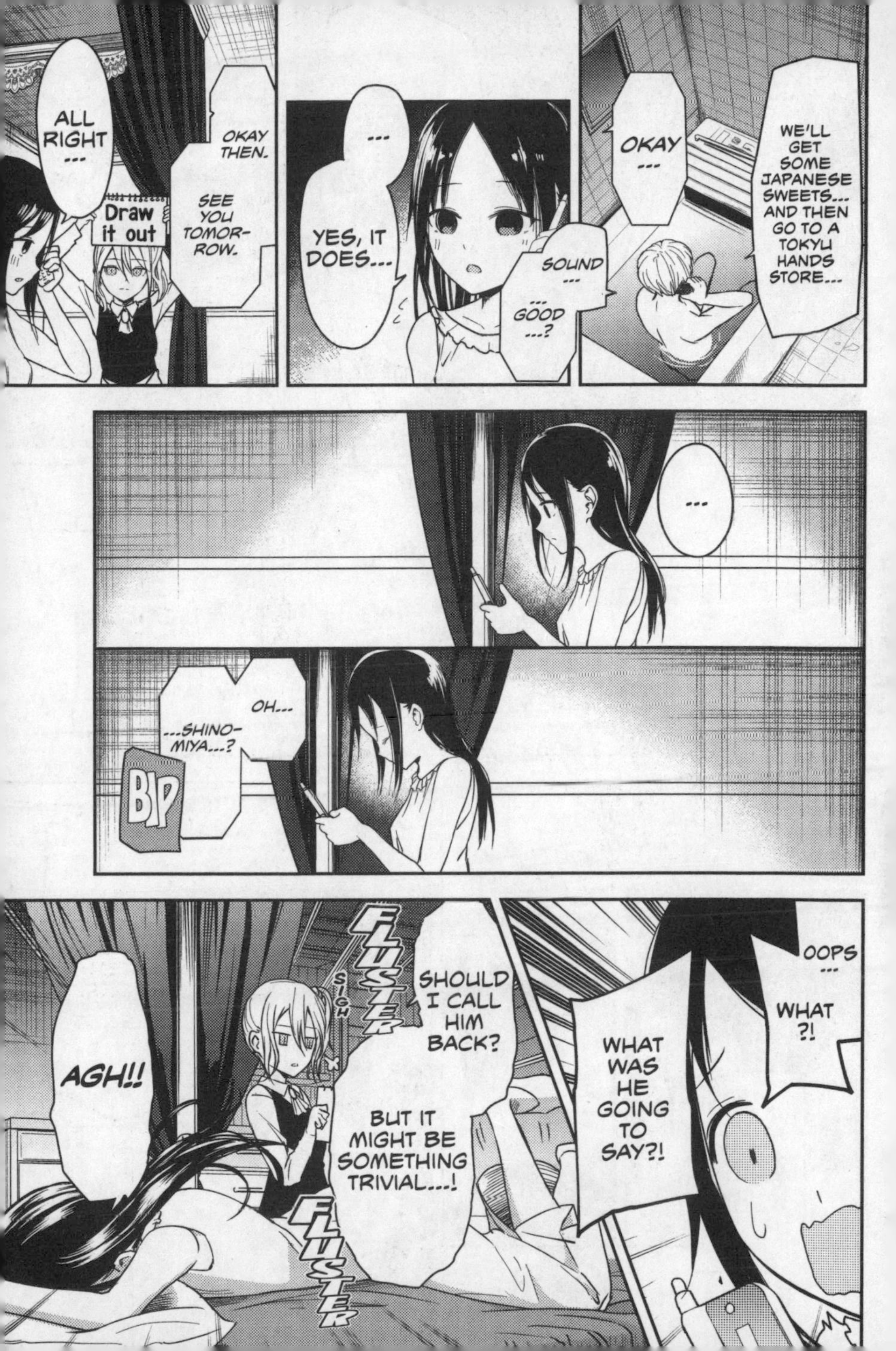
WE'LL GET SOME JAPANESE SWEETS... AND THEN GO TO A TOKYU HANDS STORE...
OKAY ...
SOUND ... ... GOOD ...?
YES, IT DOES...
...
OKAY THEN.
SEE YOU TOMORROW.
Draw it out
ALL RIGHT ...
...
OH...
...SHINOMIYA...?
BIP
OOPS ...
WHAT ?!
WHAT WAS HE GOING TO SAY?!
FLUSTER
SHOULD I CALL HIM BACK?
SIGH
BUT IT MIGHT BE SOMETHING TRIVIAL...!
FLUSTER
AGH!!

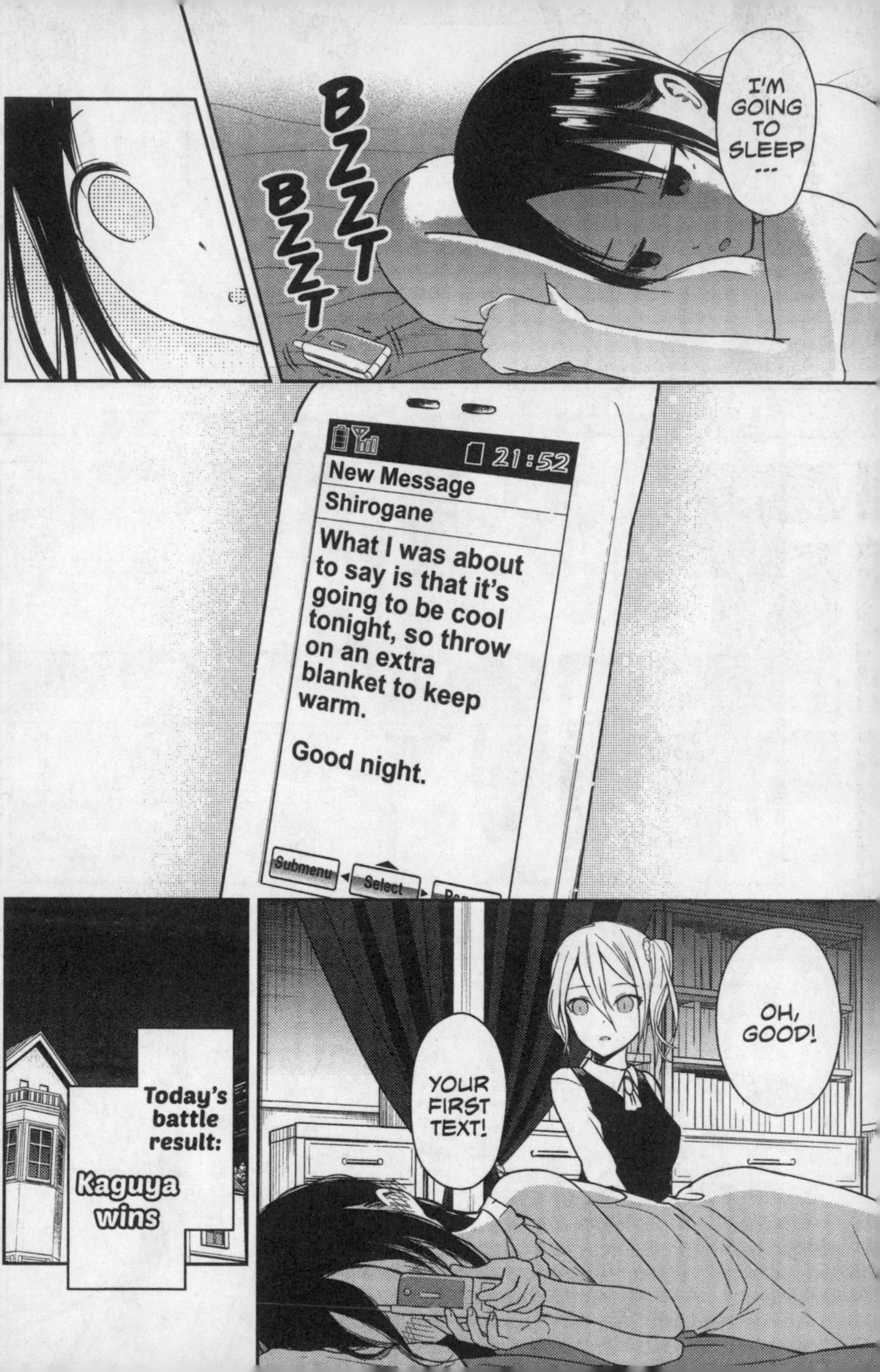
I'M GOING TO SLEEP ---
BZZT
BZZT
21:52
New Message
Shirogane
What I was about to say is that it's going to be cool tonight, so throw on an extra blanket to keep warm.
Good night.
Submenu
Select
OH, GOOD!
YOUR FIRST TEXT!
Today's battle result:
Kaguya wins

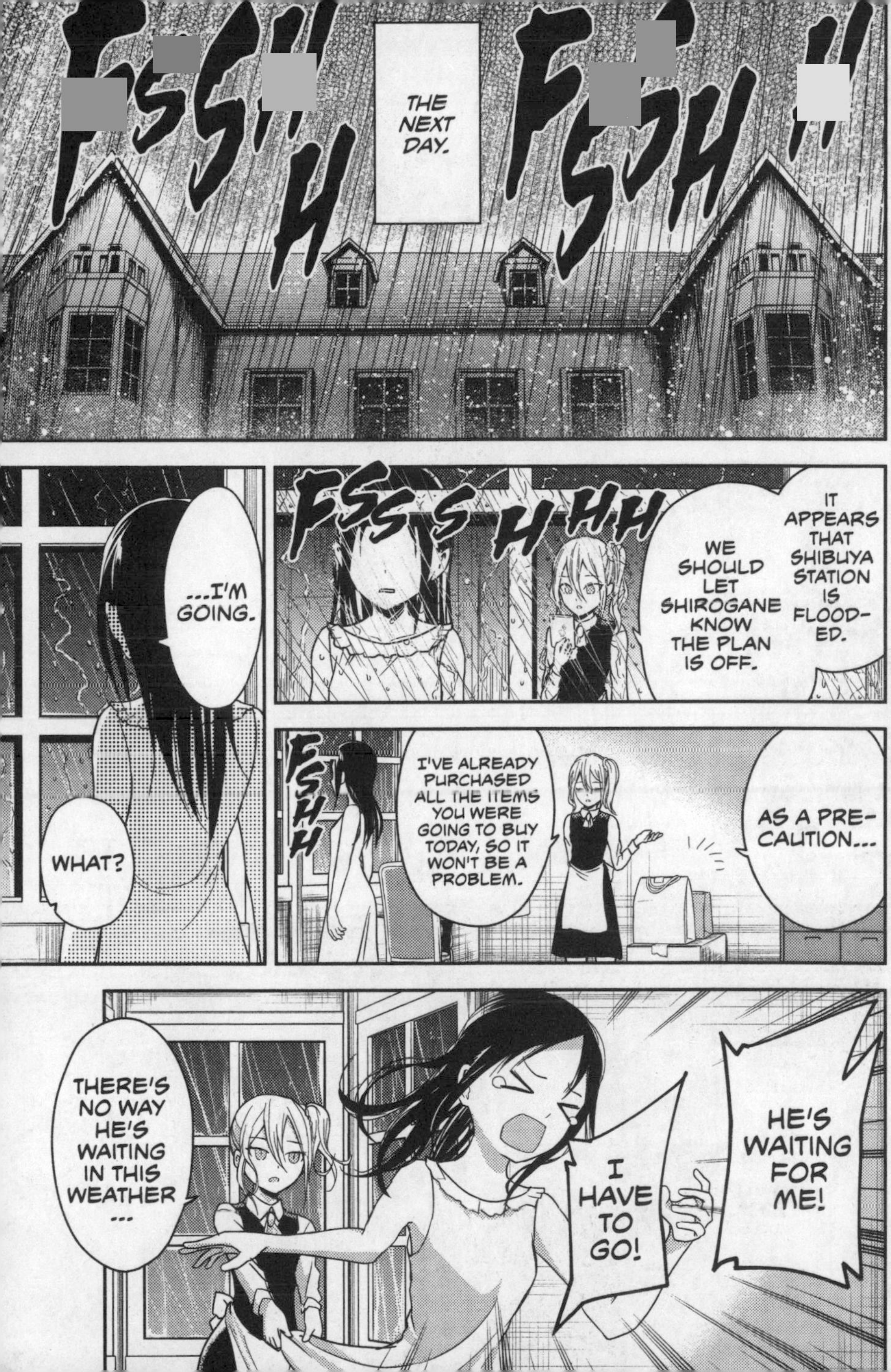
FSSH
THE NEXT DAY.
FSSH
IT APPEARS THAT SHIBUYA STATION IS FLOOD-ED.
WE SHOULD LET SHIROGANE KNOW THE PLAN IS OFF.
FSSSHHH
AS A PRE-CAUTION...
I'VE ALREADY PURCHASED ALL THE ITEMS YOU WERE GOING TO BUY TODAY, SO IT WON'T BE A PROBLEM.
FSHH
...I'M GOING.
WHAT?
HE'S WAITING FOR ME!
I HAVE TO GO!
THERE'S NO WAY HE'S WAITING IN THIS WEATHER...

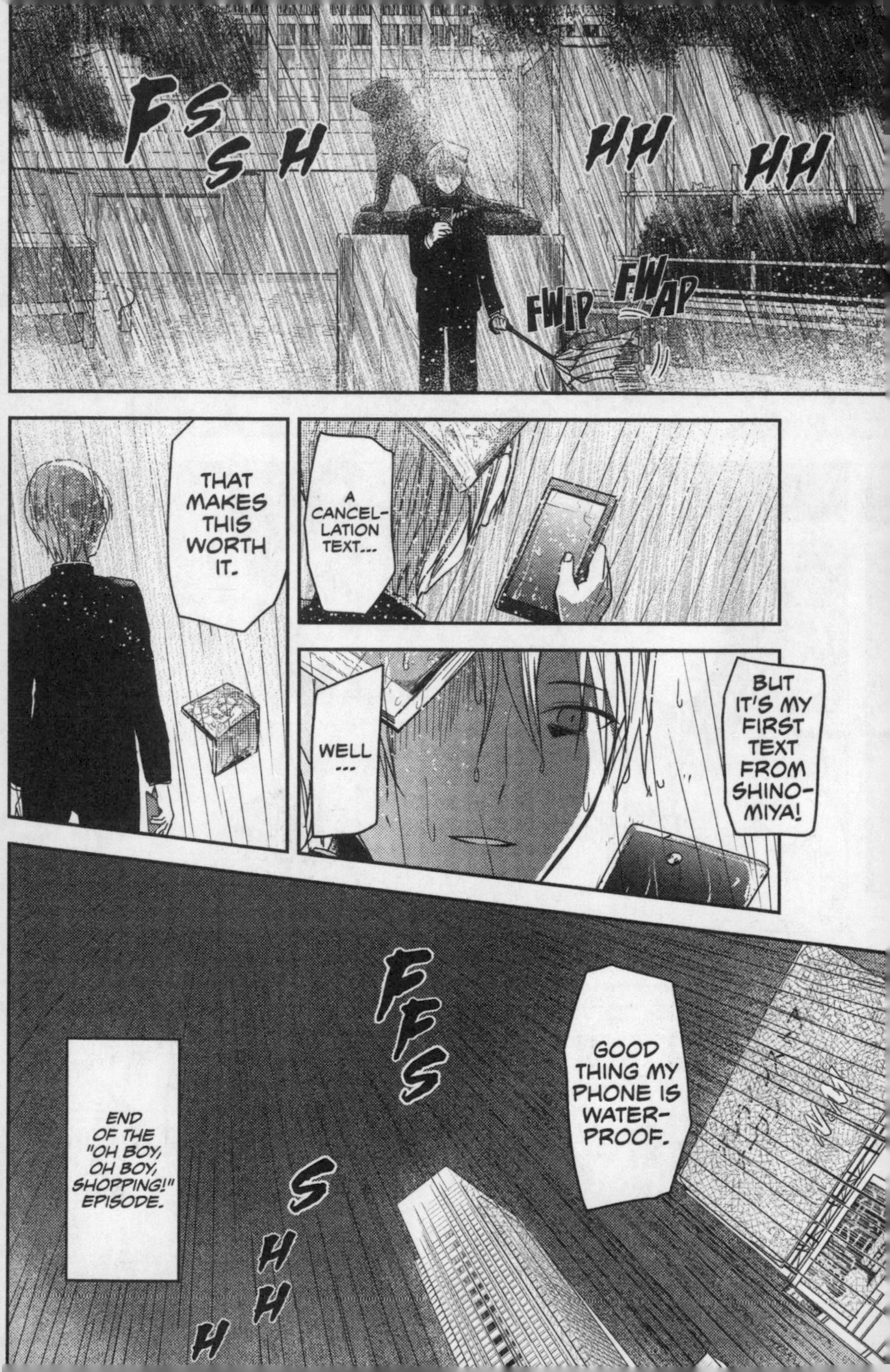
FSSH HH HH
FWAP
FWIP
A CANCEL-LATION TEXT...
WELL...
BUT IT'S MY FIRST TEXT FROM SHINO-MIYA!
THAT MAKES THIS WORTH IT.
GOOD THING MY PHONE IS WATER-PROOF.
FFSSHHHH
END OF THE "OH BOY, OH BOY, SHOPPING!" EPISODE.

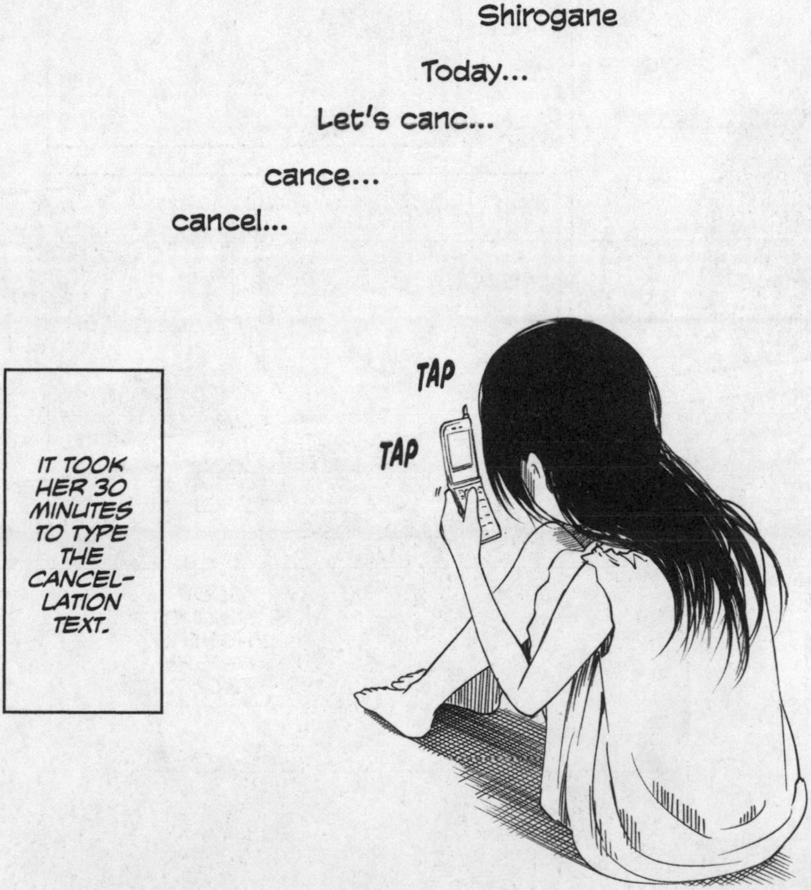

Shirogane
Today...
Let's canc...
cance...
cancel...
TAP
TAP
IT TOOK HER 30 MINUTES TO TYPE THE CANCEL-LATION TEXT.

KAGUYA-SAMA

LOVE IS WAR

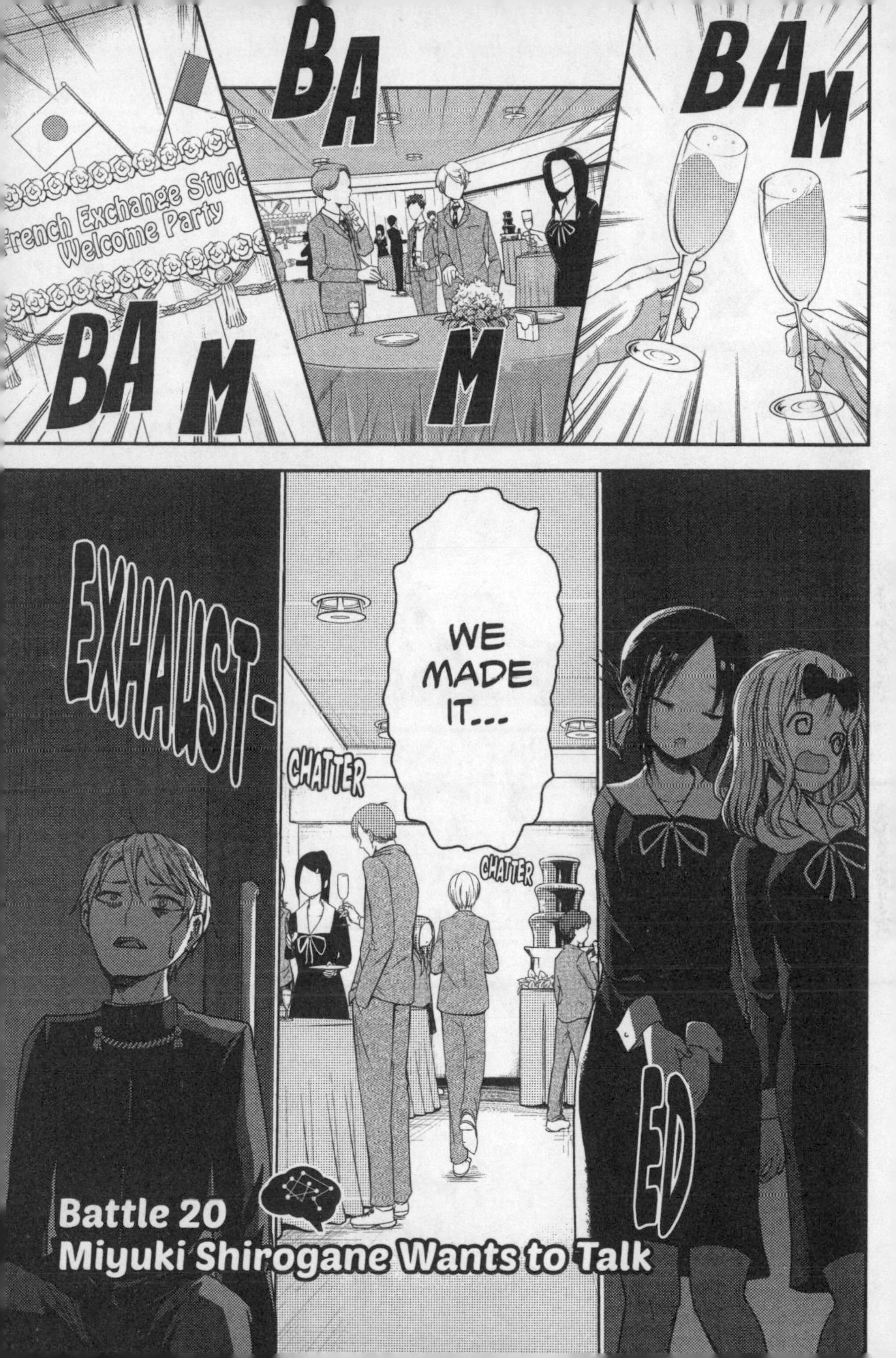
BAM
BA
M
French Exchange Stude
Welcome Party
BA
M
WE MADE IT...
CHATTER
CHATTER
EXHAUST-
ED
Battle 20
Miyuki Shirogane Wants to Talk

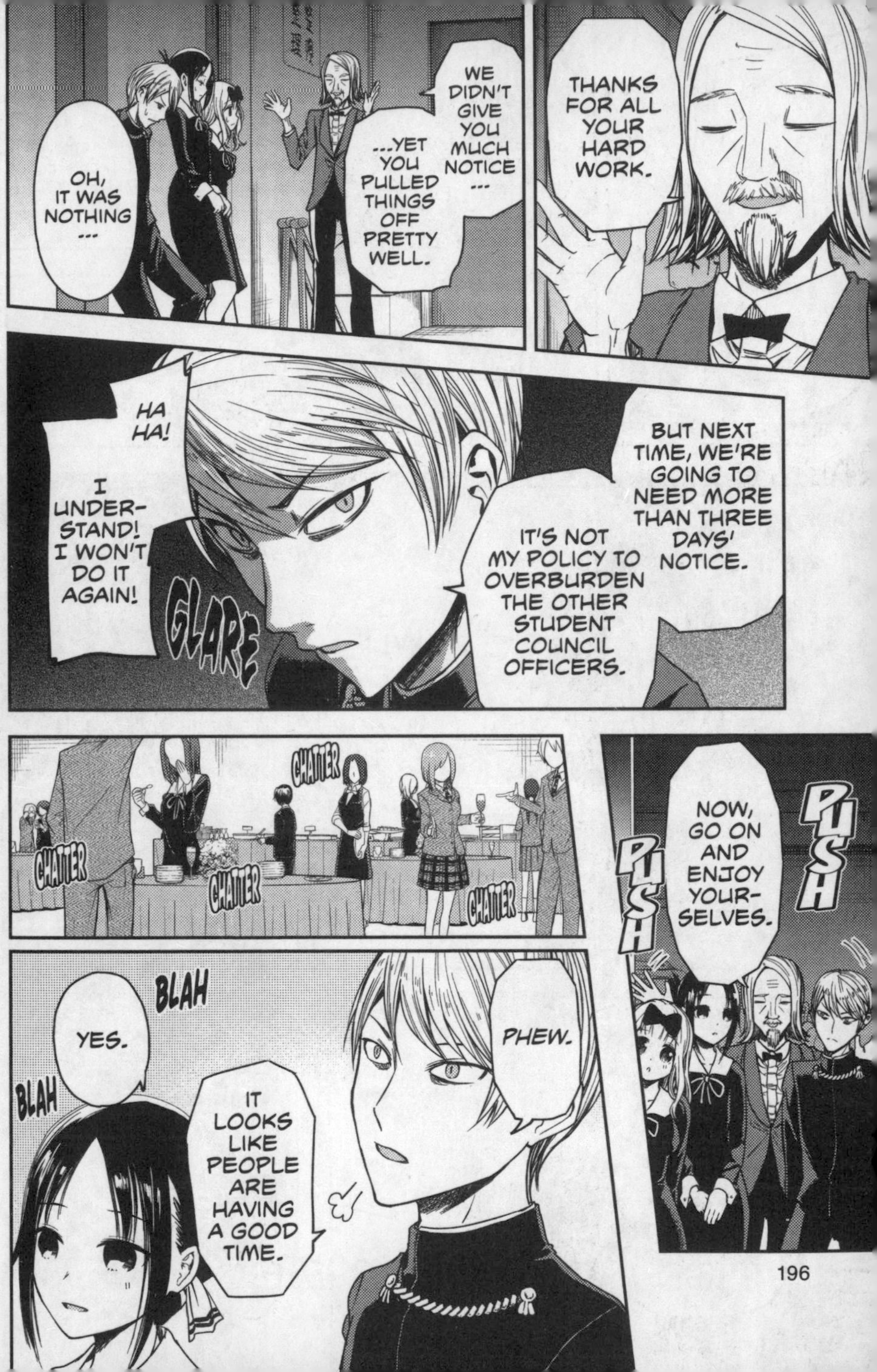
THANKS FOR ALL YOUR HARD WORK.
WE DIDN'T GIVE YOU MUCH NOTICE...
...YET YOU PULLED THINGS OFF PRETTY WELL.
OH, IT WAS NOTHING...
BUT NEXT TIME, WE'RE GOING TO NEED MORE THAN THREE DAYS' NOTICE.
IT'S NOT MY POLICY TO OVERBURDEN THE OTHER STUDENT COUNCIL OFFICERS.
GLARE
HA HA!
I UNDERSTAND! I WON'T DO IT AGAIN!
PUSH
NOW, GO ON AND ENJOY YOURSELVES.
PUSH
CHATTER
CHATTER
CHATTER
CHATTER
PHEW.
BLAH
YES.
BLAH
IT LOOKS LIKE PEOPLE ARE HAVING A GOOD TIME.

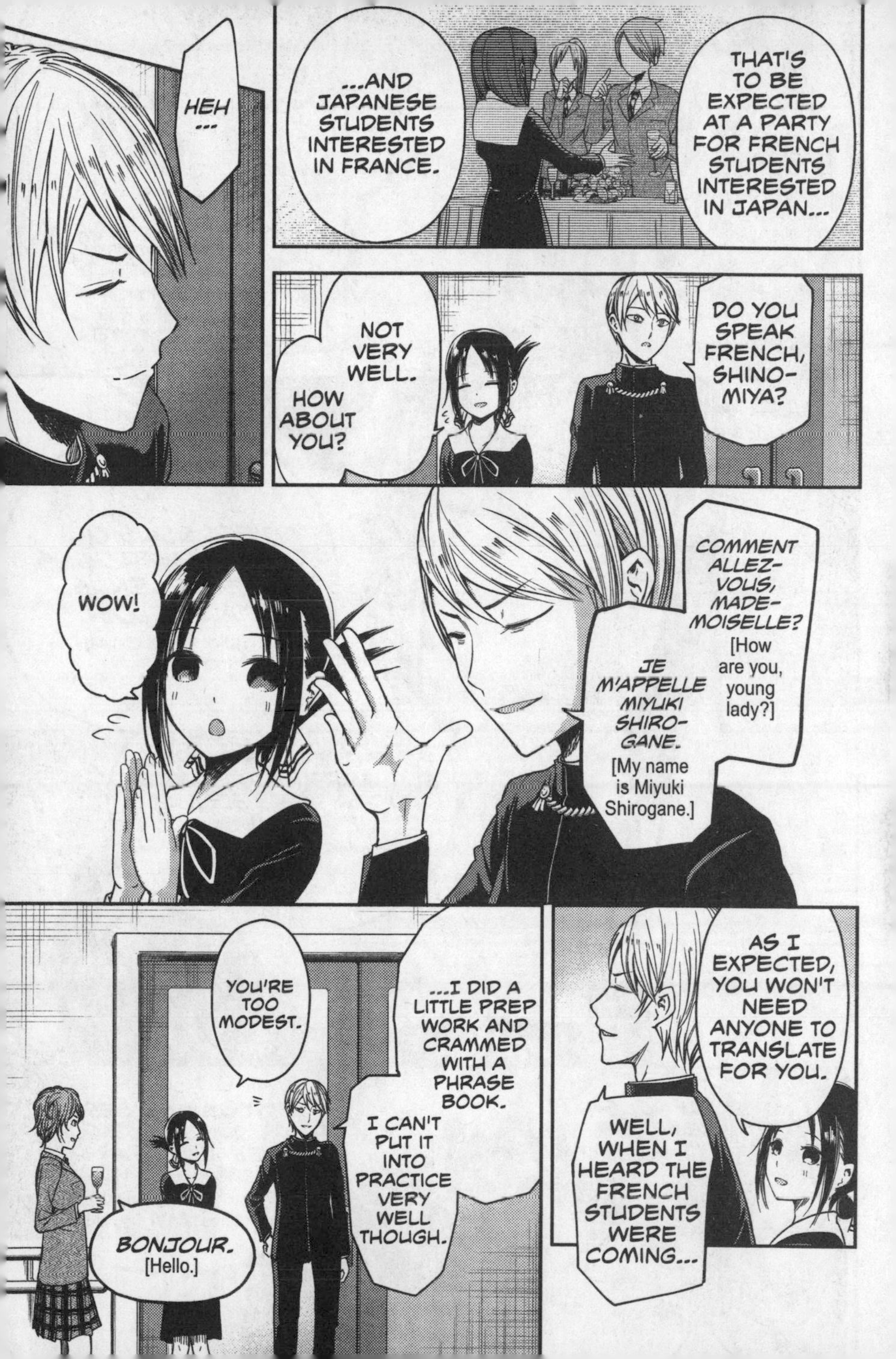

THAT'S TO BE EXPECTED AT A PARTY FOR FRENCH STUDENTS INTERESTED IN JAPAN...
...AND JAPANESE STUDENTS INTERESTED IN FRANCE.
DO YOU SPEAK FRENCH, SHINOMIYA?
NOT VERY WELL.
HOW ABOUT YOU?
HEH...
COMMENT ALLEZ-VOUS, MADEMOISELLE? [How are you, young lady?]
JE M'APPELLE MIYUKI SHIROGANE. [My name is Miyuki Shirogane.]
WOW!
AS I EXPECTED, YOU WON'T NEED ANYONE TO TRANSLATE FOR YOU.
WELL, WHEN I HEARD THE FRENCH STUDENTS WERE COMING...
...I DID A LITTLE PREP WORK AND CRAMMED WITH A PHRASE BOOK.
I CAN'T PUT IT INTO PRACTICE VERY WELL THOUGH.
YOU'RE TOO MODEST.
BONJOUR. [Hello.]

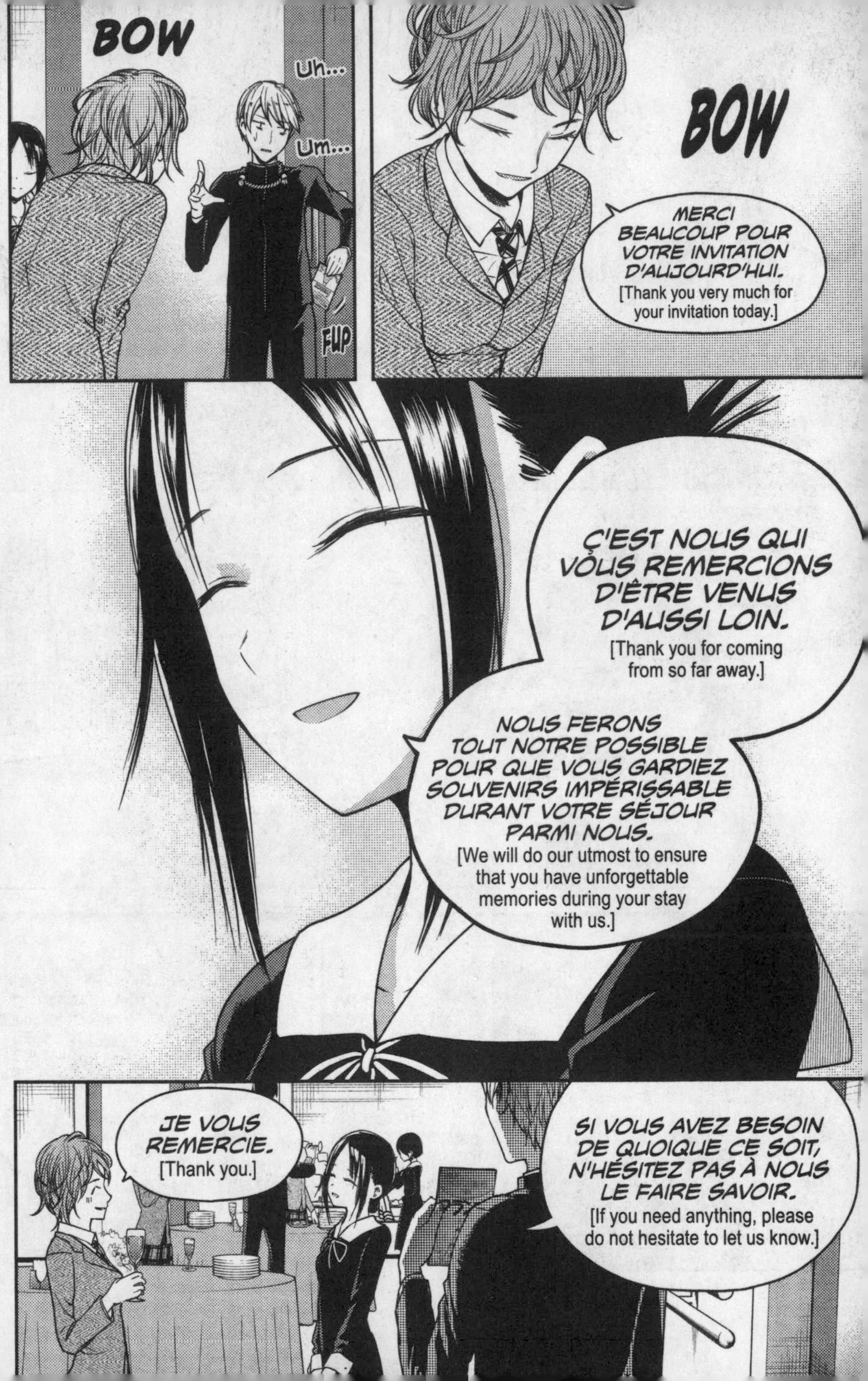
BOW
MERCI BEAUCOUP POUR VOTRE INVITATION D'AUJOURD'HUI.
[Thank you very much for your invitation today.]
BOW
Uh...
Um...
FUP
C'EST NOUS QUI VOUS REMERCIONS D'ÊTRE VENUS D'AUSSI LOIN.
[Thank you for coming from so far away.]
NOUS FERONS TOUT NOTRE POSSIBLE POUR QUE VOUS GARDIEZ SOUVENIRS IMPÉRISSABLE DURANT VOTRE SÉJOUR PARMI NOUS.
[We will do our utmost to ensure that you have unforgettable memories during your stay with us.]
SI VOUS AVEZ BESOIN DE QUOIQUE CE SOIT, N'HÉSITEZ PAS À NOUS LE FAIRE SAVOIR.
[If you need anything, please do not hesitate to let us know.]
JE VOUS REMERCIE.
[Thank you.]

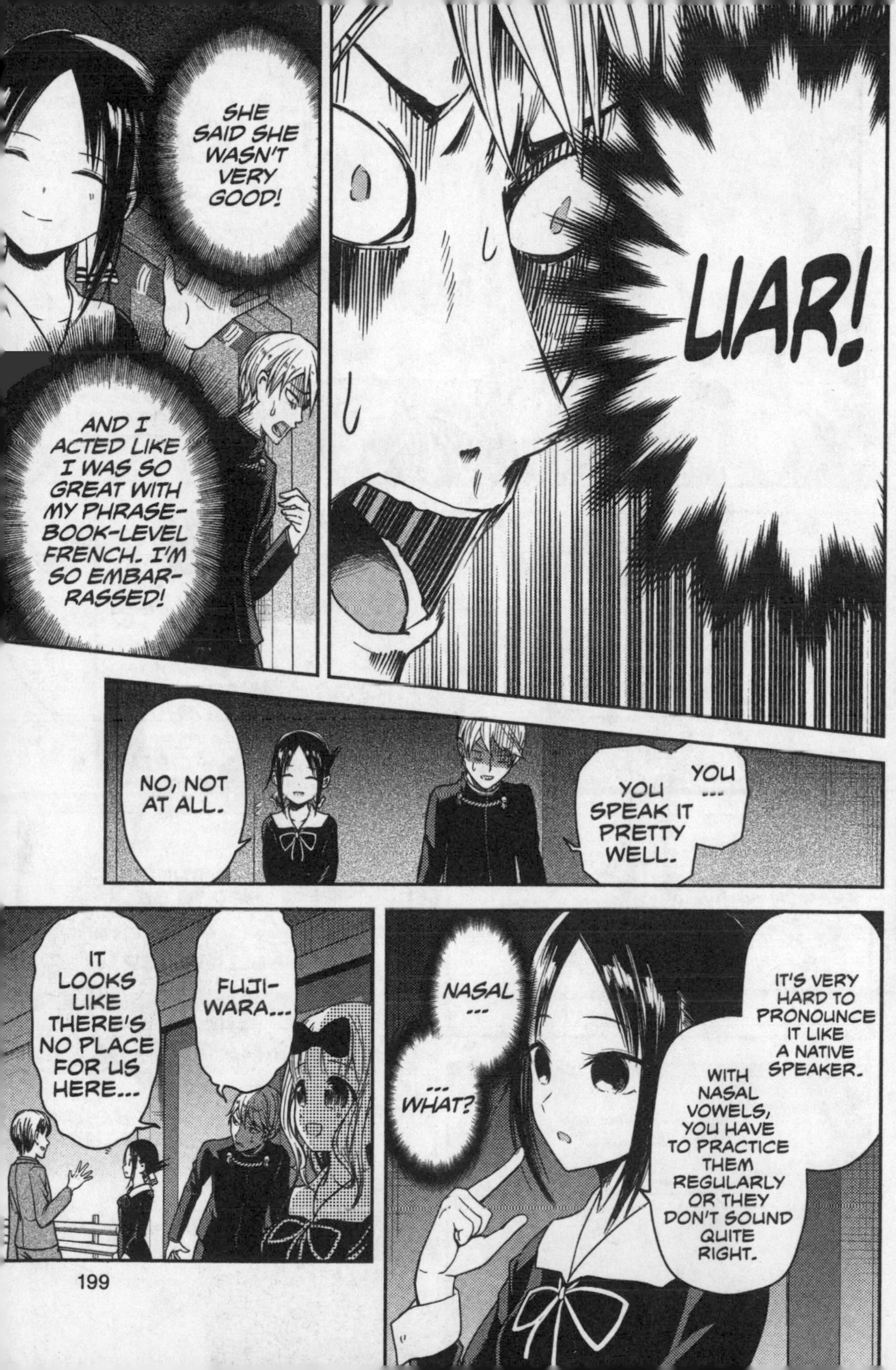
LIAR!
SHE SAID SHE WASN'T VERY GOOD!
AND I ACTED LIKE I WAS SO GREAT WITH MY PHRASE-BOOK-LEVEL FRENCH. I'M SO EMBAR-RASSED!
YOU ...
YOU SPEAK IT PRETTY WELL.
NO, NOT AT ALL.
IT'S VERY HARD TO PRONOUNCE IT LIKE A NATIVE SPEAKER.
WITH NASAL VOWELS, YOU HAVE TO PRACTICE THEM REGULARLY OR THEY DON'T SOUND QUITE RIGHT.
NASAL ...
... WHAT?
FUJI-WARA...
IT LOOKS LIKE THERE'S NO PLACE FOR US HERE...

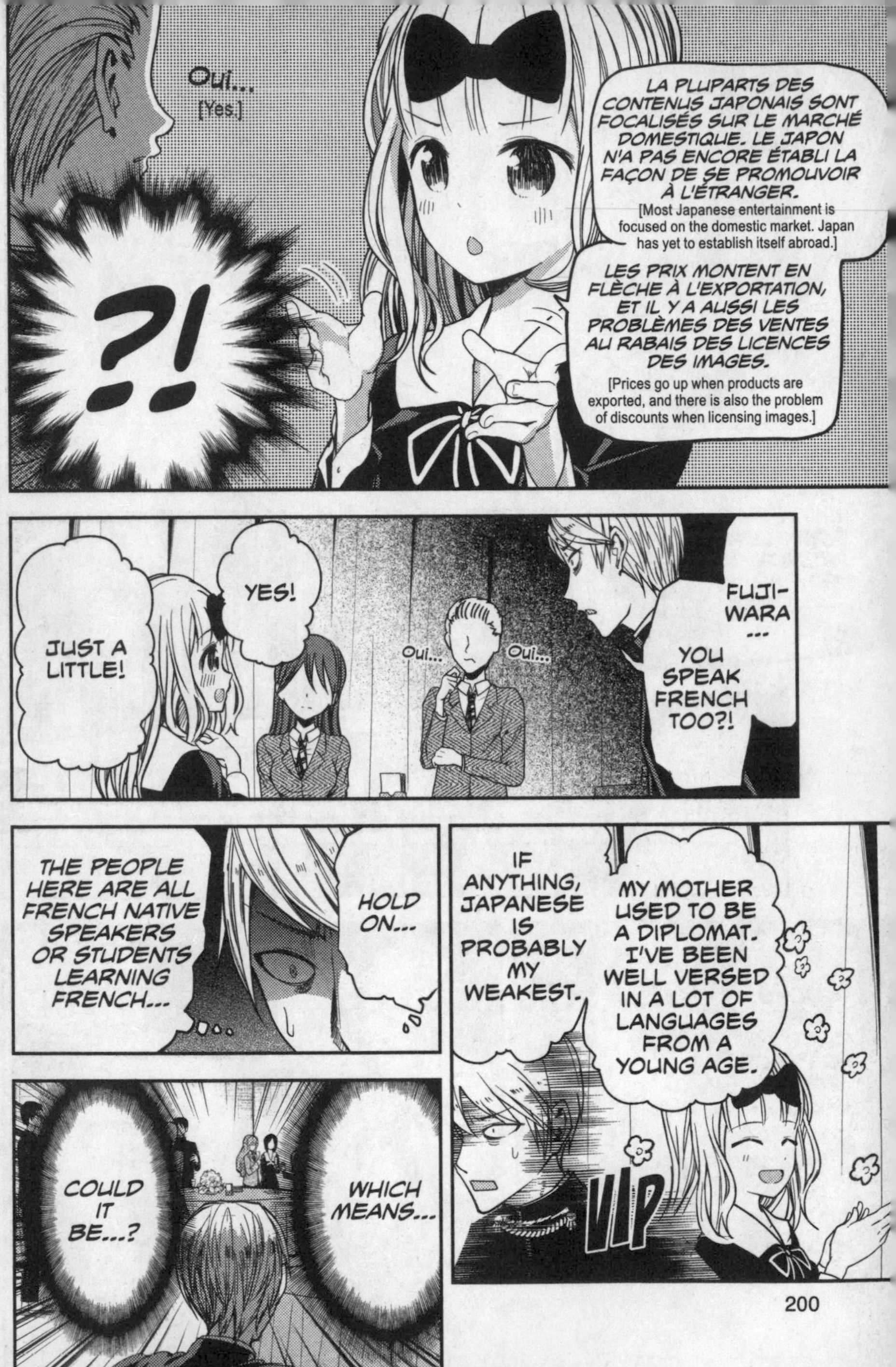
LA PLUPARTS DES CONTENUS JAPONAIS SONT FOCALISÉS SUR LE MARCHÉ DOMESTIQUE. LE JAPON N'A PAS ENCORE ÉTABLI LA FAÇON DE SE PROMOUVOIR À L'ÉTRANGER.
[Most Japanese entertainment is focused on the domestic market. Japan has yet to establish itself abroad.]
Oui...
[Yes.]
LES PRIX MONTENT EN FLÈCHE À L'EXPORTATION, ET IL Y A AUSSI LES PROBLÈMES DES VENTES AU RABAIS DES LICENCES DES IMAGES.
[Prices go up when products are exported, and there is also the problem of discounts when licensing images.]
?!
FUJI-WARA...
YOU SPEAK FRENCH TOO?!
Oui...
Oui...
YES!
JUST A LITTLE!
MY MOTHER USED TO BE A DIPLOMAT. I'VE BEEN WELL VERSED IN A LOT OF LANGUAGES FROM A YOUNG AGE.
IF ANYTHING, JAPANESE IS PROBABLY MY WEAKEST.
VIP
HOLD ON...
THE PEOPLE HERE ARE ALL FRENCH NATIVE SPEAKERS OR STUDENTS LEARNING FRENCH...
WHICH MEANS...
COULD IT BE...?

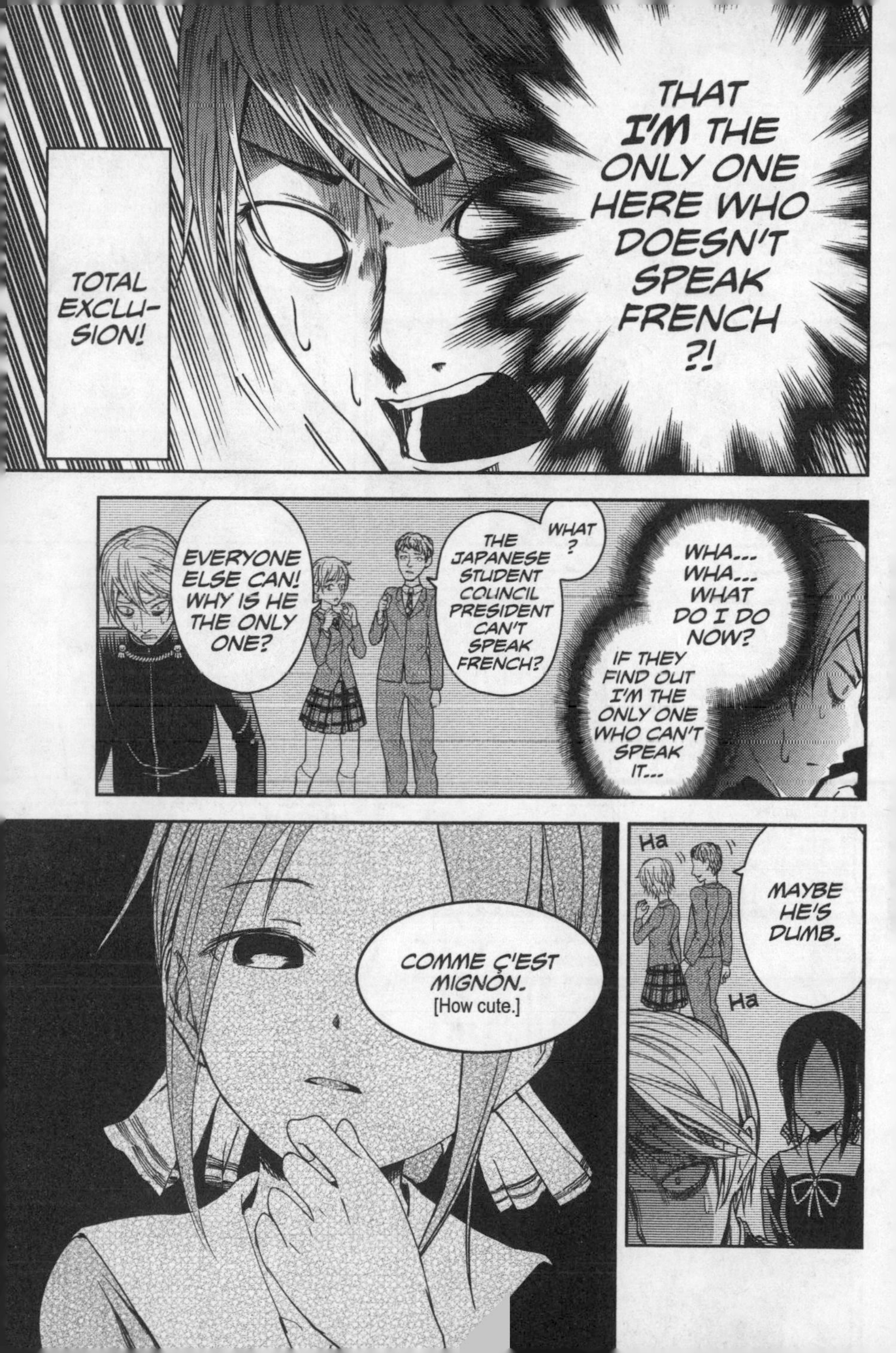
THAT I'M THE ONLY ONE HERE WHO DOESN'T SPEAK FRENCH ?!
TOTAL EXCLU-SION!
WHA... WHA... WHAT DO I DO NOW?
IF THEY FIND OUT I'M THE ONLY ONE WHO CAN'T SPEAK IT...
WHAT ?
THE JAPANESE STUDENT COUNCIL PRESIDENT CAN'T SPEAK FRENCH?
EVERYONE ELSE CAN! WHY IS HE THE ONLY ONE?
MAYBE HE'S DUMB.
Ha
Ha
COMME ÇEST MIGNON.
[How cute.]

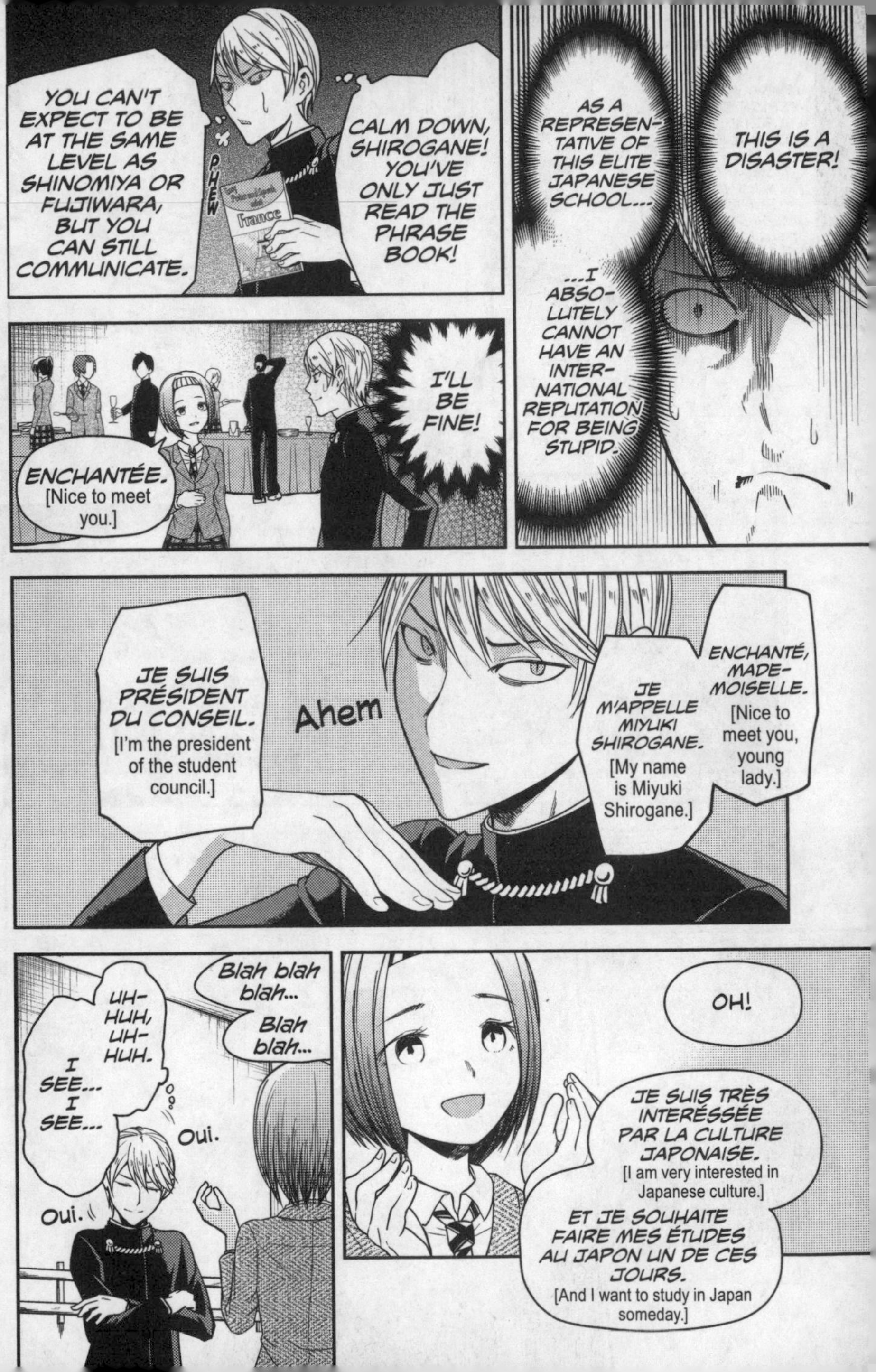
THIS IS A DISASTER!
AS A REPRESENTATIVE OF THIS ELITE JAPANESE SCHOOL...
...I ABSOLUTELY CANNOT HAVE AN INTERNATIONAL REPUTATION FOR BEING STUPID.
CALM DOWN, SHIROGANE! YOU'VE ONLY JUST READ THE PHRASE BOOK!
PHEW
France
YOU CAN'T EXPECT TO BE AT THE SAME LEVEL AS SHINOMIYA OR FUJIWARA, BUT YOU CAN STILL COMMUNICATE.
I'LL BE FINE!
ENCHANTÉE. [Nice to meet you.]
ENCHANTÉ, MADEMOISELLE. [Nice to meet you, young lady.]
JE M'APPELLE MIYUKI SHIROGANE. [My name is Miyuki Shirogane.]
Ahem
JE SUIS PRÉSIDENT DU CONSEIL. [I'm the president of the student council.]
OH!
JE SUIS TRÈS INTERÉSSÉE PAR LA CULTURE JAPONAISE. [I am very interested in Japanese culture.]
ET JE SOUHAITE FAIRE MES ÉTUDES AU JAPON UN DE CES JOURS. [And I want to study in Japan someday.]
Blah blah blah...
Blah blah...
UH-HUH, UH-HUH.
I SEE... I SEE...
Oui.
Oui.

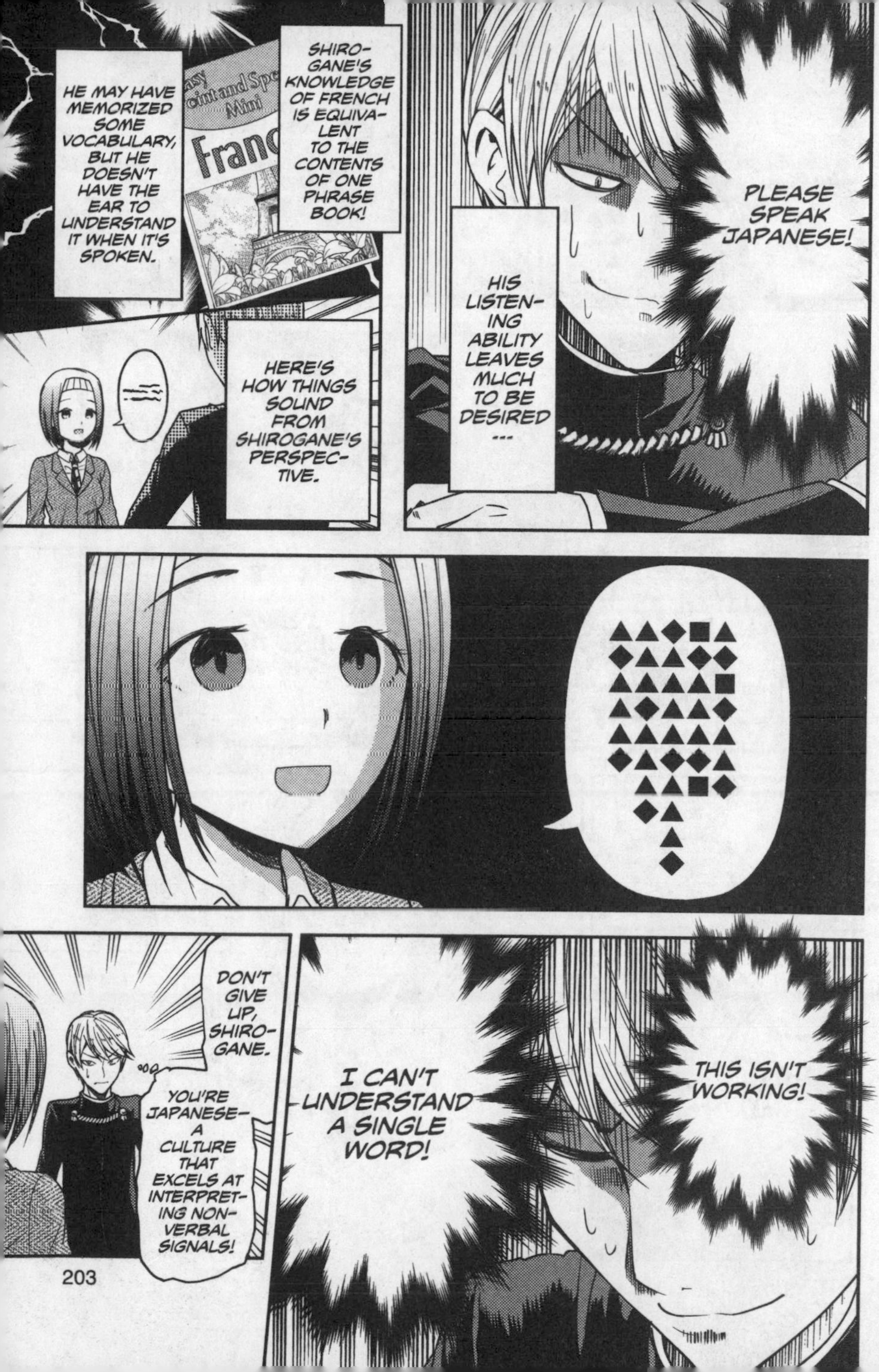
PLEASE SPEAK JAPANESE!
HIS LISTENING ABILITY LEAVES MUCH TO BE DESIRED...
SHIROGANE'S KNOWLEDGE OF FRENCH IS EQUIVALENT TO THE CONTENTS OF ONE PHRASE BOOK!
Easy ...oint and Spe... Mini France
HE MAY HAVE MEMORIZED SOME VOCABULARY, BUT HE DOESN'T HAVE THE EAR TO UNDERSTAND IT WHEN IT'S SPOKEN.
HERE'S HOW THINGS SOUND FROM SHIROGANE'S PERSPECTIVE.
THIS ISN'T WORKING!
I CAN'T UNDERSTAND A SINGLE WORD!
DON'T GIVE UP, SHIROGANE.
YOU'RE JAPANESE—A CULTURE THAT EXCELS AT INTERPRETING NON-VERBAL SIGNALS!

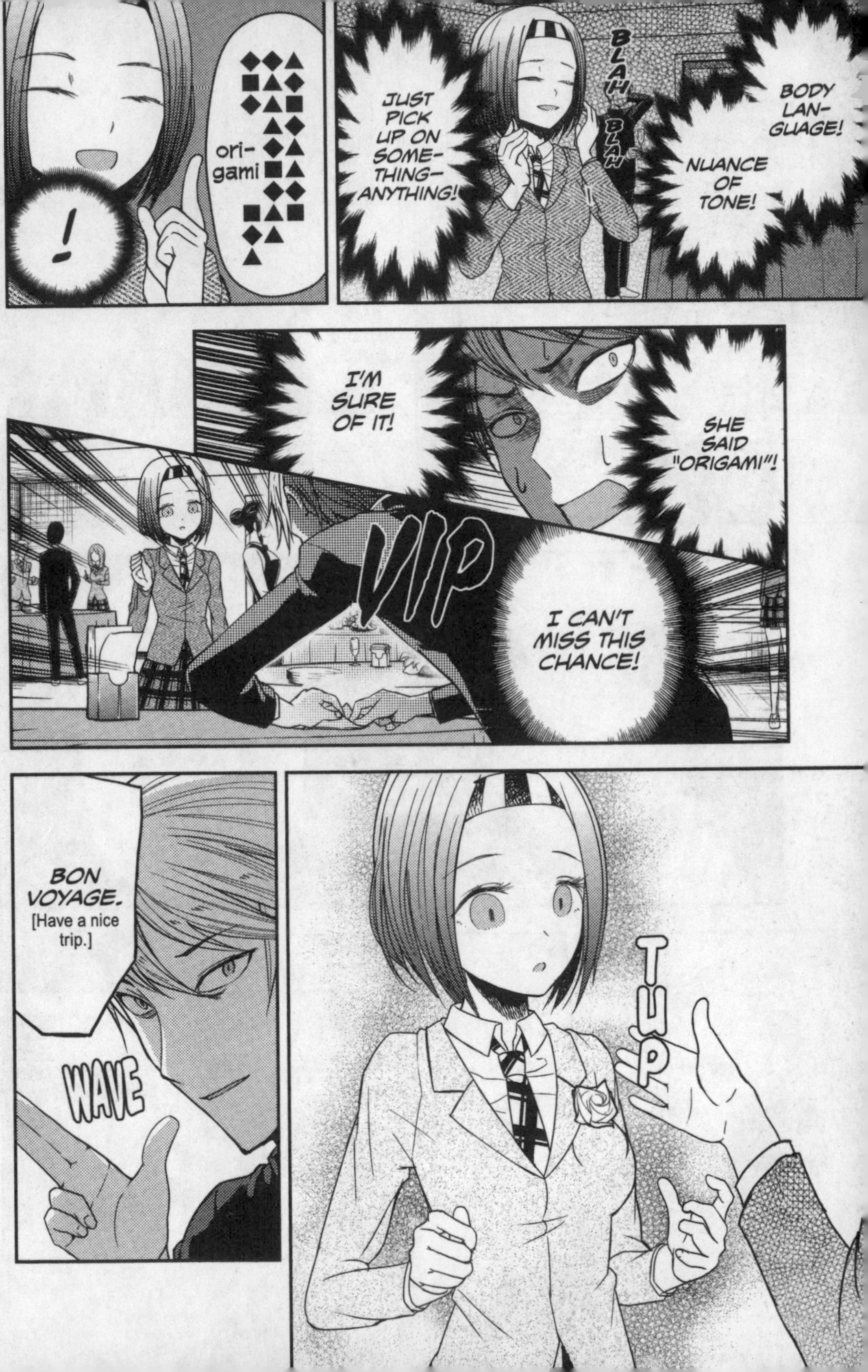

BODY LAN-GUAGE!
BLAH BLAH
NUANCE OF TONE!
JUST PICK UP ON SOME-THING—ANYTHING!
ori-gami
!
SHE SAID "ORIGAMI"!
I'M SURE OF IT!
I CAN'T MISS THIS CHANCE!
VIP
TUP
BON VOYAGE.
[Have a nice trip.]
WAVE

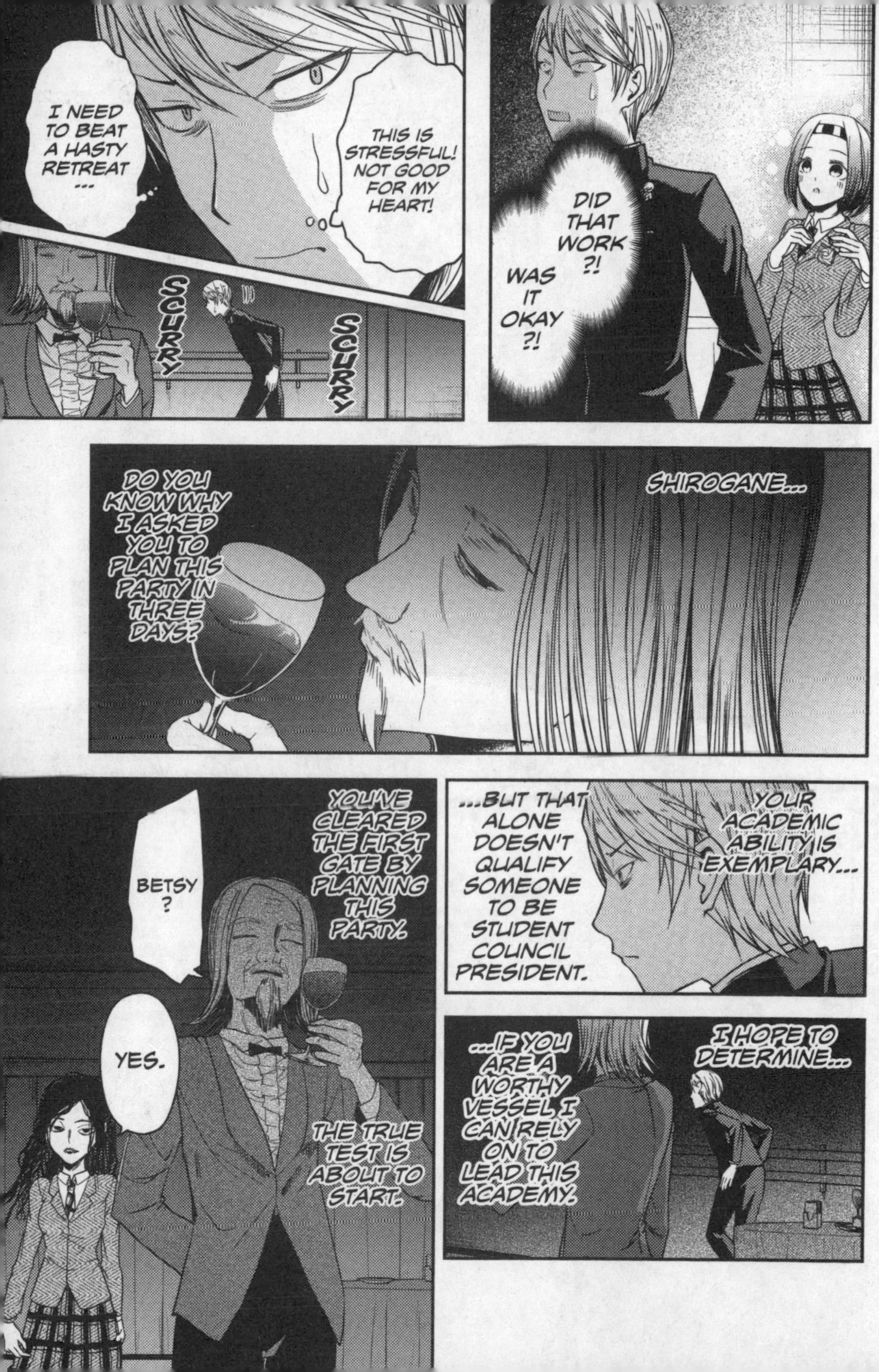
DID THAT WORK?!
WAS IT OKAY?!
THIS IS STRESSFUL! NOT GOOD FOR MY HEART!
I NEED TO BEAT A HASTY RETREAT...
SCURRY
SCURRY
SHIROGANE...
DO YOU KNOW WHY I ASKED YOU TO PLAN THIS PARTY IN THREE DAYS?
YOUR ACADEMIC ABILITY IS EXEMPLARY...
...BUT THAT ALONE DOESN'T QUALIFY SOMEONE TO BE STUDENT COUNCIL PRESIDENT.
I HOPE TO DETERMINE...
...IF YOU ARE A WORTHY VESSEL I CAN RELY ON TO LEAD THIS ACADEMY.
YOU'VE CLEARED THE FIRST GATE BY PLANNING THIS PARTY.
BETSY?
THE TRUE TEST IS ABOUT TO START.
YES.

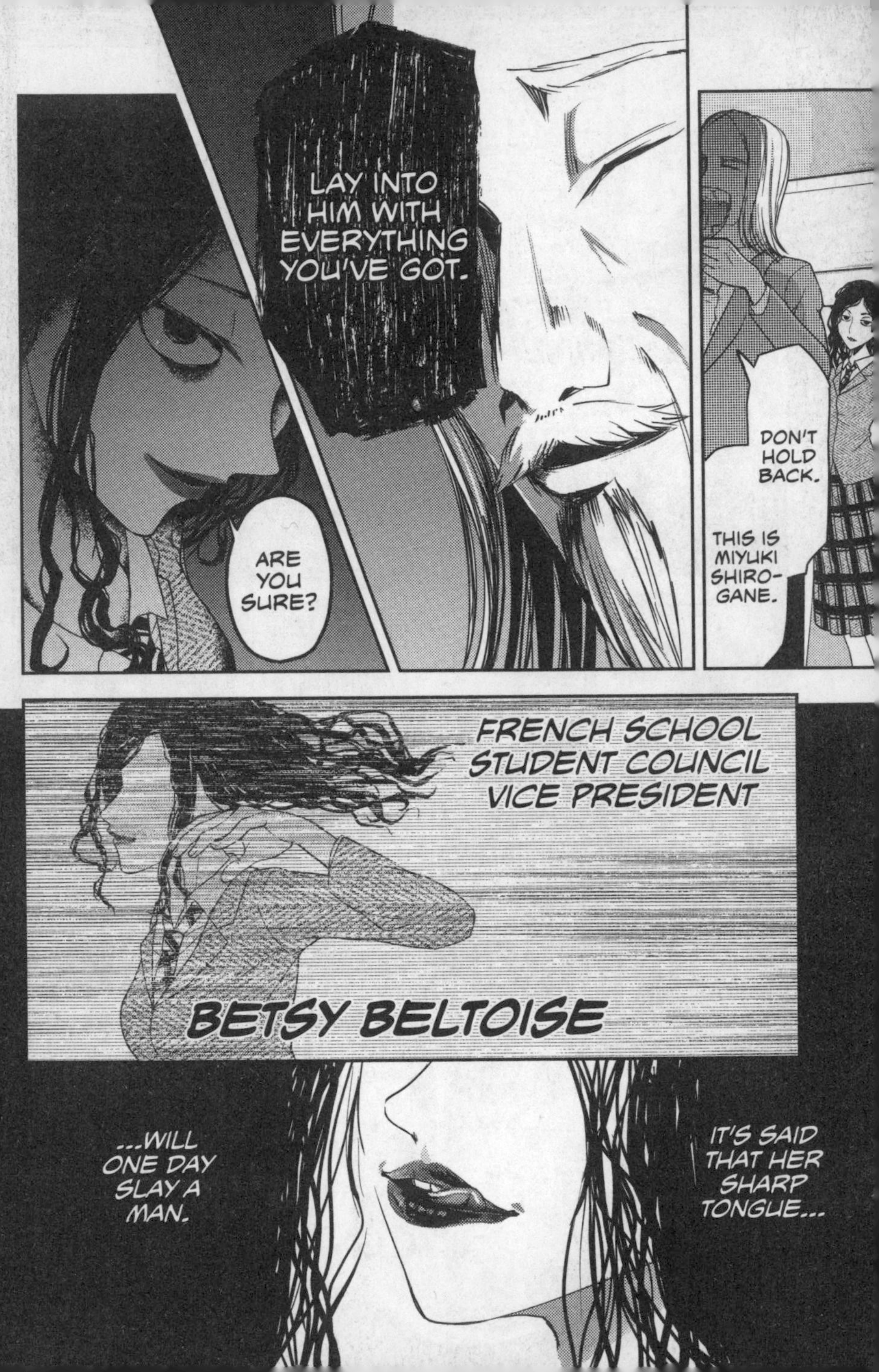
DON'T HOLD BACK.
THIS IS MIYUKI SHIROGANE.
LAY INTO HIM WITH EVERYTHING YOU'VE GOT.
ARE YOU SURE?
FRENCH SCHOOL STUDENT COUNCIL VICE PRESIDENT
BETSY BELTOISE
IT'S SAID THAT HER SHARP TONGUE...
...WILL ONE DAY SLAY A MAN.

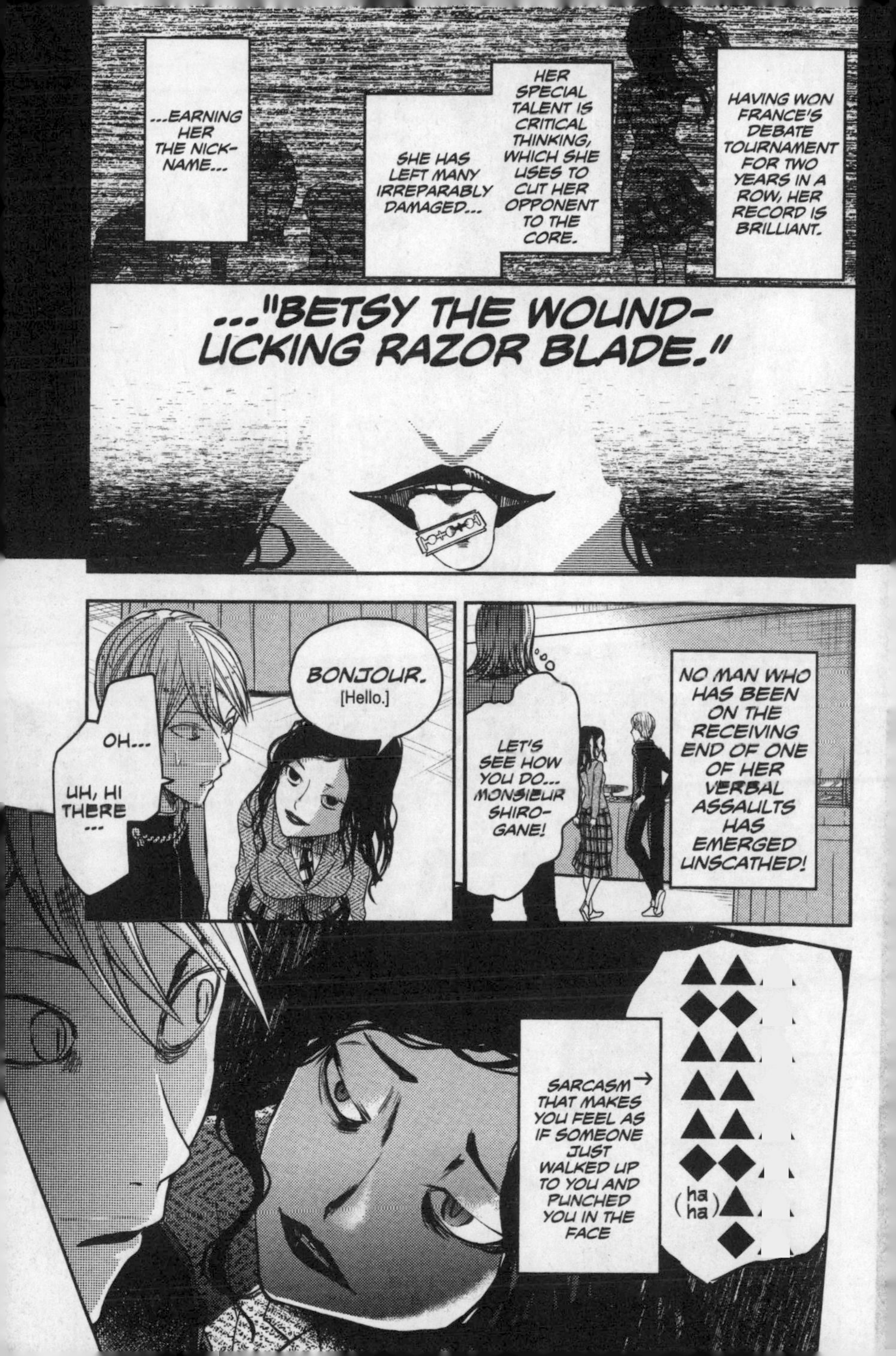
HAVING WON FRANCE'S DEBATE TOURNAMENT FOR TWO YEARS IN A ROW, HER RECORD IS BRILLIANT.
HER SPECIAL TALENT IS CRITICAL THINKING, WHICH SHE USES TO CUT HER OPPONENT TO THE CORE.
SHE HAS LEFT MANY IRREPARABLY DAMAGED...
...EARNING HER THE NICK-NAME...
..."BETSY THE WOUND-LICKING RAZOR BLADE."
NO MAN WHO HAS BEEN ON THE RECEIVING END OF ONE OF HER VERBAL ASSAULTS HAS EMERGED UNSCATHED!
LET'S SEE HOW YOU DO... MONSIEUR SHIRO-GANE!
BONJOUR. [Hello.]
OH...
UH, HI THERE...
SARCASM → THAT MAKES YOU FEEL AS IF SOMEONE JUST WALKED UP TO YOU AND PUNCHED YOU IN THE FACE
(ha ha)

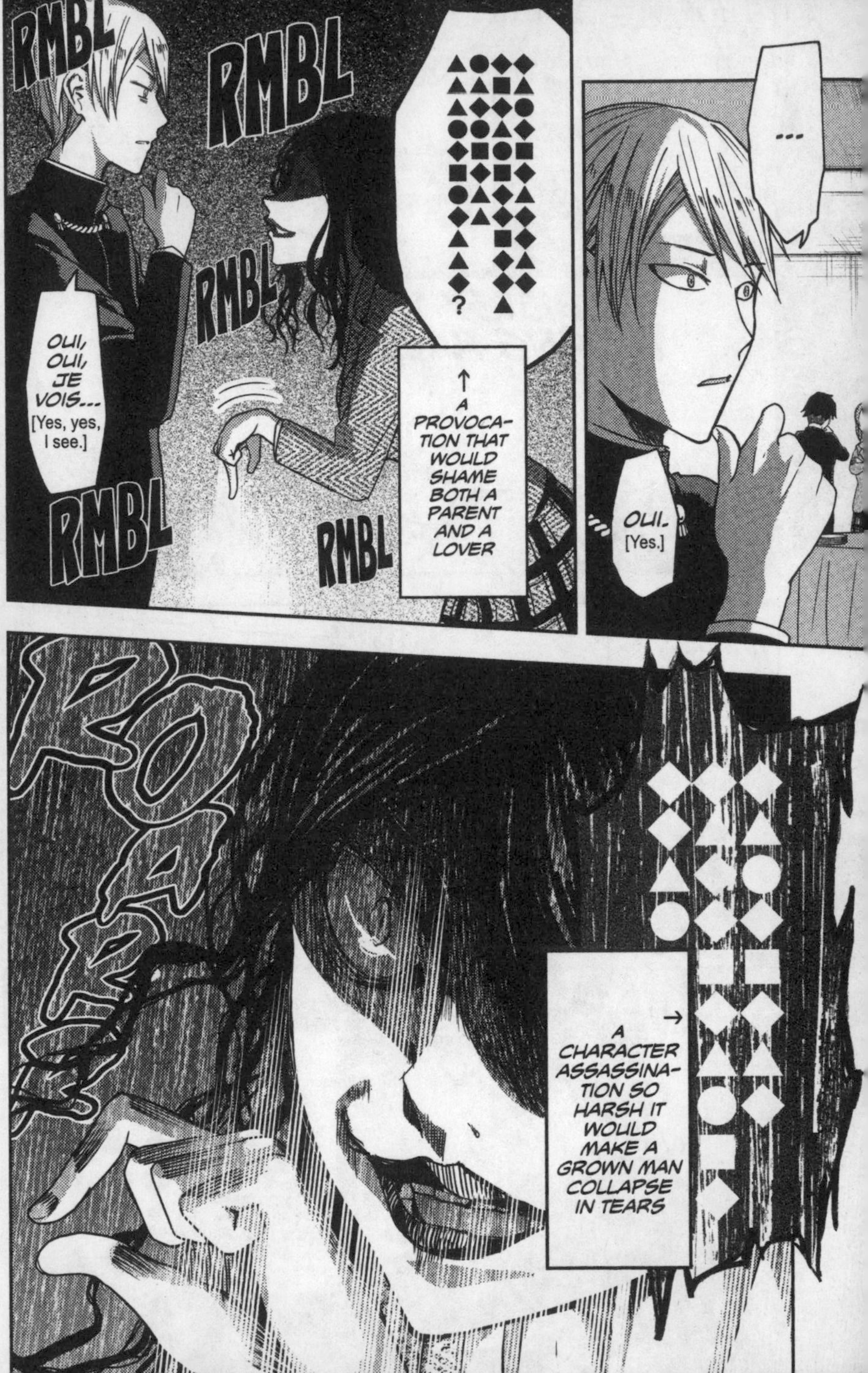
...
OUI. [Yes.]
?
↑ A PROVOCATION THAT WOULD SHAME BOTH A PARENT AND A LOVER
RMBL
RMBL
RMBL
OUI, OUI, JE VOIS... [Yes, yes, I see.]
RMBL
RMBL
→ A CHARACTER ASSASSINATION SO HARSH IT WOULD MAKE A GROWN MAN COLLAPSE IN TEARS

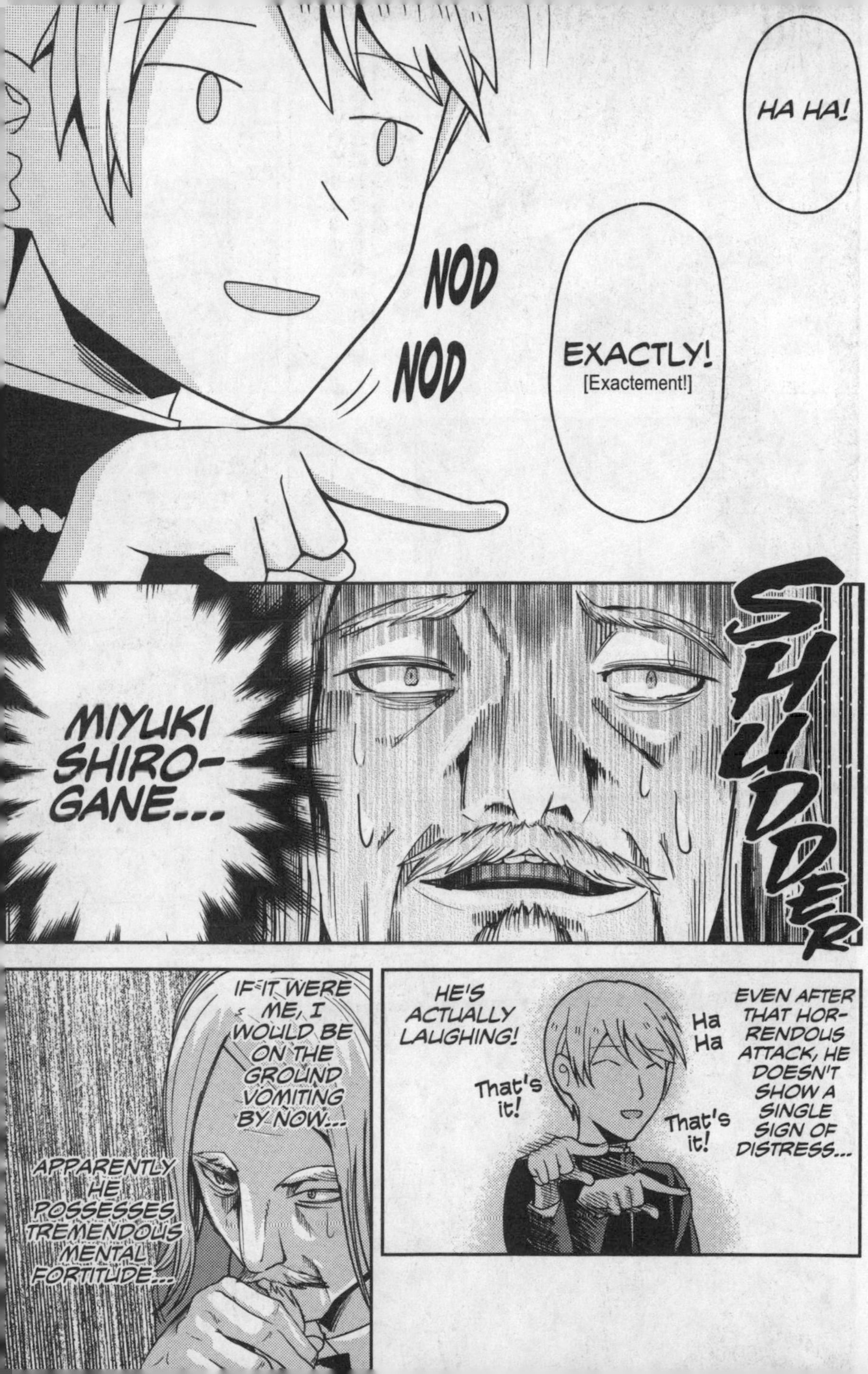
HA HA!
EXACTLY!
[Exactement!]
NOD NOD
SHUDDER
MIYUKI SHIRO-GANE...
EVEN AFTER THAT HOR-RENDOUS ATTACK, HE DOESN'T SHOW A SINGLE SIGN OF DISTRESS...
Ha Ha
That's it!
HE'S ACTUALLY LAUGHING!
That's it!
IF IT WERE ME, I WOULD BE ON THE GROUND VOMITING BY NOW...
APPARENTLY HE POSSESSES TREMENDOUS MENTAL FORTITUDE...

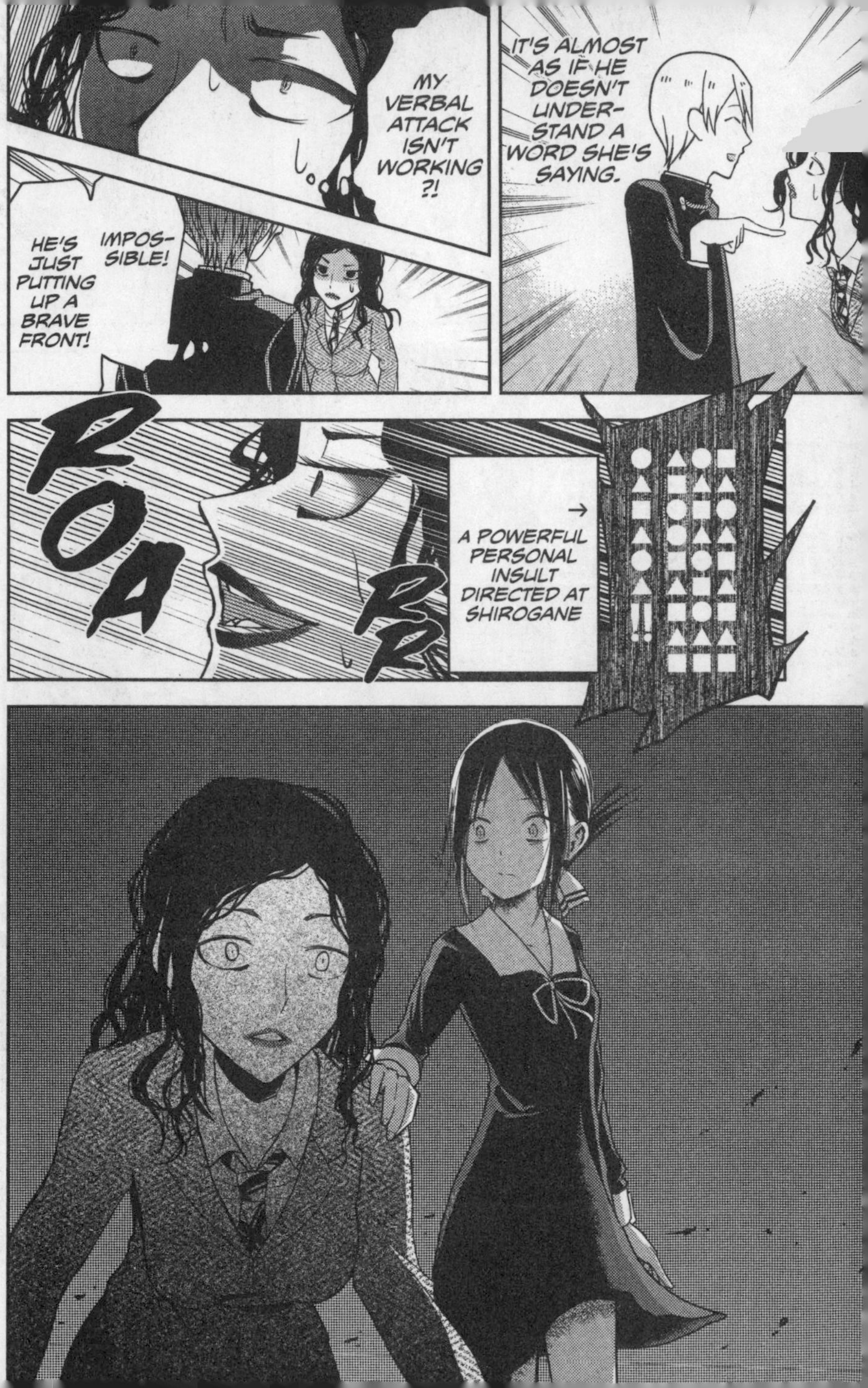
IT'S ALMOST AS IF HE DOESN'T UNDER-STAND A WORD SHE'S SAYING.
MY VERBAL ATTACK ISN'T WORKING?!
IMPOS-SIBLE!
HE'S JUST PUTTING UP A BRAVE FRONT!
→ A POWERFUL PERSONAL INSULT DIRECTED AT SHIROGANE
ROARR

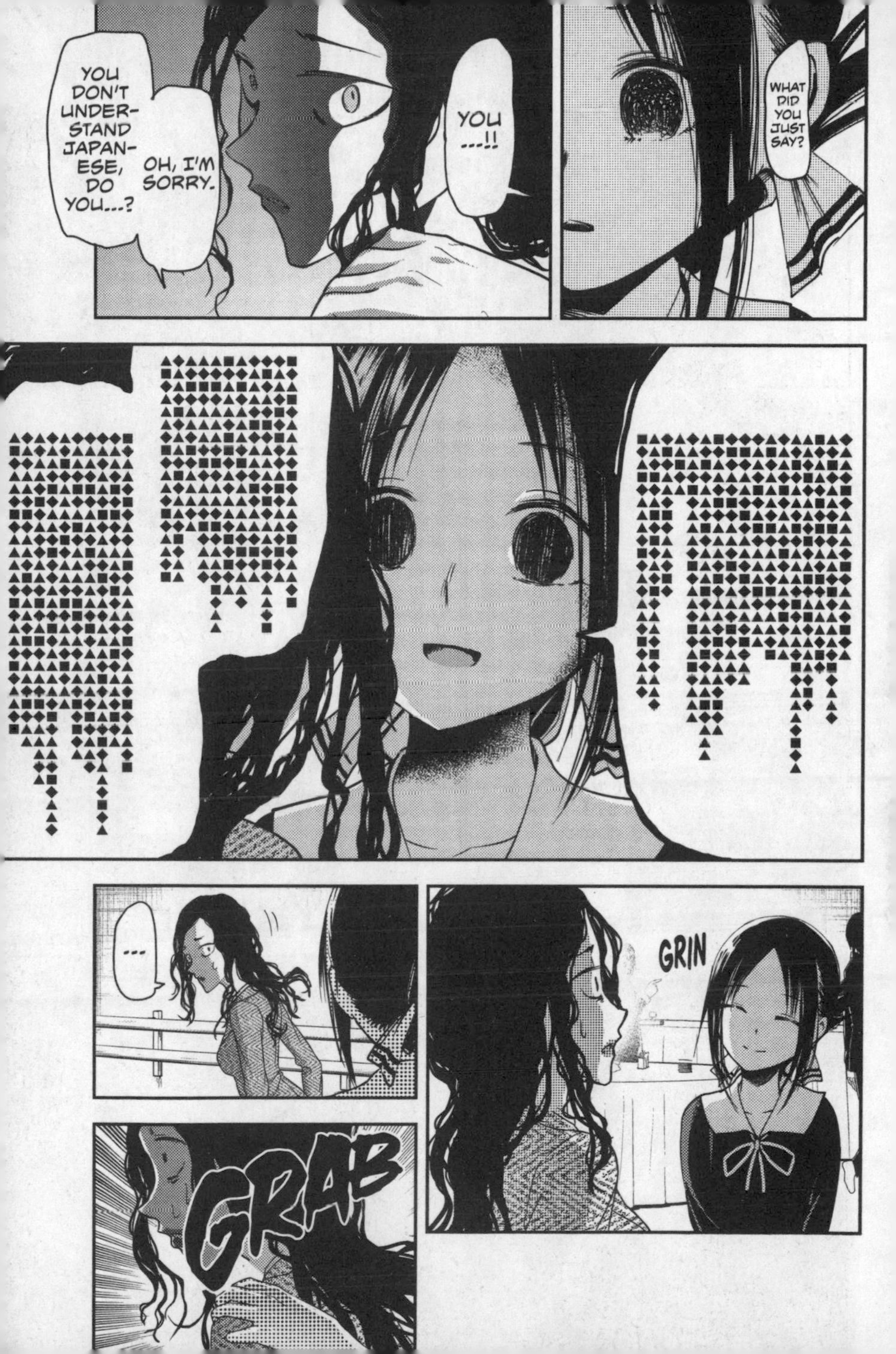
WHAT DID YOU JUST SAY?
YOU ...!!
OH, I'M SORRY.
YOU DON'T UNDER-STAND JAPAN-ESE, DO YOU...?
GRIN
...
GRAB

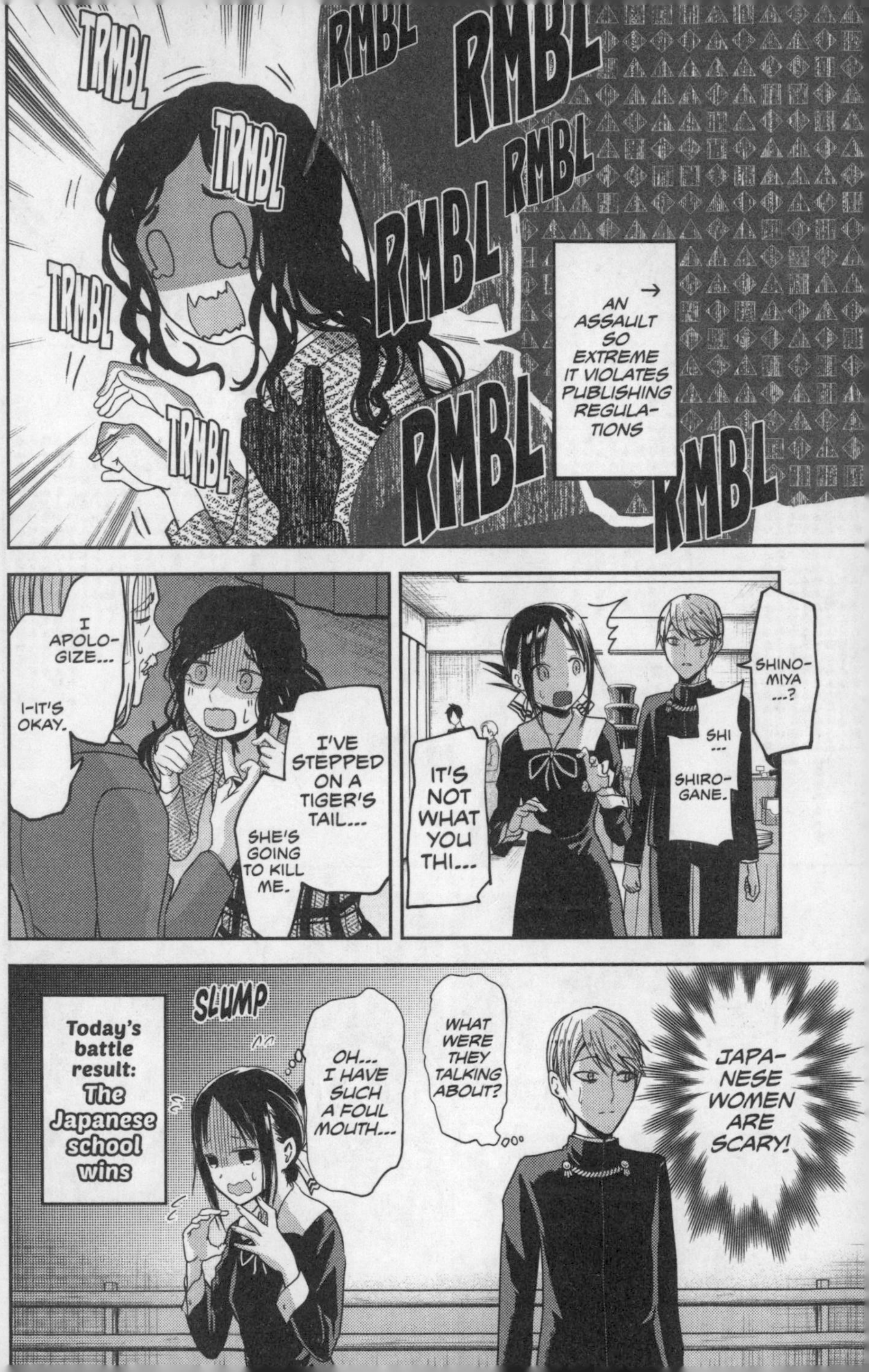

RMBL
RMBL
RMBL
RMBL
→ AN ASSAULT SO EXTREME IT VIOLATES PUBLISHING REGULATIONS
RMBL
RMBL
TRMBL
TRMBL
TRMBL
TRMBL
SHINO-MIYA...?
SHI... SHIRO-GANE.
IT'S NOT WHAT YOU THI...
I'VE STEPPED ON A TIGER'S TAIL...
SHE'S GOING TO KILL ME.
I APOLOGIZE...
I-IT'S OKAY.
JAPANESE WOMEN ARE SCARY!
WHAT WERE THEY TALKING ABOUT?
OH... I HAVE SUCH A FOUL MOUTH...
SLUMP
Today's battle result: The Japanese school wins

KAGUYA-SAMA
LOVE IS WAR

I appear in the next volume.
KLIK
KLIK
In a romantic comedy, there's no benefit to adding male characters.
We should rethink this.

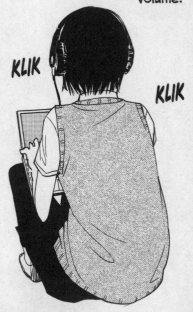

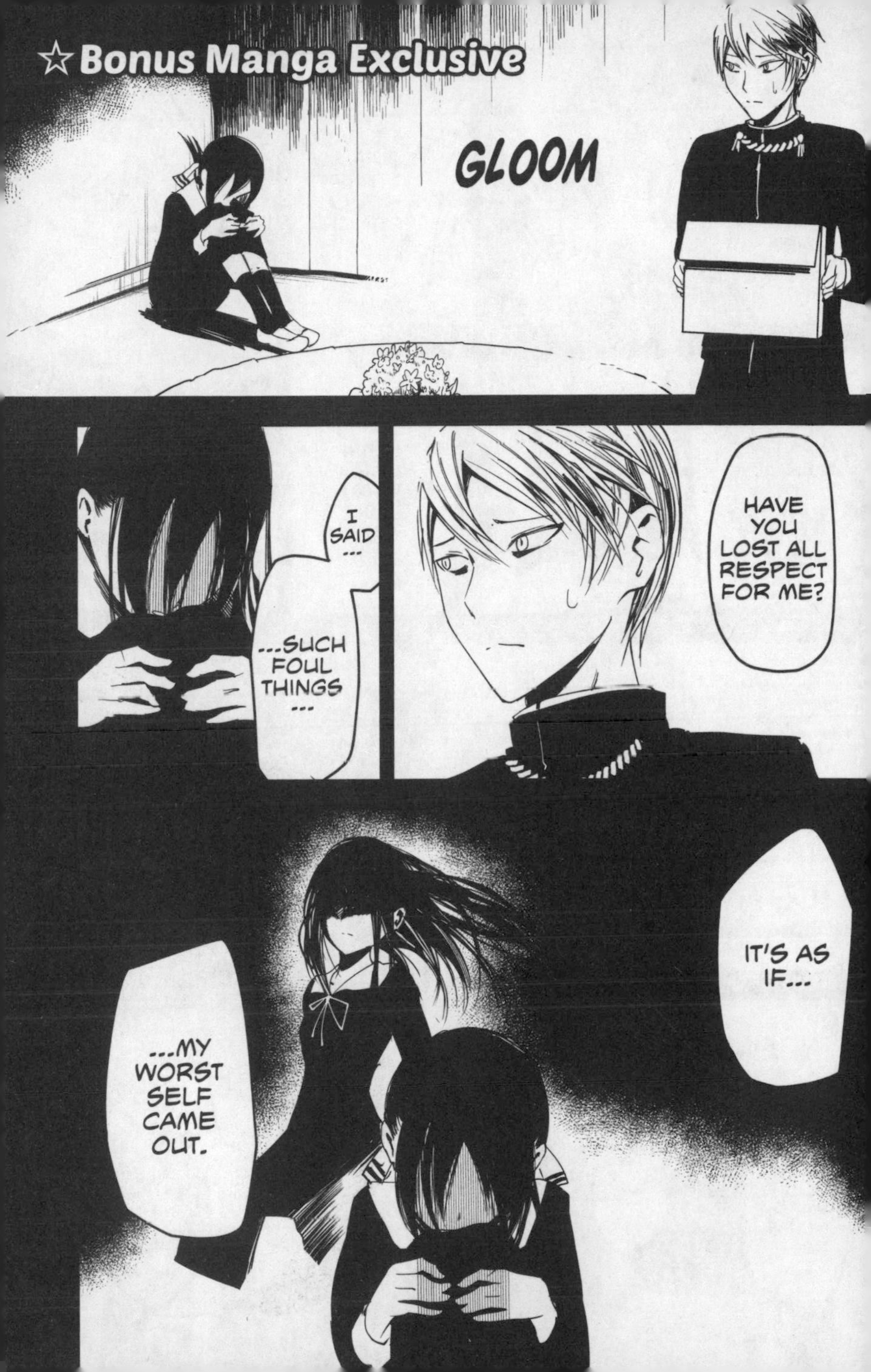
☆Bonus Manga Exclusive
GLOOM
HAVE YOU LOST ALL RESPECT FOR ME?
I SAID...
...SUCH FOUL THINGS...
IT'S AS IF...
...MY WORST SELF CAME OUT.

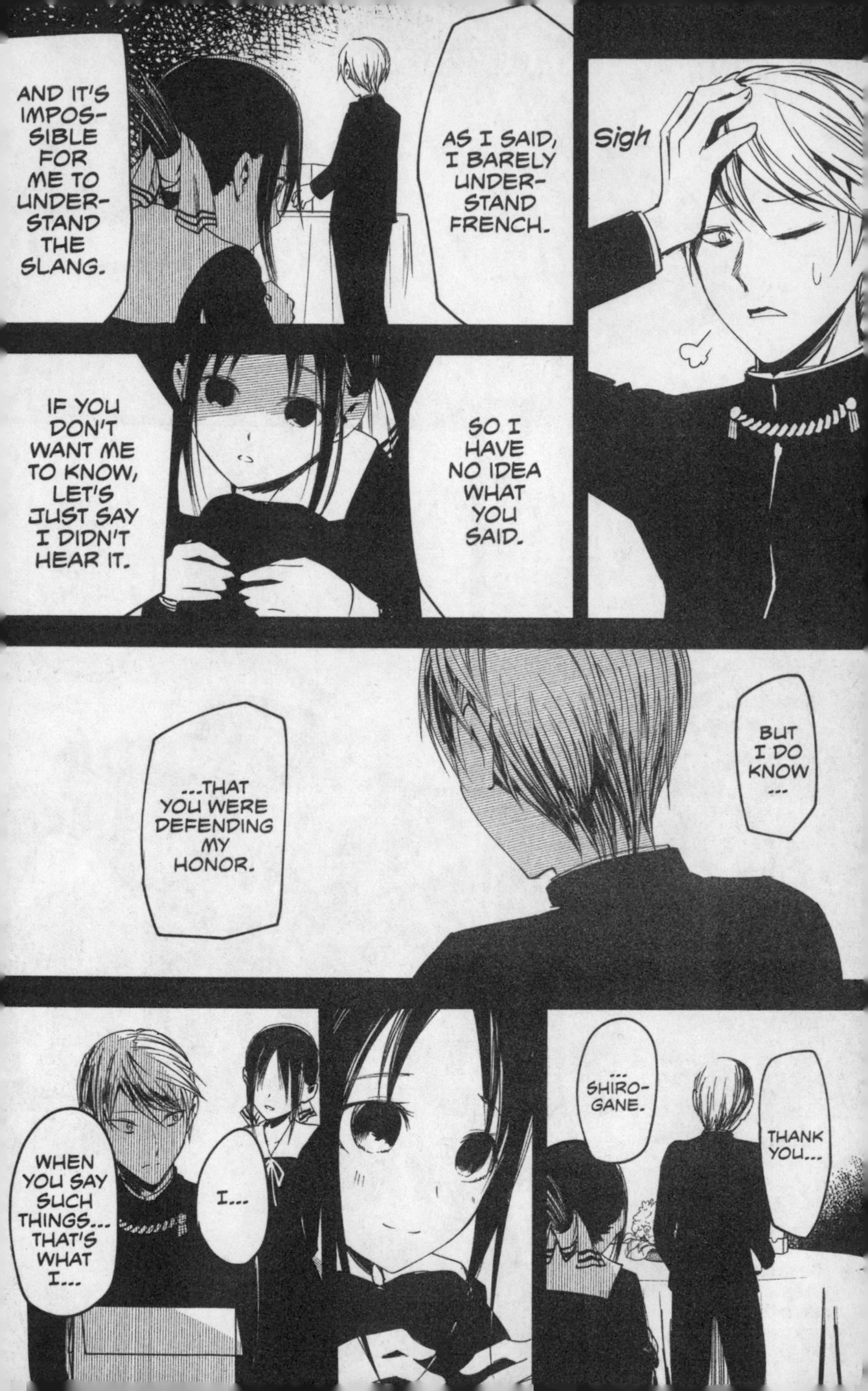
Sigh
AS I SAID, I BARELY UNDER-STAND FRENCH.
AND IT'S IMPOS-SIBLE FOR ME TO UNDER-STAND THE SLANG.
SO I HAVE NO IDEA WHAT YOU SAID.
IF YOU DON'T WANT ME TO KNOW, LET'S JUST SAY I DIDN'T HEAR IT.
BUT I DO KNOW...
...THAT YOU WERE DEFENDING MY HONOR.
...SHIRO-GANE.
THANK YOU...
WHEN YOU SAY SUCH THINGS... THAT'S WHAT I...
I...

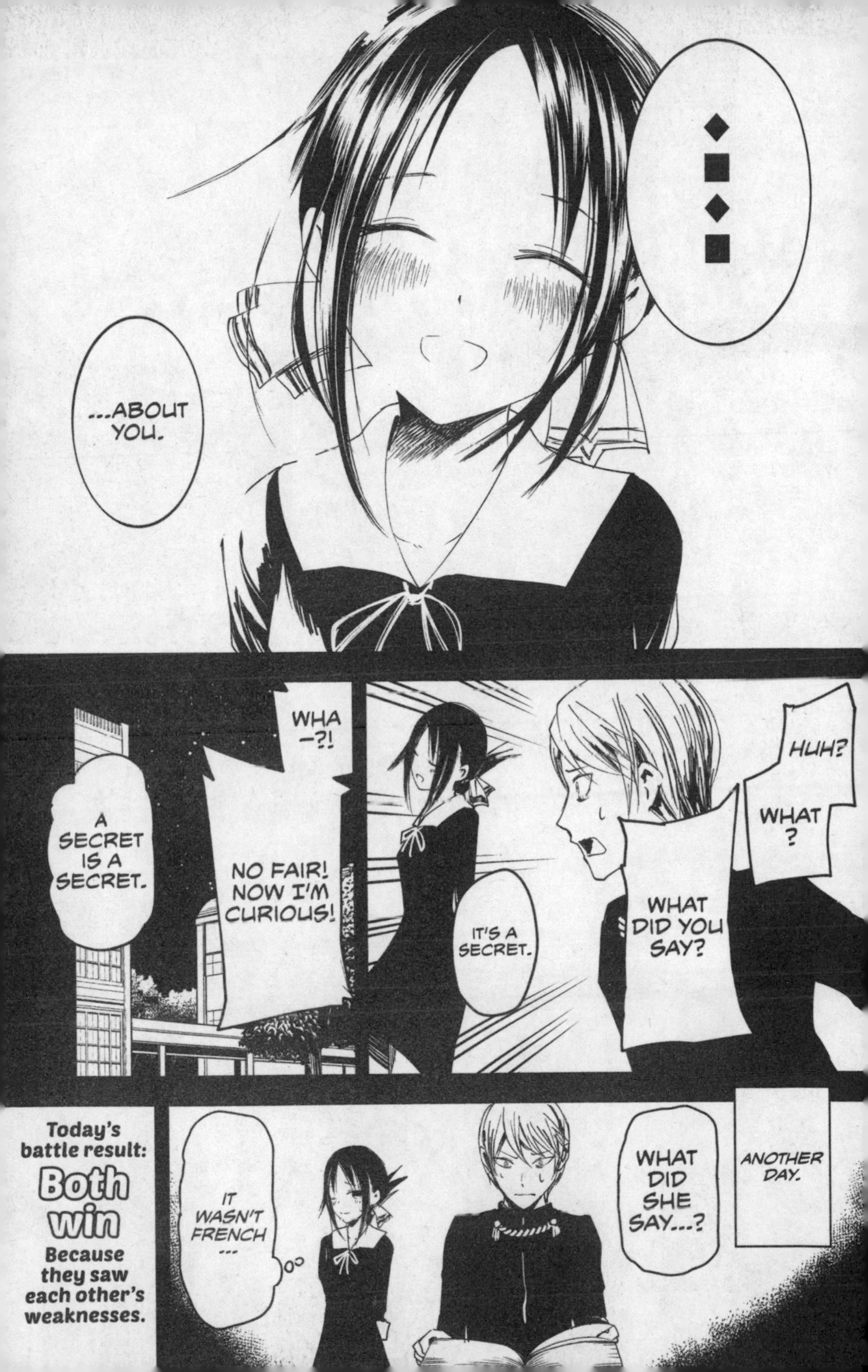
◆■◆■
...ABOUT YOU.
HUH?
WHAT?
WHAT DID YOU SAY?
IT'S A SECRET.
WHA—?!
NO FAIR! NOW I'M CURIOUS!
A SECRET IS A SECRET.
ANOTHER DAY.
WHAT DID SHE SAY...?
IT WASN'T FRENCH...
Today's battle result:
Both win
Because they saw each other's weaknesses.

A LIE REQUIRES MORE EFFORT THAN SIMPLY TELLING THE TRUTH.

AKA AKASAKA

Aka Akasaka got his start as an assistant to Jinsei Kataoka and Kazuma Kondou, the creators of *Deadman Wonderland*. His first serialized manga was an adaptation of the light novel series *Sayonara Piano Sonata*, published by Kadokawa in 2011. *Kaguya-sama: Love Is War* began serialization in *Miracle Jump* in 2015 but was later moved to *Weekly Young Jump* in 2016 due to its popularity.

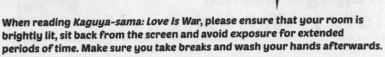

When reading
Kaguya-sama: Love Is War, Vol. 2...

When reading *Kaguya-sama: Love Is War*, please ensure that your room is brightly lit, sit back from the screen and avoid exposure for extended periods of time. Make sure you take breaks and wash your hands afterwards.

In case of accidental contact with the eyes, rinse thoroughly with water and consult a physician. Food that appears in this story will be enjoyed by the staff afterwards.

This is a work of fiction, and any resemblance to actual persons or organizations is purely coincidental. All opinions expressed are those of the author, and results may vary. While characters in this story may not all be over the age of 18, they may be considered to be so if deemed necessary due to future social mores.

This story was originally produced in 2016; thus, it may contain expressions considered outdated at the time of reading. However, the decision was made to publish the story in its original form. Due to many errors in the 2016 first printing of *Kaguya-sama: Love Is War, Vol. 1** —although the books were not officially recalled—changes have been made in subsequent printings, so it is recommended that you read the latest version.

Please be aware that there are some explicit scenes that were enacted for this manga under expert supervision. All participants are professionals who have undergone special training. To protect the privacy of the characters, voices have been altered and mosaics applied. A message to children, good and bad: do not try this at home!

*Japanese edition

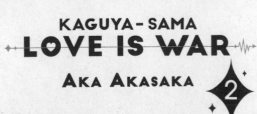

KAGUYA-SAMA
LOVE IS WAR

AKA AKASAKA

2

When not reading

Kaguya-sama: Love Is War, Vol. 2...

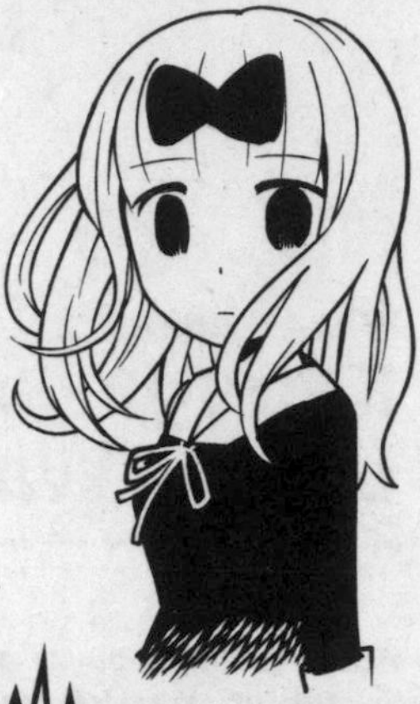

When not reading *Kaguya-sama: Love Is War*, it doesn't matter whether your room is brightly lit or not. The decision is yours.

You have free will.

KAGUYA-SAMA
LOVE IS WAR

SHONEN JUMP MANGA EDITION

2

STORY AND ART BY
AKA AKASAKA

Translation/Emi Louie-Nishikawa
English Adaptation/Annette Roman
Touch-Up Art & Lettering/Stephen Dutro
Cover & Interior Design/Izumi Evers
Editor/Annette Roman

KAGUYA-SAMA WA KOKURASETAI~TENSAITACHI NO REN'AI ZUNO SEN~
© 2015 by Aka Akasaka
All rights reserved.
First published in Japan in 2015 by SHUEISHA Inc., Tokyo.
English translation rights arranged by SHUEISHA Inc.

Printed in Canada

Published by VIZ Media, LLC
P.O. Box 77010
San Francisco, CA 94107

10 9 8 7 6 5 4
First printing, May 2018
Fourth printing, April 2021

VIZ MEDIA
viz.com

SHONEN JUMP

COMING NEXT VOLUME

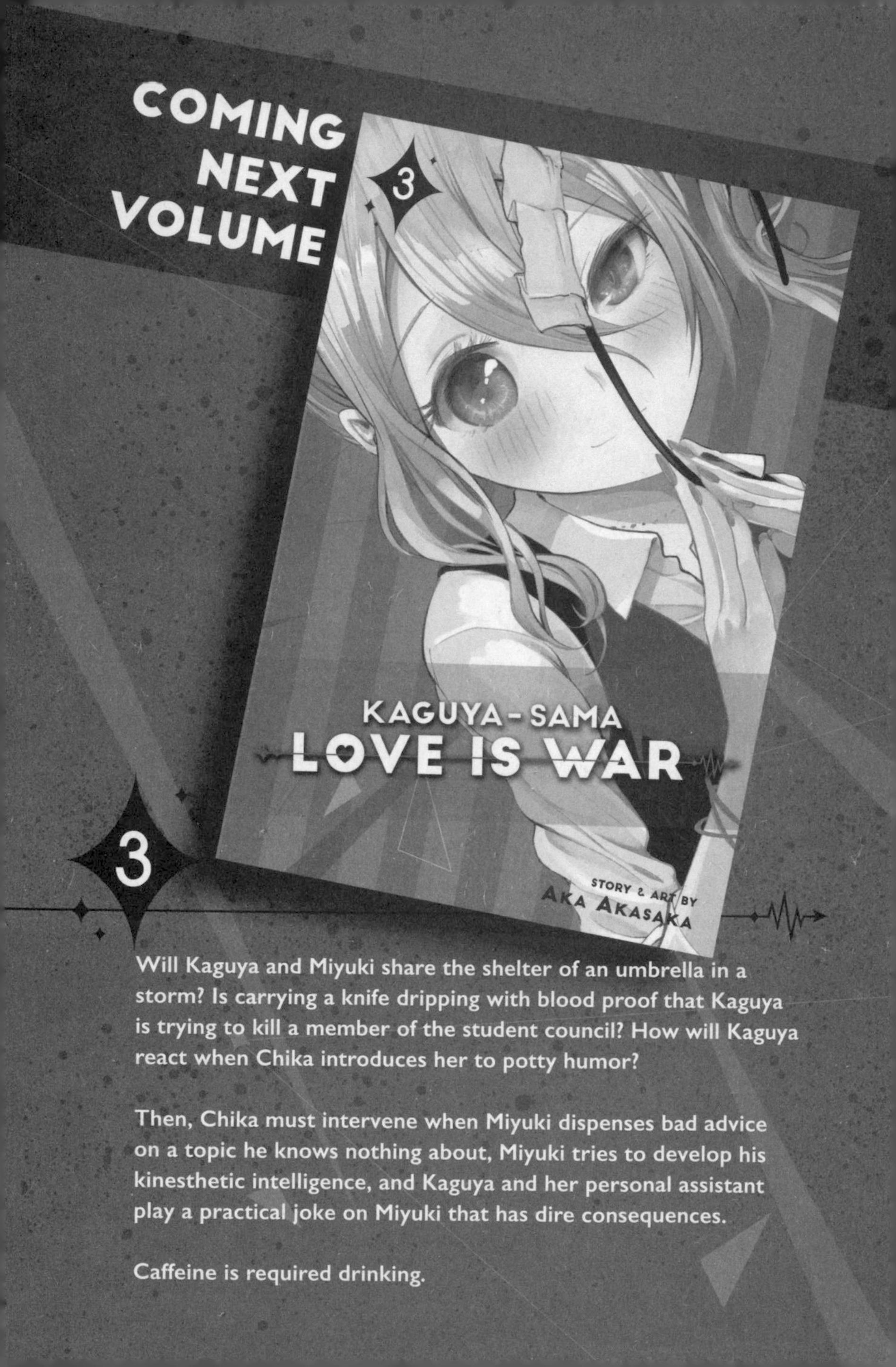
3
KAGUYA-SAMA
LOVE IS WAR
STORY & ART BY
AKA AKASAKA

3

Will Kaguya and Miyuki share the shelter of an umbrella in a storm? Is carrying a knife dripping with blood proof that Kaguya is trying to kill a member of the student council? How will Kaguya react when Chika introduces her to potty humor?

Then, Chika must intervene when Miyuki dispenses bad advice on a topic he knows nothing about, Miyuki tries to develop his kinesthetic intelligence, and Kaguya and her personal assistant play a practical joke on Miyuki that has dire consequences.

Caffeine is required drinking.

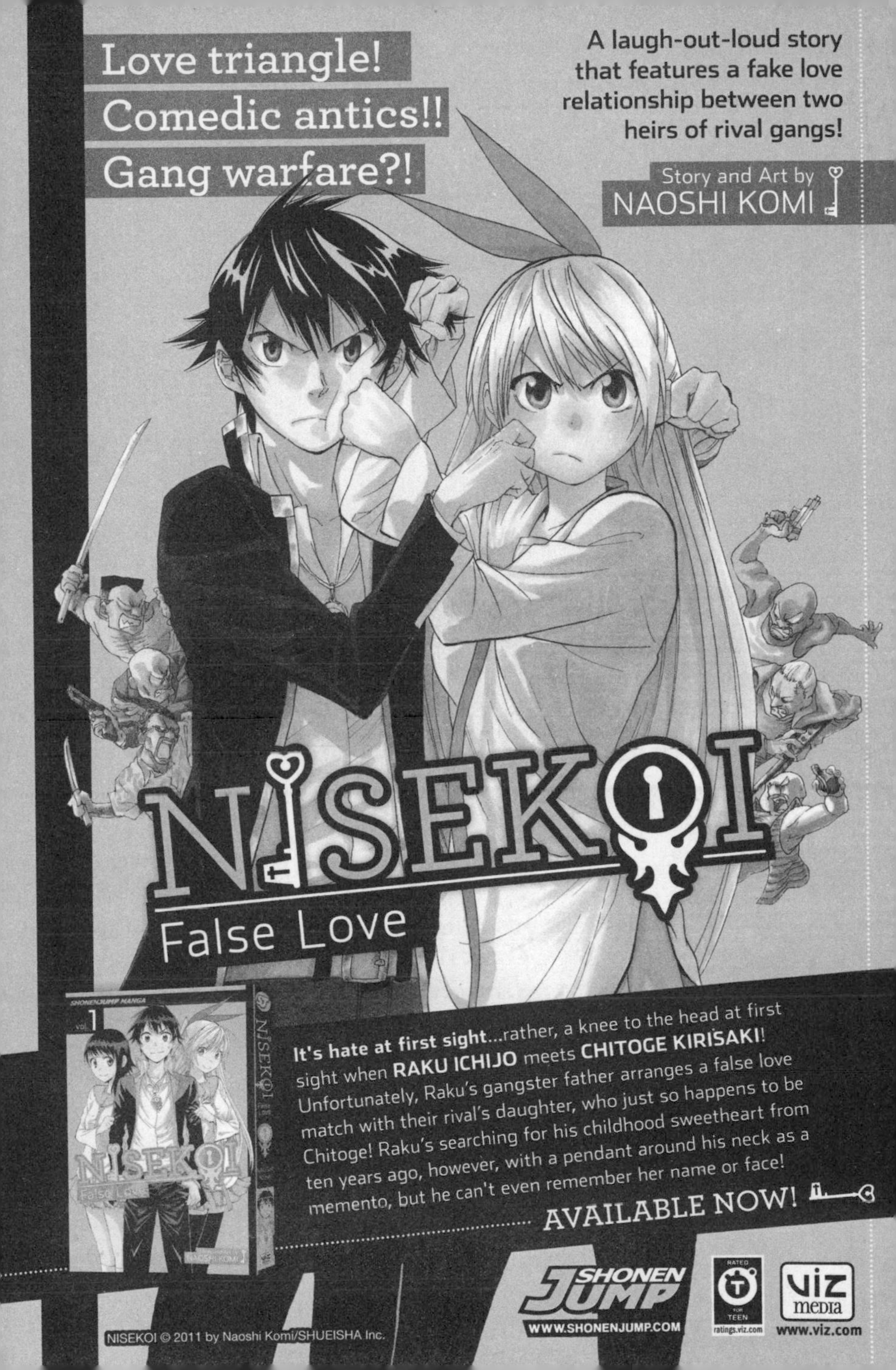
Love triangle!
Comedic antics!!
Gang warfare?!
A laugh-out-loud story that features a fake love relationship between two heirs of rival gangs!
Story and Art by
NAOSHI KOMI
NISEKOI
False Love
It's hate at first sight...rather, a knee to the head at first sight when RAKU ICHIJO meets CHITOGE KIRISAKI! Unfortunately, Raku's gangster father arranges a false love match with their rival's daughter, who just so happens to be Chitoge! Raku's searching for his childhood sweetheart from ten years ago, however, with a pendant around his neck as a memento, but he can't even remember her name or face!
AVAILABLE NOW!
SHONEN JUMP
WWW.SHONENJUMP.COM
RATED T FOR TEEN
ratings.viz.com
viz media
www.viz.com
NISEKOI © 2011 by Naoshi Komi/SHUEISHA Inc.

BORUTO
=NARUTO NEXT GENERATIONS=

CREATOR/SUPERVISOR **Masashi Kishimoto**
ART BY **Mikio Ikemoto** SCRIPT BY **Ukyo Kodachi**

A NEW GENERATION OF NINJA IS HERE!

Naruto was a young shinobi with an incorrigible knack for mischief. He achieved his dream to become the greatest ninja in his village, and now his face sits atop the Hokage monument. But this is not his story... A new generation of ninja is ready to take the stage, led by Naruto's own son, Boruto!

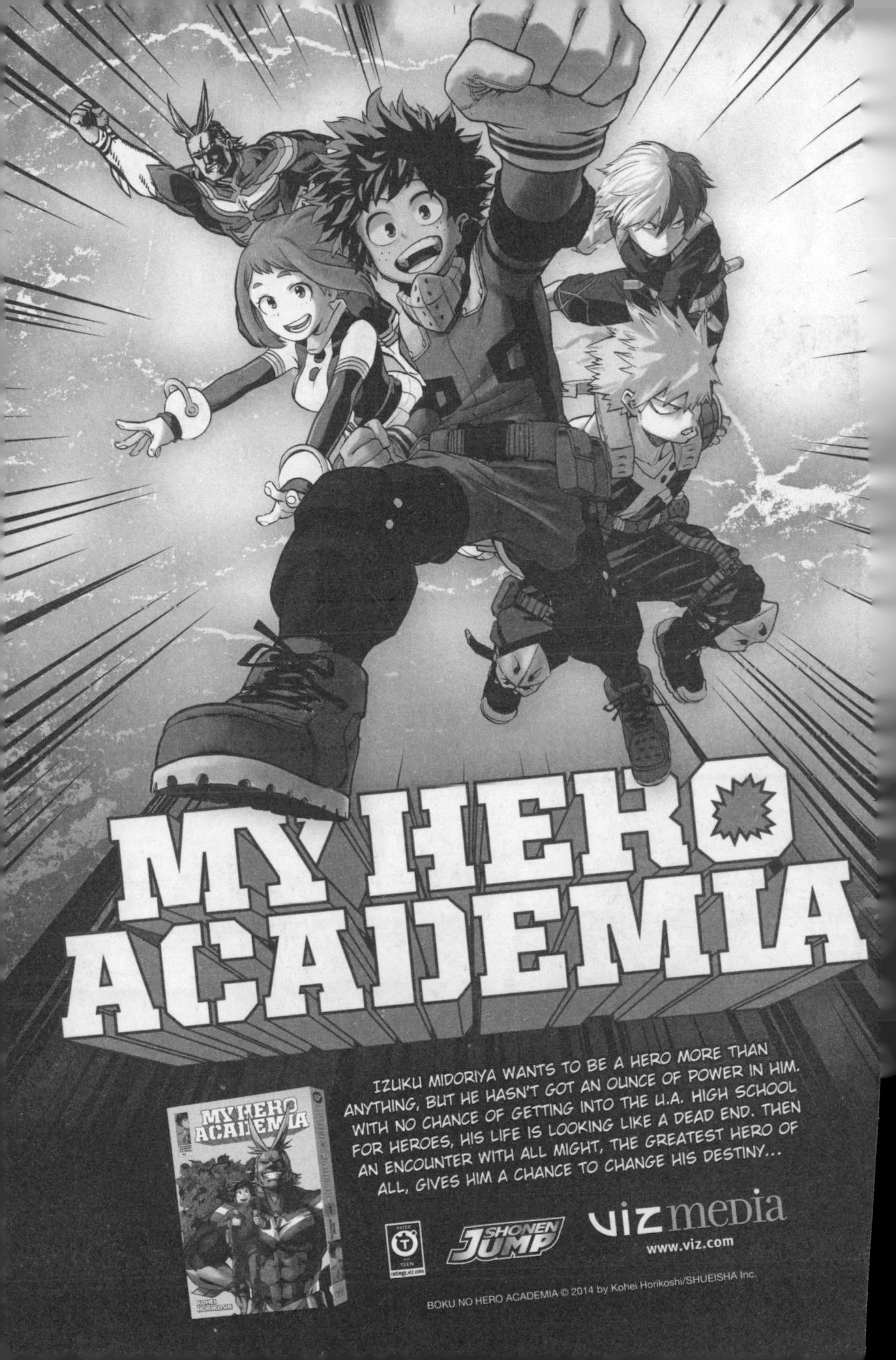
MY HERO ACADEMIA
IZUKU MIDORIYA WANTS TO BE A HERO MORE THAN ANYTHING, BUT HE HASN'T GOT AN OUNCE OF POWER IN HIM. WITH NO CHANCE OF GETTING INTO THE U.A. HIGH SCHOOL FOR HEROES, HIS LIFE IS LOOKING LIKE A DEAD END. THEN AN ENCOUNTER WITH ALL MIGHT, THE GREATEST HERO OF ALL, GIVES HIM A CHANCE TO CHANGE HIS DESTINY...
MY HERO ACADEMIA
KOHEI HORIKOSHI
SHONEN JUMP
VIZ media
www.viz.com
BOKU NO HERO ACADEMIA © 2014 by Kohei Horikoshi/SHUEISHA Inc.

YOU'RE READING THE WRONG WAY!

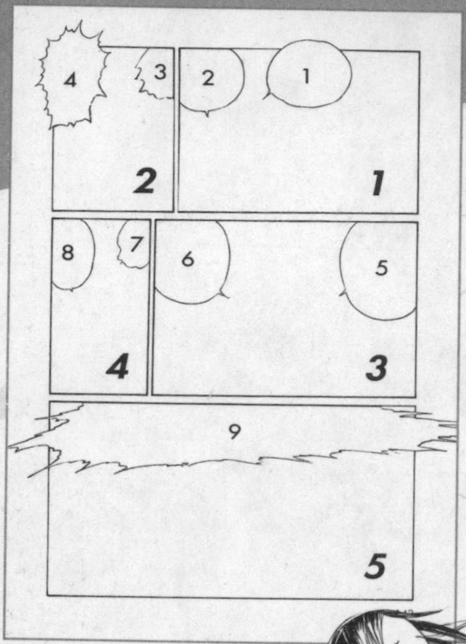
1
2
1
3
4
2
5
6
3
7
8
4
9
5

KAGUYA-SAMA: LOVE IS WAR reads from right to left, starting in the upper-right corner. Japanese is read from right to left, meaning that action, sound effects and word-balloon order are completely reversed from English order.

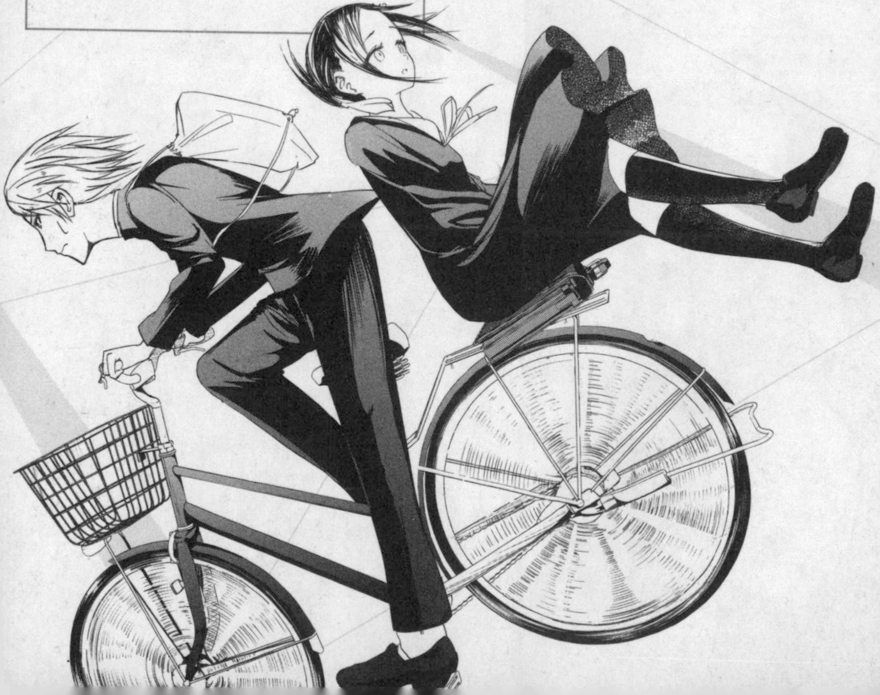